Herbs in Bloom

Plate 1. *Salvia coccinea* 'Lady in Red', Texas sage, and *Tagetes tenuifolia* 'Lemon Gem', signet marigold, growing together in an old wheelbarrow. Late summer, Gardner farm, Cape Breton Island, Nova Scotia, Canada. Photo, Alan Dorey.

Herbs in Bloom

A Guide to Growing Herbs as Ornamental Plants

JO ANN GARDNER

Illustrations by Holly S. Dougherty

TIMBER PRESS
Portland · Cambridge

Timber Press, Inc.
The Haseltine Building
133 S.W. Second Avenue, Suite 450
Portland, Oregon 97204, U.S.A.

www.timberpress.com

ISBN 0-88192-698-1

Printed in Hong Kong

Timber Press
2 Station Road
Swavesey
Cambridge CB4 5QJ, U.K.

Catalog records for this book are available from the Library of Congress
and the British Library.

To those who have inspired me

Gertrude B. Foster
Helen M. Fox
Audrey H. O'Connor

Contents

Contents

8

Acknowledgments

IT WAS a challenge to write about the large world of flowering herbs from our remote farm. I am very grateful to those who took the time to respond to me the old-fashioned way, via the United States and Canadian Postal Services. The local communication system, in lieu of a phone, should be mentioned: I am grateful to Doris Cohen, Deborah Crittenden, and Mike and Linda Rice.

Judy Kehs of Cricket Hill Herb Farm in Massachusetts was unflagging in her encouragement and helpful in the selection of flowering herbs, as was the late Madeleine Siegler of Monk's Hill Herbs in Maine. I am grateful to R. J. Siegler for permission to quote from her correspondence. Pat Bourdo of Woodland Herb Farm in Michigan was also helpful. Marjory Fortier of Meadowbrook Herb Garden in Rhode Island and Jane Kuitems of Jane's Herb Farm in upstate New York kindly advised me about bloom times in their regions, and Andy VanHevelingen of VanHevelingen Herb Nursery in Oregon wrote about favorite salvias and white borage. Peter Bouchard of Companion Plants in Ohio patiently answered all my questions, as did Louise Hyde of Well Sweep Herb Farm in New Jersey, who also granted permission to print her sweet cicely coffee cake recipe. Tom DeBaggio of T. DeBaggio Herbs in Virginia generously shared his knowledge of lavenders and rosemarys with me and granted permission to include his remarks in the rosemary portrait. The garden writer and nurseryman Fred McGourty of Hillside Gardens in Connecticut perused my allium selections, Conrad Richter of Richters Herbs in Ontario wrote me about purple basils and rosemary hardiness, and Jeanette Lowe, Secretary of the Marigold Society of America and retired plant breeder, advised me about marigolds. Lisa Crowning, horticulturist at Thompson and Morgan in New Jersey was very helpful. Timothy Ingram, a nurseryman in Britain, kindly sent me fresh seeds of *Cerinthe* before they became commercially available, and my old friend and fellow gardener John Moe in the state of Washington never let me down.

All the photographs in this book were contributed by individuals and organizations (cited in the captions) to whom I am indebted. I especially appreciate the major contribution from Brian Oke and Gisèle Quesnel who spent the good part of a summer taking photographs. I am grateful to Karen Michaud of Country Lane Herbs and Jean deGruchy of Graymalkin Farm, both in Ontario, for allowing Brian and Gisèle the free use of their gardens and for answering my questions about their plantings. I am also grateful to Alan Dorey of Halifax who spent a summer taking photographs at our farm, and to landscape architect Holly S. Dougherty of Pavilion, New York, who contributed her drawings.

I am indebted to my daughter Nellie Call of Flower Fields in Batavia, New York, for all her efforts on my behalf, as I am to Bobbe Katzman in Ohio. Her faith in "flower power" really can move mountains. I am grateful to my editor, Ellen Kussow, for her diligence and support. And to my husband, Jigs, thanks is inadequate for his editing of the original manuscript and his unstinting gift of time, which allowed me to write this book.

Preface

AS A HAND in the family's large vegetable garden, I tended culinary herbs for many years, growing parsley by the bushel and what always seemed to be more than enough basil, marjoram, and thyme than I knew what to do with in the ensuing months. My husband, Jigs, attracted by their odd names and arcane uses, dabbled in growing unusual herbs that he picked out from the Thompson and Morgan catalog (when the seeds had to be ordered from England). Although in the 1960s there was very little information about how to grow or use herbs, he raised them successfully in a small cold frame and planted them wherever he could find the space. I remember calendula—golden daisies by the kitchen door—and stately angelica, from whose many stems I learned to make a delicious confection.

Neither of us gave much care to these plants, yet they endured the neglect. Each time we moved to follow Jigs's teaching career—to Wisconsin, Maryland, Massachusetts, Vermont—a few specimens were dug up to plant in a new garden, though we thought little about what kind of garden it would be.

When we moved to the farm on Cape Breton Island, Nova Scotia, in 1971, we soon realized that Jigs would have little time for growing his plants, since reclaiming the land took top priority. I was determined that in this new setting I would at last create a garden all of flowers, the kind I had always dreamed about but had never lived long enough in one place to plant. Even after assuming my new duties in the dairy and hayfield, I had time to plan my dream garden where tall delphiniums, elegant lilies, and roses by the dozen would fill the bare ground beneath an aged apple tree. I had no intention of growing greenery—herbs could go in the kitchen garden where they belonged. I wanted color, enough to last in my memory from one growing season to the next, through the long winter months on a rugged island facing the North Atlantic.

I chose for the garden a south-facing spot not far from the house, almost directly opposite the top of our long dirt lane, the visitor's first clear sight of the farm landscape with its gently rolling hills, small apple orchard, and, on a rise, the old barn sharply outlined against a bright blue sky. My garden area, since then slightly enlarged, was about 500 sq. ft. (46 sq. m) and roughly circular in shape, covered with stones from clearing the fields many years ago and with the remains of an old wood pile, much of which had rotted into the ground over the years. The apple tree was at the back of the circle, and a solitary clump of orange daylilies survived in its shade. It was a beginning.

I raked the rubble fine, pushed away large rocks, gathered smaller ones to mark the area, then cast seeds upon the ground. As we worked around the farm that summer, we were cheered by the annuals that had germinated on the weed-free rubble; cosmos, bachelor's buttons, and poppies gaily waved to us from my first flower garden. Of course, my favorite perennial flowers, sown at the same time, would not bloom until the following season.

Early the next spring after the snow had melted, I surveyed the former rubble pile. It was bare save for the border of rocks, the apple tree, and the daylilies. Nothing at all seemed to be growing there, not even weeds. None of the perennial flowers had germinated. Looking more closely for some sign of hope, I found a few clumps of emerging greenery and recalled some herbs that in all the hubbub of the previous summer I had simply stuck into the ground. They were gifts from friends on our departure from Vermont and a few of my husband's oddities. All would be planted elsewhere when I found the time.

Caught up again in the work of the farm, I was surprised later in the season to see how the neat spears of chives had sprouted pretty, mauve flowers and how the comfrey had grown into a magnificent bush, literally smothered in blue bells that drew a pair of ruby-throated hummingbirds to the garden. By midsummer, the homely elecampane, a spreading clump of oversized leaves, had changed its appearance altogether, like the ugly duckling. What I now saw before me was a tall, distinctive plant with many bright yellow, fringed sunflowers. The once bare hyssop was now covered all along its stems with tiny purple flowers worked over daily by our resident honeybees in search of nectar.

Although these ordinary herbs were not the plants I had envisioned for my first garden, they were beautiful. Plus, I soon learned, they are easy to grow, require little maintenance, are resistant to disease and harmful insects, and most importantly, they offer a long season of varied, colorful, often deliciously scented blooms in exquisite designs. I became a devotee of flowering herbs, seeking them out and bringing them to my garden from wherever I could find them. Sometimes they were growing right under my nose as field weeds, like musk mallow with its soft pink, glistening trumpets in bloom for most of the summer. I soon found places for sweet cicely, clary sage, and the fragrant white mugwort—surely one of the most unknown and underrated of flowering herbs.

Over a period of more than twenty-five years, my garden, indeed much of the farm landscape, became a laboratory for testing flowering herbs of all types for their ornamental value. I learned, through trial and error, which herbs could be directly seeded on the ground and which had to be raised indoors as seedlings before being planted outside. My initial dream garden had failed because I had not given any thought to seeds' germination needs. The original plot was a perfect site because with part of it in the dappled shade of the apple tree and the rest of it in full sun, I could closely observe both sun- and shade-loving plants within a small area. Fortunately, the garden had inherited rich, moist, well-drained soil that had been formed over decades by decomposing organic matter. I was not so lucky elsewhere in the landscape, where I learned to cope with difficult growing conditions in order to accommodate a growing variety of plants, not all of them as easygoing as the ones in my first garden.

I came under the spell of Mediterranean herbs during trips to Israel, where for the first time I saw familiar types growing with exuberance under ideal conditions. There flourished a feast for the herb lover: pebbly-leaved salvias with beautiful candelabras of colorful blooms, yellow fringed rue embellished by flocks of swallowtail butterflies, spice-scented thymes with masses of dark pink, tubular flowers, Spanish lavender announcing its beauty to the world with dark purple flower heads topped by purple flags. I learned later that enthusiasts and specialists had been growing Mediterranean herbs for years in California, where such plants are now highly regarded for their drought resistance and landscaping role. Elsewhere, they have been grown as annuals or in containers that are brought indoors for the winter. I discovered that with care I could grow them, too. My experimentation increased to include growing frost-tender, more demanding herbs in pots and tubs, in custom-made soil, and in sheltered sites to protect them from wind.

Although I had originally conceived of my garden as purely ornamental, I could not help noticing that my flowering herbs had more to offer. I began to pick flowers and leaves to make teas, garnishes, flavorings, scented bouquets, and potpourris. There is an almost indefinable joy in knowing there is always something to harvest, on however modest a scale; I have since established a harvest bed for serious cutting. In the spring, when our stored winter cabbages give out, I dig up some bunches of succulent dandelion greens from the fertile mulch between the rows of raspberries and strawberries, and when my colander is full I head for the front of the herb garden and reach past calendula seedlings and lady's mantle to snip the growing tips of onion-flavored chives to add to our first fresh spring salad.

Flowering herbs have everything I want from a plant, both beauty and practical use. The designs and perfumes of their blossoms find favor, too, in the natural world, where hummingbirds, butterflies, and bees come to them on any sunny day—and moths come in the evening—to sample the varied bounty. I like to watch as they visit each flower, gathering pollen or sipping nectar.

These years of discovery inspired me to write *Herbs in Bloom*. Most gardeners give little serious thought to herbs as significant ornamental flowering plants. Many who might otherwise be attracted to their beauty are put off by the notion that herbs are primarily foliage plants snipped for flavoring and grown in a formal arrangement of types called "the herb garden." It is my aim to convince fellow gardeners that herbs also have beautiful flowers and can be used to advantage anywhere in the landscape. The idea is not new. Gertrude Jekyll incorporated herbs in her landscaping schemes not because they were herbs, but because she saw in them qualities that had something special to contribute to her unequaled "gardens of a golden afternoon." The main flower border at Munstead, England, considered a masterpiece, included sage—plain cooking sage—the most humble plant in the herb line. But it is undeniably beautiful, especially in flower, and Jekyll did not hesitate to show off its attributes.

Every writer on the subject is obliged to offer a definition of herbs because the subject is so vast, because, in a general sense, *all* plants are herbs: "Behold, I have given you every herb bearing seed, which is upon the face of the earth" (Gen 1:29). We obviously need to narrow the field to manageable proportions. A common and useful definition of an herb is a plant with a history of use for its culinary, medicinal, or fragrant properties. (Although there are trees and shrubs that fit this definition—some with beautiful flowers—they are, with a few notable exceptions, not included in this book for want of space.) A core group of plants, handed down from the European herbal tradition, has gradually emerged over centuries from this general definition. The familiar flavoring and scented herbs—parsley, rosemary, sage, thyme—and the old medicinals—comfrey, lungwort, yarrow—are by common consent the ones that have received virtually all the attention in the literature. Though it would be unthinkable to omit them I have also looked beyond them.

Outside the core group are the largely overlooked, native North American species—bloodroot, the lobelias, bugbane, the bergamots, and Culver's root, for instance—undeniably herbs because of their past and present uses. Also there are the herbs introduced after the core group was established: the many alliums, salvias, and thymes, as well as those more recently discovered (*Angelica gigas*) or more recently introduced (*Thymbra spicata*). Many of these occupy a tenuous place at the edges of the herb canon, residing in a category known as "ornamentals," because little is known about their herbal properties. But in their countries of origin they are often highly regarded as useful plants, and it is in this spirit that I include them in this book.

The core group itself, however, needs to be reexamined, for some of the most desirable flowering herbs have fallen by the wayside. Where are the herbs of antiquity: bugloss, bistort, and self-heal? Some, like bistort, have been rediscovered by discerning North American gardeners, although the British have been growing the superior cultivar *Polygonum bistorta* 'Superbum' for decades. But others, like self-heal, by its very name recognizable as an important herb, have been so improved in appearance by hybridization that herb enthusiasts find it embarrassing to claim them as herbs because of their showy flowers. Yet hybrids, variants, and cultivars do not necessarily lose their herbal properties; in some instances, as in double-flowered chamomile, they may actually gain. The attitude of disregarding pretty flowers as herbs is widespread among gardeners in general, for whom "herbs" brings to mind foliage plants. I think it is time for some fresh thinking on the subject.

Portia Meares, past president of the International Herb Association, observed that using herbs as garden and landscape plants "is an herb art form just beginning to be explored." You can turn them into teas and potpourri if you like, but there is no obligation to *use* the herbs in this book. It can be a liberating experience, even for dedicated herb gardeners, to grow these plants simply for their own sake, for their beautiful flowers.

> **To stand by the beds at sunrise
> and see the flowers awake
> is a heavenly sight.**
>
> Celia Thaxter, *An Island Garden*

Plate 2. *Aconitum napellus,* monkshood (See p. 62). Midsummer, Country Lane Herbs

Growing Flowering Herbs

nd Dried Flowers, Puslinch, Ontario, Canada. Photo, Brian Oke and Gisèle Quesnel.

NOTHING is mysterious about growing herbs. Of course, like any other type, they are varied plants with different requirements. Some thrive in full sun and fast-draining soil, while others need shade, heavy soil, and steady moisture—even wet feet—to grow to their full capacity. Growing herbs mainly for their flowers demands only certain adjustments, for instance, cutting back plants or enriching the soil, to produce more bloom.

Since each herb portrait in Chapter Three includes detailed growing instructions, I review here general techniques, the mastery of which leads to success in raising, maintaining, and propagating the many plants described in *Herbs in Bloom*.

Growing from seed

The advantage of growing plants from seed, aside from the satisfaction of initiating the growing process, is that for a fraction of what it would cost to purchase them, a virtual army of seedlings can be raised to satisfy every landscaping need. Seed propagation is viable for a large and varied group of herbs among annuals, biennials, and perennials.

Most gardeners welcome the variability of seed-grown plants, relishing the mystery in the phenomenon that turns up pink or white flowers among blue, or single or semidouble flowers among double. Seed strains, as distinct from vegetatively reproduced cultivars, may deteriorate over time, losing their desirable characteristics, as is the case with purple basils (*Ocimum basilicum* var. *purpurascens*). In commercial seed production, the process of restoring a named strain to its intended form is called reselection. In the garden, strains that are allowed to seed themselves over several generations may also deteriorate, for example, as tall, large-flowered *Calendula officinalis* Pacific Beauty in a range of colors will revert to shorter plants with smaller yellow and orange flowers. Then, freshly purchased seed should be reintroduced to the garden, or gardeners can practice their own reselection by saving and sowing seeds of the most desirable types.

Germination, the single most important factor in growing plants from seed, is often overlooked in general growing directions. It is crucial to keep in mind that techniques for encouraging germination vary from plant to plant. Requirements for specific plants are included in the plant portraits. For the highest germination rates, it is important to condition seeds. Conditioning may include, in any combination, (1) exposing seeds to warm, cool, or fluctuating temperatures, (2) sowing seeds on the soil surface so they are exposed to light, or covering them so they are in total darkness, and (3) chipping or soaking hard seed coats so moisture can penetrate them. Seeds may germinate even if you do not condition them properly, but germination rates will be lower and the resulting seedlings may not be as vigorous.

While it is very rewarding to grow plants from seeds you have sown yourself, nothing is more discouraging than failure—a blank space where the seeds, sown with such anticipation, have mysteriously vanished, leaving no trace. The most common reasons for germination failure, aside from a lack of conditioning, include the following:

🍃 Seeds planted too deep. A rule of thumb is to cover seeds with twice their thickness of soil. Seeds smaller than a pinhead should be just pressed into the soil. If in doubt about planting depth, sow shallow. Remember that seeds are small for the work they have to do.

🍃 Soil dried out or soggy. Provide even moisture. Seeds must be in contact with moisture to germinate, but if the soil is soggy, they will rot.

🍃 Temperatures too cold. A majority of seeds require steady, warm temperatures in the 70°F (21°C) range to germinate.

🍃 Seeds old or of poor quality. Some seeds retain their viability for years, but germination rates usually decline.

Sowing

Sowing seeds directly in the ground where you want the plants to grow is the easiest way to establish some herbs, principally fast-growing annuals that complete their growing cycle in a single season. Perennials that spend the first season as seedlings tend to get lost in surrounding growth.

Deciding which annual herbs to sow outdoors depends more on the type of soil and how it conducts heat than on the length of the growing season. For many years in northern Vermont, where the growing season is theoretically shorter than it is in northeastern Nova Scotia, we always seeded basils (*Ocimum basilicum*) and thymes outdoors, where the germination rate was high in the early-warming, loamy soil and growth was rapid. On Cape Breton Island, supposedly a warmer growing region, I must start these same plants indoors because the soil is heavy and late warming, germination rates outdoors are low, and plants grow slowly.

Sow the following herbs in weed-free and porous, prepared, ground: borage (*Borago officinalis*), calendula, German chamomile (*Matricaria recutita*), common mallow (*Malva sylvestris*), cooking sage (*Salvia officinalis*), nasturtium (*Tropaeolum*), nigella, painted sage (*Salvia viridis*), poppy (*Papaver*), purple basil (*Ocimum basilicum* var. *purpurascens*), signet marigold (*Tagetes tenuifolia*), summer savory (*Satureja hortensis*), and sunflower (*Helianthus annuus*).

The following short-lived perennials or biennials can be grown easily by direct seeding (those with an asterisk may bloom the first year): chicory (*Cichorium intybus*), feverfew* (*Tanacetum parthenium*), hollyhock (*Alcea rosea*), hollyhock mallow* (*Malva alcea* 'Fastigiata'), musk mallow* (*Malva moschata*), and sweet rocket* (*Hesperis matronalis*). All of these germinate readily and are recommended for beginning gardeners.

Seeds of perennials that require stratification—exposure to freezing temperatures to break down germination inhibitors—may be sown outdoors in prepared ground set aside for the purpose, or in a cold frame. Seeds sown in the fall should produce seedlings the following spring. A disadvantage of sowing perennials outside is that unless the cold frame is covered, the seeds are exposed to the vagaries and hazards of nature, such as heavy rains, the activities of birds, insects, and animals, or fluctuating temperatures (from which some seed types may benefit). Seeds can be sown in pots, watered well, then placed in a covered cold frame for the winter. Seedlings will form a better root system in the confines of a pot.

The easiest and most economical way to raise a large number of seedlings indoors is with a set of two 40 watt, fluorescent lights, which can be installed anywhere in the house where room temperature is about 70°F (21°C). The time needed to germinate seeds of many herbs can be dramatically shortened with bottom heat supplied by a heating cable run under germinating flats or with a heating pad set on medium. An effective way to prechill seeds requiring stratification is to place them within the fold of a twice-doubled and moistened paper towel, place the folded towel in a loosely sealed, plastic bag, and put it in the refrigerator, at approximately 40°F (4°C), or the freezer for the time recommended in Chapter Three for particular plants.

Propagation

Not every plant is suited to growing from seed. For example, seeds of cultivars (cultivated varieties of species) and hybrids (the result of cross-fertilization between species) often do not resemble the parent in every way. Some plants are discouraging to grow from seed because they take a year or more to germinate or germinate sporadically, and some, like angelica (*Angelica archangelica*), germinate best from only freshly harvested seed. To bypass these difficulties, all of these kinds of herbs are best multiplied by propagation from roots or plants.

Dividing established plants by chopping their roots into sections is the easiest way to increase many perennials. Division works best with herbs that have tender rather than woody growth at their bases. Plunge a sharp spade into an overgrown clump—dig up the whole clump or chop it in place—dividing it into smaller sections. Replant a section in the ground, watering well until new signs of growth appear. Make sure each division has a good root system and several sprouts or eyes. Large divisions generally transplant with more difficulty than smaller ones, but, as with all aspects of gardening, balance is involved. If the chunk of root is very small, replant it where it will receive more attention, such as in a cold frame, rather than in the garden where it could be overwhelmed by its more established neighbors. Plants can be divided in the spring or fall, whenever they are dormant. Some that easily divide are: chives (*Allium schoenoprasum*), bee balm (*Monarda didyma*), catmint (*Nepeta* ×*faassenii*), creeping thyme (*Thymus praecox* subsp. *arcticus, T. pulegoides*), garlic chives (*Allium tuberosum*), lady's mantle (*Alchemilla mollis*), primulas, sweet woodruff (*Galium odoratum*), wild bergamot (*Monarda fistulosa*), and wild marjoram (*Origanum vulgare* subsp. *vulgare*).

Layering is a simple way to propagate any shrubby herb with long, flexible basal branches that can be bent to the ground, such as rosemary (*Rosmarinus officinalis*), hyssop (*Hyssopus officinalis*), and santolina. Make a slit on the point of a branch and bury it in 3–4 in. (7.6–10.2 cm) of soil, pegging it down securely with a large rock, peg of wood, or length of wire so the branch will stay in place. The following season, whenever top growth appears, sever the newly rooted plant from its parent and relocate the new plant.

Taking tip cuttings is the best method for increasing woody, shrubby plants. When there is sufficient growth, in midsummer or indoors in the late winter or spring, cut a green, nonwoody stem just below a node, 3–6 in. (7.6–15.2 cm) from the tip of a healthy, nonflowering, side shoot or the main stem of the plant. Make a sharp cut at an angle, remove the bottom leaves, and dip the end of the stem in rooting hormone powder. Then insert the stem in a container or flat filled with a peat moss–perlite combination or your favorite medium. Cover the container loosely with plastic to conserve moisture, then place it out of direct light. Check occasionally to make sure the plastic tent is just holding in moisture and not creating wet conditions, which will cause the cuttings to rot. If necessary, open the tent a little to let in air. Thyme cuttings should be planted by themselves for they need to be kept drier than others. If temperatures are maintained at 70°F (21°C), cuttings should form roots in 6 weeks or less. Herbs that can be increased by stem cuttings include: bush thyme (*Thymus vulgaris*), hyssop (*Hyssopus officinalis*), lavender (*Lavandula angustifolia*), rosemary (*Rosmarinus officinalis*), salvias, and santolinas.

For some plants, water will substitute for soil as a rooting medium. When you include a few flowering stems of purple basil (*Ocimum basilicum* var. *purpurascens*) in a bouquet, the basil will have started to form roots before the bouquet is spent. The same is true of pineapple sage (*Salvia elegans*), rosemary (*Rosmarinus officinalis*), and lavender (*Lavandula angustifolia*). To root herbs in water, change the water every day, and when the roots are ¹/₂ in. (1.3 cm) long, pot up the cuttings, handling them like seedlings.

The easiest way to propagate plants with fleshy roots is to make root cuttings in the fall. Cut 2 in. (5.1 cm) sections of healthy roots, place them in an upright position in a pot 4 in. (10.2 cm) deep, and cover the sections with ¹/₂ in. (0.5 cm) of soil. Water well and place pot in a cold frame for the winter. The following spring, replant when the shoots are 3 in. (7.6 cm) tall. An alternative method of root cutting is to take a piece of fleshy root, even a small one, with some top growth. Roots will grow over the winter, producing a new plant by spring. I use this method to ensure that a variety of hollyhock (*Alcea rosea*) colors is always available. I plant the root cuttings in a cold frame, mark them with stakes to identify plants by color, then replant them where I want them in the spring. The following herbs can be increased by root cuttings: butterfly weed (*Asclepias tuberosa*), chicory (*Cichorium intybus*), comfrey (*Symphytum*), elecampane (*Inula he-lenium*), hollyhock, hop vine (*Humulus lupulus*), musk mallow (*Malva moschata*), and sweet rocket (*Hesperis matronalis*).

Planting seedlings outside

Before planting seedlings or purchased or propagated plants in their permanent place outside, consider the site and the soil conditions. Any advance thought toward alleviating or eliminating plant stress can considerably increase a plant's vigor. Providing each herb with its preferred habitat goes a long way to growing happy plants with lustrous foliage, prolific bloom, and a perky, satisfied habit. Such plants are far less prone to disease and better able to withstand insect predation.

Site requirements primarily refer to a plant's light needs. Full sun means six hours of direct sun a day; partial shade means morning or afternoon sun only, or filtered light from a high tree canopy; and shade means varying degrees of dappled light for the whole day, or a few hours of morning or afternoon sun. Many plants that do well in full sun will also grow well with only morning or afternoon light if it is direct. In choosing the planting site, consider also the topography of the land and surrounding features. Slopes provide natural drainage, and buildings and fences may create favorable microclimates with their protection from wind.

Soil conditions are generally classified with regard to moisture level; thus, soil can be described as sharply drained, well-drained, evenly moist, or boggy. Mediterranean herbs—such as lavender (*Lavandula angustifolia*), rosemary (*Rosmarinus officinalis*), and thyme—native to rocky, limestone areas, require sharply drained, light-textured, gritty, and alkaline soil. Water should quickly pass through the soil surface and off from plant roots. Other plants requiring sharp drainage such as foxglove (*Digitalis*), pinks (*Dianthus*), and hollyhock (*Alcea rosea*) will grow in richer soil, but it must be well-drained. If moisture collects at their root crowns in the winter or early spring they will not surivive.

The vast majority of flowering herbs prefer well-drained soil, sometimes referred to as garden soil, that is balanced between acid and alkaline. This is richer and loamy with a porous texture; a handful can be squeezed together in a ball and will easily fall apart when slightly shaken on the palm of the hand. Water penetrates the soil surface, bringing moisture to plant roots. Few desirable plants grow well in soil with the opposite characteristics—compacted clay.

A surprising number of herbs thrive in evenly moist or boggy conditions. Some, like chives, that grow well in garden soil, are outstanding in wet conditions. Various native wildflowers such as marsh marigold (*Caltha palustris*) and blue flag iris (*Iris versicolor*) grow best in a little standing water. Others, like meadowsweet (*Filipendula*) and dame's rocket (*Hesperis matronalis*), need moist but not necessarily wet conditions to thrive.

It is possible to amend soils to some degree in order to provide favorable growing conditions, but some amendments, such as creating a bog, are not very practical. It is inadvisable to dig up heavy soil and replace it with something better, for doing so usually creates a dip in the land that is not easily overcome. A far more successful option is to create a raised bed, to build up from the soil surface. In time, the top layer of organic matter, compost for instance, will soften the bottom layer, thereby creating new, more favorable growing conditions. Adding grit to the soil, such as rough sand, will also improve drainage.

Plate 3. *Caltha palustris*, marsh marigold, grows well in boggy conditions (See p. 112). Early summer, Memorial University Botanical Garden at Oxen Pond, St. John's, Newfoundland, Canada. Photo, Bernard S. Jackson.

To encourage healthy plants to grow to produce abundant bloom, all types of soil usually need enrichment. Compost or manure may not be sufficient although they improve the soil's tilth, or crumbly texture. Where maximum bloom is desired, plants may need additional fertilizer, such as 6-12-12, high in phosphates and potash. Nitrogen-rich soil encourages leaf production at the expense of flowers.

When planting out seedlings or more mature plants, it is most important to dig holes of sufficient size to accommodate roots. It is vital that each plant, of whatever type, establish a good root system, for it is the carrier of moisture and nutrients to the rest of the plant. Where drainage is of crucial importance, hill up the soil and position the roots so they are hanging downward. When filling in the planting hole, be sure to firm the soil so there are no air pockets. Try to plant on windless days with some cloud cover to help prevent moisture loss from roots disturbed by transplanting. If seedlings have been grown in plant cells or other containers where they develop a solid block of roots, transplanting shock is reduced virtually to zero.

Steady moisture, so important for seed germination, is also important for seedling establishment. Underground trickle irrigation is most effective but may be beyond the means of most gardeners. Overhead watering, unless prolonged, does not always reach plant roots in sufficient amounts, and it may encourage fungus disease by the overwatering of foliage. Follow these simple steps to encourage steady moisture:

- Increase the water-holding capacity of the soil by working in leaf mold or moistened peat moss. Dry peat moss will actually prevent the absorption of available moisture.
- Set transplants deeper in the ground and closer together than is ordinarily recommended, to make use of available ground moisture and to encourage shading. Water the planting hole with a dilute solution of soluble plant food high in phosphates (15-30-15). This eliminates wilting, even when planting on a dry, windy day.
- Mulch plants, especially in drought periods. A $1^{1}/_{2}$–2 in. (3.8–5.1 cm) layer of organic or inorganic material will reduce water evaporation from the soil and cool its surface.

When considering planting closer together to conserve moisture, bear in mind that some plants, such as roses, must have good air circulation since they are subject to fungus disease. Successful gardening is a balancing act that may involve the resolution of contradictory needs.

Planting ground covers is no different from planting other types of plants—the ground should be weeded well and enriched if necessary—but keep in mind that they all do not grow at the same rate. Do not imagine that in its very first season the ajugas or creeping Jenny (*Lysimachia nummularia*) will entirely fill in an area. It may take three seasons to establish a thick carpet. The process can be helped along by laying down a 1–2 in. (2.5–5.1 cm) mulch to keep the soil moist so that runners are encouraged to root. Also, push the runners into the soil, heap dirt on them here and there, peg down trailing stems, and pinch growing tips to stimulate growth.

As an alternative to planting in the ground, many aromatic herbs can be enjoyed close at hand near entrances and on patios by being grown in containers. Prime candidates are bright annuals, such as nasturtiums (*Tropaeolum*), dwarf calendulas, and signet marigolds (*Tagetes tenuifolia*). Also, frost-tender herbs such as pineapple sage (*Salvia elegans*), rosemary (*Rosmarinus officinalis*), Mediterranean rue (*Ruta chalapensis*), and others are easier to move indoors for the winter if they are grown in containers. Since containers vary considerably in size, keep in mind that the larger the volume of soil, the less it will dry out. To reduce the need for watering, which could be twice daily in hot conditions, mulch plants, place them in partial shade, and group them for ease of maintenance. Annual plants do not need to be grown in containers with drainage holes if there is a 2 in. (5.1 cm) layer of gravel in the bottom. Potting soil, amended with extra perlite and vermiculite, is a good soil mix. To conserve soil in very large containers, such as a half barrel, fill all but the top 6–8 in. (15.2–20.3 cm) with rotted sawdust or layers of newspaper. Fertilize plants every two or three weeks with soluble plant food or put a shovelful of compost in the container before adding the top layer of potting soil. Trim plants as necessary to maintain their shape and to encourage continued flowering.

Maintenance

Once plants are growing well, continued care is important for keeping them in fit condition. Ensure that plants receive steady moisture, for even drought-resistant varieties will grow better. A midsummer application of fertilizer (6-12-12) will promote continued bloom. Scratch the fertilizer into the soil surface and water it in well. Deadhead—remove spent flowers—or cut back plants to encourage a second period of flowering. Stems overburdened with bloom may need staking. And keep constant watch for disease and pest infestations.

Some herbs, like the bergamots (*Monarda*), can be encouraged to produce more flowers if exhausted flowering stalks are cut back to leaf axils, at which point more buds may form; but since such flowering is not usually heavy, it may not be worth the trouble. In such cases, it is more worthwhile to cut plants back almost to the ground to promote fresh foliage, in itself of ornamental value. Sweet cicely (*Myrrhis odorata*), for instance, which blooms only once (and that for a relatively brief period), will more readily produce a beautiful mound of ferny leaves if cut back after the flowers fade. Other herbs like feverfew (*Tanacetum parthenium*) and musk mallow (*Malva moschata*) are so eager to produce more flowers that buds form at the base before top flowers are entirely dead. As soon as the old stalks are cut back, plants shoot up, once more in full bloom. Picking flowers for bouquets is a painless form of trimming that not only encourages flower production but leads to more compact plants. Annuals, whose raison d'être is the production of flowers, readily respond to trimming and deadheading by forming yet more flowers for uninterrupted bloom. When the heads of German chamomile (*Matricaria recutita*) are picked for tea, new flowers seem to open overnight.

When cutting back plants in the fall, after their bloom cycle is complete, leave up to 24 in. (61.0 cm) of stalks as "arms" to catch snow, the best winter insulator. In harsh climates, do not trim shrubby plants in late summer, especially marginally hardy types like lavender (*Lavandula angustifolia*), since this encourages tender growth that cannot withstand freezing temperatures over the winter.

Even by pinching growing tips to encourage bushiness and cutting back naturally tall plants to dwarf them, as I advise for white mugwort (*Artemisia lactiflora*), some herbs will need staking, especially when they are heavily laden with flowers. Most annuals can support a heavy crop, but there are exceptions. Borage (*Borago officinalis*), particularly self-sown plants, tends to produce floppy stems. These are better trimmed than staked. Somewhat sprawling plants may contribute to a cottage garden aura but may take up too much room, crowding other plants. When all else fails, stake, and the sooner the better, so growing stems and foliage will cover the stake naturally.

As a general rule, support, of whatever type, should be about three-fourths the expected height of the plant. For short plants like pinks (*Dianthus*), the sprawling flower heads can be supported by strong twigs inserted in the clump here and there. Medium tall types, like a vigorous purple basil (*Ocimum basilicum* var. *purpurascens*) grown in rich soil, may need staking, especially to keep the leaves clean for harvesting. The best support for such plants is a corral of sticks—three per plant is enough—and twine. Tall plants like foxglove (*Digitalis*), monkshood (*Aconitum napellus*), and hollyhock (*Alcea rosea*) need a corral of posts of a material stronger than bamboo. Or each main stem can be tied in several places to a single stake; for the tie, use stretchy material, such as lengths cut from old T-shirts or pantyhose. Tie the lengths in a loose figure-eight between the stake and the stalk so there is no danger of the stalk being cut. Some gardeners use tomato cages for plants like monkshood, whose bushy base will cover the cage.

When the growing season approaches its end, it is time to consider preparing plants for winter survival. Snow is the best possible protection for hardy perennials in colder areas. In many climates, however, snow cover is variable, and successive freezing and thawing may occur, which can heave plants out of the ground. For added protection cover plants with a thick layer of straw or with evergreen boughs *after* the first frost. A thick layer of compost can also be used, which has the advantage of enriching the soil in the spring, when it can be carefully raked off the plants and used as a ground mulch. Whatever cover is used, do not remove it too early, or plants may suffer from freezing temperatures in the late winter or very early spring; wait until the ground begins to thaw.

Where frost-tender herbs such as rosemary (*Rosmarinus officinalis*), pineapple sage (*Salvia elegans*), and others do not survive the winter outdoors, there are ways to save the plants. If they have been grown in moveable containers, shift the whole plant indoors by stages—first to a shed or porch, then indoors—before the first frost, so it becomes acclimatized to indoor conditions. This is the best procedure to use with pineapple sage since it may not begin to bloom in cooler regions until late fall. When taking in any plants, either potted or from the ground, spray them with insecticide or wash them with insecticidal soap so you will not also be transferring bugs indoors. In the spring, cut back the plants, fertilize with a soluble plant food (15-30-15), and put them back outside, repotting if necessary.

If plants have been grown in the ground, dig them up, give them a heavy top pruning, trim the roots to fit the container if necessary, and replant them in containers to winter indoors. Another option is to propagate new plants by taking stem cuttings any time during the year when the old plants are in healthy growth but not flowering, raise the cuttings indoors through the winter, and establish the plants outside in the spring. Some Mediterranean plants, like spiked thymbra (*Thymbra spicata*), are best propagated in the fall or in early spring.

Disease and insect infestation

It is a myth that herbs are immune to disease and insect infestation. They are plants like all others, subject to the same problems. It is true that well-grown plants are less susceptible to disease and better able to withstand predatory insects. To maintain health, provide air circulation to prevent fungus attack, and in the fall after frost clean up debris around plants where insects spend the winter. Slugs will enjoy the damp conditions created by mulching, so be prepared to deal with them or to abandon mulching. Generally it is advisable not to act until something is bothering the plants. Many insects live on them and do no harm, but when plants show signs of stress, delaying treatment can only lead to further weakening or death. If nothing is done to destroy insect populations they will build up to cause even more damage, becoming ever more difficult to destroy. For chemical sprays (very effective but only when used precisely) and organic methods, follow through with each treatment according to directions. It may be necessary, for instance, to spray once a week for three weeks with a chemical spray to destroy both adult insects and hatching eggs. Consult agricultural and university extension services for the best chemical and organic methods for dealing with pests and diseases.

**Herbs reach their peak of usefulness
when treated as ornamentals in their own right,
not merely as subjects for the herb garden.**

Allen Paterson, Brooklyn Botanic Garden, *Handbook on Herbs and Their Ornamental Uses*

Plate 4. *Stachys officinalis,* wood betony, in partial shade (See p. 310). Midsummer, Count

Landscaping with Flowering Herbs

ane Herbs and Dried Flowers, Puslinch, Ontario, Canada. Photo, Brian Oke and Gisèle Quesnel.

THE PLACE where we are free as gardeners to translate the vision we see in our mind's eye into living reality—no matter how extensive and rambling or small and confined—is what we call the landscape, a broad term that encompasses our immediate outdoor living space and its adjacent surroundings. Most often, herbs are predictably grouped together in raised beds outlined with timbers, surrounded by gravel paths. There is a sense of satisfaction in creating tidy beds where plants of contrasting foliage are shown to advantage in blocks, and I would not like to discourage gardeners from establishing them (especially if a few colorful flowering herbs are added). But such a conventional notion, based on an idealized reconstruction of Colonial gardens popular in the herb revival movement of the 1930s, has become dominant, perpetuating the concept of herbs as primarily foliage plants with minor landscaping possibilities. Herbs have much more to offer. Gradually gardeners are becoming aware that the world of herbs is large and varied, and that herbs are individual plants in their own right, suggesting varied landscaping roles.

It will become apparent, in the portrait section that follows, that herbs with beautiful flowers are not exceptions. Gardeners new to growing herbs as ornamentals will be pleasantly surprised by their varied scents—sweet, spicy, or citrus, sometimes sharply penetrating—that are released when working in their vicinity or that freely flow from their opened flowers. What could be more pleasant than passing the old-fashioned, double-flowered soapwort (*Saponaria officinalis* 'Rosea Plena') on a midsummer evening and breathing in its sweet clove aroma?

Each herb's possible landscape uses are noted in the portrait section with the following shorthand terms: accent, bed and border, container, edge and hedge, ground cover, naturalized herb, and rock work. These are expanded in the text of the portraits to include pleasing plant combinations. For now, here are definitions of each function and descriptions of how they can be achieved. These functions do not in themselves create a landscape. Each individual planting is a single element, whether it is a formal bed, a cottage garden, a border, or a collection of potted plants on a sunny patio. What holds these elements together to create a harmonious landscape is their successful integration—their reference to one another, to the land itself in its varied topography and habitat, and to built structures such as houses, walls, or fences—so that plantings seem naturally linked to one another. Tall, billowy Russian sage (*Perovskia abrotanoides, P. atriplicifolia*), when used as an independent accent, can enhance an otherwise dull cement wall, or a screen of tall hollyhocks (*Alcea rosea*) can beautify the mundane compost heap.

Accent

There are flowering herbs that will not only grow, but thrive, in virtually every growing condition where accents are needed, everywhere from dry and sunny to moist and shady. And keep in mind that for many plants, the bloom period can be extended by growing different varieties. Outside the garden proper in the general landscape, an accent is achieved with plants of strong form that draw attention to themselves, thereby enhancing existing features such as walls, fences, driveways, sheds or garages, entranceways, bare banks, exposed slopes, compost heaps, storage areas, winding paths, stairways, anywhere that embellishment seems needed.

The best plants for this purpose are those that can stand alone or be combined with a few others. These include perennials of significant stature such as the tall, wide hollyhock mallow (*Malva alcea*) that offers full, uninterrupted, silvery pink bells the entire summer. The flowering artemisias, white mugwort (*Artemisia lactiflora*) and sweet Annie (*A. annua*), are shrub-like in their proportions, growing tall and wide with attractive foliage all season and at least a month's bloom of small flowers—creamy white sprays in white mugwort, bright, golden clusters in sweet Annie—that gain in effect by their sheer numbers. The advantage of growing these instead of shrubs is that they are less permanent and can be changed easily; they also combine more readily with other plants for contrast and interest.

Accents can be medium to tall vertical plants such as foxglove (*Digitalis*) laden with spotted bells all along its stalk for a month in early summer, monkshood (*Aconitum napellus*) with its purple-blue spires, or the agastaches in late summer. A single plant of angelica (*Angelica archangelica*)—an attractive mound of deeply cut leaves its first year, a tower of chartreuse umbels the second—can transform a shady corner into an asset, as can a large clump of golden, buttoned tansy (*Tanacetum vulgare*) by a shed, fence, or wall, where it will also be protected from the wind. Herbs such as brightly flowered, old-fashioned climbing nasturtium (*Tropaeolum*) and hop vine (*Humulus lupulus*) twine around supports, against walls, and over doorways or arbors, creating appealing accents wherever they are grown. Arbors, in particular, are strong linking structural elements; they invite passage from one planting to another and emphasize a formal or relaxed style with their frames, as in a classic cast iron structure or a rough wooden arch.

Within the confines of a garden, accents can be drawn from those same sorts of large plants where space permits, but where space is limited use low types that not only combine well with surrounding plants but draw attention to themselves and give interest and drama to the planting, often at seasons when fresh flowers are needed. A low-growing mat of bright crimson creeping thyme (*Thymus praecox* subsp. *arcticus, T. pulegoides*) early

Vertical foxgloves (*Digitalis*) laden with bells are combined with a mound of roses and a lavender (*Lavandula angustifolia*) hedge to create a pleasing accent at the edge of a property. This planting effectively enhances the straight picket fence boundary, providing a gentle and gradual separation between the garden proper and the landscape beyond.

in the season or medium tall and billowing lady's mantle (*Alchemilla mollis*) with chartreuse flower clusters nearly all summer are both capable of defining a corner or softening an edge. Other good accents are a medium tall mound of rue (*Ruta graveolens*), crowned by yellow clusters from midsummer until snow flies, and fall salvias suddenly appearing in wide swathes of red, blue, or purple. Accents achieve their effect within a garden setting by rising up boldly in the center of an island bed, in the middle or background of a border, or even at the very edges of such plantings, wherever strong form and bright color are needed.

Bed and border

A bed is any shape—square, rectangular, oblong, circular, curved—that lacks a backdrop, such as a wall, fence, or shrubbery. When cut into the grass, they are called island beds, a name suited to the independent, open forms, viewed from all sides. Where beds are large, a path is needed for maintenance; the path also becomes a positive element in the design, adding structure and the opportunity to grow any number of small plants along its way. Paths can be brick, paved, bark, even packed soil or grass. Laying down plastic, placing flat stones on top, then filling in with a thick layer of sawdust creates an instant path needing very little maintenance. In formal plantings, as in a raised, hedged bed in the traditional "herb garden" style, paths are usually straight; in a round or island, they curve gracefully.

Sun-loving, Mediterranean herbs such as lavenders, thymes, and gray and green santolinas that also demand perfect drainage are especially suited to raised bed plantings. These plants can provide drifts of color from massed flowers in crimsons, pinks, lavenders, and yellows. They are also well suited for low to medium hedges, stiff or loose, that can encircle and frame bushy or vertical forms like musk mallow (*Malva moschata*) and veronicas. An open sunny bed also favors signet marigold (*Tagetes tenuifolia*) at its edges, displaying golden and tangerine mounds of flowers all summer.

Beds can also be established in partial shade, where many herbs flourish. Try the clump-forming *Ajuga* 'Pink Beauty' for early bloom, medium tall and long-flowering monardas in red, pink, or lilac for midsummer, and for late summer and fall, the red or blue spires of the lobelias and the whites of Canadian burnet (*Sanguisorba canadensis*), bugbane (*Cimicifuga*), and Culver's root (*Veronicastrum*).

The classic herbaceous border is an oblong strip, even as much as 5 ft. (1.5 m) wide, backed by a wall, fence, or shrubbery. Although perennials define an herbaceous border, there is some scope for showing off bright annuals in bays where they are not overwhelmed by larger plants. Orange and yellow calendulas or nasturtiums (*Tropaeolum*), purple, pink, or white painted sage (*Salvia viridis*), or pastel viper's bugloss in the incomparable low-growing *Echium vulgare* 'Dwarf Brilliant' are splendid accents for the more substantial perennials.

Borders are usually designed with taller types such as monkshoods (*Aconitum napellus*), agastaches, fall salvias, goldenrods (*Solidago*), Russian sage (*Perovskia abrotanoides, P. atriplicifolia*), comfrey (*Symphytum*), and the meadowsweets (*Filipendula*) providing a background, with medium tall alliums, achilleas, echinaceas, musk mallow (*Malva moschata*), and betony (*Stachys officinalis*) in the middle rank, and low-growing lungworts (*Pulmonaria officinalis*), primulas, origanums, and pinks (*Dianthus*) up front. But plants should not be regimented by height, since irregularity is what gives the border its great appeal. It is the work of a lifetime, however, to find which plants together create the most pleasing impact throughout the growing season. Fortunately, flowering herbs offer great scope for herbaceous borders in their varied habits and seasonal bloom.

The cottage garden is a common form created with some of the same plants used in beds and borders. Based on an idealized version of the gardens of the rural poor in the English countryside, the convention is loosely interpreted to mean virtually any informal planting. However, those plants regarded as belonging to a cottage garden are the ones that were, in fact, most often grown by cottagers because of their ease of culture and free-flowering nature. The vast majority are herbs, some of whose common names end in "wort," meaning plant, or whose Latin species name is *officinalis*, "of the shop," signifying that it was a plant sold in apothecary shops. These include lungwort (*Pulmonaria officinalis*), soapwort (*Saponaria officinalis*), cooking sage (*Salvia officinalis*), hyssop (*Hyssopus officinalis*), the common peony (*Paeonia officinalis*), and the apothecary's rose (*Rosa gallica* 'Officinalis'). Other plants commonly grown for their perfumed flowers or practical uses were sweet rocket (*Hesperis matronalis*), sweet cicely (*Myrrhis odorata*), sweet woodruff (*Galium odoratum*), clove pinks (*Dian-*

thus caryophyllus), and cottage pinks (*D. plumarius*), as well as lavender (*Lavandula angustifolia*) and rosemary (*Rosmarinus officinalis*) whose foliage and flowers were at hand for potpourri and ceremonial occasions.

Growing even a handful of the plants described in this book can create a cottage garden atmosphere. In a border, plants are usually grown close together to create an appealing picture, a jumble of color, as cottage gardens are commonly described. Interpreted in the grand English manner,

This planting in the cottage garden style is established in a protected, sunny corner, where hollyhocks (*Alcea rosea*) can grow against the wall. Plants of varied heights and forms provide colorful blooms and scents throughout the season.

however, the humble cottage garden is well planned and carefully executed. Since many gardeners are not working in British conditions, where such plantings always appear lush and full flowering, follow the cultural directions for each plant, allowing it the air circulation it needs for healthy growth.

Container

A useful rule for gardening with containers is that for their greatest impact they should be grouped in larger rather than smaller numbers (according to one's ability to look after them). An important exception is a large tub or urn that makes a statement by itself, especially when it contains a picturesque shrub, such as rosemary (*Rosmarinus officinalis*) with its twisted stems covered with green, needle-like leaves and a multitude of tiny, blue flowers. Try placing this in the center of a raised island bed or at the entrance to a patio. A good rule of thumb in matching plants to containers is to remember that short plants look better in tall containers; tall plants look better in shorter ones. It is a challenge to plant a contained mini-garden of several different plants that complement each other in color, form, and texture. Spike, mounding, and trailing types combine well. Do not feel pressured, though, to accommodate several different plants in a single container; a container planted to a single type with a trailing accent is almost always appealing.

Flowering herbs most suited to pot culture are annuals and frost-tender perennials. If planted in light containers, they can be easily moved indoors before frost. Among appropriate annuals are several culinary herbs such as basil (*Ocimum basilicum*), sage (*Salvia officinalis*), savory (*Satureja hortensis*), and nasturtium (*Tropaeolum*), to which could be added tubs of chives (*Allium schoenoprasum*) and thyme. If these are intended for use, then the flowers are sacrificed, except in the case of nasturtiums—picking them will actually encourage more blooms. To solve this dilemma, plant extra pots to harvest and leave some to flower. The beautiful varieties of nasturtium suggest a whole collection of these delightful (and delicious) flowers in bright soft yellows and reds. Growing these at close range not only invites using them, but affords the chance to examine their variety at leisure, one of the pleasures of growing any plant in a container. Purple basil (*Ocimum basilicum* var. *purpurascens*), its tiny pink flowers showing from purplish bracts, is a complement for nasturtium in color and scent—both suggest the warm, sweet, and peppery.

Since those herbs most suited to pot culture are sun-loving sorts, containers are often grouped on sun-catching patios, decks, and terraces. Frost-tender pineapple sage (*Salvia elegans*), fruit-scented sage (*S. dorisiana*), and other less hardy salvias belong there. Also thriving in such locations is the group of Mediterranean herbs called za'atar—*Thymbra spicata, Satureja thymbra*, and *Origanum syriacum*—all are aromatic members of the mint family with camphorous, thyme- or oregano-scented leaves or spikes and clusters of small, pink, rosy mauve, or white flowers. Dittany of Crete (*Origanum dictamnus*) and other tender origanums with showy bracts and pink flowers could be added to the collection or hung in baskets on a sunny porch.

A converted wooden nail keg makes a fine planter for semitrailing nasturtium (*Tropaeolum*). The flowers and leaves are handy for picking by the back door.

Herbs for partial shade are less numerous but no less beautiful. A half dozen pips of lily-of-the-valley (*Convallaria majalis*), underplanted with sweet violets (*Viola odorata*) and other violas, purple and gold or white, will flower over a long period, the violas carrying on until halted by a covering of snow. Creeping Jenny (*Lysimachia nummularia*), a hard-working ground cover, is lovely trailing over the sides of a container with its cloak of golden flowers. And boundlessly useful lady's mantle (*Alchemilla mollis*) is frilly in flower, elegant in foliage.

Edge and hedge

There is a fine line between edge and hedge plants. The former are lower growing and used to edge, define, or frame any sort of planting, formal or informal, in a bed or border. Plants most suited to this function have a dense habit that inhibits grass and weeds from entering the garden. One of the best edgers with this singular capacity is lungwort (*Pulmonaria officinalis*), whose spreading, root-like rhizomes effectively bar unwanted growth from the garden. Only watch the spreading lungwort itself, which can be checked without great effort by chopping it away. Its clusters of vari-colored bells merge by late spring to create a spectacular, amethyst framework that is hedge-like in its relatively tall, mounded form. Cut it back after a month of flowering, when it will again assume its role as a low edge, its spotted foliage refreshed by shearing. Among temporary annual edges, *Tropaeolum majus* 'Double Dwarf Jewel' is a low-growing, bright ribbon for defining any planting.

Low shrub edges include winter savory (*Satureja montana*), a diminutive, stiff shrub with a covering of tiny, white flowers by late summer, and the taller bush thyme (*Thymus vulgaris*), both providing a pleasing, contrasting foreground for bushy, less formal plants. Lady's mantle (*Alchemilla mollis*), a mounding edge, spills over and softens hard boundaries. Medium tall *Lavandula angustifolia* 'Munstead' is compact and useful for framing an island bed. Although none of these ward off grass and weeds in the same way as lungwort (*Pulmonaria officinalis*), they do their work of defining and framing.

The edge becomes a hedge when it is used to mark a boundary. Sometimes "rooms" are created by planting hedges to divide the cultivated landscape. In formal plantings, hedges become boundaries between sections of a garden. The choices of herbs for hedging are surprisingly varied, encompassing not only the inevitable santolinas, lavenders (*Lavandula angustifolia*), and hyssop (*Hyssopus officinalis*), but also low, wide bushes such as the apothecary's rose (*Rosa gallica* 'Officinalis') and peonies (*Paeonia officinalis* and *P. lactiflora*). Massed peonies are crimson, pink, and white with handsome foliage all season.

Both annuals and perennials create useful hedges. Some sunflower (*Helianthus annuus*) types are especially bred for withstanding lodging, or falling over and intertwining, so they can be planted in a thick row as a protective hedge at the end of a vegetable garden, thereby creating an en-

Low-maintenance rose hedges are embellished here with a frilly edging of lady's mantle (*Alchemilla mollis*) for a long season of spectacular bloom. The roses will be transformed into rose hips for a second "blooming" in late summer and fall.

couraging microclimate for the other plants. A tall, self-supporting perennial like monkshood (*Aconitum napellus*), an attractive leafy mound when not in bloom, makes a beautiful, virtually maintenance-free hedge, growing up every year from its roots to perform the same function with little encouragement except for moist soil and partial shade. Bear in mind that all of these suggestions are based on allowing the plants to grow naturally without trimming, for when they are cut back, blooms are sacrificed for dense foliage. After they have flowered, of course, they should be trimmed.

Ground cover

Blessed with systems that enable them to creep—runners, rhizomes, stolons, and leafy stems that root when they touch the soil—ground covers survive and proliferate where other plants might not grow. Understanding their nature, one can admire them as they go about the job of covering the ground as rapidly as possible, obliterating weeds, and obviating the need for grass in areas where it is difficult to grow and maintain. Established around the bases of trees and shrubs, ground covers contribute to their healthy growth by keeping the soil moist and cool. Colorful carpets can even surround a collection of potted plants and tubs. Running over barren banks and slopes, where they prevent soil erosion, growing along paths, around pavings, in rocky areas, and over wasteland, ground covers not only beautify these areas, but they also unify all the separate plantings into an integrated landscape. Among the best ground covers are various herbs whose beauty of foliage and masses of flowers recommend them for general landscaping. Their pleasing scents, often released only when brushed or stepped on, are an added bonus.

Ground covers fall into three groups according to their habit: carpets, leafy covers, and carpet covers. The carpets, low-to-the-ground plants that form tight mats of growth and accept light foot traffic, include bugle (*Ajuga*), creeping Jenny (*Lysimachia*), creeping thymes (*Thymus praecox* subsp. *arcticus, T. pulegoides*), and sweet woodruff (*Galium odoratum*). Leafy covers like herb robert (*Geranium robertianum*), big root geranium (*G. macrorrhizum*), and lungwort (*Pulmonaria officinalis*) are taller, providing a canopy of foliage that shades out unwanted growth. The carpet covers are an intermediate group that combines the attributes of the other groups by creating tight carpets with leafy covers. They include sweet violet (*Viola*

42

odorata), lady's mantle (*Alchemilla mollis*), and the hop vine (*Humulus lupulus*) when it is allowed to ramble over the ground.

Ground covers are varied in their growth requirements, able to grow in dry, sunny conditions (creeping thymes, *Thymus praecox* subsp. *arcticus* and *T. pulegoides*), moist shade (bugle, *Ajuga*), or even wet areas (creeping Jenny, *Lysimachia nummularia*). A few can be planted in the garden proper (clump-forming bugles, *Ajuga genevensis* and *A. pyramidalis*) or as an accent at its edges (creeping thymes or big root geranium, *Geranium macrorrhizum*, are striking there), but as a general rule, never give them an opportunity to invade other plantings unless they are kept under strict control. With their ease of maintenance and control (cutting them back and mowing around them), gardeners should regard these plants as the single strongest ally in low-maintenance landscaping.

Ground covers have enough variety among their flowers and seasons of bloom to provide wide splashes of color from spring through fall. For great-

Plate 5. *Thymus praecox* subsp. *arcticus*, creeping thyme (See p. 333). Midsummer, Country Lane Herbs and Dried Flowers. Photo, Brian Oke and Gisèle Quesnel.

Lavender (*Lavandula angustifolia*) is used here to outline a curved, raised bed. Bugle (*Ajuga*) grows around the stone steps, obliterating all weeds and creating a carpet of blue flowers.

est contrast of color and form, establish several different kinds throughout the landscape rather than relying on only one type. Instead of choosing one bugle (*Ajuga*), for instance, try the full range of foliage types and flower-spike colors, thereby extending the bugles' bloom period by several weeks. Once having grown *Ajuga* 'Catlin's Giant', a vigorous hybrid with dark blue flower stalks and glossy bronze leaves, gardeners rejoice over their good luck in having a moist, shady spot, a spot that they formerly considered most unlucky, in which to grow this beautiful flowering herb.

Naturalized herb

Vigorous plants established anywhere in the landscape outside the garden and grown with minimum interference, allowed to return almost to a wild state, are naturalized. There is a great range of herbs suited to naturalization, because the group includes many close-to-the-wild types that may be difficult or inconvenient to grow within the confines of a garden. Sweet cicely (*Myrrhis odorata*) is undeniably lovely, with a mound of ferny leaves and masses of swaying white umbels, and where there is room for its spreading foliage, it is a grand border plant. If I could not accommodate it in a small garden, however, and I had a shady, moist piece of ground anywhere on my property, I would establish it there and let it spread wide as nature intended. When such plants return to their original habit, they reward the gardener with extreme good health that shows itself, most importantly, in improved bloom.

Naturalized plants can transform a wet meadow or bog, a dry, barren slope, or a light woodland into an asset that contributes to the overall harmony of the outdoor living space. What a pleasure it is to come upon clumps of bright yellow cowslips (*Primula veris*) and blue lungwort (*Pulmonaria angustifolia*) growing on their own in a lightly wooded spot. Add a spreading canopy of herb robert (*Geranium robertianum*) and a few clumps of bistort (*Polygonum bistorta*) and bee balm (*Monarda didyma*) to extend the season of interest.

Wild golden buttercups (*Ranunculus acris*) blooming in a piece of boggy ground signal that blue and yellow flag iris (*Iris versicolor* and *I. pseudacorus*) will also grow there. When plumy meadowsweets (*Filipendula*) and extra clumps of chives (*Allium schoenoprasum*) are added to the mix, a new "garden" is created, requiring only admiration as you pass in its vicinity, for it will take care of itself. More than that, the chives will bloom in rosier globes than in most garden settings. At the edges of the bog, where moisture is assured but not overwhelming, small blue comfrey (*Symphytum caucasicum*) will grow unhindered as a broad bush along with tall clumps of elecampane (*Inula helenium*) and the bushy sneezewort (*Achillea ptarmica*), prolific in its production of semidouble, white, daisy-like flowers, but too invasive for the garden proper.

Understanding a vigorous plant's specific needs gives one the confidence to establish it in its proper setting, after which maintenance is minimal and rewards are great. Wild marjoram (*Origanum vulgare* subsp. *vulgare*), a creeping mat one is always reducing in the garden, can become an expansive, comfortable carpet that produces a multitude of tall-stemmed,

Blue flag iris (*Iris versicolor*) grows on its own here at the water's edge. Solomon's seal (*Polygonatum multiflorum*) and a carpet of white, starry sweet woodruff (*Galium odoratum*) grow nearby in light shade.

pink and purple flower clusters in late summer. Yarrows (*Achillea millefolium*), wild bergamot (*Monarda fistulosa*), butterfly weed (*Asclepias tuberosa*), and chicory (*Cichorium intybus*) can entirely clothe a sunny slope with colorful flowers through the whole summer. This is not a garden in the usual sense, nor is it completely wild, for the plants have been introduced and they must be occasionally trimmed and mown around, but it is as close to the wild as possible in a cultivated, planned landscape.

Rock work

The association between herbs and rocks is very appealing. Rocks of varied sizes and shapes in a range of subdued colors provide a complementary background for foliage and flowers, especially many small-flowered herbs. Some plants thrive in this habitat characterized by pockets of heat, soil, and moisture. Observe the beauty of herbs growing spontaneously between rocks, in crevices of rock walls, and on rocky slopes, as naturally occurs in Mediterranean regions. The opportunities to recreate these conditions in one's own landscape, on however small a scale, are surprisingly numerous. Establish the obvious rock garden. Take advantage of a natural rocky outcropping—even a large bolder or rock pile. Situate plants by or in a stone wall, at the edges of or between pavings or stone steps, or even in otherwise unsightly ruins such as a decayed and crumbling cement foundation.

The majority of herbs suited to these habitats are sun-loving Mediterranean types that require perfect drainage, such as thymes, lavenders (*Lavandula angustifolia*), rosemarys (*Rosmarinus officinalis*), and origanums. But different conditions—deeper soil, damp or shady niches—often occur at the edges of any sunny rock work, thus allowing a more varied palette of plants. In other words, what at first glance appears to be a single habitat—sunny and dry—may actually contain numerous situations.

Rock gardening is a specialty to which gardeners may devote a lifetime. The plants most used are alpines. These high-altitude plants are difficult to establish in areas where hot, dry summers prevail. Flowering herbs with attractive foliage are far easier to grow, and with careful selection can provide colorful, often spectacular, bloom throughout the growing season. Those plants with evergreen foliage, like both creeping and upright thymes, the brilliant pink dwarf soapwort (*Saponaria ocymoides*), or creeping savory

(*Satureja montana* subsp. *illyrica*), are choice for rock garden plantings, as are herbs with drought-resistant, furry foliage, such as woolly yarrow (*Achillea tomentosa*), its sulfur-yellow flowers blooming in large clusters.

Clump-forming bugles (*Ajuga genevensis*, *A. pyramidalis*), alliums, origanums, and summer and winter savorys (*Satureja hortensis*, *S. montana*) all grow well in the vicinity of rocks in any formal or informal planting, in rock-edged raised beds, or in rock gardens. Shrubby herbs (lavenders, rosemarys, hyssops, the santolinas) as taller accents enjoy the nearness of rocks in a rock garden, in a natural rockery (the place to grow the za'atar herbs), or at the base of a rock wall, where their foliage and flowers will show to advantage.

Walls of brick or stone of whatever height are opportunities to show off flowering herbs of many kinds, from shrubby hyssop (*Hyssopus officinalis*) to low-growing origanums. Hollyhocks (*Alcea rosea*), enjoying another type of wall here, provide an impressive background.

Where walls extend into partial shade, Solomon's seal (*Polygonatum multiflorum*) well displays arching green stems and drooping ivory bells; this habitat is also favorable for the white, cupped blooms of bloodroot (*Sanguinaria canadensis*) and clumps of purple or white sweet violets (*Viola odorata*). The soil at the top of a wall can provide a home for irrepressible Johnny-jump-ups (*Viola tricolor*), for upright clumps of clove-scented Cheddar pink (*Dianthus gratianopolitanus*), bright mounds of citrus-scented signet marigolds (*Tagetes tenuifolia*), and cascades of *Thymus pseudolanuginosus* 'Hall's Woolly Thyme', its sheet of tiny, pink flowers blooming over small, fur-covered leaves.

Clumps of easygoing annual calendulas, nasturtiums (*Tropaeolum*), and love-in-a-mist (*Nigella*) can be established at the base of low walls where their beauty will not be hidden. Creeping thyme (*Thymus praecox* subsp. *arcticus, T. pulegoides*) and Roman chamomile (*Chamaemelum nobile*) accept foot traffic between pavings, releasing their scent with every step. German chamomile (*Matricaria recutita*), a mass of daisy-like flowers all sum-

Plate 6. *Sanguinaria canadensis,* bloodroot (See p. 291). Spring, Joseph Hudak garden, Westwood, Massachusetts. Photo, Joseph Hudak.

mer, grows well between rocks at the edge of a path, as does lady's mantle (*Alchemilla mollis*), which thrives virtually anywhere in the herb-inspired landscape.

Organizing flowering herbs according to the possible landscape uses suggested in this book is no substitute for the individual gardener's overarching vision, one that grows and changes over time. The following guide, based on my own experiences over more than two decades of growing herbs, should not be regarded as the equivalent of painting by numbers. And since each vision is so individual, this book supplies no ready-made garden plans. I leave the creation of the total landscape to the individual gardener, in whose hands ideas are given life.

Finally, a vision of beauty may be spiritual in origin, but it depends on the physical world, the very land, for its fulfillment. Be sure to match plants to their preferred habitat as far as possible. Such information is given in detail in the portraits.

Earth laughs in flowers.

Emerson, "Hamatreya"

Plate 7. *Achillea millefolium*, yarrow, rose-colored variant (See p. 57). Early fall, Banff,

Plant Portraits from A to Z

Alberta, Canada. Photo, Brian Oke and Gisèle Quesnel.

Introduction

The differences between botany and horticulture—which is as much an art as a science, with some mystery thrown in, too—sometimes lead to anomalies in nomenclature that we must learn to live with. As soon as people start tinkering with natural plant forms, as they have been doing for thousands of years, doubts arise as to plant identity and origin. I am neither a botanist nor a professional horticulturist, but as a garden writer and gardener, I try to keep informed of the latest changes in plant identification. My sources are the *Index of Garden Plants* (Griffiths 1994) and *Hortus Third* (L. H. Bailey Hortorium 1976). Also relevant are the names used in the most reliable plant nursery catalogs, those that arise from practices "in the field." In dealing with thymes, I have relied on the fine work of Dr. Harriet Flannery Phillips whose doctoral research on thymes at Cornell University in the 1970s has had wide influence. For those still ambiguous names, I have used in the text the ones that seem to be primary; the many synonyms are included in the index with cross references to their primary names.

Common names are used throughout the text to remind us of the herbs' salient characteristics, just as Jacob's ladder describes the ladder-like leaves of *Polemonium caeruleum*. When more than one species is discussed, I have used a general name, as meadowsweets for species within *Filipendula*; but to discuss individual species, I have used more specific common names when they exist, such as queen-of-the-meadow for *F. ulmaria* and queen-of-the-prairie for *F. rubra*. For those genera whose names have evolved into common names, when discussing multiple species in the same genus I refer to them collectively as achilleas, salvias, and so on. A list of common names with their Latin counterparts appears in Appendix I.

Each portrait includes the most vital information about each plant to show at a glance its characteristics and uses as an ornamental herb. The USDA Hardiness Zones cited are simply recommendations about a plant's ability to grow within a certain temperature range. As most mature gardeners understand, not only are zone assignments not set in stone, they vary, sometimes wildly, according to the source. For each plant description, I have tried to balance the discrepancies based on my and other gardeners' experiences. Whether a plant is aggressively invasive or not is one of the discrepancies that arise between gardeners from different regions. Several of the plants described here are on the blacklists of some botanical gardens and county extension offices. Before introducing a plant into the garden and especially before establishing it in a naturalized setting, check with experts on the plant's compatibility with local native vegetation. The portraits of remarkably easy-spreading plants include a warning and suggestions for keeping them under control.

In order to expand our view of the plants, each portrait is preceded by a brief quote from one of a wide variety of sources, past and present. Whether it is the seventeenth-century Gervase Markham writing about pinks in *The English Husbandman* or the contemporary Patrick Lima extolling the virtues of the roses blooming in his Ontario garden, the observations are fresh and apt. Their words, spanning the centuries, emphasize the impact of beautiful flowers on the human imagination. Their insights enrich our own appreciation.

One of those perceptive gardeners was Helen Fox, who died at age eighty-nine in 1974. She played a major role in the herb revival movement of the 1930s through her New York gardens, Foxden and High and Low. She explored an incredible range of herbs, most of which were grown from seeds acquired from all over the world. She grew all the basils now described as "new," as well as more alliums, salvias, and native North American plants than are generally grown today. More importantly, she grew them for their general landscaping value, although much of the stylized herb gardening from which we are only now recovering has its origin in the movement she helped launch. Those successful in finding copies of her books on herbs will appreciate her astute observations. She was able to pursue her life adventure, as she called it, of working with plants. All who celebrate the ornamental virtues of herbs are indebted to her pioneering efforts.

It is no easy task to choose the most significant from the bounteous selection of beautiful ornamental herbs. I turned for help to the classics of herb literature—the old herbals, the work of Maude Grieve, the works of early enthusiasts in North America such as Helen Fox and Rosetta Clarkson, and to Gertrude Foster, one of the most eminent contemporary authorities. And I turned to leading nurseries to learn how the herb repertoire is being expanded.

Still hoping for help in narrowing down the list, I asked professional herb growers about their favorites. They, too, were overwhelmed by the task and spouted out names and distinguishing characteristics that, despite not giving a clear list of the "best," revealed a joyous appreciation of herbs as ornamental plants, undiminished after years of growing them. The late Madeleine Siegler, former proprietor of Monk's Hill Herbs in Maine, wrote of her favorite ornamental herbs: "Number one is lavender (*Lavandula angustifolia*), of course, any variety; marsh marigold (*Caltha palustris*) because it blooms so early; calamint because it makes such a display in bloom—sort of a lavender-white haze, always covered with honeybees; clary sage (*Salvia sclarea*) because I love the fragrance of the flower bracts; annual clary (*Salvia viridis*) because it stays in bloom so long; Culver's root (*Veronicastrum*) for its white spikes and leaves clasping the stem; showy marjoram (*Origanum vulgare* subsp. *vulgare*) for its showy pink flowers and long bloom period; trailing soapwort (*Saponaria ocymoides*) for its blanket of pink flowers at the same time as *Nepeta mussinii* . . . I hope you don't omit *Monarda citriodora*. I love its stacked-up look!" I also love the stacked-up look of this seldom-grown herb. The following herbs are all favorites sure to create a splendid garden. Some portraits include related plants of interest, even more treasured selections to lead down paths of herbal beauty.

Achillea millefolium

Asteraceae, Aster Family
Yarrow, milfoil, nosebleed plant, soldier's woundwort,
thousand-leaf

Perennial
Site and soil: sun; well-drained
Hardiness: Zones 3–10
Landscape use: bed and border, naturalized herb
Height: 18–30 in. (45.7–76.2 cm)
Flower: white, light pink, rose, flat-topped cluster in
    terminal head
Bloom season: midsummer to fall

> A most beautiful rosey red-flowered variety is like an old-fashioned calico print.
>
> Rosetta Clarkson
> *Herbs: Their Culture and Uses*

The common field yarrow is among the most ancient of herbs; its well-documented use reaches back centuries, if not millennia. One of more than sixty Old World species, it is widely naturalized across North America along dusty roadsides, in old fields, and in waste places (Plate 7. See p. 52–53). It can be invasive for it increases rapidly by creeping roots, establishing colonies of attractive, ferny foliage 8 in. (20.3 cm) long and flat-topped flower clusters that bloom on straight stems into the fall. Each 3 in. (7.6 cm) wide cluster is composed of smaller flowers with pleated rays surrounding a tightly packed, inner disk of flowers with prominent yellow stamens that give the mature bloom a grayish appearance. The flowers, and to a lesser extent the leaves, release a pleasant, somewhat spicy or medicinal aroma, especially when the plant is brushed or bruised.

The genus takes its name from Achilles who is supposed to have used yarrow to staunch the wounds of his soldiers, a use preserved in the plant's many common names. The species name, meaning many-leaved, describes the way yarrow's leaves are finely divided into innumerable segments or leaflets.

Since it was an abundant weed, yarrow was easy to gather and use for a variety of complaints, so many that in the English herbal tradition it belongs to a group of plants known as all-heals; among the North American Indians it was a panacea known as life medicine. In both the Old World and the New its applications were similar: to stop bleeding, aid digestion, reduce fever, and either cure nosebleeds or induce them in order to ameliorate headaches. Modern research has identified more than 100 active compounds in yarrow, some of which are thought to be anti-inflammatory agents.

Yarrow is one of the most successful crossover herbs, a plant that started out as purely practical but was adopted as ornamental after breeding improvements. Herb enthusiasts have been slow to embrace the many faces of yarrow, perhaps because of the deeply ingrained view that pretty flowers cannot be herbs: "There is a rose-colored yarrow which is a desirable garden plant, but the field yarrow . . . with muddy white flowers . . . belongs in that portion devoted to herbs" (Kamm 1938).

Very attractive cultivars have been developed from the natural rose-colored yarrow: cherry-red *Achillea millefolium* 'Cerise Queen' (Plate 8) and deep wine-red 'Fire King', both with white or yellow centers, are tidier plants than the original, growing to 18 in. (45.7 cm) with handsome, sil-

Plate 8. *Achillea millefolium* 'Cerise Queen', yarrow. Midsummer, Country Lane Herbs and Dried Flowers. Photo, Brian Oke and Gisèle Quesnel.

very, finely divided foliage. The "muddy white" has also been improved in 'White Beauty'; larger-flowered than the wild yarrow and less invasive, it grows 18–24 in. (45.7–61.0 cm) tall with mounded, white blooms like Queen Anne's lace (*Daucus carota*). 'Paprika', to 30 in. (76.2 cm), opens ruby-red, maturing to salmon-rose; and 'Hope', to 24 in. (61.0 cm), opens creamy amber, maturing to pale, antique yellow. *Achillea* 'Salmon Beauty' is a striking plant to 30 in. (76.2 cm) with peachy salmon flowers. Also, the series of Galaxy Hybrids (*A. millefolium* × *A.* 'Taygetea'), developed in Germany, offers less invasive types in a range of exquisite colors.

In designing the garden, keep the medium tall and shorter variants near the front of a border and the taller ones toward the back, where their lovely and changing tints are refreshing all summer and into early fall. Both types can be grown in drifts of color in a generous border or bed. The wildflower can be naturalized in a meadow planting or on a dry, sunny bank or slope. I grow yarrow cultivars in a dooryard grouping with salvias, feverfew (*Tanacetum parthenium*), and catmint (*Nepeta* ×*faassenii*) so that their aroma is nearby and their blooms are close at hand for cutting.

Except for the naturally occurring wildflower, do not grow yarrows from seeds because the most dominant among a small population will inevitably be the washed-out, less desirable colors. Space plants 12–18 in. (30.5–45.7 cm) apart in full sun and well-drained soil that is somewhat thin, even gravely. Yarrows will grow in partial shade but they become leggy. In moist, rich soil they rapidly multiply. The *Achillea millefolium* cultivars, with characteristics closer to the wild, should be divided every year in spring or fall, the hybrids every 3 years. Pick off spent blooms to encourage fresh flowers all summer. The taller ones may need staking.

The yarrows make excellent cut flowers. For drying, cut them when the they are fully opened, when the inner and outer rays of each little, individual flower are flat, but pick *Achillea ptarmica* 'The Pearl' when it is freshly opened. Even the wild type makes delicate filler for posies or tussiemussies (yarrow stands for purity in the language of flowers). When you throw unwanted yarrow on the compost heap it aids decomposition.

Related plants of interest. Seeds of wild yarrow are available from wildflower sources. The other yarrows are available from perennial plant nurseries and herb sources.

Achillea filipendulina, fern-leaved yarrow, a tall plant, 3–4 ft. (0.9–1.2 m), with silvery leaves, is a focal point in an island bed or in the background of a border in early summer. Its bright yellow flower clusters, 4–5 in. (10.2–12.7 cm) across, are highly prized for dried floral arrangements and wreaths but its contribution to the garden is reason enough to grow it. 'Coronation Gold' has brighter yellow flowers.

Achillea 'Moonshine' (*A.* 'Taygetea' × *A. clypeolata*) is one of the most popular garden yarrows because it is not invasive. It grows to a tidy 12 to 24 in. (30.5–61.0 cm) with large, long-lasting, lemon-yellow flowers above silvery foliage. Where summers are very hot it should be grown as an annual.

Achillea ptarmica, sneezewort, an Old World medicinal for treating toothaches, epilepsy, and headaches, bears small, off-white, daisy-like, sometimes semidouble flowers. 'The Pearl' (Plate 9), developed by the

Plate 9. *Achillea ptarmica* 'The Pearl', sneezewort. Midsummer, Gardner farm. Note the fully doubled flowers of the true cultivar with no center showing. Photo, Alan Dorey.

French nuseryman Victor Lemoine in the late nineteenth century, produces abundant sprays of pure white, fully double pompons over a long period beginning in early summer. The flowers are prized for cutting, lasting more than a week indoors. 'The Pearl' should never be grown from seed for it will produce flowers closer to the wild type.

Achillea tomentosa, woolly yarrow (Plate 10), is a low creeper that loves sun and dry, even drought-like, conditions. It blooms in late spring to midsummer with repeat bloom in late summer if plants are cut back after their first flowering. 'Maynard's Gold' is 6 in. (15.2 cm) tall with rich yellow flowers and silver-green foliage; it creates beautiful mats around rocks and pavings. A good place to grow 'Maynard's Gold' is at the top of a wall, or lacking that, on a heaped up mound of soil so the roots are kept dry. Woolly yarrow tends to die out in patches where growing conditions are moist.

Plate 10. *Achillea tomentosa,* woolly yarrow. Early summer, Graymalkin Farm, Caledon East, Ontario, Canada. It blooms all summer if spent flowers are picked. Photo, Brian Oke and Gisèle Quesnel.

Aconitum napellus

Ranunculaceae, Buttercup Family
Monkshood, aconite, English monkshood, wolfsbane

Perennial
Site and soil: partial shade; evenly moist
Hardiness: Zones 3–9
Landscape use: accent, bed and border, edge and hedge,
   naturalized herb
Height: 4–6 ft. (1.2–1.8 m)
Flower: amethyst, blue, pink, bicolor, hooded panicle
Bloom season: midsummer to fall

The monkshoods, all native to the Northern Hemisphere, are so named because of their distinctive flowers (Plate 2. See p. 16). These grow on lax to erect stems above a shiny mound of palm-shaped leaves. The plant looks very similar to delphinium, but when it blooms there is no mistaking its identity. The flowers, variable in color, are borne in loose to tight spikes at the top of the stem and on many small branches, assuring a long season of bloom that starts in midsummer with the 3–4 ft. (0.9–1.2 m), azure-blue common or true monkshood, *Aconitum napellus*, and ends in the fall with the taller, purple-blue *A. carmichaelii* to 6 ft. (1.8 m). Each delicately veined flower is composed of five sepals: the upper one forms a hood that either perches atop the four sepals or snugly clasps them. The slight, curiously formed flower petals inside—often compared to monkeys on sticks—provide amusement for those who enjoy lifting the hood to look for the flower. Bees and hummingbirds are fond of the flowers' nectar.

The common name wolfsbane refers to the plant's past use as a poison. Powerful alkaloids, present in every part except the flowers, are especially concentrated in its turnip-shaped, tuberous roots, the source of the medicinal drug aconite. These distinctive roots, most pronounced in common monkshood, are noted in the name *napellus*, meaning little root. Despite monkshood's association with poison (Medea is supposed to have used aconite to poison Theseus, and Romeo to poison himself), ointments made from the roots have been used to treat neuralgia and rheumatism.

But the plant is considered very poisonous and should never be consumed in the least amount.

Monkshoods were English cottage garden favorites because of their ease of culture and showy, long-lasting blooms. A staple of the institutional medicinal garden, they hardly fit the concept of "the herb garden" if that means a collection of gray-leaved plants. With the rise in popularity of perennials and interest in the informal cottage garden style, however, the monkshoods are gaining a wider audience. They are healthiest in cooler climates, where they offer late and beautiful color.

Monkshoods have always been grown in New World cottage gardens, where one can still find the amethyst, deep blue, and light pink sorts, most of them variants of *Aconitum napellus*. At abandoned homesteads monkshoods are sometimes all that is left to mark a spot of human habitation. All mine, collected from old gardens, are very welcome in my own cottage garden among similar easygoing types like soapwort (*Saponaria officinalis*) and elecampane (*Inula helenium*). Common monkshood first blooms along with orange-bronze daylilies (*Hemerocallis*), then carries on with dark pink bergamots (*Monarda*) and nicotianas in dappled shade. The packed clusters of flowers on the later-blooming *A.* ×*cammarum* 'Bicolor' (Plate 11) are particularly beautiful, each large flower darkly edged with purple-blue. The late-blooming, azure monkshood, *A. carmichaelii*, known in the countryside as autumn lilac, brings the season to a glorious end, its rich purple-blue stalks mingling among the white-flowering wands of bugbane (*Cimicifuga*) and Canadian burnet (*Sanguisorba canadensis*) through several light frosts. In an old garden I saw common monkshood grown as a hedge marking garden rooms; after more than 60 years it showed no sign of age, growing up every year from new roots to bloom once more.

Although some of the monkshood species can be grown from seed, germination may be slow and plants may take 3 years to bloom; therefore, it is best to grow them from roots. These should be planted in cool weather in the fall or early spring in evenly moist, humusy soil in sun or shade; they do best where some shade is offered. Never plant any of the monkshoods where children are likely to sample them. Set plants 12–18 in. (30.5–45.7 cm) apart with the crowns just below the soil's surface. Although one is often warned not to divide monkshood, propagation by division is easy as long as the plant is dormant, the soil is moist, and the site

Plate 11. *Aconitum* ×*cammarum* 'Bicolor', monkshood. Late summer, Gardner farm. Photo, Brian Oke and Gisèle Quesnel.

protected from drying winds. Wear gloves or wash hands afterwards if you handle the actual roots; juice from any part of the plant should never come in contact with an open wound. Through more than two decades of growing monkshoods, I have never even seen the roots since when a division is made it is usually accompanied by a large chunk of moist soil, inseparable from the roots. Be prepared to stake most types since stems tend to be too weak for their burden of bloom. Use wire cylinders (tomato hoops), or surround the plant with three or four stakes that reach at least up to the flower spikes; encircle the stakes with a network of twine over which the foliage will grow. Cut back spent flower stems to encourage modest rebloom in the earlier kinds. Or, cut the flowers before they wither for long-lasting bouquets and colorful dried spikes.

Related plants of interest. Monkshoods are available from perennial plant nurseries and a few herb sources. The following have similar growth requirements to the monkshoods discussed above, and they all have poisonous properties and should be handled with care.

Aconitum henryi, autumn monkshood, is deep blue to 6 ft. (1.8 m). 'Spark's Variety' is violet-blue. Both bloom in early fall.

Aconitum lycoctonum is the original wolfsbane of folk tales. It grows 3–4 ft. (0.9–1.2 m) and is unusual for its large, creamy yellow flowers produced in midsummer.

Aconitum napellus 'Bressingham Spire' grows to 3 ft. (0.9 m) and is valued for its long-flowering, stiff spikes of violet-blue in mid- to late summer.

Aconitum napellus 'Ivorine' is a compact plant to 24 in. (61.0 cm) with beautiful, creamy white spires, blooming in early fall.

Aconitum napellus 'Newry Blue' is a cultivar, to 4 ft. (1.2 m) tall, favored for its deep, marine-blue, midsummer flowers.

Agastache foeniculum

Lamiaceae, Mint Family
Anise hyssop, blue giant hyssop

The herb is decorative enough for the flower garden.
Gertrude Foster
Park's Success with Herbs

Perennial
Site and soil: sun; well-drained
Hardiness: Zone 4–8
Landscape use: accent, bed and border
Height: 30–48 in. (76.2–121.9 cm)
Flower: lavender, white, small tube whorled on spike
Bloom season: late summer to fall

Anise hyssop belongs to a group of plants known collectively as giant hyssop. The only connection between these and the herb commonly known as hyssop, *Hyssopus officinalis*, is that they are all members of the mint family. Anise hyssop occurs in North America in dry, open woodland and prairie country from Ontario to Illinois to Washington state. It is a handsome plant, maintaining its narrow, upright habit throughout its growth cycle. The leaves, pleasantly scented like anise, are ovate and toothed, mostly growing along the lower stem. The flowers, small and tubular with prominent stamens, are borne in whorls on rounded spikes at least 6 in. (15.2

cm) long. Even after the flowers fall, the spikes are attractive with the remaining light purple bracts.

The Plains Indians made tea from the leaves of anise hyssop to alleviate the symptoms of colds and coughs. Also, it is a phenomenal attraction for bees (one of its more obscure common names is wonder honey plant); they prefer it to all other plants in its season of bloom. All the giant hyssops are popular with bees, butterflies, and hummingbirds.

There are few wildflowers so adapted to cultivation as anise hyssop. It is suitable for formal or informal perennial beds and borders or for accent plants inside and outside of the garden proper. With its slender, upright habit it fits perfectly in the tightest planting, but if room is available, the massed spikes make quite a show. Pairing the lavender with the white types, such as the elegant and hardy *Agastache foeniculum* 'Snow Spike', offers a pleasing, long-lasting contrast of colors; try the lavender with late, white phlox for an effective contrast of forms and colors.

Information about growing anise hyssop from seed is contradictory;

Plate 12. *Agastache foeniculum*, anise hyssop. Late summer, Country Lane Herbs and Dried Flowers. Photo, Brian Oke and Gisèle Quesnel.

from one source it is easy, from another, germination may take from 1 to 3 months. The secret of success may lie in sowing the seeds on the surface of the growing medium, whether indoors or out. Indoors, sow seed 12 weeks before the last frost for possible first year bloom; seeds sown at 70° F (21°C) should germinate in 7 days. After the last frost, space plants outdoors 12–18 in. (30.5–45.7 cm) apart in well-drained garden soil in full sun. Very light shade is acceptable. Outside, seed may be sown in the fall for spring germination. Where winters are severe, anise hyssop will not survive in heavy, moist soil, nor does it usually set seed in regions colder than Zone 5. In Zone 7, where summers are very hot, anise hyssop is short-lived but self-sowing. Plants can be propagated by division every 3–5 years or by stem cuttings taken any time during the season. Plants can be moved, even in bloom, with no sign of stress as long as sufficient soil is taken with them and they are well-watered.

The giant hyssops are fine cut flowers spectacular in fall bouquets; try lavender spikes with flowers of a golden or orange hue. Leaves of all the types make soothing teas (dried leaves have a more penetrating flavor and scent). Use dried leaves and flowers for potpourri.

Related plants of interest. Anise hyssop is the hardiest of the giant hyssops, but the curious gardener in cold regions should try growing the following kinds in containers that can be moved indoors over the winter. Or take stem cuttings in late summer to winter indoors. The compact cultivars are good for borders, but the tall species are best naturalized on banks or slopes. Seeds and plants are available from general and specialty seed sources and perennial plant and herb sources. Anise hyssop is the most widely available.

Agastache 'Apricot Sunrise', 12–15 in. (30.5–38.1 cm) with peach-pink flowers, is a hybrid developed from species native to the American Southwest and Mexico.

Agastache barberi 'Firebird', to 24 in. (61.0 cm) with brilliant coral or coppery orange flowers, and 'Tutti-frutti', also to 24 in. (61.0 cm), are useful compact plants. 'Tutti-frutti' may be the hardiest, possibly in areas as cold as Zone 6.

Agastache cana, called mosquito plant for its use as a repellent, is native to New Mexico and western Texas and grows 18–24 in. (45.7–61.0 cm). It has loose spikes of dark pink flowers and sweet, minty leaves. A boon for gardeners with shorter growing seasons, 'Heather Queen' (Plate 13), to 30 in. (76.2 cm), blooms the first year from seed. Grown as a perennial, *A. cana* may be hardy in Zone 8. It requires very well-drained soil on the dry side.

Agastache foeniculum 'Fragrant Delight', to 3 ft. (0.9 m), is an interesting cultivar that can be raised from seed, perhaps hardy in Zone 8. Flower colors include blue, yellow, red, pink, and white, and the foliage of each color is supposed to have a different fragrance.

Agastache mexicana, Mexican giant hyssop or Mexican lemon hyssop, 24–36 in. (61.0–91.4 cm) or taller, is very showy with rosy purple flower spikes and lemon-scented leaves, probably hardy in Zone 9. It grows easily from seed and may be grown as an annual where winters are severe if plants are started indoors by late winter.

Agastache nepetoides, yellow giant hyssop, native from Quebec to Ontario and south to Georgia and Kansas, is a tall, striking plant to 6 ft. (1.8 m)

Plate 13. *Agastache cana* 'Heather Queen', mosquito plant, grown from seed as annual. Late summer, Country Lane Herbs and Dried Flowers. Photo, Brian Oke and Gisèle Quesnel.

with yellow-green flowers and catnip-scented leaves. A rather invasive plant, it is hardy in Zone 4.

Agastache rugosa, Korean mint, native to Asia, hardy in Zone 5, grows 4–6 ft. (1.2–1.8 m). It is a robust plant that resembles anise hyssop but is broader and more vigorous, with violet to rose flower spikes and a strong, minty scent. Pinching it back will encourage bushy growth. Space plants to 24 in. (61.0 cm) apart.

Ajuga

Lamiaceae, Mint Family
Bugle

Perennial
Hardiness: Zones 4–9
Site and soil: partial shade, sun; evenly moist
Landscape use: accent, bed and border, ground
   cover, rock work
Height: 5–12 in. (12.7–30.5 cm)
Flower: sky-blue, deep blue, rose, white, small, two-lipped whorls
Bloom season: spring to early summer

> **It has much to recommend it, fresh glossy rosettes which are . . . always attractive, and sturdy spikes of blue flower.**
> Margery Fish
> *Ground Cover Plants*

Two species of bugle, introduced from Europe, have been naturalized in North America. One, *Ajuga reptans* (Plate 14), is a creeping type, as its species name suggests; the other is *A. genevensis*, tufted bugleweed, which forms clumps and spreads more slowly. A third type, *A. pyramidalis* (Plate 15), pyramid bugle, not naturalized in North America, is also clump forming. These three species readily interbreed, resulting in many hybrids with variations in leaf and flower color. The habits of these hybrids vary also, from very low carpets to more compact, slowly spreading types, all with striking flowers.

All bugles grow by short rhizomes that produce rosettes of downy, outward-spreading, oval leaves 2–4 in. (5.1–10.2 cm) long, often crinkled and tinged with bronze or purple. The early spring flowers are sky blue to deep blue, almost purple, or white to rose and are borne in dense terminal spikes with the small flowers arranged in whorls around erect, square-sided stems to 12 in. (30.5 cm). Each ½ in. (1.3 cm) bloom is two lipped, with a short upper lip and a three-lobed lower lip, and very inviting to bees who enter the flowers to collect nectar from the base of the long tube of the corolla.

Plate 14. *Ajuga reptans*, bugle, creeping type. Early summer, Gardner farm. Photo, Alan Dorey.

The odd name bugle is explained by some as a corruption of *Ajuga*, meaning not yoked, a reference to the shape of the flower's calyx. Carpet bugle is a very descriptive common name for *A. reptans*, for during the growing season it sends out runners with paired leaves, which at intervals develop roots. These effectively nail down the carpet to create a growing mat of dense foliage. Over the winter the older plants die out, but the next season the young plants develop and send out more runners. Bugle is always on the move.

For centuries, both bugle and self-heal (*Prunella vulgaris*) were equally regarded as healing herbs for wounds of all sorts due to their astringent properties (they both contain tannin), as the common names for *Ajuga reptans* attest—carpenter's weed, middle comfrey, and sicklewort. Bugle was also recommended for coughs, ulcers, rheumatism, and liver disorders. It also yields a black dye for wool. Although it is rarely claimed as an herb anymore, it is considered an indispensable and beautiful ground cover.

Bugle does an excellent job of smothering weeds. It is most useful under trees and flowering shrubs that bloom at the same time, especially aza-

Plate 15. *Ajuga pyramidalis*, pyramid bugle, clump-forming type. Late spring, Joseph Hudak garden. Photo, Joseph Hudak.

71

leas and rhododendrons. It is a pleasing alternative for those difficult places were grass does not grow or cannot be easily maintained, such as tight corners or between walls and walkways; bugle always creates a very favorable impression in what would otherwise be a dreary, weedy spot. The less vigorous, clump-forming types, *Ajuga genevensis* and *A. pyramidalis*, can be planted at the front of a bed or border or in a rock garden where their brilliant, long-lasting blooms show to advantage.

Bugle is usually grown from pieces of root but can be raised from seed. It prefers evenly moist soil and some shade, although most bugles will grow even in full sun and dry soil. Helen Fox once described it as marching across the ground, but it will do so only where conditions are most favorable, that is, in prepared, relatively weed-free ground. Plants can be divided in spring or fall and the new clumps set 9–12 in. (22.9–30.5 cm) apart. All will accept some foot traffic when not in bloom. Even the carpeters are not pestily invasive, since the shallow-rooted runners are pulled up easily.

Related plants of interest. A selection of bugles is readily available from the best perennial plant nurseries. Herb nurseries rarely carry them. Keep in mind that the blue-flowered bugles are the heaviest flowering and are slightly more vigorous than others.

Ajuga genevensis 'Pink Beauty' spreads slowly and bears light pink flowers on 5 to 6 in. (12.7–15.2 cm) stems with lustrous, green foliage.

Ajuga pyramidalis is a compact, 6 in. (15.2 cm) tall bugle with evergreen foliage and deep blue flowers.

Ajuga reptans 'Alba' (Plate 16) forms a white-flowered carpet with dark green foliage 8 in. (20.3 cm) high. This most elegant form with small but plentiful, pure white spires, blooming at least a week before the blue type, finds a welcome home in a shady nook with pink, old-fashioned granny's bonnet (*Aquilegia vulgaris*).

Ajuga reptans 'Burgundy Glow' is the most popular bugle. Its foliage changes over the season from deep red to dark pink, is variegated with creamy white, and is complemented by bright blue flower spikes. Growing to 8 in. (20.3 cm), it creates a glowing carpet, especially in sunlight.

Ajuga reptans 'Catlin's Giant' is a vigorous hybrid and the showiest of all bugles. It has dark blue flower stalks to 12 in. (30.5 cm) and glossy, bronze leaves. It spreads fast and is best grown in shade and moist soil.

Plate 16. *Ajuga reptans* 'Alba', bugle, creeping type. Early summer, Gardner farm. Photo, Alan Dorey.

Alcea rosea

Malvaceae, Mallow Family
Hollyhock, holyoke, jagged mallow

Biennial
Site and soil: sun; sharply drained, well-drained
Hardiness: Zones 3–10
Landscape use: accent, bed and border, edge and hedge, naturalized herb
Height: 6–8 ft. (1.8–2.4 m)
Flower pink, purple, rose, yellow, white, large saucers solitary up the stalk and in clusters at the tip
Bloom season: midsummer to late summer

The origin of the garden hollyhock, probably introduced from Asia, is uncertain because it has been cultivated for so long that its wild form is unknown. A tall, stately plant, it grows from a fleshy taproot and produces a clump of large leaves the first year, each leaf up to 12 in. (30.5 cm) wide and 10 in. (25.4 cm) long, scalloped, and nearly heart-shaped. The second year the hollyhock produces a stout stem bedecked with leaves that diminish in size as they ascend and lovely saucer- or bell-shaped flowers from midsummer to fall.

Tucked into leaf axils, tightly wrapped in bud, their pointed tips just showing from their light green sepals, the flowers begin mid-way up the tall stalk, clustering at the top. Each five-petaled bloom of overlapping, silky petals, slightly curled back at their edges, is about 4 in. (10.2 cm) wide, revealing the showy, tubular column of stamens that is typical of all plants in the mallow family. As the flower matures, it changes in shape from cupped to flat before folding up fanwise and dropping off the stalk. The main flower color is rose, as the name *rosea* suggests, but many centuries of cultivation, selection, and hybridization have produced pastel shades on the rose theme from the lightest of pinks to the darkest of purples, as well as yellow and white, some with a distinctive darker eye in their centers. Flared and ruffled petals also occur.

The genus name comes from the Greek *altho*, to cure, placing hollyhocks in the category of healing plants, although they are seldom regarded as herbs by herb authorities. In common with all members of the mallow family, hollyhocks contain a mucilaginous substance that has a soothing effect on lung and urinary tract ailments. The contemporary medicinal herb authority John Lust adds that hollyhock flowers—viscous to the touch when wet—are used in cosmetic preparations to soften rough skin. The cultivar *Alcea rosea* 'Nigra' (Plate 19) or black hollyhock has been used as a dye to color wine and tea (the flowers bleed purple when wet). These almost black, dark purple flowers are impressive with a glowing quality that is remarkable. The chocolate-maroon 'The Watchman' is aptly named, for the dark, out-facing flowers on tall stalks do appear as sentinels in the landscape.

Plate 17. *Alcea rosea*, hollyhock, grown from seed mix. Midsummer, Country Lane Herbs and Dried Flowers. Photo, Brian Oke and Gisèle Quesnel.

Plate 18. *Alcea rosea*, hollyhock, self-sown variant. It enjoys protection from wind at the front of the house. Midsummer, Gardner farm. Photo, Alan Dorey.

Although the classic form remains the tall, single-flowered type, *Alcea rosea* Chater's Double is a famous and enduring, double-flowered, Victorian hybrid group in an extraordinary range of colors—rose, salmon, red, buff, yellow, maroon, white, and scarlet—that come true from seed. In the Victorian era hollyhocks became florists' flowers, objects of intensive breeding in the insatiable search for new forms, but all the many cultivars have been lost except for the Chater's Double Hybrids and the older, very rare *A. ficifolia* 'Antwerp Hollyhock'.

Alcea rosea 'Indian Spring', a cultivar introduced before 1939, is a fine selection of old-fashioned types with single and semidouble flowers in the pastel range, some with wavy edges; they usually do not exceed 5 ft. (1.5 m)

Plate 19. *Alcea rosea* 'Nigra', black hollyhock. Midsummer, Gardner farm. Photo, Alan Dorey.

and may not need staking. Others that will not need staking are the widely available dwarf types, but their short stalks, burdened with overstuffed flowers, lack all dignity and appeal.

The opportunities for using hollyhocks in their towering glory include massing them in front of fences or walls, by the sides of buildings, near any significant structure such as a trellis or arbor, or grouping them in front of a shrubbery where they are given some wind protection. Massed hollyhocks can also be used as a screen to hide functional features such as a compost heap. A conventional device is to plant them in the rear of a border in back of dahlias, which serve to hide the lower, straggly-leaved hollyhock stalks. Wherever they are planted, hollyhocks will need staking: they may manage very well most of the season but one hard blow will transform them into horizontal monsters.

Sow seeds outside in a cold frame in late summer where they will germinate the following spring, or raise seedlings indoors to germinate in 10 days at 70°F (21°C). Space plants 24 in. (61.0 cm) apart in enriched, well-drained soil. This latter requirement is very important for hardiness; more hollyhocks are probably lost from wet root crowns during late winter or early spring than from any other cause. Well-situated hollyhocks grow as perennials, self-sowing from year to year on their own in early-warming soil, such as near building foundations (Plate 18). Hollyhocks are described as short-lived perennials in Zones 3–8 and as biennials in Zones 9–10; wherever they are planted, survival depends a great deal on specific growing conditions. It is a good idea to cut back flowering stalks at the end of the season to prolong the life of the plant.

New plants can be grown from plantlets that begin to form at the base of a mature plant. Using a sharp knife, separate them as root cuttings and plant them in a cold frame for the winter. Transplant the root cuttings in the early spring before the plants have had a chance to develop long taproots. Raising plantlets is the best procedure for ensuring the return of favorite hollyhock colors; saving seeds may be variable because of cross pollination.

The most common affliction of hollyhocks is rust, a fungus disease that appears as rusty or orange-colored areas on hollyhock leaves, usually when the plants are in flower during prolonged periods of humidity. To prevent and treat rust, provide good air circulation and spray or dust leaves with agricultural sulphur according to the manufacturer's directions. If the disease is too far advanced, destroy the plants and try growing new ones in a different location.

Away from the garden, dried hollyhocks of all species give texture and color to potpourri and are easily harvested, since the flowers partially dry as they mature. Black hollyhock flowers impart a warm tea color to any brew and blend assorted flavors. I use three parts lemon balm to one part chamomile and add three dried blossoms of hollyhock for each cup of tea.

Related plants of interest. Seeds of the tall, single hollyhock and the black hollyhock are increasingly available from general seed sources but not usually from herb sources. Seeds and plants of the Chater's Double Hybrids and *Alcea rosea* 'Indian Spring' are available from general seed and perennial plant sources, although the latter is harder to find.

Alcea ficifolia 'Antwerp Hollyhock', a naturally occurring hybrid, is similar to *A. rosea* except its color range includes copper, yellow, red, rose, and white, and the foliage is deeply lobed or fig leaf shaped, as the Latin name notes.

Alcea rugosa, rugosa hollyhock, is a beautiful plant native to the Ukraine and southern Russia, with fig-leaf foliage and large, pale yellow flowers. It has narrower, more abundant canes than *A. rosea* and appears more bushy when massed. Unlike *A. rosea*, it does not reproduce thriftily, so care should be taken to ensure its continued appearance.

Althea officinalis, marsh mallow, is a native to Europe that grows perennially in marshy ground and on river banks. It bears the genus name by which the hollyhock was once known. Marsh mallow is a widely recognized medicinal, as its species name, "from the apothecary," indicates. All parts of the plant are edible and have been used for food in time of need; every part has been used medicinally, especially the roots, which are richly mucilaginous. These roots were the original source for making marshmallows. Now enjoying a revival as a cottage garden flower and a medicinal, the marsh mallow grows to 4 ft. (1.2 m) or more and blooms in late summer. It has distinctive, velvety, gray-green leaves with small, $1\frac{1}{2}$ in. (3.8 cm) across, pale, lilac-pink flowers borne in groups along lax stems. It is suitable for a mixed, informal border or, even better, for naturalizing in damp ground. The marsh mallow should be grown and propagated like hollyhock and is hardy in Zone 4.

Alchemilla mollis

Rosaceae, Rose Family
Lady's mantle, dewcup, lion's foot

Perennial
Site and soil: sun, partial shade, shade; evenly moist
Hardiness: Zones 3–8
Landscape use: bed and border, container, edge and
  hedge, ground cover, naturalized herb, rock work
Height: 12–18 in. (30.5–45.7 cm)
Flower: chartreuse star in cluster
Bloom season: spring to early summer

> **The leaves are delightfully fan-shaped and pleated, and the pale green flowers open in June.**
> Margaret E. Brownlow
> *Herbs and the Fragrant Garden*

Lady's mantle, originating in Europe and Asia, is now sometimes found as a garden escape in the northeastern United States where it has been cultivated since colonial times. One of the plant's distinctive features, from which it derives its common name, is its nearly circular, toothed, pleated, and cloak-like leaves. Tiny silver hairs that cover the leaves and give them a grayish cast also catch drops of rain or dew that glisten like jewels, a characteristic that gave rise to the popular belief that the liquid was magic water. By early summer, the clumps of spreading foliage are embellished by loose clusters of very small, star-like flowers, greenish yellow or chartreuse, that appear above the foliage, bringing the height of the plant to 18 in. (45.7 cm).

According to some authorities, *Alchemilla mollis* never had any medicinal use. Lady's mantle's reputation as an astringent and styptic to dry up wounds, stop bleeding, and alleviate excessive menstrual flow belongs to other species: *A. alpina*, alpine lady's mantle, and *A. xanthochlora*. Virtually identical to *A. mollis* in appearance, neither has a history of cultivation in North America.

Lady's mantle is still relatively unknown despite its ease of culture, refined habit of growth, adaptability, and long-lasting, frothy blooms whose unusual color blends with and complements most others in the landscape. Lady's mantle is a quiet plant whose subtle beauty must be given the opportunity to show itself. Its greatest impact comes, when massed, from the total ensemble of foliage and flowers. It is an incomparable, eye-catching, and elegant edge along a generous border or beside a path where its flowers gracefully spill over to soften boundaries. In partial shade it is effective among hostas or beneath rhododendrons; in the sun it looks good in colonies beneath dark pink roses or among salvias and lavenders (*Lavandula angustifolia*) in a garden setting. Lady's mantle is stunning billowing over the sides of a large tub, where both its foliage and blooms can be appreciated at close range. It may bloom until late summer in wet years, or repeat bloom in late summer and fall if cut back after its first flowering.

Seeds are difficult to germinate and need to be fresh. Plant seeds $^1/_8$ in. (0.3 cm) deep to germinate over the winter in a cold frame. Space plants 24 in. (61.0 cm) apart, 8–10 in. (20.3–25.4 cm) for a ground cover, in moderately fertile, evenly moist soil in sun, partial shade, or shade. In very rich, moist soil lady's mantle rapidly multiplies. To control its growth, give it more sun and drier soil. In hot, humid conditions provide good air circulation, otherwise the water that collects in the leaves may cause fungus

Plate 20. *Alchemilla mollis*, lady's mantle. Early summer, Country Lane Herbs and Dried Flowers. Some of the flowers will be dried to use in wreaths. Photo, Brian Oke and Gisèle Quesnel.

disease. Divide plants after flowering, taking separate pieces of the crown with attached roots.

Sprays of lady's mantle make fine cut flowers and bouquet filler. Dried, they stay a soft light green that is very useful in dried bouquets and wreaths.

Related plants of interest. Seeds of lady's mantle are available from a few seed and herb sources, and plants are available from perennial plant and herb sources.

Alchemilla erythropoda, dwarf lady's mantle, is a choice, 6 in. (15.2 cm) replica of its larger cousin with the same delicate flower clusters, but these turn reddish as they fade. It grows best in cool conditions, is hardy in Zone 4, and is perfect for small plantings tucked at the foot of stairs or between pavings. It also makes a good ground cover.

Allium schoenoprasum

Liliaceae, Lily Family
Chives

Perennial
Site and soil: sun; well-drained, evenly moist, boggy
Hardiness: Zones 3–10
Landscape use: bed and border, container, edge and
   hedge, naturalized herb, rock work
Height: 12 in. (30.5 cm)
Flower: lavender-rose ball in terminal head
Bloom season: spring to early summer

> As an ornamental plant, chives are as nice as anything in the perennial border.
> John Williamson
> *Perennial Gardens*

Chives have been cultivated for at least 4000 years, beginning in China. Of the 700 or more alliums that grow in the Northern Hemisphere, none is so well known for its practical and ornamental qualities as chives, sometimes seen growing wild in meadows and along stream banks. Since pioneer days they have been an early, reliable, and nutritious spring vegetable. Clusters of small bulblets sprout 10 in. (25.4 cm) mounds of narrow, hollow-stemmed, tapering leaves. The flowering stems just above them bear small, round globes of tightly packed florets in early summer that are very attractive to bees.

The virtues of chives as flowering plants must have been apparent to the colonial housewife who tended them in the kitchen garden. Wherever they are grown, and for whatever purpose, they are admired for their free-flowering, delicately colored blooms, a sea of rosy lavender among clumps of blue-green foliage. *Allium schoenoprasum* 'Forescate', 18–20 in. (45.7–50.8 cm), has larger, brighter flowers. 'Profusion' is a sterile form that flowers over a longer period than the species. Dwarf and taller cultivars are also available.

When it comes to placing chives, gardeners have many choices. If the soil is very rich, chives will spread rapidly and be difficult to control. Otherwise, they can be an edge for a garden of culinary herbs or vegetables or a single specimen accent in virtually any type of planting. In a rock garden they complement mats of rose-flowered creeping thyme. A few clumps are

Plate 21. *Allium schoenoprasum*, white and mauve chives. Early summer, culinary bed, Country Lane Herbs and Dried Flowers. Photo, Brian Oke and Gisèle Quesnel.

handy to have near the door for snipping leaves and flowers to toss over summer salads. Chives in bloom combine well with the late spring and early summer pastels of columbine (*Aquilegia vulgaris*) and dame's rocket (*Hesperis matronalis*). Naturalize them in a bog, where they will bloom in colorful drifts; it is surprising how well chives grow in really wet ground where the blooms take on a darker, rosier hue. White-flowered chives, though hard to find, are a charming plant whose mass of nearly white globes is best appreciated at the front of the border with a low mound of *Geranium* 'Johnson's Blue' or as a single accent in the landscape next to any structure or large rock.

Chives take two or three seasons to grow from seed to the flowering stage, but it is not difficult. Sow seeds about $^1/2$ in. (1.3 cm) deep in a prepared seed bed outdoors or in a cold frame where they will germinate by spring. Transplant the wispy seedlings in small clumps spaced 6 in. (15.2 cm) apart in evenly moist, garden soil in full sun. If cutting back the plants to invite a second flowering do not cut close to the ground, and be sure to work in fertilizer (6-12-12) or compost at the base to encourage the production of fresh growth. Divide clumps after flowering every 3 years or as needed.

The flowers and leaves of chives can be picked at any time to add to salads or to work into cream cheese for a sandwich spread; pick apart the florets before use. Both the pulled-apart flowers and finely cut leaves retain their flavor if they are quickly dried (I use the pilot light warmth in a gas oven). Mixed with dried parsley, celery, and lovage leaves, it is an important ingredient in a general, all-purpose, salt-substitute mix. Most of the alliums' flowers or seed heads can be dried for arrangements. The following recipe for pickled chives is from the local French-Acadian cuisine:

Pickled Chives

Cut the fattest, most succulent leaves, rinse, and pack them whole in a wide-mouth jar in which you have mixed $1^1/2$ cups salt and 1 gallon cold water. Put a weight on the chives so they remain submerged, cover the container, and refrigerate. Let the chives ripen for 2 weeks before using. To use, squeeze the brine from a handful of chives, rinse them (or not and add no additional salt to the dish) and cut up the leaves in soups, stews, and vegetable and egg dishes. Pickled chives are traditionally used to flavor fricasseed rabbit.

Plate 22. *Allium shoenoprasum*, chives. Early summer, Graymalkin Farm. Photo, Brian Oke and Gisèle Quesnel.

Related plants of interest. None of the multitude of alliums in cultivation can match the brilliance and beauty of the group known as ornamental onions. Virtually all of them are useful as well as attractive, having been used for food or medicine in their country of origin. Those with the strongest onion flavor have the highest concentration of sulfur oil, considered antiseptic and helpful in lowering blood pressure. Most allium flowers are lightly and sweetly scented; only the bulbs and foliage smell oniony when bruised. Summer-dormant types have strap-like foliage close to the ground that withers as the flowers bloom on strong, leafless stems. All types thrive in sun and well-drained soil. They increase by bulblets that form close to the mother bulb or by seeds or bulbils that form at the top of the plant in fruiting clusters. The planting depth of the bulbs should be three times their width, spaced 6–18 in. (15.2–45.7 cm) apart, depending on type.

The following is a selection of alliums available for early to midsummer bloom. Seeds are available from general and herb sources; plants are available from perennial plant and herb sources. Look for nodding onion from wildflower sources. Siberian onion is hard to find.

Allium cernuum, nodding onion or lady's leek, was once food, medicine for asthma and coughs, and insect repellent for North American Indians and the early settlers. It is the prettiest of the native alliums, growing to 24 in. (61.0 cm) in rocky soil in the midwestern United States with slender, grass-like leaves as tall as the stems. By midsummer, these bear bell-shaped, rose-pink flowers in clusters that nod because of a crook at the top of the stem. This is a very desirable plant for a rock garden or for naturalizing, but it requires sandy, even gravely soil; it is hardy in Zone 5.

Allium christophii, star-of-Persia, the largest of the allium flowers, is summer dormant with space-age globes of purple florets with a metallic sheen; 8–12 in. (20.3–30.5 cm) across, the flowers perch on strong stems to 24 in. (61.0 cm). Show it off at the front of a border in rich, well-drained, mulched soil with sweet alyssum (*Lobularia maritima*) to hide the dying foliage in late spring. Its ornamental value lasts well into summer as the flowers form decorative fruits.

Allium moly, lily leek or golden garlic, is also summer dormant. Its butter-yellow stars grow in loose clusters 2–3 in. (5.1–7.6 cm) across on stems 8–12 in. (20.3–30.5 cm) tall. Plant the bulbs close together in clumps in rich, well-drained soil. It looks lovely among blue pansies (*Viola ×wittrockiana*) and irises or massed beneath shrubs in spring. This species was once regarded as a good luck charm, a floral talisman of prosperity.

Allium ramosum, Siberian onion, grows to 20 in. (50.8 cm) and bears honey-scented, smallish flower heads of a reddish lilac tinged with gray. It bears some resemblance to garlic chives (*A. tuberosum*) with which it is sometimes confused. It blends well in a garden setting with other herbs such as painted sage (*Salvia viridis*) and nepetas. It readily self-sows.

Allium tuberosum

Liliaceae, Lily Family
Garlic chives, Chinese chives, Chinese leeks, oriental garlic, gow choy

Perennial
Site and soil: sun; well-drained
Hardiness: Zones 3–9
Landscape use: accent, bed and border
Height: 30 in. (76.2 cm)
Flower: white star in umbel
Bloom season: late summer to fall

Native to China, garlic chives grow by means of three little bulbs attached to a horizontal rhizome, a construction which produces spaced clumps of bulbs rather than rounded clumps like ordinary chives. The leaves, too, are different, flat rather than round. For much of the season, all that is seen of garlic chives is a low, somewhat arching mound of long, narrow leaves. By late summer the plant is transformed into round, white umbels at the tops of long stems. The flower heads are composed of many small, white, star-shaped florets, each one delicately lined with green on its undersides. The seed head with its green, then beige fruiting knobs is attractive into late fall. The leaves have a mild garlic flavor, the flowers a sweet scent that verges on the garlic.

In North America, garlic chives have been grown mostly by herb enthusiasts, and the plant's uses have not been much explored. It is seldom considered an ornamental, perhaps because it is overshadowed by such big-headed types as *Allium christophii*. This is a shame because it is an elegant, late-blooming perennial. The primary use of garlic chives has been as an important vegetable. In oriental cuisine, virtually every part—stalks, buds, flowers, seed heads, even the oil—is used; consequently, most cultivars emphasize large leaves. At least one type, *A. tuberosum* 'Flowering', has been selected for its edible flowers; and 'Mauve' has been selected for its different-colored flowers.

Visitors to my garden always want to know about this plant, so rarely seen in fall gardens. It can be combined effectively with both annuals and

Plate 23. *Allium tuberosum,* garlic chives. Late summer, edible flower bed, Country Lane Herbs and Dried Flowers. Some of the flowering stems will be cut for dried flower arrangements. Photo, Brian Oke and Gisèle Quesnel.

perennials. I grow it near spreading colonies of painted sage (*Salvia viridis*) and the taller nicotianas such as the chartreuse *Nicotiana* 'Limelight'. Among perennials, I grow garlic chives near *Sedum* 'Autumn Joy', a perfect pairing of form and color; elsewhere, it combines well in front of bright rudbeckias and purple coneflower (*Echinacea purpurea*). The easygoing garlic chives are an invaluable late-blooming flower—and there are many leaves to spare for use in the kitchen.

Sow seeds indoors 6–8 weeks before the last frost, where they will germinate in 14 days or less at 70°F (21°C); or sow seeds in a cold frame in the fall, where they will germinate in the spring. Space each plant, with its three bulbs attached to a rhizome, about 12 in. (30.5 cm) or more apart, or leave it in the cold frame for another season until it has gained some size. Once established, cut back seed heads to discourage self-sowing, though in areas colder than Zone 5 the seeds will not germinate.

Use the leaves of garlic chives in salads, sour cream dips, soups, stir-fries, and meat, egg, and fish dishes, wherever a mild garlic flavor is desired. Steep the leaves in white or cider vinegar for about 2 weeks, then strain the vinegar through two layers of cheesecloth and rebottle; use garlic vinegar in salads, with cooked greens, and in marinades. Flowers of most alliums can be dried for decoration, but dry the flowers of garlic chives out of the way for they give up their garlic scent as they dehydrate.

Related plants of interest. The following alliums, variously regarded as ornamental onions or as wildflowers, have all been used as food or medicine. They are hardy, easy to grow, and very desirable in the herb-inspired landscape. Seeds or plants of garlic chives are generally available from seed and herb sources. The other alliums are harder to find; look for them at plant and wildflower nurseries.

Allium senescens var. *glaucum,* silver curly chives or corkscrew chives, is an arresting little plant 8–12 in. (20.3–30.5 cm) tall. It is a variant of the chives called *sekka-yama-negi* in Japan, where the bulbs, leaves, and young shoots are used as food. Small, rose-lilac umbels grow up from rosettes of silvery, twisted leaves, making the plant very attractive for the front of a border or in a rock garden.

Allium stellatum, prairie onion or autumn wild onion, is a wildflower of rocky slopes and prairies from Saskatchewan south to Illinois and Texas. Rosy lavender flower clusters, similar in form to garlic chives, top leafless stems to 24 in. (61.0 cm); the foliage is narrow and grass-like. The bulbs were used for food and medicine, even insect repellent, by North American Indians and the early settlers. This is a good subject for naturalizing on dry slopes or in light shade with white coralbells (*Heuchera micrantha*).

Allium thunbergii, from eastern Asia, is *yama-rakkyo* in Japan, where it is preserved in salt, pickled in brine, or eaten raw as a flavoring herb. 'Ozawa's Variety', 8–10 in. (20.3–25.4 cm), is a low-growing clump of thin foliage, topped late in the season by bright red-violet flower clusters.

Anchusa

Boraginaceae, Borage Family
Bugloss, alkanet

Biennial, perennial
Site and soil: sun, partial shade; well-drained
Hardiness: Zones 3–10
Landscape use: bed and border, container,
  naturalized herb, rock work
Height: 1 1/2–6 ft. (0.5–1.8 m)
Flower: blue, purple, violet, tubular cluster
Bloom season: early summer to midsummer

> **After all is said and done, the mystery of the blue flower . . . by its heavenly color, lifts the heart toward heaven.**
> Mrs. Francis King
> *From a New Garden*

The biennial common bugloss, *Anchusa officinalis* (Plate 24), is an Old World medicinal. Naturalized from Maine to Michigan, it can be recognized by its basal cluster of coarse leaves to 8 in. (20.3 cm) long and its bristly stems 12–36 in. (30.1–91.4 cm) tall that carry delicate, five-petaled flowers in bright blue, purple, or violet, in profusion most of the summer. Italian bugloss, *A. azurea*, is a short-lived perennial also of European origin, with similar rough leaves but with larger, bright blue, clustered flowers on stems 5–6 ft. (1.5–1.8 m) tall. It mimics an overgrown forget-me-not (*Myosotis scorpioides*), blooming in early summer.

Both these plants, closely related to comfrey (*Symphytum*) and borage (*Borago officinalis*), are known as bugloss, a word derived from Greek, meaning ox tongue, because of the shape and texture of the leaves. They are also known as alkanet, from the Arabic *alhenna*, the same word that prefigured the name of henna, the famous red dye once extracted from bugloss roots. Bugloss has been used to treat coughs and fevers, to soothe sore throats, and to ameliorate skin conditions. Common bugloss was once listed in the U.S. Pharmacopeia. Anchusas were popular cottage garden flowers because of their relative ease of culture and profusion of beautiful and useful flowers. Their sweet, rich nectar was used in restorative conserves and as flavoring in wine and beverages. The leaves, musk-scented when dried, were preserved for medicinal use.

Plate 24. *Anchusa officinalis*, common bugloss. Early summer, Graymalkin Farm. Photo, Brian Oke and Gisèle Quesnel.

Because of their ungainly habit of toppling over from the weight of their blooms, anchusas fell from favor as popular ornamentals, but they have remained in gardens because of their irresistibly beautiful flowers, which are also good in bouquets. Cultivars such as *Anchusa azurea* 'Loddon Royalist', no taller than 3 ft. (0.9 m), and 'Little John', a dwarf version to 18 in. (45.7 cm) with masses of flowers, have been bred from Italian bugloss. 'Loddon Royalist' belongs at the back or middle of the border, and 'Little John' should be right up front or grown in a rock garden. The bugloss blues stand out best among the pale yellows and whites of vertical irises, lupines, and foxgloves (*Digitalis*). Common bugloss is best grown in a billowy cottage garden or naturalized in a dry, sunny meadow.

Sow seeds of the biennial common bugloss where they are to bloom, as soon as the soil can be worked. After they have sprouted, thin seedlings to 12 in. (30.5 cm) apart. They will take a year to flower from seed, and if conditions are favorable—light, well-drained soil and full sun—they will continue to self-sow. Space Italian bugloss 18 in. (45.7 cm) apart and stake the taller kinds in their early growth. Italian bugloss grows in the same conditions as common bugloss and may not survive over the winter if there is excessive moisture in the ground. Anchusas are short-lived plants, so divide them in early spring or fall to assure a fresh supply since the self-sown plants may not come true to type. Cut back plants after their first flowering to encourage a second, more modest bloom later in the season.

Related plants of interest. Seeds and plants of common bugloss and viper's bugloss are available from herb sources. Cultivars of Italian bugloss are available from perennial plant nurseries, and dwarf forms of viper's bugloss are available from a few seed sources.

Echium vulgare, viper's bugloss, a biennial from Europe, is sometimes seen growing along roadsides and in old fields. It is easily naturalized, and occasionally will make itself at home near cultivated ground. It grows to 3 ft. (0.9 m) or more, on bristly stems from a basal growth of rough, pointed leaves. The delicate, funnel-shaped flowers on curved spikes are rose, becoming bright blue as they mature, and plentiful. It takes its genus name from the Greek for viper and was once used to treat snakebites (its roots contain allantoin, a substance used to heal wounds). Infusions of the leaves were used to relieve dysentery, fevers, headaches, and nervous complaints. Nowadays, viper's bugloss is useful as a dried flower (it dries blue) and in potpourri. The annual 'Dwarf Brilliant' (Plate 25) to 18 in. (45.7 cm) flowers the first year from seed, blooming all summer in elongated, colorful spikes that curl over the edges of beds and borders. Just a few plants create a wide mass of flowers, forming a weed-smothering edge for rose beds or any mixed planting.

Plate 25. *Echium vulgare* 'Dwarf Brilliant', viper's bugloss. Midsummer, Gardner farm. Photo, Alan Dorey.

Angelica archangelica

Apiaceae, Celery Family
Angelica, archangel, wild celery, wild parsnip

Biennial
Site and soil: sun, partial shade, shade; moist and well-
    drained
Hardiness: Zones 3–8
Landscape use: accent, bed and border, naturalized herb
Height: 6–8 ft. (1.8–2.4 m)
Flower: chartreuse, wheel-like umbels
Bloom season: early summer to midsummer

> Angelica . . .
> is a plant of
> the angels.
> Kay Sanecki
> *The Complete
> Books of Herbs*

The Eurasian angelica, one of fifty species native to the Northern Hemisphere, is the most celebrated for its herbal use and adaptability to cultivation. The first year it forms a handsome mound of medium green, toothed,
divided leaves up to 20 in. (52.1 cm) long; the second year it sends up a
tall, hollow stem with side stems sprouting at intervals, all bearing large,
dome-shaped umbels of tiny, chartreuse flowers in early summer. These
flowers gradually ripen to form oblong green fruits, which turn darker
over time, finally dropping to earth as the plant itself begins to die. The
whole plant is aromatic, combining the scents of celery and gin.

Many legends are attached to angelica, so named, some say, because of
its angelic properties: it relieved stomach disorders, colds, and coughs; its
leaves and stems were cooked in many recipes; and its oil was distilled for
flavoring wines (vermouth and chartreuse) and scenting perfumes. Its
name is associated with the archangel St. Michael, whose feast day coincides with the plant's flowering.

Angelica is a spectacular flowering herb that takes imagination and experience to grow in the right place, but do not be inhibited—in the language of flowers it signifies inspiration. Angelica is a stately presence at the
back of a border. It also makes a bold accent by the corner of a building,
in a semiwild setting among lower-growing plants, or in a formal herb garden or island bed. The plant remains a focal point well over a month,
from the beginning of its long bloom period until the seed heads are
formed. And only one plant is needed to make a grand statement. Helen

93

Fox grew it in an unexpected situation along a walk with auratum lilies (*Lilium auratum*)—the effect was stunning. When massed, angelica makes a fine screen with its many umbels reaching upward and outward, highlighted by a backdrop of blue sky.

Plants are most easily established by roots set 3 ft. (0.9 m) apart in rich, moist, well-drained soil in sun, partial shade, or shade, wherever its roots can be kept cool and moist. After flowering and dying, angelica will maintain itself by dropping its own seeds. Since they lose significant germinating strength after they ripen, however, it is safest to gather the seeds, store them in the freezer until needed, and establish seedlings. In a prepared seed bed in early spring or fall, drop several seeds every 30–36 in. (76.2–91.4 cm) for a screen or hedge; then thin to the strongest plants every 3 ft. (0.9 m). Plants can be propagated by detaching new shoots that form at the base of a second-year plant after it has been cut back to prevent flowering; plants are difficult to move after a year because of their long taproot.

Fresh leaves or stems add a unique flavor to stewed rhubarb or gooseberries. The leaves also enhance fish dishes. The following recipe makes the well-known angelica candy:

Angelica Candy

Cut stems $^1/_2$ in. (1.3 cm) in diameter from a second-year plant early in its growth. Cut them into 2 in. (5.1 cm) pieces and boil them in salted water until tender. Drain, and scrape off the outer skin so the stems are bright green. Weigh the stems and make a syrup of the same weight, using 1 cup of water for every 1 pound of sugar. Let the stems sit in the syrup for 3 or 4 days. Twice a day bring the syrup to a boil and pour it back over the stems until the syrup is nearly absorbed. Drain the stems and dry them on paper, turning them often until they feel completely dry. Stems preserved this way will keep almost indefinitely in a tightly closed jar stored in a cool, dry place away from light. Use the stems to decorate cakes or eat them after a meal in the same way as after-dinner mints, to aid digestion. They have a sweet, clean taste. The leftover syrup is delicious in summer fruit cups or over ice cream.

Related plants of interest. Angelica plants are available from perennial plant and herb sources. Korean angelica is harder to find but, when offered, is at the same sources.

Angelica gigas, Korean angelica, carries out the purple theme suggested in the wild native species, *A. atropurpurea*. Also biennial, it sends up purple stems 4–5 ft. (1.2–1.5 m) tall its second year and bears impressive, dense, red-violet to deep purple, spherical heads in late summer. It may survive as long as 3 or 4 years in partial shade. It is a very striking plant, hardy in Zone 4.

Artemisia lactiflora

Asteraceae, Aster Family
White mugwort, ghost plant, sweet mugwort

Perennial
Site and soil: sun, partial shade; moist and well-drained
Hardiness: Zones 3–9
Landscape use: accent, bed and border, naturalized herb
Height: 4–6 ft. (1.2–1.8 m)
Flower: creamy white, small head in loose panicle
Bloom season: late summer to fall

> Hardy and handsome at the back of the herb border.
>
> Helen Fox
> *The Years in My Herb Garden*

White mugwort was brought to North America from China by Ernest Wilson in 1901. A superhardy perennial of shrub-like proportions, it bears masses of tiny, creamy white, perfumed flowers in loosely panicled plumes at the ends of long, reddish stems that are covered with deeply toothed, green leaves. The flowers have a grape-like, camphor-overtoned aroma that has been described as resinous. Called *yomogi-na* in Japan and *junn jui choi* in China, white mugwort is important in Asian cooking as a potherb and a flavoring for rice cakes. In the West, where it is largely unknown as an herb or as an ornamental, its uses are confined to flower arrangements and dried flower decorations.

White mugwort has everything one could want in a distinctive garden plant. Its feathery sprays bloom in late summer when fresh flowers are most needed in the landscape, and the foliage remains handsome all season. And though it is very easy to grow, it is not invasive, unlike its dowdy cousin common mugwort, *Artemisia vulgaris.*

This flowering mugwort is extraordinarily adaptable to a variety of landscaping situations. In the back of a perennial border it complements colorful monardas all season; in a sheltered dooryard garden it contrasts with tall, purple hollyhocks; in an island bed it is an unparalleled centerpiece in late summer when its arching white sprays dominate the scene. White mugwort is also suitable for an informal or wild garden where it will light up a shady corner along with the white-flowered black cohosh (*Cimicifuga racemosa*) and Canadian burnet (*Sanguisorba canadensis*), vertically blooming plants in bottle-brush and poker designs. Like other vigorous, shrublike herbs it can be used as a shrub substitute, especially in a difficult spot where real shrubs would languish, such as moist, heavy soil and partial shade; it also makes a fine, informal hedge.

White mugwort attains its maximum height in rich, moist, well-drained soil and sun or partial shade. For a shorter, bushier plant, cut it back when it has reached 24 in. (61.0 cm) or plant it in dry soil and full sun. Since white mugwort is sterile, it can only be grown from root cuttings. Space

Plate 26. *Artemisia lactiflora*, white mugwort. Late summer, Country Lane Herbs and Dried Flowers. Photo, Brian Oke and Gisèle Quesnel.

new plants 3 ft. (0.9 m) apart or closer for a hedge. Plants are easily propagated by division either in the spring or fall. Tall plants may need staking.

For fresh and dried flower arrangements, cut the stems of white mugwort when the flowers are still white and fresh. Cut the stems of *Artemisia annua* when the flowers are bright yellow. Little bunches of the flowers can be tied around a form to make aromatic sweet Annie wreaths.

Related plants of interest. Both artemisias are hard to find. White mugwort is available from the best perennial plant nurseries and herb sources; sweet wormwood is available from specialty seed and herb sources.

Artemisia annua, sweet Annie or sweet wormwood, is a Eurasian species that is little known in the West except by herb fanciers and those who have discovered it for decorating. It is a fast-growing annual that reaches 6 ft. (1.8 m) in one season. By the fall it looks like a fern-leaved tree, wide at its base, pointed at its tip, bearing many supple, tapering stems laden with clusters of small, bright yellow flowers. The whole plant exudes an unusual and unforgettable, warm, citrus-camphor scent. In China, sweet wormwood is used in the wine-making process and as a medicinal, having properties similar to quinine. Start plants indoors by sowing seeds 10–12 weeks before the last frost; germination should occur in 7 days at 70°F (21°C). After the last frost, plant seedlings 24 in. (61.0 cm) apart. Plants do not start growing until warm temperatures prevail, but then they shoot up fast. Sweet wormwood belongs in the perennial border, a surprise accent for the fall, or against a fence or wall for a general landscape accent. Once established it will self-sow.

Asclepias tuberosa

Asclepiadaceae, Milkweed Family
Butterfly weed, pleurisy root

Perennial
Site and soil: sun; sharply drained, well-drained
Hardiness: Zones 3–10 (with winter protection
 colder than Zone 6)
Landscape use: accent, bed and border, naturalized
 herb
Height: 12–36 in. (30.5–91.4 cm)
Flower: red, yellow, usually orange, compact cluster
Bloom season: midsummer to late summer

Butterfly weed, a common sight on the North American prairies, also grows from New Hampshire to Florida along roadsides, in dry fields, and at the edges of woodland. Its adaptability and beauty account for its popularity as a cultivated plant. Growing from a deep taproot that enables it to reach moisture in dry conditions, butterfly weed sends up five to ten erect, flowering stems. Each one is topped by numerous, brightly colored, fragrant, and nectar-rich clusters of small flowers that attract monarch and swallowtail butterflies—swallowort is an older of its common names—as well as hummingbirds and bees. Each little flower, long-lasting when cut, consists of five fused petals with upright crowns. Unlike other milkweeds, butterfly weed's slender leaves are not borne in pairs but are scattered along the rough, hairy stems, which contain watery juice rather than milky sap. The distinctive boat-shaped seed pods, characteristic of the milkweed family, expand in maturity to release multitudes of airborne seeds, carried aloft by silky, white threads. The remaining decorative seed pods are often used in wreaths and dried bouquets.

As an herb, butterfly weed was more commonly known as pleurisy root because of the numerous preparations from its root that were used to treat respiratory ailments. Settlers to North America learned these uses from the local Indians who had long regarded butterfly weed as a medicinal. In the nineteenth century it was still listed in the U.S. Pharmacopeia, but it fell out of use because the plant contains toxic glycosides.

Butterfly weed has several attributes that highly recommend it to contemporary gardeners: a natural look, ease of maintenance, more than a month of bloom, and the attraction of hummingbirds and butterflies. Butterfly weed is a perfect choice for a naturalized planting in an open, sunny site, where it can be combined with herbs and flowers that similarly prefer dry growing conditions, such as wild bergamot (*Monarda fistulosa*), chicory (*Cichorium intybus*), and shasta daisies (*Luecanthemum* ×*superbum*). Within the confines of a border, butterfly weed can be grown with stunning effect among other hot-colored flowers—true lilies (*Lilium*) and daylilies (*Hemerocallis*)—with deep blue borage for contrast.

Of the several seed strains that have been developed, Gay Butterflies Mixed is the most significant and lasting. Always advertised as a mix of red, orange, and yellow, the strain is dominated by orange. The wild form of *Asclepias tuberosa*, variable enough, is a more rugged, carefree type.

It usually takes two seasons for butterfly weed to bloom from seed. If the seeds are fresh, stratification is unnecessary, otherwise germination is

Plate 27. *Asclepias tuberosa*, butterfly weed. Midsummer, butterfly bed, Country Lane Herbs and Dried Flowers. Photo, Brian Oke and Gisèle Quesnel.

triggered by moist stratification outdoors over the winter or indoors when seeds are stored in moist conditions at 40°F (4°C) for 3 months. Outdoors or in, seeds germinate at 75°F (21°C) in 3 weeks. Cuttings are easiest to make by slicing the taproot into 2 in. (5.1 cm) pieces, then replanting them in a vertical position in light, sharply drained or well-drained soil. Space plants 8–12 in. (20.3–30.5 cm) apart in a dry, sunny site. Moist, rich soil is the most common cause of early death. Established plants are most easily moved when they are dormant in the fall, but care must be taken not to damage the long taproot; if sufficient soil is dug up with the root, plants can be moved or divided in the spring. When the spent blooms are cut back, flowering is extended 5–6 weeks. Since butterfly weed does not begin to grow until temperatures warm, do not be alarmed by its non-appearance in the early spring—be patient and do not disturb the soil.

Related plants of interest. Seeds and plants of butterfly weed are widely available, although not usually from herb sources. Of blood flower, seeds only (with few exceptions) are available from specialty seed sources. Seeds and plants of swamp milkweed and its cultivars are available from a variety of sources, general and specialty.

Asclepias curassavica, blood flower, 24–36 in. (61.0–91.4 cm), is a bright crimson annual native to South America, where its root and sap have been used as a laxative. The upright, narrow plant carries spectacular flowers of scarlet petals with bright yellow crowns in the same design as butterfly weed. It is grown as an annual in areas colder than Zone 7. Plants can be wintered indoors, then cut back and replanted in the spring after the last frost. Or start seed in late winter. Flowers are produced over a long period, from midsummer through early fall, and are very attractive to Monarch butterflies and hummingbirds.

Asclepias incarnata, swamp milkweed, also once a medicinal herb, bears its reddish pink flower clusters on stout, 4 ft. (1.2 m) stems. Although it grows wild in damp conditions, it is adapted to well-drained garden soil. 'Soulmate' has deep rose-pink flower clusters and is supposed to bloom the first year, 3 months after sowing. 'Ice Ballet' is an elegant all-white version. A week's stratification at 40°F (4°C) speeds germination.

Borago officinalis

Boraginaceae, Borage Family
Borage, bee bread, cool tankard, star flower

Annual
Site and soil: sun; well-drained
Landscape use: bed and border, naturalized herb,
   rock work
Height: 24 in. (61.0 cm)
Flower: cornflower-blue star in cluster
Bloom season: early summer to midsummer

> **In all the plant realm, there is no more beautiful blue than that of borage flower with its dancing starlike blooms.**
>
> Priscilla Sawyer Lord
> "The Beauty of Herbs"
> *Handbook on Herbs and Their Ornamental Uses*

Borage is an herb from the sunny Mediterranean region. It might be dismissed as a weed of no account, with its coarse fuzzy stems and large oval leaves covered with silvery hairs, except for its lovely, star-shaped flowers—said to reflect the blue skies of its native habitat—that nod in clusters atop each plant in early summer. It takes an effort to examine them since they face downward as if embarrassed by their beauty: five pointed petals frame a central mauve-white, inner ring with a core of jet-black stamens, altogether about ³/₄ in. (1.9 cm) across. The nodding habit, a challenge to gardeners but a bonus for foraging bees, protects the flowers' considerable supply of nectar from both rain and dew.

Ever since someone discovered that borage flowers and leaves impart their fresh, cucumber-like flavor to alcoholic drinks, the plant has been associated with courage and cheerfulness, because such fortified beverages were thought to make people glad and merry. First-century writers like Pliny the Elder also extolled borage's ability to alleviate the pains of rheumatism, to cure hoarseness, and to reduce fevers.

Although its starry blue flowers are cheering, little thought was given to the landscaping role of borage except as a plant that belongs in the herb garden. But a few writers of the past, such as Helen Fox and Helen Webster, mention a white-flowered form as well as red and violet variants, thinking they might make nice color combinations. For some years herb enthusiasts have been sharing seeds of the white *Borago officinalis* 'Alba', circumventing its lack of commercial availability.

Season after season I hopefully grew borage in my herb garden, but their promising buds never seemed to deliver. Then one summer I threw some seed at the back of the vegetable garden on a slight rise. The effect was startling: a mass of blue stars, brilliant in the sun, cast a benevolent glow over

Plate 28. *Borago officinalis*, borage. Midsummer, Country Lane Herbs and Dried Flowers. Photo, Brian Oke and Gisèle Quesnel.

rows of greenery below. Surely one of the most rewarding moments for a gardener is to realize a plant's potential: from this experience I learned that one should always plant borage so the nodding flowers can be seen from below. Choice locations include rock gardens and mass plantings on a slope or hillside with other sun-loving herbs such as wild bergamot (*Monarda fistulosa*), musk mallow (*Malva moschata*), and feverfew (*Tanacetum parthenium*). Try Helen Fox's method of mixing borage seed with nigella and calendula seeds to create what she called a flowery tapestry.

Sow borage seeds about a week before the last expected frost and cover them since they require darkness to germinate, which should occur in 5 days at 70°F (21°C). Roots resent transplanting, so sow seeds where you want the plants to bloom in full sun and ordinary, even thin, soil with moderate moisture; thin seedlings to 1 in. (2.5 cm) apart. Overrich soil produces thick-stemmed plants with fewer flowers. To assure continued flowering all summer, sow a small amount of seeds every 4 weeks. Pull out old plants by midsummer or cut them back to encourage fresh flowers and trimmer plants. Self-sown seedlings are huskier plants than the originals.

Borage is a fine cut flower as long as the bouquet is placed where the flowers can be seen. In the kitchen, crushed leaves and whole flowers lifted from the calyx add fresh flavor to cool drinks. The flowers can be used as a salad garnish or they can be candied according to the following directions:

Candied Flowers

Pick the flowers on a sunny day after the dew has gone. Remove the green calyx and carefully lay the flower heads on waxed paper. Lightly brush both sides of the petals with egg white and water beaten to a froth. Then sprinkle both sides with granulated sugar, shake off the excess sugar, and place the flowers on fresh waxed paper to dry. Turn them occasionally, and when they feel dry to the touch store them in a waxed paper-lined tin, checking occasionally to make sure they have not reabsorbed moisture. Use the flowers within 2 weeks. Gently press the crystallized flowers into cake frosting, gelatin, or whipped desserts as a garnish.

Related plants of interest. Seeds of borage are widely available from general seed and herb sources; the white-flowered variant is rare. Seeds of the perennial *Cerinthe* are also rare.

Cerinthe, honeywort, is a little-known member of the borage family from southern Europe that has been known in England since the 1500s. John Gerard described two species, *C. major* and *C. minor,* in 1633. The genus name comes from the Greek *keros,* meaning wax, a reference to the belief that bees obtain wax from the flowers. I first saw an annual species, *C. palestina* (Plate 29), at the Jerusalem Botanical Garden and admired its semicoiled, drooping, yellow bells. It was not until I had read about *C. minor,* very similar to the Middle Eastern species, from Gertrude Foster in *Park's Success with Herbs* that I realized annual *Cerinthe* could be grown in North America. Foster's plants, originally grown from seed collected in Portugal, self-sowed in her garden for over 20 years.

Thompson and Morgan has introduced the perennial *Cerinthe major* 'Purpurascens', an admired flower in English gardens. It grows 12–18 in. (30.5–45.7 cm) tall, its fleshy, blue-green leaves spiraling up the stem with clusters of showy flowers growing in their axils. The flowers hang down in coils, each drooping, tubular bloom purplish blue on the outside and cream at the base, enfolded by purplish bracts. Gardeners in colder regions

Plate 29. *Cerinthe palestina,* honeywort. Late spring, Jerusalem Botanical Garden, Israel. Photo, Carolin Göhler.

should start plants indoors by February. Some sources (Timothy Ingram of *The Hardy Plant*) regard *Cerinthe* seeds as having short viability; some freshly harvested seed did germinate for me especially quickly, in 4 days. Thompson and Morgan describes germinating seeds at 70°F (21°C) in 5 to 21 days. The plants should be grown in a sheltered, sunny site in sharp-draining, alkaline soil, spaced about 12 in. (30.5 cm) apart. The fleshy roots will rot over the winter in moist conditions. Place honeywort at the front of any planting, in a rock garden, along a border, or in a container. Propagate by seeding (or allow to self-sow). Although its hardiness is not yet known, gardeners in regions colder than Zone 7 or 8 should grow this species as a summer-blooming annual.

Calamintha grandiflora

Lamiaceae, Mint Family
Calamint, large catnip, mountain balm, ornamental savory, showy calamint, showy savory

Fragrant and desirable.
Louise Beebe Wilder
The Fragrant Garden

Perennial
Site and soil: full sun; well-drained
Hardiness: Zones 5–9
Landscape use: accent, bed and border, container, rock work
Height: 14–24 in. (35.6–61.0 cm)
Flower: bright pink, magenta, purple-mauve, small, tubular in spike
Bloom season: midsummer to late summer

Calamint is the showiest of several species of highly aromatic herbs originating in Europe and Asia. Its common name showy savory is a reference to its former classification as *Satureja grandiflora*. The Latin *cala* means beautiful, which is an apt description for this lovely herb, but *cala* is derived from the Greek *kale*, meaning good, and probably refers to the ancient belief in the calamints' magical powers to drive away evil demons. Also well known in the Middle Ages were the calamints' healing virtues as expectorants and perspiration inducers. The sixteenth-century John Gerard maintained that drinking calamint tea "cureth the infirmities of the heart and taketh away sorrowfulness which cometh of melancholie" (1633).

The plant grows in a fragrant mat of soft, downy, light green, serrated leaves, smaller but the same shape as those of catnip (*Nepeta cataria*). By midsummer, the mat sends up many square-sided stems typical of the

Plate 30. *Calamintha grandiflora*, calamint. Midsummer, Country Lane Herbs and Dried Flowers. Photo, Brian Oke and Gisèle Quesnel.

mint family, each one bearing small, tubular, bright pink, purple-mauve, or magenta flowers on 6 in. (15.2 cm) spikes, bringing the height of the plant to as much as 24 in. (61.0 cm), depending on the richness of the soil. The effect is a mass of bloom from only a few plants. All parts are pleasingly aromatic with a fruity scent somewhat like pineapple—like catnip, thyme, and pennyroyal (*Mentha pulegium*) rolled into one—without a hint of sharpness or cloying sweetness. *Calamintha grandiflora* 'Variegata' offers white-speckled leaves that highlight the dark flowers.

Considering its beauty and value as a garden subject, calamint has been underused by both herb gardeners and gardeners in general. An elderly gardener who specialized in collecting choice, unknown plants introduced it to me without telling me anything about it; I guessed wrongly that it should be treated as a mint and be planted in shady, damp ground. I could not have given it a worse reception, and it is a testimony to its essentially low-maintenance nature that it managed to linger on. The variegated form, on the other hand, does better in partial shade, where its leaves retain their speckles.

Grown in rich soil, calamint produces a profusion of bloom that tends to force the many long stems downward to sprawl in every direction; in this case plant it on a bank, near paving, or atop a wall where it can tumble gracefully. In the lean soil that it prefers, calamint grows as a tidy plant suitable for the front of a border, for containers, for lining a path, for filling in around rocks, or for footing a low stone wall where its soft texture is an asset. As for all aromatic types, plant calamint and its relatives where you will be able to benefit from their fragrance.

For best results, plant calamint in full sun and dry soil with perfect drainage. Sow seeds in the spring, or propagate by division in the spring or fall or by stem cuttings in early summer. Where winters are harsh, calamint may die back, but it usually leaves seeds behind which germinate the following spring. All calamints and related species thrive in warm weather and drought-like conditions.

Besides being a pleasure for the eye, calamint makes a very soothing tea. Pour 2 cups boiling water over 1 to 2 teaspoons dried leaves and steep only a few minutes (steeping any herb too long usually produces an unpalatable drink). Add sugar or honey to taste, and serve with lemon as desired.

Related plants of interest. Calamints and the closely related species of *Acinos* are worth investigating. Calamint and lesser calamint are available from perennial plant and herb sources. Alpine calamint and basil thyme are rare but available from herb sources that have a large and varied inventory.

Acinos alpinus, alpine calamint, is a spreading perennial only 4 in. (10.2 cm) tall with grayish leaves and small, purple-blue flowers in late summer. It is great for edging, rock gardens, or any foreground planting.

Acinos arvensis, basil thyme, is a self-sowing annual (or a short-lived perennial in warm climates) with pungently scented flowers and foliage. The flowers, typically small and two-lipped, are violet with purple markings and a white throat on stems to 12 in. (30.1 cm). The plant's upright to spreading habit and long blooming period (from early summer to fall) shows to advantage in rock work of any type. Its essential oil is reputed to lessen the pain of neuralgia and it soothes nerves when added to baths. Its culinary uses are similar to those of thyme.

Calamintha nepeta, the more widely grown lesser calamint, is somewhat shorter than calamint, more upright, and bushy on rugged stems 12–18 in. (30.5–45.7 cm) tall. *Calamintha nepeta* subsp. *nepeta* is a more robust version. Both bear from late summer onward clouds of dainty, pale lavender, almost white flowers similar to baby's breath (*Gypsophila paniculata*). The whole plant exudes a tart, minty aroma when crushed or simply brushed.

Calendula officinalis

Asteraceae, Aster Family
Calendula, holigold, marybud, pot marigold

Annual
Site and soil: sun, partial shade; well-drained
Landscape use: bed and border, container, rock work
Height: 12–24 in. (30.5–61.0 cm)
Flower: yellow, orange, daisy-like, solitary head
Bloom season: early summer to fall

> The marigold that goes to bed wi' the sun
> And with him rises weeping.
>
> Shakespeare
> *A Winter's Tale*
> Act IV, scene iv, lines 105–106

In their native Mediterranean habitat, calendulas bloom almost every month of the year. This unusual characteristic is preserved in the plant's name, derived from the Latin *calendae*, meaning "through the months." Plants grow on erect and brittle stems with oval, light green, clasping leaves as long as 6 in. (15.2 cm) at the base. Each stem carries a daisy-like flowerhead 1½–3 in. (3.8–7.6 cm) across, with pale yellow to deep orange rays in several rows and sometimes with a chocolate-brown center. In common with other members of the family, calendulas close at sunset and open in the morning, damp with dew as Shakespeare described. The whole plant is covered with little hairs that give it a sticky feeling. When bruised, the flowers and leaves give off a peppery aroma.

This plant, rather than the French or African marigold (*Tagetes*), is the marigold of past literature. It was primarily valued as an easily accessible and edible vegetable with nearly evergreen leaves. Its petals, high in vitamin A, were stored in barrels and sold by the ounce to impart their rich, orange-yellow color to cheese and butter or to give a smooth texture to soups and stews. Their lathering, thickening, and soothing properties are due to the presence of saponin, for which calendula flowers were and still are used in preparations to soothe and heal cuts and bruises.

Because of its easygoing disposition and its ability to produce blooms over a long period—from early summer through successive frosts or from winter to spring in warmer areas—it has been called a workhorse of the ornamental garden. Variations of the simple cottage garden flower come and go, some with double flowers to 4 in. (10.2 cm) wide with quilled petals like mums, others with unusual crested centers. Some are dwarf to 12 in. (30.5 cm), need less deadheading, and are suitable for containers. One of the most popular *Calendula officinalis* seed strains is the vigorous Pacific Beauty Mixed that produces plants 18–24 in. (45.7–0.6 m) tall, with large, wide, double flowers that remain loose enough to reveal an occasional dark center. These come in the full range of calendula colors — cream, bright yellow, brilliant orange, apricot, and even orange petals with mahogany-red undersides. In the cultivar 'Touch of Red' (Plate 31) the theme is elaborated so that the backsides of petals in the full color range are all literally touched with red.

Various calendulas are suitable for different situations. The old-fashioned, cottage garden flower can be left to self-sow in a dooryard planting with other annuals such as poppies (*Papaver*) and larkspur (*Delphinium*); the heirloom cultivar *Calendula officinalis* 'The King', large, double, and orange, can be interplanted along a narrow border with dark blue cornflower (*Centaurea cyanus*) and spreading mats of white sweet alyssum (*Lobularia maritima*). As temperatures fall in late summer these colors gain intensity. The dwarf 'Bon Bon' will grow attractively in a tub with other herbs handy for picking. In the cutting and harvesting bed I plant a solid block of bright orange and yellow calendulas between blocks of light green lemon balm (*Melissa officinalis*) and scarlet bee balm (*Monarda didyma*). The tall, elegant Pacific Beauty Mixed and 'Touch of Red' plants, with their harmonious blend of colors, are easiest to fit into a perennial planting. 'Touch of Red' and the hardy red rose, *Rosa* 'Champlain', are striking companions in a perennial bed (Plate 31).

Sow calendula seeds outdoors in late spring or whenever the soil temperature reaches 60°F (16°C). Choose a site in full sun or in partial shade in warmer climates. In Zones 8–10, sow seeds outdoors in late summer for winter bloom. Calendulas will grow in a wide range of soils but will produce the most flowers in well-drained, rich loam. Thin seedlings 9–15 in. (22.9–38.1 cm) apart. Once established, calendulas will self-sow, eventually all reverting to the original cottage garden flower. Combat this degeneration by saving seeds of favorites or by refreshing the planting with purchased seed. The old-fashioned cottage garden calendula, the cultivars, and the strains are available from general seed, specialty seed, and herb sources.

Plate 31. *Calendula officinalis* 'Touch of Red', calendula, and *Rosa* 'Champlain'.
Midsummer, Gardner farm. Photo, Alan Dorey.

Dried and powdered calendula petals, called poor man's saffron, can be used in rice and grain dishes for flavor and color. Small, whole flower heads or petals can be candied as described for *Borago officinalis*. Dried flowers and petals are colorful additions to citrus-scented potpourri with lemon balm and bee balm. The Pacific Beauty flowers are exceptional in bouquets; pick them when the buds are just opening.

Caltha palustris

Ranunculaceae, Buttercup Family

Marsh marigold, American cowslip, kingcup, meadowbright

Perennial

Site and soil: sun, partial shade, shade; evenly moist, boggy

Hardiness: Zones 3–9

Landscape use: bed and border, naturalized herb

Height: 8–24 in. (20.3–61.0 cm)

Flower: bright gold cup in cluster

Bloom season: spring to early summer

Marsh marigold is a variable species which grows wild throughout the North Temperate Zones of the world (Plate 3. See p. 24). In North America it grows along streams and brooks and in marshes and wet meadows from Labrador to Alaska and South Carolina to Nebraska. Its bright gold flowers herald the onset of spring. The heart-shaped, glossy, 2–3 in. (5.1–7.6 cm) leaves, largest at ground level, form a clump from which grow branching, succulent stems that bear clusters of golden, goblet flowers. Deriving their genus name from the Greek for cup, these oversized buttercups, about 1 1/2 in. (3.8 cm) across, hold numerous stamens surrounded by five to nine shining, petal-like sepals. By midsummer the entire plant disappears until the following spring.

This water-loving plant is not a marigold (neither *Calendula* nor *Tagetes*) but acquired its common name because it was one of the flowers dedicated to the Virgin Mary in the spring of the year. Medicinally, marsh marigold has been used as a laxative and diuretic. Nowadays use of the plant as a food of any sort is discouraged because all parts are potentially poisonous unless properly cooked.

Variants of the species include the tightly double-flowered *Caltha palustris* 'Flore Pleno' (Plate 32), showier than the wildflower and more compact to 9 in. (22.9 cm). The flower sprays are carried on semiprostrate stems and are framed by glossy leaves. White-flowered *C. palustris* var. *alba* is a choice compact form.

A bog or any sodden ground can be turned into a stunning asset by naturalizing marsh marigold along with other plants that thrive there, such as bistort (*Polygonum bistorta*), blue and yellow flag iris (*Iris versicolor* and *I. pseudacorus*), monkshood (*Aconitum*), Joe Pye weed (*Eupatorium purpureum*), boneset (*Eupatorium perfoliatum*), and cardinal flower (*Lobelia cardinalis*). I long admired marsh marigold in my friend's carefully cultivated perennial border before daring to try it, because I had incorrectly assumed that it *must* be grown in a bog. It is quite adaptable to ordinary garden soil on the moist side, where the longer lasting, double type is preferable. The white form is quite suitable for the border, too, if you can find it.

Marsh marigold will grow in full sun as well as shade as long as the soil is evenly moist. Seeds take 2 years to produce flowering plants and should be sown as soon as they ripen or in early spring. Space plants one foot apart in moist, humusy, acid soil with a pH between 5.0 and 7.0 and keep the ground soggy until the plants are established. Divide them every 3 years in early summer after they become dormant. It is most important not to let the deep roots dry out during the plant's blooming period. To be

Plate 32. *Caltha palustris* 'Flore Pleno', double-flowered marsh marigold. Early summer, Memorial University Botanical Garden at Oxen Pond. Photo, Bernard S. Jackson.

113

sure to get water to the roots during prolonged drought, sink a perforated can to soil level near the planting and top it with water every few days. Young plants should be mulched over the winter.

Plants of the single marsh marigold are easiest to find from perennial plant nurseries specializing in wetland or wild plants; seeds are available from wildflower sources. The double yellow and white are harder to find; look for them in perennial plant sources.

Capparis spinosa

> **The caper is the persevering among the trees . . . as Israel is among the nations.**
>
> *Talmud*
> (Babylonian)
> Beitza 25b

Capparidaceae, Caper Family
Caper bush

Shrub
Site and soil: sun; sharply drained
Hardiness: Zones 7–10
Landscape use: container, ground cover, rock work
Height: 2–5 ft. (0.6–1.5 m)
Flower: white, cupped, solitary
Bloom season: late summer to fall

The caper bush, native to the Mediterranean area, grows in the crevices of rocks, stone walls, and rocky ground, where few other plants could survive. A multitude of large-petaled flowers are borne on spiny, lax, reddish stems with waxy, green, nearly heart-shaped leaves notched at their tips. The four-petaled flowers, similar in construction to those of honeysuckle, open from rounded buds to spread 3 in. (7.6 cm) across. Purplish pink stamens in profusion extend beyond the petals, considerably adding to the flowers' beauty.

During its flowering period, bushes produce both new flowers and new fruits every day. The show begins in late afternoon when the white tips of the petals can just be seen in the caper bush's round, fat buds; by evening the fragrant flowers open; and by the following morning, as the heat of the day increases, the petals wilt, then fall, revealing the embryonic fruits. Over 2000 years ago Rabbi Gamaliel took his skeptical students to the field to show them this phenomenon as proof that in the world to come trees (as the ancients categorized the caper bush) could bear new fruit every day, since one already fulfills the prophecy.

The caper bush buds, young fruits, and tender branch tips have been preserved by pickling since ancient times. Great skill is needed in harvesting them because of the bush's rapid growth. Buds not picked one day will be too mature for pickling the next day. In North America the caper bush is gaining followers because of its beauty and use.

I first became aware of the caper bush while studying biblical flora. In Israel the long, skeletal branches hang down from ancient walls (including the Western Wall) and produce spectacular summer bloom. Returning home from one of these trips, I discovered that herb enthusiasts were already growing the caper bush as an ornamental, in cold areas as a potted plant and in warmer areas as a slightly arching shrub. Where it can be grown in the ground, it is best established among rocks or between the crevices of rocks or walls, as it grows in its native Mediterranean region. A high wall would provide the perfect backdrop (and habitat) for the cascading branches laden with their lovely blooms.

The caper bush is difficult, but possible, to establish from seed. If you want to try growing it as an annual, start plants in the winter. Freezing premoistened seeds for 2 weeks helps, as does nicking the seed coat. Sow, cover well, and maintain at 70°F (21°C). Germination is slow. When seedlings are large enough to handle, transplant to small pots and place them under florescent lights. Shift growing plants as needed to larger contain-

Plate 33. *Capparis spinosa*, caper bush. Late summer, Jerusalem, Israel. Photo, Avinoam Danin.

ers—1 and 3 gallon (3.8–11.4 liters) tubs work well. Place these outdoors in a protected, sunny spot once temperatures have warmed. If plants do not form buds their first season, winter them indoors or take cuttings during the summer and winter these indoors. In Zones 7 and 8 potted plants can be left outdoors if protected. In Zones 9 and 10, where the caper bush can confidently be grown in the ground, provide sun and dry conditions and do not overwater. Cut back previous season's growth 2–3 in. (5.1–7.6 cm) to maintain a more shrubby appearance. In its native habitat, new plants sprout even from exposed roots. Unfortunately, caper bush seeds and plants are generally hard to find.

For kitchen use, pickled capers are widely available in food stores. They are tender and piquant, a delicious condiment with meat, fish, and cheese dishes, a traditional flavoring for eggplant and tomatoes, and a great addition to sauces, butters, and salads of all kinds. The pickled young fruits and tender branch tips are available from specialty food stores, especially those specializing in Middle Eastern foods. To make your own capers, follow the recipe below:

Pickled Capers

Make a brine by stirring pickling or kosher salt into water, using 1½ cups salt to 1 gallon water. Pick unopened, full buds and soak them in the brine for 3 days, changing the liquid daily. Drain the buds and drop them into pickling vinegar that has been brought to the boiling point. Pour the buds and hot vinegar into clean jars, seal, and store in a cool place.

Cichorium intybus

Asteraceae, Aster Family
Chicory, blue sailors, succory

Biennial, perennial
Site and soil: sun; well-drained
Hardiness: Zones 3–10
Landscape use: bed and border, naturalized herb
Height: 2–5 ft. (0.6–1.5 m)
Flower: sky-blue, dandelion-like, close to stem
Bloom season: midsummer to late summer

> **The flowers attract because of the clarity and perfection of their color.**
>
> Kay N. Sanecki
> *The Complete Book of Herbs*

Chicory, a hardy perennial or biennial of Eurasian origin, transforms waste places and roadsides into a clear, sky-blue haze all summer, beginning as early as March in the South and Pacific Northwest and as late as midsummer in the cooler parts of the United States and Canada. The common names for *Cichorium intybus* are very similar in most languages, all of which derive their word from the Arabic *chicoruey*. The more colloquial name "blue sailors" comes from the legend that tells of a blue-eyed maiden who is waiting in vain by the roadside for her sailor lover to return.

An ugly duckling until it blooms, its long taproot sends up stiff, angular stems as tall as 5 ft. (1.5 m), usually shorter, from a basal rosette of green leaves very similar to the dandelion (*Taraxacum*) in their lush early growth. These nearly disappear farther up the stem as the plant matures, becoming very narrow and pointed, and bearing in their axils the awkward chicory's redeeming feature: attractive blue flowers 1 1/2 in. (3.8 cm) across with narrow, square-edged, toothed petals, almost fringed in appearance, of a light, clear blue that is unrivaled for its exquisite coloring. Bracts at the base of each flower operate with precision, opening the blooms at dawn and closing them 5 hours later, except when cloudy weather keeps them open longer.

Tender chicory greens have been eaten as a tonic or restorative for centuries. It is one of the bitter herbs of Passover, eaten not in its tender growth but in its most unpalatable, bitter form as a reminder of the Exodus experience in Egypt. Chicory was valued for treating liver complaints, sore eyes, and external inflammations; a mild laxative prepared from its roots, syrup of succory, is especially recommended for children. Chicory root is cultivated commercially for the roasted and ground preparation brewed as a coffee substitute or additive. Gardeners are more familiar with witloof, the colorless salad leaves grown from forcing the root of a strain of chicory, and the dark red and white heads known as radicchio, the Italian common name for *Cichorium intybus*.

The rose breeder J. H. Nicholas is supposed to have seriously considered hybridizing chicory for its ornamental potential, because "he considered it to be among the handsomest of all plants" (Fox 1953). He did not live to carry out his plans, but possibilities abound: compact plants with double, fringed, light blue daisies; a wider range of colors based on the white and delicate pink, natural variations, as well as the bright red sometimes found on plants growing in the acid soil of ant hills; dwarf types from a cross between *Cichorium intybus* and the Mediterranean species *C. pumilum* whose blue flowers are scattered on the ground like stars in the morning hours. And then there is the possibility of flowers with longer daily bloom.

For many years I have grown the "coffee" chicory strain *Cichorium intybus* 'Magdeburgh' with its large, white, carrot-like roots. The second year, if the roots are not harvested, or if some have been left in the ground, they will produce the desired bloom. Chicory does well at the fringes of the kitchen garden, naturalizing itself among scarlet-red bee balm (*Monarda didyma*). Do not hesitate to grow this plant in the back of a border or in an island bed featuring other sun-loving wildflowers, such as butterfly weed (*Asclepias tuberosa*), purple coneflower (*Echinacea purpurea*), and yarrow (*Achillea millefolium*).

Chicory seeds are available only from sources specializing in wildflowers or herbs, but 'Magdeburgh' is often listed with vegetables in general seed sources. Sow seeds in early spring when you sow lettuce, covering them 1/4 in. (0.6 cm) in ordinary garden soil in full sun. If the roots will be harvested, be sure the soil is also deep and friable. Thin young plants to 12 in. (30.5 cm) apart. In cooler regions, new plants will flower the second year. Populations maintain themselves by self-sowing, only requiring thinning in the spring when old, dead stalks should be cleaned up as well.

Greens of first-year plants can be picked for salad in earliest spring but they soon become too bitter to eat. For the coffee substitute, harvest only roots of first-year plants since older roots become woody and knobby. Dig up roots in the fall; they should be the shape and length of a good-sized carrot. Scrub and peel the roots, cut them in small pieces, and slowly roast them at 325°F (165°C) until they turn from white to dark brown, not black. Then grind the roasted pieces as you would coffee beans. Top off every scoop of coffee with a generous amount of chicory to produce a stronger drink without added caffeine; chicory may have a mildly sedative effect. For a delicious morning drink, add cocoa to taste. Roots can also be dug up in the fall and forced in a dark, cool place to produce blanched salad greens during the winter months.

Cimicifuga racemosa

Ranunculaceae, Buttercup Family
Bugbane, black cohosh, fairy candles, rattletop, snakeroot, squawroot

Perennial
Site and soil: sun, shade; evenly moist and well-
    drained
Hardiness: Zones 4–9
Landscape use: accent, bed and border, naturalized
    herb
Height: 6 ft. (1.8 m)
Flower: creamy-white, round in narrow plume
Bloom season: midsummer to late summer

> **Their long, graceful fingers add a sublime touch to large borders or woodsy corners.**
> Amos Pettingill
> White Flower Farm
> Litchfield, Connecticut

Bugbane is found in rich, moist ground in and at the edges of woodland, mostly in the Appalachian Mountains. Growing up from a knotty black root or rhizome, it spends a good part of the summer producing a 24 in. (61.0 cm) tall, leafy base of large, thrice-divided, dark green leaves. By mid- to late summer, the wand-like stems have soared to 6 ft. (1.8 m) or more, each bearing several tapered spikes packed with pearly, round buds. As the flowers open, the petals, actually sepals, start to fall, leaving behind bushy stamens that give the spikes a fluffy appearance. Although bugbane's actual bloom period may last only 2 weeks or so, its vertical form is attractive for more than a month, even before it shows its buds and after it has formed its pea-like pods.

It is unfortunate that so beautiful a plant has acquired such plebeian names, although these are descriptive of its herbal history. The genus name from the Greek *cimex*, meaning bug, and *fugure*, "to drive away," refers to the fact that the plant's odor, not readily apparent to humans, repels most insects. Preparations from its rough, black roots were used by North American Indians to alleviate menstrual cramps and relieve the pain of childbirth, hence the names cohosh, meaning rough, and squawroot. The bruised root was also used externally to treat snakebites, leading to the name snakeroot, and even the peculiarity of its dried pods is aptly preserved in the name rattletop. Modern research suggests that bugbane is effective in treating pain associated with rheumatism and neuralgia.

Plate 34. *Cimicifuga racemosa*, bugbane. Midsummer, Joseph Hudak garden. Photo, Joseph Hudak.

Bugbane takes center stage when it blooms, whether as a tall, dramatic accent at the back of a wide perennial border, blooming among *Lilium* 'Journey's End' and colorful red and blue salvias, or as a rising centerpiece for an island bed of bushy rudbeckias. Its tall, vertical form and fluffy flower spikes combine well with wide-leaved hostas in partial shade. The bugbanes are fine cut flowers, too, and the seed stalks are attractive in dried bouquets. A most satisfactory way to grow bugbane is to naturalize it in moist, humusy ground at the edge of light woodland among a colony of ferns. It will carry on for years without any interference.

The easiest way to grow bugbane is from roots, spaced at least 12 in. (30.5 cm) apart in deep, humusy, somewhat acid soil. Partial shade is ideal, but bugbane is fairly adaptable and will grow in full sun if the soil is evenly moist but well-drained. Plants in bloom may need staking; simply secure each flower spike to a tall, thin stake that will be hidden by the foliage. Propagate by division in early spring, being sure that each chunk of root has three eyes. Once plants are established, if you want to try growing bugbane from seed sow freshly collected seed in a cold frame in late summer and let it naturally stratify over the winter—it needs a period of warmth followed by a period of cold to germinate. To raise seedlings indoors follow the procedure outlined in Chapter One.

Related plants of interest. *Cimicifuga racemosa* is the earliest blooming of several cultivated species, none of which are widely grown despite the beauty of their late-season, flowering spires and their handsome appearance at all seasons. A striking cultivar sold as 'Purpurea' with deep burgundy stems and leaves blooms a little later. Bugbanes are available from perennial plant nurseries and a few herb sources.

Cimicifuga simplex 'White Pearl', kamchatka bugbane, is an Asian type very late to bloom in harsh climates (by September in Zone 6). Shorter than the North American species and valued for its 2–4 ft. (0.6–1.2 m), dense, fluffy spikes, it is grown the same way. It is hardy in Zone 5.

Colchicum autumnale

Liliaceae, Lily Family
Meadow saffron, autumn crocus

Bulb
Site and soil: sun, partial shade; well-drained
Hardiness: Zones 4–9
Landscape use: bed and border, naturalized herb,
 rock work
Height: 8 in. (20.3 cm)
Flower: rosy-lilac, white, globe in cluster
Bloom season: late summer to fall

Meadow saffron, not to be confused with the real source of saffron, *Crocus sativus*, is native to Europe and North Africa, and belongs to the group of fall-flowering bulbs. It grows from an oval corm that sprouts two or three glossy, strap-shaped leaves in the spring that soon die back, leaving nothing to mark the spot. In the fall, as if by magic, a flame-shaped, pointed bud appears on the bare ground, the tube arising straight from the corm below. The six petals, translucent with a silvery sheen and white base, are lightly flushed with color, but as the cupped flower opens, its color deepens to mauve, then to rosy-lilac. Fully opened blooms to 3 in. (7.6 cm) across are star-shaped, revealing the six golden-orange anthers within (the true saffron crocus has three). As each flower withers new buds arise and new flowers open, continuing for at least a month from an established colony of clustered corms.

The genus name comes from Colchis, a port on the Black Sea where meadow saffron flourished. The plant's active ingredient, colchicine, is poisonous and is present in all its parts, especially the corms and seeds. As with other plants that contain powerful substances, meadow saffron has a long history of use as a medicinal and is still used in the treatment of gout. Applied to the seeds or plants to double the number of chromosomes a plant carries, colchicine is used to produce types with stronger stems and larger flowers with richer colors.

Meadow saffron's absence of foliage at the time of blooming means it should be planted with this characteristic in mind. Naturalized plantings in grass are very successful; the early foliage and late, "naked" blooms are complemented by the grass itself. Colonies of meadow saffron are most attractive at the grassy foot of a wall or fence, near a shrubbery, or in a rock garden busy with foliage all season. It is also effective naturalized in a woodland setting, along walks, on banks too difficult to mow, or amongst a ground cover such as periwinkle (*Vinca minor*) whose fairly loose habit allows room for the bulbs' natural growth. In a garden setting try pairing it with *Sedum telephium* 'Red Chief', whose leaves and flowers complement meadow saffron (Plate 35). The double flowers can be planted up front in a generous border or bed, where their foliage will be covered by other plants during the summer, and where their large flowers will be appreciated in the fall.

Meadow saffron is hardy in Zone 4 and even some areas of Zone 3 if plantings are protected over the winter. Plant the corms as soon as you re-

Plate 35. *Colchicum autumnale*, meadow saffron, and Sedum telephium 'Red Chief'. Late summer, Joseph Hudak garden. Photo, Joseph Hudak.

ceive them—they tend to bloom even before they are planted—in late summer or early fall, 3 in. (7.6 cm) deep and 6–9 in. (15.2–22.9 cm) apart; they will bloom the first season and will soon multiply. They grow best in full sun or partial shade in well-drained, moderately enriched garden soil that is not allowed to dry out. When establishing a planting you would like to naturalize, keep in mind that it will be more successful if you prepare the ground to meet these conditions. It is vitally necessary for the plantings' future health that the foliage be allowed to die back undisturbed. If colonies become overcrowded, divide them in the early summer or after the foliage has withered; baby corms, developed at the base of larger ones, can be replanted. It is advisable to wear gloves when handling the corms.

Related plants of interest. Choice cultivars of meadow saffron include the vigorous *Colchicum autumnale* 'Majus', with abundant, oversize, purple-pink flowers; 'Roseum', rosy pink; 'Plenum', double lilac-pink (Plate 36); and the peony-shaped, double, white 'Alboplenum'. In common with other double-flowered kinds, these last two hold their petals longer than do single flowers.

Of the following plants, the hybrids—all results of crosses involving *Colchicum speciosum*—are especially suitable for growing in the garden proper or in containers with annuals, such as sweet alyssum (*Lobularia maritima*) or edging lobelia (*Lobelia erinus*), where their larger forms can be seen to advantage. The meadow saffrons are available from bulb specialists and perennial plant nurseries. Saffron crocus bulbs are available from bulb specialists and herb sources.

Colchicum speciosum, showy autumn crocus, cultivated extensively in Turkey for commercial use, has large, rosy-purple, tulip-shaped blooms and is suitable for naturalizing.

Colchicum 'The Giant', a late bloomer, is 8–12 in. (20.3–30.5 cm) tall with large, rose-colored flowers.

Colchicum 'Violet Queen', 7 in. (17.8 cm) or taller, has rich purple flowers, somewhat tessellated, or checkered with light and dark purple.

Colchicum 'Waterlily' is late blooming and very showy with large, double, mauve flowers similar in form to true waterlilies (*Nymphaea*).

Crocus sativus, saffron crocus, is a true crocus belonging to the iris family that has been prized for centuries for the orange powder collected from its threads or stigmas that is used for flavoring or dyeing. It is smaller in all its parts than meadow saffron: first it is a tuft of narrow, grass-like foliage, then later it displays cupped, pale mauve or bluish lilac, veined, 2 in. (5.1 cm) flowers, loveliest when they open on sunny days to reveal their elongated, bright orange threads. Saffron crocus has been grown in North America at least since the eighteenth century when Dutch settlers cultivated it for its flavoring as well as medicinal uses—it treated fainting spells, jaundice, and heart irregularities. It is grown in full sun and well-drained soil with 4 to 6 in. (10.2–15.2 cm) between corms. It is hardy in Zone 6.

To harvest your own saffron powder, first consider that it takes thousands of dried stigmas from thousands of flowers to accumulate a pound. On the other hand, a little of the seasoning goes a long way; the harvest

Plate 36. *Colchicum autumnale* 'Plenum', double-flowered meadow saffron. Fall, Robison York State Herb Garden, Cornell Plantations, Ithaca, New York. Photo courtesy of Cornell Plantations.

125

from six plants should produce enough saffron to use in most recipes. Pick the threads as soon as the flowers open and dry them on paper out of direct light. Store them, whole if possible, in a well-sealed jar, also out of the light. Crush the threads to use the powder in breads, rice, and oriental dishes, where they add flavor as well as color.

Convallaria majalis

> It has an ethereal beauty unknown in any other flowers.
> Roy Genders
> *The Cottage Garden*

Liliaceae, Lily family
Lily-of-the-valley, convall-lillie, May lily, our lady's tears

Bulb
Site and soil: sun, partial shade, shade; evenly moist and well-drained
Hardiness: Zones 3–8
Landscape use: accent, bed and border, container, ground cover, naturalized herb
Height: 8–10 in. (20.3–25.4 cm)
Flower: white bell in cluster on one-sided raceme
Bloom season: spring to early summer

Lily-of-the-valley, native to Europe and Asia, grows from horizontal rhizomes called pips that send up purple-sheathed stems in late spring. These unfold to reveal glossy, lance-shaped, broad leaves, which in turn enfold arching stems embellished with small, waxy, intensely fragrant little bells, white with a faint greenish tinge, scalloped at their edges. The hawk moth fertilizes the flowers in the evening when their scent is strongest. The genus name means "of the valley"; the species name describes its May blooming time. Most of the folk names it has accumulated over the centuries draw attention to these characteristics.

A well-loved flower, once highly valued as a healing herb, lily-of-the-valley was described by the seventeenth-century Nicholas Culpeper as a plant that "restores lost speech, helps the palsy, and . . . comforts the heart" (1652). Preparations from its dried root or flowers do, in fact, contain two powerful glycosides that, like digitalis, slow and strengthen the heartbeat. But these properties are also dangerous and potentially lethal when self-

126

administered; thus, the plant is considered poisonous. The flowers' well-known fragrance is distilled and used to scent soaps and toiletries.

Poets, herbalists, and garden writers never tire of celebrating the beauty of this woodland plant, so amply endowed by nature with every attribute one could want: glossy foliage; abundant, beautiful, long-lasting, scented blooms; and ease of culture. Several different forms elaborate on the classic lily-of-the-valley: *Convallaria majalis* 'Fortin's Giant' has very large bells, about fifteen per stem, and is recommended for forcing; the double, white 'Flore Pleno' has longer lasting flowers and spreads more slowly; 'Variegata' with green and creamy yellow, variegated leaves grows best in the sun; and *C. majalis* var. *rosea* has mauve-pink, some say washed out, flowers.

It is wonderful to inhale the scent of lily-of-the-valley from a terrace or porch when a population has been established under shrubs or in a semi-shaded spot near the house. Under these conditions, however, the creeping rhizomes will probably find their way into the lawn or a nearby bed. See below for techniques that will control lily-of-the-valley. With its waxy whiteness and evening scent, this is also the plant for the evening or moonlight garden, where it should be grown either in containers or as a contained ground cover. The slower-spreading 'Flore Pleno' can be grown in a bed or border if later-blooming plants cover its dying foliage. Lily-of-the-valley is striking in a strawberry jar—a wide-mouth container with pocketlike openings at intervals around and up and down the jar—where it can be replanted with trailing nasturtiums (*Tropaeolum*) after its own blooms are spent; the rhizomes should be either discarded or replanted in the garden.

In the fall or early spring, plant lily-of-the-valley roots 6 in. (15.2 cm) apart in rich, moist, well-drained, slightly acidic soil in a shady situation; it will tolerate full shade but flowering will be adversely affected. Though it is regarded as easy to grow, do not neglect to prepare the bed in advance by clearing out weeds and loosening and enriching the soil. Cover the pips with 1 in. (2.5 cm) of soil, then leave the planting undisturbed, or propagate by division when the foliage dies back by late summer. Fertilize annually with rotted compost if necessary, but lily-of-the-valley will grow and bloom as long as the soil is moderately rich in nutrients, loose, and moist. To prevent invasiveness, mow around the planting, grow plants in a drier, sunnier location, or vertically sink 6 in. (15.2 cm) wide, heavy-gauge plastic around the planting.

According to folklore, lilies-of-the-valley are associated with purity, gentleness, and a return to happiness. For this reason, and because they can be forced to bloom indoors at any season, they are highly prized at weddings, in bridal bouquets, and in table settings. The pips can be stored in the refrigerator for several months mixed with moistened peat moss, compost, and a little top soil, covered loosely with plastic, and packed in a container. If they begin to grow under these conditions, water them, possibly daily. After removing the pips from the refrigerator, trim root growth as needed to fit the container, repot—six to ten pips nicely fill a 6 in. (15.2 cm) bowl—and move them into the light, watering as needed to maintain steady moisture. Allow 21 days from planting to flowering.

Plants of the classic lily-of-the-valley are widely available from perennial plant and bulb nurseries, as well as some herb sources. The cultivars and varieties are harder to find, but are available from the same sources.

Cytisus scoparius

> When these plants are in full bloom the large expanse of brilliant yellow is gorgeous.
>
> Donald Wyman
> *Wyman's Gardening Encyclopedia*

Fabaceae, Bean Family
Scotch broom

Shrub
Site and soil: sun; well-drained
Hardiness: Zones 5–8
Landscape use: accent, bed and border, edge and
   hedge
Height: 6 ft. (1.8 m)
Flower: bright yellow, pea-like cluster
Bloom season: spring to early summer

One of thirty-three *Cytisus* species, mostly native to the Mediterranean region, Scotch broom is the only one indigenous to the British Isles. Grown in the New World since the colonists brought it over in the seventeenth century, it has escaped cultivation and naturalized itself, especially in the sandy, coastal areas of Massachusetts, Virginia, and the Pacific Northwest, even to the point of choking out native vegetation and causing environmental problems. Watch vigilantly for self-sown seedlings so as to keep the planting under control.

In mid- to late spring, Scotch broom bears showy, 1 in. (2.5 cm), rich yellow flowers, closely set on a dense mass of supple, bright green, slender branches. Each pea-like bloom looks like a butterfly in flight; each tripartite leaf is almost invisibly small. After the shrub has bloomed and the little leaves have fallen, the grassy green stems remain all winter to give the appearance of an evergreen bush. The name *Cytisus* may be derived from the Greek *kytisos*, trefoil, a reference to the shrub's leaves; *scoparius*, meaning broom-like, graphically describes its stiff, upright, twiggy branches.

At one time, nearly every part of Scotch broom was pressed into daily service. In Scotland, whole fields were harvested for fuel or sheep fodder. Smaller amounts went for thatching, making cloth and paper, veneering cabinets, dyeing, tanning, manufacturing potash, and above all, for making brooms. Medicinally, Scotch broom was used as a diuretic and purgative. During World War II, the tops were collected to produce an extract used to treat kidney and liver complaints. All parts of the plant, however, especially the seeds, are considered poisonous and should never be used for internal consumption.

Because it was so common, Scotch broom was not horticulturally cultivated in Europe until the late nineteenth century, when Edouard André, a French landscaper and horticulturist, discovered a variant with red wings, from which a multitude of hybrid forms eventually developed. The enduring cultivar *Cytisus scoparius* 'Dorothy Walpole' has flowers a little smaller than the species, a beautiful crimson and rosy cream. 'Moonlight' is more upright in habit with masses of primrose-yellow flowers.

With its delicate form, Scotch broom is effective in a shrubbery as contrast for darker, heavier shrubs such as *Viburnum*. It can also be used as a focal point behind a perennial border, as an informal hedge, or as a windbreak, if kept well trimmed and compact. Even try a single-specimen accent planting, for few shrubs can match its golden glory in full bloom or its bright green stems through the winter.

Scotch broom sprouts readily from seed, which should be chipped and soaked before planting. Germination takes 25–30 days at 70°F (21°C). Grow plants in pots to establish strong roots; purchased plants should be small and pot grown because larger, field-grown ones transplant poorly.

Plant Scotch broom in full sun, in well-drained, slightly acidic, light soil. In exposed areas, branches may die back over the winter. Prune after flowering.

To make a rough broom, cut a number of branches from Scotch broom, trim them evenly, and tie them securely around the end of a stick. Also, the flowering stems make fine cut flowers. Complete and clear directions for using both Scotch broom and dyer's broom to produce a bright yellow or green dye can be found in *Dye Plants and Dyeing* (Cannon 1994).

Related plants of interest. Both Scotch broom and dyer's broom are available from perennial plant and shrub nurseries. Seeds of both are sometimes available from general or herb seed sources.

Cytisus ×*praecox*, warminster broom is a natural hybrid discovered in England in 1867. It is earlier flowering and hardier than Scotch broom. Also fast-growing, it has profuse, creamy yellow flowers on bushy plants to 5 ft. (1.5 m). 'Allgold' blooms a beautiful lemon color and is hardy in Zone 5 with winter protection.

Genista tinctoria, dyer's broom, is closely related to Scotch broom. The most noticeable difference in the bright yellow, pea-like flowers is the protuberance that forms on the fruits of *Cytisus* species. Dyer's broom, as the common name suggests, was a very important dye plant, one that is now being rediscovered for its landscaping potential. A superhardy shrub, growing in Zone 2, it reaches 3 ft. (0.9 m), has green, twiggy stems, and blooms profusely a bit later than Scotch broom. The double-flowered 'Plena' is highly desirable for its brilliant mass of long-lasting bloom and its low habit, 8–12 in. (20.3–30.5 cm); it is especially striking in a rock garden setting. Cuttings from new wood root readily in a mix of peat and sand in late summer or early fall.

Dianthus

Caryophyllaceae, Pink Family
Pink, carnation, gillyflower

Perennial
Site and soil: sun; sharply drained
Hardiness: Zones 3–8
Landscape use: bed and border, container, ground
   cover, rock work
Height: 4–18 in. (10.2–45.7 cm)
Flower: red, pink, rose, white, fringed in cluster or solitary
Bloom season: spring to early summer

> **Gilliflowers are of all other flowers, most sweet and delicate.**
> Gervase Markham
> *The English Husbandman*

"Pink" describes the way the petals of all plants in the family are crimped and has nothing to do with the color pink, which was not introduced to the English language until the eighteenth century. The genus name is derived from the Greek for divine flower.

One species particularly useful ornamentally and one of the pinks of herbal history in the West is *Dianthus caryophyllus*, clove pink. Native to rocky limestone areas in the Mediterranean, it has been cultivated for thousands of years for its beauty and fragrance. Plants are branching to 24 in. (61.0 cm) with narrow, gray-green leaves attached at swollen intervals along wiry stems. The red, pink, or white flowers are broad-petaled, serrated at their edges, usually very doubled, long-lasting, and in the best types most true to the flesh-colored wildflower, strongly scented with the fabled clove sweetness. As with any plant cultivated over millennia, there is wide variation in flower size and form, from over 1 in. (2.5 cm) wide to 4 in. (10.2 cm) wide in the long-stemmed, unscented, florist sorts.

Another significant dianthus is *Dianthus plumarius*, cottage pink (Plate 37). Native to rocky, limestone areas from central and southern Europe to the Caucasus, its many long, silvery green, grass-like leaves grow in wide mats. In late spring or early summer innumerable stems to 9 in. (22.9 cm) bear in profusion jagged-petaled, feathery flowers $3/4$–$1^{1}/2$ in. (0.75–3.8 cm) wide. These are single, semidouble, or double, colored in shades of pink and white, sometimes with a darker eye or band. These are also blessed with a powerful, clove-scented perfume. In contrast to some carnations, which bloom repeatedly, cottage pinks have one month-long season of bloom, beginning in late spring or early summer.

Both the clove and cottage pinks were introduced to England from France as a result of the Norman Conquest and were called gillyflowers after the French *giroflé*, meaning clove. In time, gillyflower became a generic term to describe similarly scented flowers, all prized for flavoring. In times past, spices that we now take for granted were not widely available and were very expensive. Thus, tavern keepers raised pinks as a cheap way to flavor their wines. From this use, both pinks were also known as sops-in-wine, a graphic description of their mundane use.

Pinks belong among rocks, in natural rocky outcroppings, in rock gardens, or near stone walls, where they benefit from the warmth and quickly draining soil that such conditions provide, as in their native habitat. Pinks should also be grown along paths and walkways, featured as a ground cover beneath roses—use the old double or single cottage pink—or exposed on a sunny bank. I grow an old, double-flowered cottage pink—a multitude of feathery, pink-colored flowers over a weed-smothering mat of grassy foliage—at the edges of a raised dooryard garden where its semiprostrate form softens the straight lines of wooden timbers. The long-flowering hybrids bloom in masses in sunny borders and beds, in front of the purples and blues of veronicas and catmints (*Nepeta*). Their bright pink and rose-colored flowers are complements for herb greenery in a culinary garden. Grown in containers, pinks can be placed on decks, patios, and porches where their fragrance will be enjoyed and they will benefit from the sunny exposure.

Pinks require a sunny location

Plate 37. *Dianthus plumarius*, cottage pink. Midsummer, Gardner farm. In warmer areas, cottage pinks bloom by late spring or early summer. Photo, Alan Dorey.

and sharply drained, gritty soil on the alkaline side. To raise indoors, sow in late winter and just cover the seed to germinate in 7 to 14 days at 70°F (21°C). Freezing seeds beforehand, as often advised, does not seem to affect germination. In early spring, space plants outside 18 in. (45.7 cm) apart or 12 in. (30.5 cm) to establish a ground cover. In early spring, trim plants to encourage fresh growth. Trim them again after flowering for a fresh round of leaves and possible second flowering in the fall. Propagate pinks by cuttings every few years or as needed: pull off side shoots after flowering, taking a bit of the main stem, trim off lower leaves, dip stem ends in rooting hormone powder, and plant them in a mixture of sand and peat where they should root in 6 weeks. After they have established good roots, the new plants can be grown over the winter in a cold frame; they will bloom the following season. Never mulch pinks since this encourages moisture around the root crown and leads to untimely death, but they can be protected over the winter with a covering of evergreen boughs.

Breeding of clove and cottage pinks has given rise to border pinks, hardy kinds with characteristics of both parents, although not always heavily perfumed. In the early 1900s Montague Allwood, an English breeder, widened the pink repertoire by further crossings and selections. His creations, known as *Dianthus* ×*allwoodii*, are long blooming but not as hardy as older types.

Although many of the older hybrids have disappeared, there are still enough hardy pinks available to satisfy the most devoted aficionado. They show mixed parentage in their rounded or fringed flowers, in their range of colors, including red, in their types of foliage, and in their long-blooming habit. *Dianthus* ×*allwoodii* 'Doris' to 10 in. (25.4 cm) has carnation-like flowers, a soft pink with a deeper rose center, and a long-blooming habit; *Dianthus* 'Clove Pink' (Plate 38), the most fragrant border type, also has carnation-like, soft, rose-pink flowers over a mat of silvery gray foliage on 5 in. (12.7 cm) stems; 'Essex Witch' is low growing to 5 in. (12.7 cm) with rose-pink, semidouble, lacy flowers; 'Helen', vigorous and free-flowering, is salmon-pink to 10 in. (25.4 cm); the old and rare 'Mrs Sinkins' to 12 in. (30.5 cm) has so many white petals its flowers have been described as cabbage-like and its scent as almost overwhelming; and 'Sweet Memory', also low-growing, has semidouble, unfringed flowers with pink centers. All these should be propagated vegetatively rather than by seed to keep their colors and forms.

Fragrant, hardy, and large-flowered seed strains include the vigorous *Dianthus* 'Sonata' series, single or double in a broad color range—salmon, rose, red, pink, white, and bicolor—some with a central eye. 'Spring Beauty' is an older, double-flowered strain in pink, rose, salmon, and white. Both these types grow to 12 in. (30.5 cm) and are free-flowering all summer and into the fall.

All the pinks make fine cut flowers. The larger-flowered types dry well for dried bouquets and wreaths, although they do not retain their scent. To preserve the scent and flavor, infuse two handfuls of washed and trimmed petals (cut out the bitter white part near their bases) from the most fragrant flowers in a hot sugar syrup of 1 cup sugar to $^{1}/_{2}$ cup water. Bring the mixture to a boil and simmer a few minutes. Leave the petals in the mixture until the syrup cools, then strain them out and use the syrup to sweeten fruit cups or stewed fruit. Increase or decrease petal amount as desired.

Plate 38. *Dianthus* 'Clove Pink'. Early summer, Graymalkin Farm. Photo, Brian Oke and Gisèle Quesnel.

Related plants of interest. The perennial pinks are available from perennial plant and herb sources. Seed strains are available from general and specialty seed sources.

Dianthus arenarius, sand pink, is a low-growing, hardy plant from northern and eastern Europe with small, fragrant, fringed flowers growing over a hummock of foliage that makes a good ground cover. The white 'Snow Flurries', to 8 in. (20.3 cm), is strongly scented.

Dianthus chinensis, China pink, native to Asia, is usually grown as an annual. It is used in *qu mai,* a drug of Chinese medicine, to treat various complaints. A dainty plant growing to 12 in. (30.5 cm), its foliage is slender and pointed. Flowers are numerous, produced all summer in bright pink, red, and white, often with a central band or eye. They have prominent stamens and very pinked petals. Many seed strains exist, among them the heat-tolerant 'Baby Doll' with blooms up to $2^{1}/_{2}$ in. (6.4 cm) wide.

Dianthus gratianopolitanus, Cheddar pink, is named for its native habitat in Cheddar Gorge, England. Like sand pink it is a low plant with silver-blue foliage and pink flowers with a clove scent, also a good ground cover. 'Pink Star' is double, grows to 4 in. (10.2 cm), and is very fragrant.

Dianthus 'Rainbow Loveliness' (*D. allwoodii* × *D. superbus*), 12–15 in. (30.5–38.1 cm), is an improved strain of fringed pink that includes carmine, pink, lilac, and white flowers with darker bands. It is a short-lived perennial but self-sows and is easily propagated by stem cuttings. It is hardy in Zone 4. 'White Loveliness' to 10 in. (25.4 cm) is a cultivar from the late 1920s.

Dianthus superbus, sweet John or fringed pink, native to Europe, has been used in Chinese medicine to treat various ailments. The plant's fragrance is extraordinary, a warm, all-enveloping, jasmine aroma, from wholly fringed, lilac flowers, their petals widely separated.

Digitalis purpurea

Scrophulariaceae, Snapdragon Family
Purple foxglove, deadmen's bells, fairy's glove, fairy's thimble

Biennial
Site and soil: sun, partial shade; sharply drained, well-drained
Hardiness: Zones 3–9
Landscape use: accent, bed and border, naturalized herb
Height: 4–8 ft. (1.2–2.4 m)
Flower: purple, pink, white, cream, tubular in spike
Bloom season: early summer to midsummer

Purple foxglove is an impressive and robust European wildflower, often found naturalized in North America near abandoned homesteads, in open fields, or at the edge of woodland. A plant of biennial habit, the first year it forms a basal rosette of soft, downy, oval-shaped leaves to 12 in. (30.5 cm), the next year producing a tall stalk with many down-facing, bell-shaped flowers crowded along one side of a spike, the ends of the petals slightly flared to reveal a dark, mottled, or spotted interior. Flowers, from 1 to 3 in. (2.5–7.6 cm) long, vary in color from white or cream to pale pink, but in the wild the vivid purple is dominant. In well-grown specimens the giant speckled bells are too large for a fairy's thimble but appear to be straight out of a fairy tale, nevertheless.

Common names abound, most of them calling attention to the flower's distinctive shape, while others recall the plant's potent and deadly effect when misapplied medicinally. Its genus name is from the Latin *digitabulum,* meaning thimble. Despite its fame as a heart stimulant, foxglove was used primarily to treat sores and wounds until the eighteenth century, when an English doctor, William Withering, discovered it as the active ingredient in a folk remedy for dropsy. In the nineteenth century, further research revealed precisely how its powerful glycoside digitoxin strengthens the beat of the heart muscle. So effective is the plant extract that no synthetic preparation has taken its place, but other species are now also used for medicinal purposes. Bees enjoy the flowers without any ill effects, but never should any part of this beautiful plant be ingested, as the name deadmen's bells suggests.

Purple foxglove has been grown as a garden ornamental for many centuries, admired for its early and prolific bloom and relative ease of culture. Although biennial, it produces so many seeds that some are bound to germinate if the habitat is agreeable, so that once well-situated it can be regarded as perennial. Its abundance of easily germinating seeds has made it unwelcome in many areas where it has overpowered native vegetation. Keep the planting under control by pulling up unwanted seedlings.

Choice selections from the wildflower include the white-flowered *Digitalis purpurea* 'Alba', a favorite of Gertrude Jekyll, and the soft pink 'Apricot'. Breeding has produced several seed strains worthy for their larger flowers in a wider range of colors. 'Giant Shirley' (Plate 39), the creation

Plate 39. *Digitalis purpurea* 'Giant Shirley', purple foxglove. Midsummer, Gardner farm. Photo, Alan Dorey.

of the Rev. Henry Wilkes of Shirley poppy fame, is vigorous with closely packed bells in white, dark rose, purple, maroon, and crimson, all heavily spotted. It can attain 9 ft. (2.7 m). In 'Gloxinoides' the tubular flower has become open-faced, to some a violation of the classic form, and the Excelsior Hybrids have bells that are outfacing. Both of these strains have a wider range of colors from cream, primrose, and pink to carmine and purple, all well-spotted. They grow 4–5 ft. (1.2–1.5 m) tall. The Foxy Hybrids have outfacing bells in a wide color range and will bloom within 5 months of seeding; they can be grown as annuals if started early enough.

Foxgloves are the first really tall plants to provide showy flowers in early summer, and all are outstanding, long-lasting cut flowers. The true wildflower, combined with hollyhocks, is the ultimate cottage garden plant. In an island bed the showier *Digitalis purpurea* 'Giant Shirley' creates a focal point among shorter, bushier plants such as feverfew (*Tanacetum parthenium*) and musk mallow (*Malva moschata*). The wildflower is the choice for naturalizing at the woodland edge or in a meadow planting. Any of the foxgloves are effective accent plants within the garden or near buildings, walls, and fences, where their tall stalks are protected from wind. Their spires stand out when backed by an evergreen border.

Sow seeds in early spring in a prepared bed outdoors or in a cold frame, mixing in a little sand before broadcasting the tiny seeds over the soil; just press them in without covering. Thin seedlings 6–12 in. (20.3–30.5 cm) apart, and when they are 2–3 in. (5.1–7.6 cm) tall, plant them 12–24 in. (30.5–61.0 cm) apart in their permanent position where they can establish a good root system over the summer and be ready to bloom the following season. Foxgloves need perfect drainage or their roots will rot over the winter. Also give it a sunny exposure, though partial shade will suffice where early summer is very warm. To prolong flowering on side stems, cut down the main stalks after the flowers have faded and before they have formed seeds. If plants are allowed to self-sow without interference, purple-flowered seedlings will dominate. Save seeds of favorite colors or take stem cuttings almost any time from the base of the plant; replant these in fine soil, where they will quickly establish good roots.

Related plants of interest. Note that all *Digitalis* species contain powerful alkaloids and should never be ingested. Seeds of purple foxglove and its variants are available from general, specialty, and herb seed sources; plants are available from herb sources. The seed strains are available from general and specialty seed sources. The perennial foxgloves can be found in perennial plant and herb sources.

Digitalis feruginea, rusty foxglove, to 4 ft. (1.2 m), is a perennial with lance-shaped leaves and coppery bells with rusty red, interior veining and a noticeably furry lower lip. The flower color is a refreshing change from the many pink and purple spring and early summer flowers, but for this reason it is difficult to combine with other plants. It is stunning with feather reed grass (*Calamagrostis* ×*acutiflora* 'Karl Foerster'), an early-blooming plant with cinnamon flowers. Rusty foxglove is hardy in Zone 4.

Digitalis grandiflora, yellow foxglove, is one of the most desirable of the perennial types. Only 24 in. (61.0 cm) tall, it forms tidy clumps of attractive, dark green leaves whose flower stalks are heavy with large, 3 in. (7.6 cm), creamy yellow bells, somewhat open and speckled brown inside. If stalks are cut down before the flowers set seed, there may be repeat bloom in the fall. It is hardy in Zone 3.

Digitalis lanata, Grecian foxglove, is a commercial source for digitoxin, 300 times more potent than digitalis powder, quicker acting, and more stable. A perennial, it grows to 3 ft. (0.9 m) with spikes of small, bronze-yellow to purplish, tubular flowers with a pearl-gray lip. This plant is an effective complement for gray-leaved *Artemisia*.

Digitalis lutea, straw foxglove, is a slender perennial to 3 ft. (0.9 m) with numerous narrow, light yellow bells along its spike. The flower sprays are highly prized in fresh arrangements. According to some authorities it is a primary source for digitoxin.

Digitalis ×*mertonensis*, merton foxglove, is a tetraploid hybrid between purple foxglove and yellow foxglove that comes true from seed. The large, coppery pink flowers are produced over a long season on stems that rarely grow taller than 3 ft. (0.9 m). Although it is described as a perennial, it is short-lived, so plants should be divided every other year or propagated from seed. It is hardy in Zone 3.

Echinacea purpurea

Asteraceae, Aster Family
Purple coneflower, sampson root

Perennial
Site and soil: sun, partial shade; well-drained
Hardiness: Zones 3–8
Landscape use: accent, bed and border, naturalized herb
Height: 24–36 in. (61.0–91.4 cm)
Flower: purplish pink, daisy-like, solitary head
Bloom season: midsummer to fall

Of the three species which comprise the genus, purple coneflower is the showiest, like a giant daisy. Especially abundant on the midwestern prairies, it grows from a central clump of coarsely toothed, tapered leaves on stiff but sturdy, unbranching stems. Its glory is in its wide flower head, to 4 in. (10.2), which first appears with short, stiff, greenish rays upturned around a prominent dark cone of compressed tubular flowers. Gradually, as the rays elongate, to horizontal then to drooping, they turn a rich, rosy pink, as the cone itself turns to coppery brown. Butterflies show a strong attraction to the flowers. If you run your fingers across the prickly head, you will know why its genus name is derived from the Greek for hedgehog, *echinos*.

The roots of purple coneflower and the other echinaceas were highly regarded by North American Indians who used them as a general panacea, mainly for infections of all kinds. After being displaced by antibiotics in the 1930s, the drug echinacea is once more gaining popularity for its antiinflamatory properties, which are thought to bolster the body's own immune system.

In the landscape, purple coneflower has long been a mainstay of the late summer border, especially with the improved cultivars. Mostly of European origin, these play on natural variants, some with white petals like the elegant, compact *Echinacea purpurea* 'White Swan' to 24 in. (61.0 cm), others with horizontal, flaring petals such as 'Magnus'. 'Bright Star', a variable, seed-propagated type has smaller, 3 in. (7.6 cm), but abundant, flowers. The version 'Dwarf Star' is shorter and more compact than others, useful in tight situations. 'Robert Bloom' bears handsome, wide flowers to 5 in. (12.7 cm).

Purple coneflower's self-sustaining, upright form in its several versions is adaptable for formal and informal plantings and complements every bloom in the garden. It is traditionally grown with its close relative *Rudbeckia*, but it also combines attractively with long-blooming, pink hollyhock mallow (*Malva alcea* 'Fastigiata') and garlic chives. In partial shade try it with crimson, pink, and lime *Nicotiana*. The unimproved wildflower is a good choice for naturalizing on a dry bank with wild bergamot (*Monarda fistulosa*), black-eyed Susan (*Rudbeckia hirta*), and butterfly weed (*Asclepias tuberosa*), which enjoy the same conditions. The echinaceas are outstanding cut flowers, and after the petals fall, the naked cone on its stalk is harvested for dried flower arrangements.

Plate 40. *Echinacea purpurea*, purple coneflower. Midsummer, Country Lane Herbs and Dried Flowers. Photo, Brian Oke and Gisèle Quesnel.

For best results, stratify seeds in the refrigerator for 4 weeks before sowing at 70°F (21°C); make sure to cover seeds. Germination should occur in 10 to 21 days. Outdoors in the early spring—a light frost will not hurt—space seedlings about 15 in. (38.1 cm) apart. Plants will grow in partial shade as well as full sun, but they must have well-drained soil or they will die over the winter; in areas colder than Zone 5 give winter protection. Cut back plants after blooming to maintain vigor. Propagate by division, not too often since it seems to weaken plants, or by root cuttings in the spring or fall, or plant seeds. Seed-grown plants are variable but always attractive.

Related plants of interest. Purple coneflower is widely available as seed from general seed and some herb sources; the seed strains and cultivars are less widely available but can be found from general seed sources and from perennial plant nurseries. The other echinaceas are generally only available as seeds from wildflower, specialty, and a few herb sources.

Echinacea angustifolia, narrowleaf echinacea or black sampson coneflower, is native to the Plains states and grows to 5 ft. (1.5 m) with orchid-pink to violet rays on 2 in. (5.1 cm) wide flowers. Seed germination is tricky and rarely exceeds 50 percent; stratify seeds for 30 to 90 days.

Echinacea pallida, pale purple echinacea, grows from Illinois to Texas and is later blooming. It grows on stems to 4 ft. (1.2 m) and bears a pronounced cone, embellished with spidery, rose-pink, drooping petals. The flower has a distinctive, honey scent. It, too, is difficult to raise from seed and should be treated the same as narrowleaf echinacea. It is hardy in Zone 5.

Filipendula

Rosaceae, Rose Family
Meadowsweet

Perennial
Site and soil: sun, partial shade; moist, boggy
Hardiness: Zones 3–8
Landscape use: accent, bed and border, naturalized herb
Height: 4–8 ft. (1.2–2.4 m)
Flower: creamy white, peach-pink, frothy terminal cluster
Bloom season: early summer to midsummer

> There are few sights in the garden more pleasing and spectacular.
> Harry R. Phillips
> *Growing and Propagating Wild Flowers*

There are two meadowsweets, both handsome plants, one from the Old World, the other from the New. The common name may have evolved from "meadwort," a word describing herbs used to flavor mead and beer. John Gerard called the Eurasian species, *Filipendula ulmaria*, queen-of-the-meadow because it dominates the English countryside in early summer, covering moist meadowlands, marshes, and wet woods with its frothy mass of creamy, sweet-scented blooms. Plants grow by creeping rhizomes but they increase slowly, producing hollow, reddish stems 4–6 ft. (1.2–1.8 m) tall that branch irregularly near the top, bearing terminal clusters of very crowded tiny, soft, creamy white flowers with protruding stamens. Any movement causes them to pour forth a shower of pollen that gathers on the plant's handsome, divided, dark green leaves, silvery on the reverse. Unlike the flowers, the leaves have a sharp wintergreen aroma when bruised, but when dried they exude a vanilla-like sweetness due to the presence of coumarin, the same scent-giving substance found in new-mown hay. The double-flowered *F. ulmaria* 'Plena' is most often grown. A less rangy plant, its rosy white buds open to fluffy, white, double buttons.

A little later blooming, queen-of-the-prairie, *Filipendula rubra*, is a bold plant that thrives in moist meadows and bogs in the eastern United States as far south as Georgia, decorating the land with its plumes of tiny, sweet-scented, peach-rose flowers in spreading terminal clusters atop stems as tall as 8 ft. (2.4 m). Its leaves are deeply divided, jagged, and crinkled, silvery on the underside. Although enjoyed in British and European gardens since the eighteenth century, it is not so well known in its native land. The type most cultivated is *F. rubra* 'Venusta', Martha Washington's plume.

143

Like many sweetly scented plants, queen-of-the-meadow was highly regarded as a strewing herb. It was also popular for bridal bouquets and garlands, hence the common name bridewort. An eminently useful plant from every point of view, it was employed in the kitchen to flavor wines, in the household it was used as a dye plant, and in the family's pharmacopeia its leaves, roots, and flowers were pressed into service to treat a number of ailments. Its greatest achievement, however, rests on its role in the development of aspirin, to which it gave its name: aspirin means "from spirea," a reference to the genus under which meadowsweet was once classified. It was from the plant's flower buds that scientists in 1839 first obtained a source of salicylic acid, later synthesized into the familiar white pills we take to alleviate headaches, pains, and fevers, the same ailments for which queen-of-the-meadow had been a folk remedy for centuries.

Queen-of-the-prairie roots were used by North American Indians to treat heart trouble. As a plant high in the astringent tannin, it was also effective in treating diarrhea and wounds. Chemically, its makeup is similar to the Old World species.

Consider yourself lucky to have a piece of ground so sodden, either in sun or partial shade, where nothing else will grow, because both meadowsweets, spectacular when massed, will love these conditions and repay you with weeks of lovely, scented blooms from early to midsummer. In partial shade, as long as the soil is evenly moist, flowers bloom longer. Try meadowsweets in a naturalized bog garden with the earlier-blooming blue and yellow flag iris (*Iris versicolor* and *I. pseudacorus*), bee balm (*Monarda didyma*), and lobelias. The meadowsweets are happy by any body of water, from a large pond to a ditch. In a more formal setting, they are background for daylilies (*Hemerocallis*) and astilbe or companions for monkshood (*Aconitum napellus*). In an island bed they become a focal point for a month, after which they can be replaced by white mugwort (*Artemisia lactiflora*) whose creamy white plumes are similar in form.

Sow seeds in the fall in a cold frame and plant seedlings early the following spring, spacing them 24–36 in. (61.0–91.4 cm) apart in rich, moist soil. The cultivars should be grown from roots planted in early spring. Pick off spent blooms to stimulate the production of more flowers. When the plant is finished flowering, cut it back to about 12 in. (30.5 cm). Divide in late summer or early spring. To stake queen-of-the-prairie, if necessary, place stakes in a square around the planting and weave on them a supporting network of strong twine.

All meadowsweets are attractive cut flowers. They dry well for winter bouquets; queen-of-the-meadow dries to a deep cream with a chartreuse cast. The fresh leaves of *Filipendula vulgaris* are perfect for encircling nose-gays or tussie-mussies.

Related plants of interest. Seeds of queen-of-the-meadow are available from specialty seed and herb sources; seeds of dropwort are available from specialty seed sources. Meadowsweet and dropwort cultivars are available from perennial plant nurseries.

Filipendula vulgaris, dropwort, is an Old World plant 12–24 in. (30.5–61.0 cm) tall with small, airy clusters of creamy white flowers on slender,

Plate 41. *Filipendula vulgaris* 'Flore Pleno', dropwort. Midsummer, Gardner farm. Photo, Alan Dorey.

wand-like stems that grow up from a mound of beautiful, emerald green, ferny leaves 6–20 in. (15.2–50.8 cm) long. Juice from its small, drop-like tubers (that suggest its common name) was once used to treat menstrual cramps as well as kidney and lung ailments. A native of dry pastures, it grows in a wider range of conditions than the meadowsweets, but it does not appreciate wet soil. The double-flowered 'Flore Pleno' (Plate 41) is the one most often grown. A shorter plant to 10 in. (25.4 cm), it is beguiling with its tight clusters of buds, like miniature, antique-rose-tinted pearls, that open to perfect, little, white, rose-like blooms, but the thin stems can only support their freight in windless situations. Space plants 12 in. (30.5 cm) apart in the front of a border or among rocks, where the attractive leaves and flowering stems will show well. The flowering plumes combine beautifully with purple mullein (*Verbascum phoeniceum*).

Galium odoratum

The tiny white flowers are also stars.
Rosetta Clarkson
Herbs: Their Culture and Uses

Rubiaceae, Madder Family
Sweet woodruff

Perennial
Site and soil: partial shade, shade; moist and well-drained
Hardiness: Zones 4–8
Landscape use: container, ground cover, naturalized herb, rock work
Height: 6–8 in. (15.2–20.3 cm)
Flower: white star in cluster
Bloom season: spring to early summer

Sweet woodruff is one of about 400 *Galium* species native to woodlands of temperate regions of the world. Plants grow by creeping roots, quickly creating horizontal stems to 15 in. (38.1 cm). Each stem carries whorls of six to eight lance-shaped, shiny leaves and masses of small, white, star-shaped flower clusters from May to June. Although the flowers themselves are odorless, the leaves exude a sweet, vanilla-like scent when bruised or dried, due to the presence of coumarin, the same substance found in meadowsweet (*Filipendula*). "Wood" in its common name refers to its preferred

146

habitat, while "ruff" is a good description of the leaves that ascend, like a series of ruffs, up each stem.

In Elizabethan times, sweet woodruff was the strewing herb par excellence, releasing its scent as it was crushed underfoot. It was also dried for sachets to scent linens and to keep insects from woolens. Medicinally, it was used as a poultice on fresh wounds, as a tea for headaches, and as an aid to digestion. It was most famously used to flavor May wine, a traditional drink to welcome the spring.

In England at the turn of the century, Gertrude Jekyll championed planting sweet woodruff as an ornamental, an idea that apparently met with astonishment because decades later Marjory Fish still felt obliged to justify its cultivation: "Some gardeners may be shocked to see our little native woodruff . . . as a cultivated plant in the garden, but I think it is as pretty as many garden plants" (1964). Since then the little, unimproved sweet woodruff has become highly regarded by gardeners in North America for its ease of culture and glossy beauty as a weed-smothering ground cover. Its mass of white, starry flowers, blooming in sheets, lights up shady areas. Plantings are especially effective beneath azaleas (*Rhododendron*) and the pink-flowering Sargent crab tree (*Malus sargentii*). Sweet woodruff has many other uses in the landscape, including clothing a shady bank or bordering a naturalized woodland planting of sweet cicely (*Myrrhis odorata*), purple honesty (*Lunaria annua*), and the ivory-belled Solomon's seal (*Polygonatum multiflorum*). I plant it beneath a hedge of wild roses where mowing is difficult. Sweet woodruff, with its cascading stems, is a fetching container plant; containers can be placed almost anywhere as long as their soil is kept moist.

Sweet woodruff is not difficult to grow from seed, but seeds must be fresh. Condition seeds in the refrigerator for 2 weeks, then sow on the soil surface. Seeds should germinate in 21 to 42 days at 50°F (10°C). Outdoors in early spring, plants should be spaced 12 in. (30.5 cm) apart in moist but well-drained, acidic soil in shaded conditions. Sweet woodruff will grow in drier soil and a sunny site, but it will not spread as rapidly and may die out in exposed situations. Plants can be increased by stem cuttings after flowering. Take stems with two whorls of leaves and root them in sand in a shaded cold frame, keeping them well-watered. Or divide plants by disentangling the roots of a single clump in the spring. Water well the transplanted clumps. For indoor culture, use an acid soil mix (three parts loam, two parts sand, one part peat moss) and expose potted plants to a few hard frosts before bringing them indoors.

Sweet woodruff offers various home uses. For potpourri, cut stems before they flower for best scent. The foliage with its flowers is useful in wreaths and swags. The flowers of lady's bedstraw are an effective filler in fresh bouquets. To make May wine, steep a handful of partially dried leaves overnight in a bottle of white wine—Sautern, Rhine, or Reisling is best. Add orange pieces or a handful of crushed strawberries. Strain and chill.

Related plants of interest. Sweet woodruff is widely available as seed or plants from general seed and herb sources; a few general and specialty seed sources may carry seeds of oriental woodruff; and lady's bedstraw is available from perennial plant nurseries and herb sources.

Asperula orientalis, oriental woodruff, is a self-sowing annual, upright to 12 in. (30.5 cm) with small, sky-blue, scented flowers. Seeds should be sown where you want the plants to bloom, then thin them to 6 in. (15.2 cm) apart. It is a lovely ground cover to cascade over a wall, to grow in a rock garden, or to fill in around stone pavings. It also will grow indoors in a container over the winter.

Galium verum, lady's bedstraw, a hardy perennial, is an ancient strewing herb containing coumarin. Somewhat weedy, growing in full sun or light shade with wiry stems to 3 ft. (0.9 m), it bears many tiny, frothy, yellow, scented flowers in early to midsummer. It is best grown as an informal ground cover on a slope where the lax stems can trail along. Otherwise, stake it for the flower border. This is the legendary mattress filler associated with the baby Jesus' manger bed. It was used extensively as a dye—red from the roots, yellow from the tops—and to curdle milk and cheese.

Geranium robertianum

Geraniaceae, Geranium Family
Herb robert, bloodwort, fox geranium, red robin

Annual, biennial
Site and soil: partial shade, shade; evenly moist
Hardiness: Zone 4
Landscape use: ground cover, naturalized herb
Height: 10–12 in. (25.4–30.5 cm)
Flower: purplish pink, round-petaled in pairs
Bloom season: spring to early summer

It's a weed to some, but the little pink flowers are charming . . . The less self-conscious the garden becomes, the better I like it.

Rob Proctor
The Herb Companion

Herb robert is the daintiest of the hardy geraniums (not to be confused with the tender geraniums in the genus *Pelargonium*). Native to Europe, Asia, and Africa it has made itself at home in shaded rocky woods and ravines from Newfoundland to Maryland and west to Illinois. Its light green, finely cut, downy leaves spread out close to the ground, while above them masses of small, five-petaled, pink flowers on 1 in. (2.5 cm) stems are produced in profusion over a long period beginning in late spring or early summer. Although each blossom lasts but a short time, new ones are always opening. Just behind the spent petals, round, puffed fruits form; as the petals fall, the pod extends a reddish-tipped beak to $^{3}/_{4}$ in. (1.9 cm) and bursts open, spilling its contents to the ground and assuring successive generations of plants. This seed-forming and -dispersing habit is shared by all members of the genus.

The genus name is from the Greek *gheranos,* meaning crane, a bird whose beak the plant's mature fruits resemble. There are many fanciful legends concerning the origin of the common name "robert," but the more sedate explanation is that it comes from the Latin *ruber,* meaning red, a reference to herb robert's reddish stems, fruits, and mature leaves. According to the seventeenth-century *Doctrine of Signatures,* herb robert's reddishness signified its use to regenerate blood and to heal wounds. In fact, its high tannin content was effective in treating a number of disorders and afflictions.

I first found herb robert in its favorite habitat, covering the steep bank of a wooded ravine on our farm. The mass of soft greenery had natural-

149

ized itself among the trees. Watching through the season as the pretty, pink flowers finally spent themselves and the foliage gradually turned a lovely bronze-purple-red, I decided to take advantage of this natural planting by creating a spring woodland garden with plants that prefer the same habitat, such as spotted-leaved lungwort (*Pulmonaria officinalis*) and bright yellow cowslips (*Primula veris*). Other herb fanciers have dealt creatively with this interesting plant, using it as a ground cover in damp ground with ostrich ferns (*Mateuccia struthiopteris*) and meadowsweet (*Filipendula*). Although it forms a light, airy canopy rather than a tight mat, it is an effective weed-smotherer. It can be grown at the edges of a garden or in a shady corner of the garden itself, since it pulls up easily when it has overstepped its boundaries.

Sow seeds, preferably freshly ripened, in early fall. Space plants 1 in. (2.5 cm) apart, in rich, moist, acidic soil, in shade or semishaded conditions, protected from strong wind; if the soil is moist, herb robert will grow in full sun. Newly established plants must be well-watered until they show signs of growth. Herb robert will self-sow from year to year and can be regarded almost as perennial.

Related plants of interest. Both of these hardy geraniums are long-flowering and hardy in Zone 4. Plants and seeds of herb robert are available from herb sources; wild geranium is available from perennial plant and wildflower sources; large-rooted cranesbill is available from perennial plant nurseries.

Geranium macrorrhizum (Plate 42), large-rooted cranesbill or big root geranium, is a hardy perennial from southern Europe, 10–15 in. (25.4–38.1 cm) tall. Just a few plants make a wide, dense, leafy mound that slowly turns red in the fall. The leaves, whose extracted oil is used in the perfume industry, are soft and velvety, exuding a refreshing, lemon-apple scent when crushed or dried. The magenta flowers with prominent, golden pistils rise just above the canopy of leaves and are decorative over a long season, from flowering to seed formation. The most popular cultivar is 'Ingwersen's Variety' to 12 in. (30.5 cm) with clear, prominent pink flowers; 'Album', 15–18 in. (38.1–45.7 cm), bears apple blossom-like, pink-white flowers; and 'Bevan's Variety' is 12 in. (30.5 cm) tall with deep magenta flowers. This greatly undervalued perennial is elegant wherever it is grown, as a mounded groundcover, in a rock garden, in a bed or border, or as a corner accent. It thrives in virtually every condition—in shade, partial shade, even full sun—and in almost any soil, even on the dry side. The leaves of large-rooted cranesbill can be harvested all summer for potpourri. Just rubbing fresh leaves on one's skin will leave a lasting, pleasant fragrance.

Geranium maculatum, wild or spotted geranium, is a perennial species native to North America. It grows to 24 in. (61.0 cm) with large, deeply-cut green leaves that become blotched with light green as they age. The flowers are 1 in. (2.5 cm) wide, pale pink to rosy purple, delicately veined, and cupped. Following them appear the upward-thrusting beaks typical of the genus. The white-flowered 'Album' has somewhat larger flowers. One

Plate 42. *Geranium macrorrhizum*, big root geranium. Early summer, Gardner farm. Photo, Alan Dorey.

151

of this species' common names, alumroot, attests to its use as an astringent with the same properties and uses as herb robert. Wild geranium grows in similar conditions as herb robert and is a good choice for a shade garden among ferns, wild bleeding heart (*Dicentra eximia*), and the red cardinal flower (*Lobelia cardinalis*); it creates a long-flowering accent at the base of shrubs. As long as the soil is moist and deep, it will grow well in less shaded conditions. Plants can be grown from seed, preferably fresh, sown outside in the summer or fall. Space seedlings 10–15 in. (25.4–38.1 cm) apart and cover the planting with light mulch until it is established. Propagate from rhizomes planted 1 in. (2.5 cm) deep, in early spring or fall.

Helianthus annuus

> This beautiful plant . . . lifts its yellow flowers sunward in pale imitation of the great lifegiver itself.
>
> Mrs. William Starr Dana
> *How to Know the Wildflowers*

Asteraceae, Aster Family
Sunflower, common sunflower

Annual
Site and soil: sun; well-drained
Landscape use: accent, bed and border, container, edge and hedge, naturalized herb
Height: 10 ft. (3.0 m)
Flower: yellow, daisy-like, solitary
Bloom season: late summer to fall

The sunflower native to North America is a plant of far more modest proportions than the type that is now synonymous with it. Growing in prairies, rich soil, waste places, corn fields, and arid regions of the west as far south as Mexico, it has rough, erect stems 3–10 ft. (0.9–3.0 m) high that carry rough, nearly heart-shaped leaves 3–12 in. (7.6–30.5 cm) long and, at the top, one or several round flower heads 3–6 in. (7.6–15.2 cm) wide. Flower rays are yellow, sometimes tinged with red or purple, and the center disk is red or purple to match, as in a real daisy. As the petals fall and the head is at last crowned by its own brown, curling bracts, the face becomes a mass of seeds, really fruits, variable in color from white and purple to black, some striped, all tightly packed in a concentric pattern.

The stereotypic sunflower is larger in all its parts, growing to 12 ft. (3.7 m) with huge leaves and a huge, solitary head at least 10 in. (25.4 cm) wide that in maturity bears hundreds of seeds. The flower head is dominated by the disk, with the yellow petals as a sort of fringe. One of the best of these plants is *Helianthus annuus* 'Mammoth Russian' (Plate 43), a cultivar developed in Russia for seed production, and introduced to North America in the 1880s. It and similar types are referred to by commercial growers as confectionery sunflowers for the plants' ample supply of seeds destined for the food industry.

There is probably no other native plant with a longer history of use— North American Indians have grown it for 3000 years—yet the sunflower

Plate 43. *Helianthus annuus* 'Mammoth Russian', sunflower. Late summer, vegetable garden, Gardner farm. Photo, Alan Dorey.

has rarely been mentioned in popular herb literature. Virtually every part has a use. The seeds are left whole and roasted as a substitute for coffee. Fresh seeds are ground to make butter and meal or pressed for their oil. The seed receptacles are used for blotting paper. The dried stalk is used for fuel, and the prepared stalk makes fine writing paper, coarse ropes, and silky fabric. The stalk's lightweight pith is used in scientific laboratories. And in China the plant is used in acupuncture.

For years there were only a few ornamental types that had any use beyond a vegetable garden screen. Among these shorter, branching, multiflowered plants, *Helianthus annuus* 'Italian White', now regarded as an heirloom strain, is especially striking. It bears lovely 4–5 in. (10.2–12.7 cm) wide flowers—pearly white to cream petals surround a chocolate brown center—on 4 ft. (1.2 m) stems. 'Teddy Bear' is another one of these first few ornamentals, but its dwarf stature and huge, oversize pompons does not much enhance the landscape.

Many seed strains are now available for finding the perfect sunflower for any location. *Helianthus annuus* 'Autumn Beauty' is an older and still very desirable branching type with solid and bicolored, single flowers 8 in. (20.3 cm) wide. To 5 ft. (1.5 m) tall, it is a good background or accent. 'Hopi Black Dye', tceqa, is a confectionery type best adapted to cool, high desert regions, but it can be grown elsewhere. It grows 6–8 ft. (1.8–2.4 m) with a 5–8 in. (12.7–20.3 cm) wide, yellow flower head and some side heads. Its purple-black seed hulls yield red to blue dye, depending on the mordant. 'Moonwalker' may grow 5–10 ft. (1.5–3.0 m), depending on conditions, and bears multiple, as many as eight to ten, large, pale yellow flowers on top-branching stalks. A strong, vigorous strain, it is useful as a windbreak. 'Music Box' is dwarf to 30 in. (76.2 cm) and is very free-flowering, with solid and bicolored single flowers 4 in. (10.2 cm) wide, suitable for smaller spaces, tubs, and window boxes. 'Orange Sun' (Plate 44) carries its large, double-flowered head, 5½–6 in. (14.0–15.2 cm) across, on single, 3½ ft. (1.1 m) stalks. One plant is sufficient for bed or border. 'Sun 891' is a sturdy, high-yield, seed-producing type to 7 ft. (2.1 m). It is especially suitable for growing in a row as a hedge. It takes 110 days to mature, however, compared to the 80 days of 'Mammoth Russian', making it too late for gardeners in Zone 4. 'Sunspot' with its classic head on 2 ft. (0.6 cm) stems creates a whimsical hedge, like something out of a fairy tale. It also yields a fine crop of seeds. 'Valentine', a particularly fine cut flower, grows to 5 ft. (1.5 m), bearing lovely 6 in. (15.2 cm) wide flowers with lemon-yellow petals surrounding a black disk.

The introduction of these and more new types in the Sunflower Revolution has considerably expanded landscaping possibilities. The tall branch-

Plate 44. *Helianthus annuus* 'Orange Sun', sunflower. Late summer. Photo courtesy of Thompson and Morgan.

ing sorts with multi-colored flowers are beautiful, late-summer accents in the back of a flower bed or border, in front of a garden fence, or as a screen. Shorter, sturdier types make great hedges, and three of them planted in a tub and placed on a patio or deck create a sensation—a bright, daisy-flow-ered little shrub. Very dwarf kinds with single, rather than double, flowers can be planted in a window box. Any of the sunflowers are suitable for a children's garden or for a single accent by the back door, shed, mailbox, or as a final row in the vegetable garden. The unimproved wildflower should not be ignored; it can be naturalized or used as a charming accent near doorways.

Few things are easier or more enjoyable than planting a sunflower seed. After all danger of frost has passed and when the ground has warmed (at the same time for planting corn), plant three sunflower seeds $1/2$ in. (1.3 cm) deep every 12–24 in. (30.5–61.0 cm), then thin out the extra plants after germination. Full sun and dry growing conditions produce the best results. To encourage branching and longer stems for cutting, pinch out the first buds. In rich ground, the taller sunflowers may need staking.

Those sunflowers with long stems are very desirable cut flowers—cut them when the bud is barely opened. A very easy way to add sunflower decor indoors is to cut a single, large head before the birds eat the seeds and display it where it will have the most impact. The seeds retain their flavor for a long time if they are left in the head. The edible roots of the perennial sunflowers are prepared the same as tubers of Jerusalem arti-choke, *Helianthus tuberosus*, raw, roasted, or boiled.

Related plants of interest. Look for the confectionery types with general vegetables or from specialty seed sources; the ornamental types are listed with other flowers. The perennials are available from specialty seed sources for prairie- and wildflowers and from a few perennial plant nurseries. The perennial species are grown the same way as annual sunflowers and should be cut down at the end of the season; they are hardy in Zone 4.

Helianthus ×laetiflorus (*H. pauciflorus × H. tuberosus*), showy sunflower, is a natural hybrid of the Central Plains and a perennial whose tuberous roots are edible. It grows on stems to $6^{1}/2$ ft. (2.0 m) with large, tapered leaves and bright yellow flowers 4 in. (10.2 cm) across. Cultivars, not yet avail-able in North America, include 'Miss Mellish' with clear yellow, semidou-ble flowers and 'Semiplenum' with semidouble, orange-yellow flowers.

Helianthus maximilianii, Maximilian's sunflower, was named for Prince Maximilian of Germany who discovered it on the American prairies in the 1830s. Also perennial, it, too, has edible tubers, and grows 5–8 ft. (1.5–2.4 m) with 3 in. (7.6 cm) blooms of orange centers surrounded by golden-yellow petals. It looks great against walls and fences and even at the back of a border.

Hesperis matronalis

Brassicaceae, Mustard Family
Sweet rocket, dame's rocket, evening rocket, mother-of-the-evening

> **It is easy to fancy its white stars gleaming about the Temple of Love.**
> Louise Beebe Wilder
> *The Fragrant Garden*

Biennial, perennial
Site and soil: sun, partial shade; evenly moist
Hardiness: Zones 4–9
Landscape use: bed and border, naturalized herb
Height: 24–36 in. (61.0–91.4 cm)
Flower: pink, purple, mauve, white, phlox-like in cluster
Bloom season: early summer to late summer

Sweet rocket (not to be confused with garden rocket, *Eruca sativa*) is native from south and central Europe to Siberia. It is widely naturalized in North America, especially in damp meadowlands where it appears as a sea of fluffy blooms in early summer. The flowers are phlox-like in appearance, with four rounded, pink, purple, mauve, or white petals in loose terminal clusters atop stalks that grow from a taproot. The lower leaves are plentiful and rather coarse—long and pointed with sharp edges–but they diminish in size as they ascend the plant. The cylindrical seed pods which form behind the flowers point upwards, like small rockets just waiting to discharge their load of seeds.

The dried leaves of sweet rocket, rich in vitamin C, were once used as an antiscorbutic, and in Europe the young leaves are still used like salad rocket (*Eruca sativa*) to add a spicy, mustardy flavor to spring salad. Sweet rocket's enduring fame, however, rests on its powerful, clove-scented aroma that is released in the evening air. It is this characteristic that is preserved in all sweet rocket's folk names, as well as in the genus name which means evening. The plant is pollinated by moths attracted to the flowers' nectar.

The pure-white-flowered *Hesperis matronalis* 'Alba' is less common than the pastels. Devotees of sweet rocket would love to have the legendary double white 'Flore Pleno' because of its beauty and powerful aroma; the flower head is so large that the stems need staking. It is notoriously difficult to grow, however, and can only be propagated vegetatively. As far as I know, it has not been offered for sale in North America since the late nineteenth century, although it is still found occasionally in Britain.

As an addition to a theme garden, sweet rocket is an obvious choice for a scented or fragrant garden, perhaps among artemisias, lavenders (*Lavandula angustifolia*), and sweet cicely (*Myrrhis odorata*). Sweet rocket will enhance an informal island bed or a cottage garden where its flowers outlast foxgloves, mallows (*Malva sylvestris*), and clary sage (*Salvia sclarea*). Though the combination sounds odd, sweet rocket's pastel flower clusters complement and soften the bright reds of oriental poppies (*Papaver orientale*); like musk mallow (*Malva moschata*), it blends and harmonizes harsh col-

Plate 45. *Hesperis matronalis*, sweet rocket. Early summer, Toronto, Ontario. It blooms all summer if trimmed of spent flower stalks. Photo, Brian Oke and Gisèle Quesnel.

ors. Sweet rocket can be naturalized in damp conditions, either in bright sun or partial shade, where with virtually no attention it will return year after year to sweeten the evening air and bloom all summer.

Sow seeds indoors in late winter or early spring, uncovered, where they will germinate at 70°F (21°C). Or sow the seeds in a cold frame in the summer, where they will germinate by the following spring. Space plants 15–18 in. (38.1–45.7 cm) apart in sun or partial shade in evenly moist soil. These may produce flowers late the first year, after which they will bloom earlier and self-sow from year to year. New plants also sprout at the base of mature plants, which usually do not last more than two seasons. Keep control of the planting by pulling up escaping seedlings since sweet rocket has a history of crowding out native vegetation. After several years, mauve flowers may dominate the population, so save seeds of favorite colors or separate plantlets from mother plants and replant them in early spring, watering them well until they have recovered from temporary wilting. Sweet rocket benefits greatly from trimming all season. When the old flowering stalks are cut back, new leaves and buds form quickly, so the plant is in constant bloom.

Related plants of interest. Sweet rocket is usually only sold as seeds, which are widely available from general seed sources. *Hesperis steveniana* is rare.

Hesperis steveniana grows to 30 in. (76.2 cm) and produces clouds of lightly scented, loose, lilac flower clusters in early spring. It winds down when sweet rocket begins to bloom. It is grown the same way as sweet rocket.

Humulus lupulus

Cannabaceae, Hemp Family
Hop Vine

Perennial
Site and soil: sun, partial shade; well-drained
Hardiness: Zones 3–9
Landscape use: accent, ground cover,
  naturalized herb
Height: 25 ft. (7.6 m)
Flower: pale yellow cone in loose panicle
Bloom season: midsummer to fall

The European hop vine is widely naturalized throughout the Northern Hemisphere. A remarkably vigorous plant, it grows from a fleshy root, twining its long, weak stems clock-wise around any support by means of its anvil-shaped prickles or hooks. Its dark green leaves on reddish stems are large, deeply lobed, and veined, providing dense cover in a single season. The cone-shaped, insignificant female flowers or strobiles are covered by overlapping, papery bracts; the male flowers, which appear on separate plants, are small and green. By midsummer, the vine is covered with many hanging clusters of tight, light green cones. As the season advances and the cones partially open, their color gradually changes to lime or chartreuse, then to amber-bronze by late summer or early fall. This is when the cones have their most pungent scent, from the yellow-grained powder deep within the light, papery bracts. Hop aroma varies from very strong and pungent to spicy and mellow.

The hop vine has been cultivated at least since the ninth century to flavor and preserve beer; the mature flower heads, the hops, house substances that prevent the growth of bacteria while lending their bitter flavor. Most often associated with their sedative powers, the prepared cones have been used medicinally to treat a number of ailments. For the North American settler, the hop vine was indispensable for making barm to raise bread; for this purpose hop vines were moved from one homestead to another. Eventually, its ornamental qualities became appreciated and it was planted to embellish the outside of the home or to quickly create a screen to shade porches, verandahs, or arbors. As tastes changed, the hop vine was discarded as old-fashioned, but now it is chosen more and more often for that very same quality. *Humulus lupulus* 'Sunbeam Golden' is an especially good ornamental with superior aroma that shows its golden foliage off against the hop vine's reddish stems. *Humulus japonicus*, Japanese hop vine, is an annual grown mostly for its foliage. Hop vine roots and those of various cultivars, mostly developed for their flavor, are available from herb sources.

The hop vine's phenomenal growth rate, 6–12 in. (15.2–30.5 cm) in a day, makes it ideal for quickly covering the sides of buildings, porches, or wherever shade is needed. When grown over an arbor, it makes a wonderful entryway to any garden. In my local area, the hop vine is a homesteader's remnant, growing today as it was in the late 1800s, neatly trained to climb up a long pole by the side of the house. Given about 6 ft. (1.8 m) of support from a fabric trellis secured to the side of a building, the cone-laden vine will frame a doorway by attaching itself to last season's hard-

Plate 46. *Humulus lupulus*, hop vine, growing against a cedar rail fence. Midsummer, Country Lane Herbs and Dried Flowers. Photo, Brian Oke and Gisèle Quesnel.

ened stems; it also looks good supported by a wooden teepee, one sturdier but similar to those used for propping tomato vines. If given no support, it will sprawl along the ground as a long-season cover for "unsightly" areas.

It is easiest to grow the hop vine from roots, which should be planted in the spring when the ground has warmed in humusy, enriched, and well-drained soil in full sun or light shade. Light shade is best for *Humulus lupulus* 'Golden Sunbeam'. Space roots 3 ft. (0.9 m) apart and bear in mind that one well-established plant will provide a lifetime supply of offspring from the new shoots that grow up from the ever-spreading roots. In the spring, these new shoots can be detached from the mother plant and re-planted elsewhere. When considering a planting site, choose one that will allow you to mow around the vine during the growing season—this is the easiest means of controlling its rapid expansion. Cut down old canes in the fall—they make good compost—leaving some for next season's support. It is best to keep plantings clear of debris to discourage insect infestation. The leaves are sometimes attacked by leaf-suckers, for which a rotenone-pyrethrum spray is effective if used every 4 or 5 days for 2 or 3 weeks in order to catch the insects during their life cycle. Diazinon can also be used.

For wreaths and swags, cut the flower clusters when they are still light green, otherwise they will shatter, and air dry them; the stems can be used for a wreath base. To harvest hops, cut the clusters when the cones are pale yellow, then spread them to dry on newspaper, away from light. To make a sleep pillow, stuff a miniature pillow case with dried hops and slip it inside your pillow case.

Hyssopus officinalis

Lamiaceae, Mint Family
Hyssop

Perennial
Site and soil: sun; well-drained
Hardiness: Zones 3–9
Landscape use: accent, bed and border, edge and
  hedge, rock work
Height: 24–36 in. (61.0–91.4 cm)
Flower: blue-violet, pink, white, small, tubular in spike
Bloom season: early summer to late summer

> **Like the lavender, the santolina and the rosemary, the hyssop is a plant to give beauty to the shrub border.**
>
> Roy Genders
> *The Cottage Garden*

Hyssop is indigenous to southern and eastern Europe. It is shrub-like, woody at its base, and covered with numerous narrow leaves on square-sided stems. From early summer to fall flowers bloom on one side of the last 6 in. (15.2 cm) of the stems. Each leaf axil produces from six to fifteen densely packed flowers, giving the plant a very full appearance. The flowers are two-lipped and funnel shaped or tubular, with protruding stamens; the petal color is usually deep bluish violet, occasionally dark pink, and only rarely white. All summer bees, butterflies, and hummingbirds hover around the flowers, busily harvesting their nectar. The whole plant has a peppery, pungent, and sharply minty aroma similar to thyme.

The common name is derived from the Hebrew *ezov,* translated as holy herb because it is mentioned so many times in the Bible, where it is called hyssop. But the plant that corresponds to *ezov* in Israel as well as in the Hebrew Bible and New Testament, is *Origanum syriacum; Hyssopus officinalis* is unknown in the Middle East. The hyssop of the Western world is an ancient herb, used for strewing and to flavor heavy meat dishes; it may also be helpful in digestion. Hyssop's extracted oil has been used in perfumery. Since medieval times it has been used for flavoring liqueurs, most notably Chartreuse. And since the time of Hippocrates hyssop has been used to soothe mucous membranes irritated from coughs and bronchitis, a remedy with which modern pharmacological investigation concurs.

Once a staple of monastery plantings and Tudor knot gardens, hyssop has spent most of recent history relegated to the herb garden despite its ornamental virtues, which include hardiness, low maintenance, disease-resistance, long season of bloom, and most of all, the beauty of its densely packed, blue-violet flowers set off by attractive green foliage. Far easier to maintain than lavender (*Lavandula angustifolia*), but with upright spikes of similar color, it is a plant to be treasured by all serious gardeners. Variations include the very dense and showy, dark pink *Hyssopus officinalis* 'Roseus', the choice white 'Albus', and the later-blooming, dwarf rock hyssop, *H. officinalis* subsp. *aristatus*, that grows to 10 in. (25.4 cm) with color similar to the species.

Hyssop provides a strong vertical accent, stunning in wide swaths with other aromatic, shrubby types, especially the prolific, yellow-flowered santolinas. It can be planted in the foreground of a flower or shrub border, near the edge of a sunny island bed, or lined out along paths, stairways, and entrances. By itself it provides a low to medium hedge that needs little trimming if an informal appearance is desired. Closer trimming for a neater hedge, however, will destroy many flowering stems. Both types, regular and dwarf, grow well among rocks in an exposed situation. For many years, I have grown hyssop by an old boulder to mark the entrance to a mixed planting, combining it with the golden-flowered dyer's chamomile (*Anthemis tinctoria*) and a bright ribbon of deep scarlet nasturtiums.

Hyssop grows readily from seed sown $^1/_4$ in. (0.6 cm) deep in early spring at 70°F (21°C). Plants should be spaced 24 in. (61.0 cm) apart, 12 in. (30.5 cm) for a hedge or the dwarf type, in well-drained, garden soil in a sunny spot. In hot climates where hyssop suffers from high humidity, it will tolerate partial shade. Water well during dry spells or flower production will be sparse. Hyssop survives harsh winters but only if drainage is perfect, which can be assured by incorporating grit into the soil and planting on a slope. Cut back flowering stalks for a second bloom in late summer; clip established plants almost down to the ground in early spring to encourage fresh, vigorous growth. Plants become woody after 3–5 years and should be replaced by division in the spring or fall, or by stem cuttings during the summer. The cultivars and dwarf forms are best grown from roots, since seed-grown plants are variable. Seeds of hyssop are widely available from general seed sources, plants from herb sources, and the cultivars from perennial plant and herb sources.

Hyssop can be used sparingly, like thyme, in cooking. It also is a fine cut and dried flower and is useful in potpourri.

Inula helenium

Asteraceae, Aster Family
Elecampane, horse-heal

Perennial
Site and soil: sun, partial shade; evenly moist
Hardiness: Zones 3–8
Landscape use: accent, bed and border, naturalized
  herb
Height: 4–6 ft. (1.2–1.8 m)
Flower: yellow, fringed sunflower, solitary or in groups
Bloom season: midsummer to late summer

> **An herbaceous plant with a thick root and showy yellow flowers.**
> Christoph Jakob Trew
> *The Herbal of the Count Palatine*

Elecampane is an Old World medicinal herb whose common name is a corruption of the Italian *ala Campania*, a reference to the farming area near ancient Rome where the plant once flourished. In North America, it grows along roadsides and clearings from Ontario and Nova Scotia to North Carolina and Missouri, a reminder of its past role as a healing herb among settlers. Elecampane grows from a long, thick, root—the source of its curative powers—from which sprouts a large basal clump of light green, tapered leaves, as long as 20 in. (50.8 cm) and as wide as 8 in. (20.3 cm), covered with soft down on their undersides. The strong, felty stem, mostly unbranching, is topped by bright yellow flowers, informal versions of the familiar sunflower—elecampane is sometimes called wild sunflower. Many thin, almost spidery, rays are loosely arranged around a brownish disk, each flower head supported by broad, light green bracts, and framed by small, pointed, light green, clasping leaves, the whole flower 2–4 in. (5.1–10.2 cm) across. Although the plant is coarse and rather homely, it is attractive in bloom, and the dried flower or seed head enhances wreaths, swags, and other arrangements.

At one time the United States imported annually 50,000 pounds (22,680 kg) of dried elecampane roots to meet the demand for their use in various medicinal preparations, especially in regard to healing horse ailments (thus the name horse-heal). Since ancient times, elecampane has been associated with soothing coughs and bronchitis and aiding digestion. Research suggests that it has antiseptic properties.

Elecampane was reintroduced to cultivation during the 1930s herb revival and is still featured in herb gardens. Its rough beauty stands out wherever it is planted. It is fine for a wide border where its large clump of leaves is not crowded and where its stalks can rise up, unfettered, in the background among monkshood and other tall types. Featured in the center of an island bed, it complements the flowers and forms of lower-growing clary sage (*Salvia sclarea*) and bergamot (*Monarda*). Elecampane takes readily to naturalizing in a damp, sunny spot with the vivid red cardinal flower (*Lobelia cardinalis*). On drier ground, it creates a pleasing accent when paired with the much shorter and bushy, white-flowered sneezewort (*Achillea ptarmica*). This planting could be expanded to include butterfly weed, chicory, and wild bergamot (*Monarda fistulosa*), making an effective, low-maintenance, wild garden with colorful midsummer bloom.

Sow seeds outside in the fall, where they will germinate in the spring. Transplant seedlings when they are 2–3 in. (5.1–7.6 cm) tall, spacing them 24–48 in. (61.0–121.9 cm) apart. Divide established plants every 3 years or when blooms decrease. Though a mature elecampane root is fearsomely difficult to remove, only a small piece is needed to start new plants. Cut a 2 in. (5.1 cm) piece of root with a bud or eye, and replant it in a weed-free spot, watering well until it shows signs of growth. If you do manage to dig up a significant portion, store it outside away from the sun for a few days and you will soon notice that the surrounding area is permeated with a wonderful, violet scent released from the old, drying root. In cooler regions, elecampane grows best in sun and deep, moist, clay loam. Elsewhere, where the summers are very hot and the soil is dry, provide partial shade to prolong blooming.

Related plants of interest. Several species of *Inula* are now regarded as choice perennials. They deserve more attention for their beautiful flowers and hardiness. All grow well in ordinary garden soil. Seeds or plants of elecampane are widely available from herb sources, but look for the other species from perennial plant nurseries or, on the rare chance, seed and herb sources.

Inula ensifolia 'Compacta', swordleaf inula, is a wonderful dwarf, bushy version of elecampane with bright yellow, daisy-like flowers in low, 8–10 in. (20.3–25.4 cm) mounds, effective in a rockery or up front in a border.

Inula magnifica, fringed elecampane, grows 3–5 ft. (0.9–1.5 m), producing even larger leaves than ordinary elecampane, up to 24 in. (61.0 cm) long by 12 in. (30.5 cm) wide. The flowers are bright yellow and thinly rayed like threads.

Inula orientalis, Caucasian inula, is striking for its bright orange flowers 3–4 in. (7.6–10.2 cm) across with rays slightly quilled and lacy, growing on sturdy, 24 in. (61.0 cm) stems.

Inula royleana, Himalayan elecampane, is a stunning garden flower, growing to 30 in. (76.2 cm) on sturdy, straight stems topped by orange-yellow flowers 5 in. (12.7 cm) across. Try it with white astilbe. This species, along with Caucasian inula, makes especially good cut flowers.

Iris germanica var. *florentina*

Iridaceae, Iris Family
Florentine iris, orris, white flag iris

Perennial
Site and soil: sun; well-drained
Hardiness: Zones 4–10
Landscape use: bed and border, naturalized herb, rock work
Height: 30 in. (76.2 cm)
Flower: silvery white fleur-de-lis on multiflowered stalk
Bloom season: spring to early summer

> **Its pearly iridescent color and delicate . . . fragrance make it one of the most desirable irises.**
>
> Helen Fox
> *Gardening with Herbs for Flavor and Fragrance*

The origins of the Florentine iris are uncertain, but it is probably native to the eastern Mediterranean area, from which it spread to Europe. Sturdy stems sheathed in sword-like, blue-green leaves almost as tall as the flower stalk grow up to 30 in. (76.2 cm) from bumpy rhizomes. Each stalk produces two to five flowers, first appearing as tightly wrapped, grayish buds. These unfurl in late spring to reveal the classic fleur-de-lis design—three upright petals (standards) and three drooping, incurved, lower petals (falls)—in a delicate, silvery white with a light blue or pearl gray cast. The lower petals are delicately veined and spotted with a golden beard of raised hairs that guide insects deep within the flower for nectar. The lightly

Plate 47. *Iris germanica* var. *florentina*, Florentine iris. Spring, VanHevelingen Herb Nursery, Newberg, Oregon. Photo, Andrew VanHevelingen.

scented flower heads are relatively large, 2^1/$_2$–3 in. (6.4–7.6 cm), for the short stature of the plant.

The Florentine iris is named after the Italian city of Florence, where the commercial production of orrisroot began in the thirteenth century. The name "orrisroot" is a corruption of "iris root," the dried and chopped or powdered iris rhizome which has the remarkable ability to preserve the fragrance of other essential oils as well as to impart its own violet-scented fragrance. It is used in perfumery, potpourri, and cosmetic products and is added to soft drinks, candy, and chewing gum. The rhizomes also have medicinal applications, both internal and external, mainly for treating coughs and healing wounds. Some people, however, have an allergic skin reaction to orrisroot. All parts of any iris are considered potentially harmful and should never be ingested.

The distinctive flowers and sturdy, upright form of the Florentine iris show to advantage in a formal herb garden of mounded, silvery gray plants, or in an informal cottage garden where it is allowed to form a drift of pearly white. If left on its own, it will produce large mats useful at the base of shrub roses, which bloom at the same time. An open, sunny rock garden or rockery that simulates its natural and preferred habitat is the best of all planting sites. It combines well with flowers of a darker hue, especially purple-flowered *Iris germanica* (Plate 48).

Like other iris native to the Mediterranean region, the Florentine iris must have plenty of sun, good air circulation, and perfect drainage, under which conditions it will produce the maximum number of flowers per stem. The rhizomes need baking in the summer, so only half bury them in well-drained soil on the lean and alkaline side. Space them 8–12 in. (20.3–30.5 cm) apart, fans pointing outward and the feeder roots spreading downward, in a site protected from heavy wind. Cut the stems after flowering but leave the foliage to ripen. Unless the planting is naturalized, divide the rhizomes every 3 years immediately after the plants have bloomed, selecting and replanting only the fattest. Trim leaves to a 6 in. (15.2 cm) fan in the shape of an inverted V so as not to disturb new leaf growth which forms in the center of the fan.

The rhizomes of Florentine iris can be dug up and prepared as orrisroot to use as a fixative in potpourri. Wash and peel them and put them in the sun to dry or lay them on newspaper near a gentle source of heat. Then

Plate 48. *Iris germanica*. Spring, VanHevelingen Herb Nursery. Photo, Andrew VanHevelingen.

store the roots for 2 years until they develop their characteristic violet scent, after which, chop or grind them into powder. Wear gloves to avoid an allergic reaction.

Related plants of interest. The Florentine iris is mainly available from herb sources. Yellow flag iris is available from perennial plant and herb sources, and the others are available from perennial plant, wildflower, or herb sources.

Iris cristata, crested iris, native to the southeastern United States, is a North American Indian medicinal plant. An early-blooming, dwarf iris, 4–8 in. (10.2–20.3 cm) tall, it bears exquisite, somewhat flattened, light blue flowers, 2$^{1}/_{2}$–3 in. (6.4–7.6 cm) across, with fluted, golden crests on their falls. The flowers are short-lived, but appear in masses when the slender rhizomes are planted in moist, rich soil, in shade or partial shade. With arching green leaves that retain their appeal all season, crested iris looks best in a naturalized, light woodland planting, or in a lightly shaded rock garden or rockery. The white form, 'Alba', is choice. Crested iris is hardy in Zone 3.

Iris pseudacorus, yellow flag iris, is a vigorous Old World medicinal and dye plant that grows to 4 ft. (1.2 m) or taller under optimum conditions, which are moist or wet soil and sun or light shade. In late spring it produces bright yellow, 4 in. (10.2 cm) flower heads with very lightly veined, violet-brown falls on stems heavily sheathed in sword-like foliage as high or higher than the flowers. Double forms, lacking yellow flag's simple and appealing character, are available. It does very well in low, wet spots, either alone or combined with blue flag iris. It can also be grown in a garden or as a single accent, since its leaves remain attractive over a long period. It is hardy in Zone 4.

Iris versicolor, blue flag iris, is native to the northeastern United States and is also a North American Indian medicinal herb. Preparations from its roots have been used to treat a number of ailments, such as liver and gall bladder disorders and skin diseases. Even more than yellow flag, it prefers a wet habitat. It blooms a little earlier but overlaps with yellow flag so the two make a spectacular splash when combined in a bog garden. Blue flag's flowers are half the size of yellow flag's but beautiful, nevertheless—slender, delicate, violet-blue, sometimes red-violet petals are streaked with gold and white and overlaid with darker veins. It also grows in sun or partial shade and is hardy in Zone 2. Since the roots are considered poisonous, it is advisable to wear gloves and wash your hands after handling them. The large seed pods of blue flag iris are decorative in winter bouquets.

Lamium maculatum

The little creeping mint of old-fashioned gardens.
Minnie Watson Kamm
Old-time Herbs

Lamiaceae, Mint Family
Spotted dead nettle, cobbler's bench, false salvia

Perennial
Site and soil: sun, partial shade, shade; well-drained, evenly moist
Hardiness: Zones 4–9
Landscape use: bed and border, ground cover, naturalized herb
Height: 6–18 in. (15.2–45.7 cm)
Flower: violet-purple, pink, white, hooded in whorl
Bloom season: spring to late summer

Dead nettle is a daunting name to describe a desirable plant, one of fifty species mostly native to Asia and Europe. "Dead" here means harmless, having no ability to sting as does the real stinging nettle, *Urtica dioica*, with sharp hairs on its leaves. In contrast, spotted dead nettle has soft, almost heart-shaped leaves spotted white along the mid-rib and creeping stems that bear whorls of small, long-lasting flowers in late spring. These are so arranged that the upper lip arches over the three-lobed lower lip like a hood or a turtle's head. One stem can spread out as far as 4–5 ft. (1.2–1.5 m) from the original plant. False salvia aptly describes the plant's showy flowers, which appear especially large arising from a low mat of foliage.

The astringent, tannin-rich spotted dead nettle belongs to a group of plants, like bugle (*Ajuga*) and self-heal (*Prunella vulgaris*), once highly regarded for their ability to staunch bleeding and heal wounds, bruises, and burns. Although no longer needed as an herb, it is a popular ground cover, valued for its summer-long flowers and its ability to thrive in the most difficult of all sites, dry shade. *Lamium maculatum* 'Beacon Silver' is an older cultivar with green leaves overlaid with a shimmering, white sheen and whorls of purplish pink flowers; 'Pink Pewter' is an improved form with silvery gray, gray-edged leaves and clear pink flowers; the popular 'White Nancy' (Plate 49) with marbled leaves, bears an abundance of long-lasting, clean, white flowers and is stunning in a hanging basket; and 'Chequers', also with marbled leaves, has deep pink flowers.

With such an amazing capacity to roam, albeit slowly in my experience, it is an invaluable ground cover, particularly for dry shady places where nothing else will succeed. It can be grown as a wide, weed-smothering accent in front of an informal planting, as long as its entry into the garden itself is barred. For boundaries, use old truck tire rims, cut in half and sunk into the ground; here the marbled and striped leaves of two different forms can grow side by side, creating striking semicircular patterns. Try *L. maculatum* 'Beacon Silver' at the base of a clove currant bush (*Ribes odoratum*) for great effect. Any type makes a good cover for the withering leaves

Plate 49. *Lamium maculatum* 'White Nancy', spotted dead nettle. Early summer, perennial garden, Graymalkin Farm. Photo, Brian Oke and Gisèle Quesnel.

of spring-flowering bulbs. The slower-growing cultivars can be planted in the garden proper. Wherever it is grown, dead nettle is an asset in the landscape.

Space plants 6–12 in. (15.2–30.5 cm) apart in ordinary garden soil, in sun, partial shade, or shade. Dead nettle does well in the sun if the soil is moist; it will grow in the shade in moist or dry soil. In warmer regions, give plants some shade for best foliage appearance and longer flowering. Propagate by division in the early spring or early fall; plants also self-sow, but do not encourage the cultivars to do so. If the planting looks tired in midsummer, mow it back for a second, refreshed bloom.

Related plants of interest. Dead nettle and yellow archangel are available from perennial plant and herb sources.

Lamium galeobdolon, yellow archangel, is a variable dead nettle with splotched leaves, yellow flowers, and the same herbal applications as spotted dead nettle. There are two cultivars of interest. 'Hermann's Pride', silver archangel, is a later-blooming type to 10 in. (25.4 cm), and since it is non-creeping, it can be planted directly in a garden where it forms a mound of foliage and flowers; its leaves are silvery with green veins and its flowers are yellow. The quickly spreading 'Variegatum', to 14 in. (35.6 cm) with variegated leaves and yellow flowers, blooms in late spring. It can be used as a vigorous cover under trees, but will overrun everything in its wake, so plant it and tend it with care.

Lavandula angustifolia

Lamiaceae, Mint Family
English lavender, hardy lavender, true lavender

Perennial, shrub
Site and soil: sun; sharply drained, well-drained
Hardiness: Zones 4–10
Landscape use: accent, bed and border, edge and
  hedge, rock work
Height: 18–36 in. (45.7–91.4 cm)
Flower: lavender, purple-violet, dark purple,
  tubular in whorl
Bloom season: early summer to midsummer

> **Lavenders are truly the "sweet herbs" among the simples, and they belong not to the herb garden alone.**
>
> Helen Noyes Webster
> "Lavenders"
> *The American Herb Grower*

Called English lavender because of its popularity in English gardens and for the English production of its perfume, this hardiest species is native to the western Mediterranean, probably introduced to northern Europe by the Romans. A shrubby plant with square branches woody at their base, English lavender may reach 4 ft. (1.2 m) high and almost as wide under optimum conditions, but it usually grows 24–36 in. (61.0–91.4 cm) in most gardens. Stems are clothed with slender, down-covered leaves, gray-green in their early growth and medium green, but still cast with gray, in maturity. In early to midsummer the small, lavender, purple, or violet flowers (rarely pale pink or pure white) are carried in dense whorls of six to ten flowers in a ring on straight, broom-like spikes 2–24 in. (5.1–62.2 cm) long, depending on growing conditions.

Lavender's penetrating aroma, arising from the entire plant, better known than the plant itself, is complex. Different, opposing notes compose the scent; a sweetness like heliotrope and jasmine and a sharpness like balsam and rosemary create a stimulating, invigorating, refreshing, and at the same time, tranquilizing effect. The genus name is derived from the Latin *lavare*, to wash, from the Greek and Roman tradition of adding lavender scent to bath water. Hardy lavender produces the finest, most desirable essential oil, used for centuries in perfumes, toiletries, and potpourri. It was also used medicinally as an antiseptic with other herbs in the

Plate 50. *Lavandula angustifolia*, lavender, and *Thymus praecox* subsp. *arcticus*, creeping thyme (See p. 333, and Plate 5, p. 43). The lavender was grown from collected seed and the creeping thyme was self-sown, producing flowers from light pink, here, to dark

pink. Midsummer, Country Lane Herbs and Dried Flowers. Photo, Brian Oke and Gisèle Quesnel.

once popular palsy drops for treating headaches, insomnia, and nervous digestion. The American herbalist Helen Webster writing in 1947 remembered having to drink steaming cups of lavender tea to treat a cold: "It was sugary and pink and tasted just the way lavender flowers smell."

The inevitable attention to English lavender's fabled fragrance should not obscure the fact that it is also a very desirable garden plant for general landscaping. The hardy lavenders are neat in habit, are drought resistant, have evergreen leaves and masses of beautiful flowers, and are pretty even in bud.

English lavender survives winter temperatures of −30°F (−34°C) without winter protection if the site is sunny with perfect drainage. I have seen decades-old plantings of the species growing on their own in northern Vermont, where winter temperatures may plunge to −35°F (−37°C). A good snow cover evidently carried the plants over many winters. Equally hardy, perhaps even more so because of their smaller size, are two reliable cultivars excellent for hedging: *Lavandula angustifolia* 'Hidcote'—a slow-growing lavender with beautiful, deep purple-blue flowers, blackish violet in bud, 18–20 in. (45.7–50.8 cm) tall with narrow, silvery leaves—and 'Munstead' (Plate 51), developed by Gertrude Jekyll, 12–18 in. (30.5–45.7 cm) tall, very early- and long-blooming with closely packed, true lavender flowers over compact mounds of light green leaves.

Among the less hardy (Zone 5 or 6) is *Lavandula angustifolia* 'Twickel Purple', to 18 in. (45.7 cm), which blooms just after 'Munstead' with long, fan-like spikes of soft purple flowers above a mound of gray-green leaves. The rare, white 'Alba', grown in England since the seventeenth century, is vigorous like the species with long spikes of pure white flowers and soft, silvery gray foliage; 'Nana Alba', dwarf and compact in 6 to 12 in. (15.2–30.5 cm), is similar in flower and leaf. Both these white lavenders need winter protection. One of the best hardy cultivars with recurrent bloom is 'Irene Doyle', which grows to 18 in. (45.7 cm) with lavender-blue flowers, greenish lavender in bud. It blooms from June through July with strong reblooming in the fall and is hardy in Zone 5 or 6.

Lavandula angustifolia 'Lady' is a unique lavender for it blooms the first year from seed. This characteristic is a blessing for gardeners who cannot winter lavender in the ground, either because young plants do not attain the maturity needed to withstand freezing temperatures or because of soil conditions. A 1994 All-America Selection, 'Lady' was introduced in the spring of that year. First trying seeds of 'Lady' in Nova Scotia, I was very skeptical of its performance in cool damp ground where summers are short and cool, but it astonished me with its rapid growth, very unusual in lavenders. It did, indeed, bloom the first season from seed, and has proved reliably hardy in the ground, too. 'Lady' is compact with a 10 in. (25.4 cm) mound of silvery green foliage and 6 in. (15.2 cm), dark blue flower spikes above.

Several lavenders grown together reward the landscape with a long season of bloom, from early June through the fall. In my daughter's upstate New York garden (Zone 4) various forms of English lavender enhance a series of island beds in full sun. The house and a retaining wall create a

Plate 51. *Lavandula angustifolia* 'Munstead', lavender. Early summer, Cricket Hill Herb Farm, Rowley, Massachusetts. Photo, Judy Kehs.

protective microclimate where Mediterranean plants thrive in otherwise inhospitable conditions. The taller lavenders are strong accents among wide mounds of yellow button santolinas; *L. angustifolia* 'Munstead' is used throughout as a low-growing edge for mixed-herb or -flower plantings. Lavenders also belong with roses, especially the soft pink, old roses which bloom at the same time. Try growing them together in a wide raised bed where each can grow to its fullest extent without interfering with the other. I grow 'Lady' in a sheltered, corner garden, raised above ground level by a low, stone wall. Here it enjoys the same conditions as lemon thyme (*Thymus* ×*citriodora*) and dwarf soapwort (*Saponaria ocymoides*). Lavenders are always healthy among rocks or near stone walls, where they benefit from captured heat and moisture. Taller lavenders are handsome in a shrub foundation; all types make excellent hedges to outline paths or divide garden spaces, especially useful in formal designs. To protect less hardy kinds from winter damage, plant them near buildings or shrubs, or on elevated ground away from frost pockets. Or grow them in containers, either sunk in the ground or grouped near entryways, on decks, and on patios. 'Nana Alba' is especially suited to container culture.

Lavenders do not come true from seed, but variations may be desirable. Start plants indoors 10–12 weeks before the last frost. One is often advised to prechill seeds for at least 2 weeks before sowing but I have not found this procedure necessary. Supply bottom heat and barely cover seeds at 70°F (21°C) to hasten germination, which could occur in one week or less. Plant seedlings outside only when the ground has warmed, spacing plants 24 in. (61.5 cm) apart all around, or 12–18 in. (30.5–45.7 cm) apart for a hedge. They must have full sun and sharply drained or well-drained, loose, gritty, neutral soil. Overrich soil tends to encourage leaf growth at the expense of flower production.

Cut off buds that form on first year plants to encourage strong root growth. On mature plants, cut back spent flower stalks but not severely, just to give plants a trim look. Serious pruning should be done in early spring, when new growth at the base is strong, to maintain the plant's shape and to stimulate the production of flower spikes. Never cut below new growth or you may weaken the plant as well as reduce flowering. Mature plants can be divided if their roots are carefully separated and replanted. Tip cuttings, taken early in the season before blooming, are the fastest way to make new plants. Cut 3 in. (7.6 cm) from the tips of the most vigorous growth and root the cuttings in moist sand and damp peat moss or your favorite medium using rooting hormone powder. Sometimes lavenders can be left in place for many years, but with age they usually become a dense mass of woody stems with few blooms and some dead patches. It is always best to propagate them every few years.

Harvest flowers for potpourri when they are just beginning to open. Cut spikes in midday, bunch them, and hang them in an airy room away from bright light—they will dry quickly. Use the whole spikes in dried bouquets, rub off the flowers for potpourri, and break up the flowering stalks for use in sachets. Lavender is one of the herbs with thyme, fennel, basil, and savory in the salt-free blend known as Herbes de Provence used for flavoring meat, fish, salads, sauces, and egg dishes, or as I use it in the following recipe for Honor's herbed potatoes:

Honor's Herbed Potatoes

Cut up the desired amount of peeled, raw potatoes in bite-size pieces, coat them with olive oil, and sprinkle them liberally with Herbes de Provence. Bake the potatoes at 375°F (190°C) for 30 to 40 minutes or until golden brown. The herbs will be baked into the potato crust.

Related plants of interest. Seeds of the species English lavender, as well as *Lavandula angustifolia* 'Hidcote', 'Lady', and 'Munstead' are available from general seed sources. Plants of all the lavenders are available from perennial plant sources, but the widest selection is from herb sources.

Lavandula ×*intermedia*, lavandin, the French name, is the sterile hybrid produced from crossing English lavender with spike lavender (*L. latifolia*). It has been grown for centuries in France for the production of oil. As a garden plant it performs better in warmer regions where English lavender may suffer fungus infections. Lavandin and its cultivars are vigorous with spikes longer than either parent and compact foliage that looks good all season. 'Grosso' bears an abundance of long, fat spikes of deep violet flowers, heavily scented. In plantsman Thomas DeBaggio's Zone 7 garden the flower spikes, which he describes as voluptuous, reach 3 ft. (0.9 m) and bloom in late June and early July, later in Zone 6 where they reach 24 in. (61.0 cm). Give lavandin winter protection in areas colder than Zone 6.

Lavandula stoechas (Plate 52), Spanish or French lavender, the hardiest

(Zone 7) of the tender lavenders, 24–36 in. (61.0–91.4 cm) tall, is well worth growing as a pot plant in colder zones where it may grow to 18 in. (45.7 cm). The flowers, above attractive silvery leaves, are different from all other lavenders with their oblong, short heads covered by tiny, purple flowers whose petals just show from tightly packed, rosy bracts. As if to make up for its modest form, the flower head is topped by two or three flamboyant, vivid purple plumes, as long as 1 1/2 in. (3.8 cm). The scent is slightly camphorous, and the plant has been an important medicinal. The species name is derived from the ancient name for a group of islands off the French coast where this lavender flourishes. I first saw Spanish lavender growing as a roadside weed in Israel and was quite struck by its beauty. With the Hebrew name *ezov kokhli*, it belongs to a small group of aromatic plants regarded as false hyssops in the Talmud. (See *Thymbra spicata* for more on hyssops and za'atar plants.)

Plate 52. *Lavandula stoechas*, Spanish lavender, wild. Late winter to early spring, Israel. Elsewhere, Spanish lavender blooms from summer to fall in the ground or in containers. Photo, Avinoam Danin.

Lobelia cardinalis

Campanulaceae, Bluebell Family
Cardinal flower, Indian pink

Perennial
Site and soil: sun, partial shade; evenly moist, boggy
Hardiness: Zones 4–9
Landscape use: accent, bed and border, container, naturalized herb
Height: 2–5 ft. (0.6–1.5 cm)
Flower: scarlet, tubular in elongated cluster on terminal spike
Bloom season: midsummer to late summer

> **America's favorite.**
> Roger Torey Peterson
> *A Field Guide to Wildflowers*

Roger Torey Peterson's brief accolade sums up the cardinal flower's popularity as a wildflower. It grows in wet meadows, along streams, and in swamps from southern Ontario to New Brunswick and south to Florida. Its slender flower spikes, considered to be among the most brightly colored in nature, are a vivid splash in the uncultivated landscape.

The cardinal flower's unbranching stems grow up from a basal rosette of irregularly toothed, lance-shaped leaves. These are prominent when the plant is dormant, but, as if to acknowledge the flowers' dominance, the leaves are often absent when the cardinal flower comes in bloom in late midsummer. The two-lipped flowers are 1½ in. (3.8 cm) long, composed of five petals—two upper petals through which the glistening white stamens protrude, and three spreading, lower ones. The tubular, scarlet flowers are mostly pollinated by hummingbirds, since other insects find it difficult to reach the pollen. The juice of the plant is considered poisonous.

North American Indians, and later the settlers, used the cardinal flower interchangeably with great lobelia, *Lobelia siphilitica*, to treat syphilis, fevers, stomach complaints, coughs, and hard-to-heal sores, although it was not considered as effective as the latter plant. By the eighteenth century it was in general use, but today both plants are regarded solely as ornamentals. Cardinal flower cultivars include the deep scarlet *L. cardinalis* 'Bees' Flame', the pinkish 'Rosea', the rare white 'Alba' or 'Gladys Lindley', and the bicolored white and coral 'Janet French'.

Despite its natural habitat, cardinal flower does not require a bog to induce its beauty, just a damp spot. There, it will not only grow well, but look stunning when combined with New England aster (*Aster novae-ang-liae*) and the dainty nodding onion (*Allium cernuum*), both of which bloom at the same time; later, its flaming flowers, which are also excellent for bouquets, will provide a vivid contrast to goldenrods (*Solidago*) and the muted Joe Pye weed (*Eupatorium maculatum*). Singly or in small groups, it can be used as a bright accent in the landscape when planted near shrubs or trees or even in a large tub set on a patio or wherever you will be able to enjoy hummingbird visits. The cardinal flower is a focal point in a raised bed cut into an expanse of green lawn. In the border try pairing it with a bushy rudbeckia.

Grow the cultivars from plants, but for the species, stratify seeds for 2 months, either indoors in the refrigerator or outdoors planted in a cold frame. Germination occurs in one week at 70° F (21° C) if seeds are sown on the surface of the soil and only lightly pressed into the sowing medium. Transplant seedlings in the late spring, spaced 8–10 in. (20.3–25.4 cm) apart, in moist, even submerged soil, or ordinary garden soil that is not allowed to dry out. Place them where they will receive some afternoon shade, though in cooler regions full sun is acceptable. Some plants may blossom the first year; flowering can be extended well into the fall by cutting back the spent flowering stems, which will encourage more flowers to form on side shoots. The cardinal flower is a short-lived perennial that propagates itself by self-sowing. This is fine in an informal or naturalized setting, but in a more formal garden that looks unkindly on indiscriminate seedlings, it is advisable to establish new plantings by dividing basal offshoots from the mother plant in the spring or fall. Replant them at once and keep them well-watered. Winter protection is advisable.

Related plants of interest. Seeds and plants of the cardinal flower are widely available, especially from wildflower sources. The cultivars are available from perennial plant and specialty nurseries, but the Compliment Hybrids are available from general seed sources.

Lobelia Compliment Hybrids are a vigorous, tetraploid, F_1 hybrid series growing on strong stems and blooming the first season from seed. All under 3 ft. (0.9 m), the mix includes blue-purple, deep red, and scarlet, the last sometimes sold separately. They are hardy in Zone 5 and need winter protection in colder zones.

Lobelia siphilitica

Campanulaceae, Bluebell Family
Great lobelia, blue cardinal flower

Perennial
Site and soil: sun, partial shade; evenly moist
Hardiness: Zones 4–9
Landscape use: bed and border, naturalized herb
Height: 3 ft. (0.9 m)
Flower: blue, tubular in elongated cluster on terminal
  spike
Bloom season: late summer to fall

> I love to grow this lobelia, partly as a challenge, but more essentially as a plant which will give my late summer borders a blue look.
>
> Rosemary Verey
> "My Plant of the Year"
> *The Hardy Plant*

A surprising number of our native flowers bloom in the late summer, brightening woods, meadows, and wetlands. Great lobelia, a later-blooming, blue counterpart to the cardinal flower, grows in the same habitat, favoring swamps, ditches, and wet places from western New England to Minnesota. Its lance-shaped leaves are more rounded at their tips, and the flowers—of varied blues, from clear to purplish, and occasionally white—are not quite the same as the red lobelia. Although both plants bear long, open, tubular flowers, the stamen tube of great lobelia is hidden within its upright top petals, while its lower ones are broader and striped with white. The flowers of both lobelias grow in showy, 6–8 in. (15.2–20.3 cm) terminal spikes.

The native lobelias have a long history of use among the North American Indians. Great lobelia's species name is derived from its former use to treat syphilis, but this is only one of several applications: its leaves were smoked as a treatment for asthma and bronchial ailments and in a poultice they were applied to heal persistent sores. The plant is considered poisonous, however, from the strong alkaloids in its roots and should never be ingested in any form.

The two lobelias, red and blue, have naturally crossed to produce *Lobelia* ×*gerardii* 'Vedrariensis', a most beautiful hybrid with rich purple flower spikes that is more adaptable to dry growing conditions. The natural variant, *L. siphilitica* 'Alba' is reported to be less hardy than the blue

185

form. These plants make longer lasting cut flowers, too, though all great lobelias are good in bouquets.

Great lobelia has always had a following among discerning gardeners for its late color, upright form, and longevity. Its blue spikes are choice for bed or border, especially the hard-to-find, sparklingly clear blue. Growers have discovered that it tolerates drier conditions far better than its red counterpart and is longer-lived. The purple-flowered hybrid is especially tolerant of drier soil. In a tame setting, its late-blooming flower spikes combine well with the lower, rounded forms of late-blooming sedums. Great lobelia is especially suited to a cultivated or naturalized planting near a stream or pool with cardinal flower, or in drier soil with rudbeckias, goldenrods (*Solidago*), and Joe Pye weed (*Eupatorium maculatum*). When choosing a site, bear in mind that one of great lobelia's virtues is its ability to grow, even thrive, in ground that may change from wet in spring to dry later in the season.

Great lobelia is grown the same way as the red cardinal flower. Stratify seeds for 2 months, either indoors in the refrigerator or outdoors in a cold frame; the tiny seeds should be sown on top of and lightly pressed into the medium's surface, where they should germinate in about one week. Outdoors, space seedlings 8–10 in. (20.3–25.4 cm) apart in moist or ordinary garden soil in partial shade; great lobelia will take more sun in accordance with more moist soil and more shade in accordance with drier soil. Cut back spent flower stems, since like the cardinal flower this plant self-sows prolifically. Propagate by making divisions of the basal offshoots in the spring or the fall; use this method to save desired colors, especially true blue or white. Great lobelia is available as seed from general and wildflower seed sources, and plants are mostly available from perennial plant nurseries and a few herb sources.

Lysimachia nummularia

Primulaceae, Primrose Family
Creeping Jenny, meadow runnagates, moneywort, string-of-sovereigns

Perennial
Site and soil: sun, partial shade, shade; moist
Hardiness: Zones 3–10
Landscape use: container, ground cover, naturalized
  herb, rock work
Height: 2 in. (5.1 cm)
Flower: bright yellow, solitary cup
Bloom season: early summer to midsummer

> Moneywort . . . is pretty but prudently left out of the garden.
> H. Lincoln Foster
> *Rock Gardening*

Creeping Jenny, introduced to North America from Europe, grows wild from Newfoundland to Georgia and west to the Pacific coast, an extraordinary range for such a diminutive herb. It is an amazing creeping plant with single stems extending for 5 ft. (1.5 m) by means of rooting stolons, which negate the need to produce seed. Shiny, rounded, coinlike leaves grow in pairs along the stems, creating a tight, low-to-the-ground, spreading carpet of bright green foliage. By early summer golden yellow flowers—five deeply cut petals joined at their base to form a cup—develop in the leaf axils, blooming in sheets for over a month.

In the sixteenth century John Gerard maintained that there was not a better wound-healing herb than creeping Jenny. From medieval times it was widely used externally in ointments and compresses to heal sores, and taken internally, when boiled with wine or honey, to alleviate whooping cough. It was also recognized as an antiscorbutic. Its many folk names preserve its rampant growth, coinlike leaves, and unique flowers.

The gardening historian Ann Leighton includes it among those herbs planted in New England by seventeenth-century settlers. By the nineteenth century, although it was no longer needed for its herbal properties, it was grown for its ability to easily cover and brighten damp places. Old plantings are often found around abandoned homesteads. Nowadays, it is largely neglected, although its landscaping virtues have not changed—it

187

still speedily covers the ground as it was meant to do. The golden-leaved variant *Lysimachia nummularia* 'Aurea' is especially bright, its golden cups lavishly blooming in masses above a ruffled mat of golden foliage.

As H. Lincoln Foster observed, moneywort is not a garden plant, but it and the choice 'Aurea' are extremely useful as ground covers to smother weeds around the base of shrubs and trees. Their golden sheets of bloom transform an old tree stump into a positive landscape feature or beautifully frame grouped containers, where it may be difficult to mow closely, and moneywort itself is attractive trailing over the sides of containers. Moneywort forms a barrier to weeds or grass by stone walks and walls and shows itself off spilling over rocks or growing in rock crevices. It grows in and around pavings, obliterating weeds, and unlike other plants suggested for this job, it will grow in damp conditions anywhere, in full sun or full shade. 'Aurea' is perfect for shady spots, lighting up dull areas. Both kinds are easily naturalized near streams or ponds.

Once you have obtained a root, creeping Jenny's future is assured. Plant it in weed free, moisture retentive ground and let it go. Periodically pinch off the tips of the trailing stems to encourage leafy growth. Control its spread by mowing throughout the summer.

Related plants of interest. Creeping Jenny, *Lysimachia nummularia* 'Aurea', and *L. japonica* var. *minutissima* are available from specialty plant nurseries.

Lysimachia japonica is a miniature version of creeping Jenny, 1 in. (2.5 cm) tall with the same bright yellow flowers over a flat mat of bright green foliage. It is a neater, less rampant plant suitable for rock gardens or around rocks anywhere in the landscape where the soil is moist. *Lysimachia japonica* var. *minutissima*, the form usually offered, is especially choice for its smaller leaves and larger flowers (or so they seem in relation to the foliage). This is the plant for rock crevices; both versions are hardy in Zone 3.

Malva sylvestris

Malvaceae, Mallow Family
Common mallow, blue mallow, cheeses, high mallow

Annual, biennial, perennial
Site and soil: sun, partial shade; well-drained
Hardiness: Zones 4–9
Landscape use: accent, bed and border, naturalized herb
Height: 3–6 ft. (0.9–1.8 m)
Flower: mauve, creamy pink, rose-purple bell in cluster
Bloom season: early summer to fall

> **The etched lines on the sheen of the petal are exquisite.**
> Kay Sanecki
> *The Complete Book of Herbs*

The Eurasian common mallow, the true mallow, has naturalized itself along roadsides in the United States. It should not be confused with the rampant weed of the same genus, *Malva neglecta*, low mallow, which grows in disturbed ground. An annual, biennial, or even short-lived perennial in warm climates, the strong, round stalks and their side branches grow from a long fleshy taproot characteristic of mallows. The leaves are broad, crinkly, heart- or ivy-shaped, and numerous. The five-petaled delicate flowers —1 1/2 in. (3.8 cm) wide with gracefully waved, narrow petals, pink to purplish mauve with dark purple veining—are among the most beautiful of any in the mallow family, and although small by comparison with others, they are produced in abundance. Growing from leaf axils, they appear above them in showy clusters, except for those near the bottom of the stalk that are nearly hidden by a profusion of foliage. The pink-tipped buds are jammed together, but do not open all at once, thus promising a long season of bloom from early summer until late fall.

As a familiar wildflower of the English countryside, the common mallow has accumulated many folk names associated with its round, flat fruits, like little cheeses or buttons. All parts of the plant have soothing properties based on their mucilaginous character. The leaves and roots have been used for teas to alleviate coughs and bronchitis; external poultices were used to treat inflammations and skin irritations. In times of famine, the evergreen leaves were a reliable source of nourishment. Even its seeds, sweet and nut-like in their early development, are edible. Mallows are considered innocents because all parts are edible, but large doses are laxative. All mallows provide plentiful pollen and nectar for bees.

The cultivar *Malva sylvestris* 'Zebrina' (Plate 53), zebrina mallow, an improvement over the rangy wildflower, is more compact with larger flowers and smaller leaves that obscure none of the flowers. On the contrary, the stems are merely a vehicle for the all-season display of creamy pink flowers with broad petals that just overlap to form a bell, each one enhanced by purple-black veining that spreads like a radiating flame from the center of the bloom. At different seasons, in different lights, the flowers seem to change color, from nearly white to rosy pink. They begin to open when the plant is less than 12 in. (30.5 cm) tall, and continue as the stalk grows until the whole plant, like a diminutive hollyhock, is smothered in upturned bells. These continue to open each morning, even when the leaves are covered with snow, until sometime in November or December. *Malva sylvestris* subsp. *mauritiana*, tree mallow, is a taller plant to 6 ft. (1.8 m). Blooming a little later, it bears larger, glossy flowers, $2^1/_2$–3 in. (6.4–7.6 cm) wide, rose-purple to magenta, purple veined, and loosely double like an old-fashioned rose. The cultivar *M. sylvestris* subsp. *mauritiana* 'Bibor Felho' is less rangy with the large flowers held above the leaves. Though

Plate 53. *Malva sylvestris* 'Zebrina', zebrina mallow. Midsummer, Gardner farm. Photo, Alan Dorey.

the beautiful mallows are not widely grown, they are virtually maintenance and disease free, resistant to drought, and tolerant of both cold and
hot growing conditions, producing phenomenal flowers over a very long
season.

All the mallows are attractive when massed against a fence, wall, house,
or structure of any kind where they show off their flowers and gain some
protection from the wind. *Malva sylvestris* 'Zebrina' is tame enough to grow
in the flower border. I plant seedlings in the sun to cover up bare spots left
by the oriental poppy (*Papaver orientale*) and in partial shade to fill in after bleeding heart (*Dicentra spectabilis*). When grown in a tub, the plant is
dwarfed 24–30 in. (61.0–76.2 cm). The tree mallow is an excellent background plant, either against a fence or in a border. The common mallow
lends itself to naturalizing in a semiwild garden or on a dry, barren piece
of ground where it will produce an abundance of bloom.

For early bloom, sow seeds indoors 6–8 weeks before the last frost, to
germinate in 15 to 21 days at 70°F (21°C). Plant seedlings outside in
warm, well-drained, not overly rich soil, spacing plants 12–18 in. (30.5–
45.6 cm) apart, or more for tree mallow, in sun or partial shade. Or sow
seeds outside when the soil has warmed. Plants can only be moved before
their long taproots have developed. Plantlets that form at the base of mature plants can be removed and replanted. The mallows will self-sow prolifically from year to year. To keep strains pure propagate them by stem
cuttings in the spring or sow fresh seeds. In rich soil mallows will need
staking. *Malva sylvestris* 'Zebrina' can be wintered in a cool greenhouse
where it will bloom all winter, then bloom again when replanted outside.

For use in the household, mallow flowers are a sweet and decorative
garnish for desserts. Press them lightly into jellies, mousses, or puddings
made with any purple-black fruits, for best effect, such as blueberries,
blackberries, or black currants, or arrange the flowers on a frosted cake. All
mallow flowers press well and are highly prized in floral crafts.

Related plants of interest. Seeds or plants of common mallow are available from herb sources; seeds of *Malva sylvestris* 'Zebrina' are available
from general seed sources. Seeds or plants of poppy mallow are hard to
find—look for them in general and wildflower seed sources and specialty
plant nurseries. Seeds or plants of musk mallow and hollyhock mallow
are available from some general seed and perennial plant sources.

Callirhoe involucrata, poppy mallow, is a native flower that grows on dry prairies and grasslands in the Midwest and Southwest. It was once widely used by the Dakota Indians, whose name for it is "the smoke-treatment medicine," a reference to its use as a soothing vaporizer for bronchial congestion when smoke from its burned roots was inhaled. Only 6–12 in. (15.2–30.5 cm) tall, it is firmly anchored to the ground by its taproot, from which grow thin, sturdy stems bearing silky, chalice-shaped flowers

Plate 54. *Malva moschata*, musk mallow, and *Papaver somniferum*, opium poppy. Midsummer, Country Lane Herbs and Dried Flowers. Original pink poppies have self-sown to produce double, single, and fringed variants. Photo, Brian Oke and Gisèle Quesnel.

2¹/₂ in. (6.4 cm) wide, wine-purple with a white center. A sprawling, trailing plant, it spreads in a 24 in. (61.0 cm) wide mat covered with flowers from midsummer to fall. The poppy mallow needs perfect drainage in light, sandy soil on the acid side. Seeds sown in the spring will bring flowering plants late the first summer that will return to bloom in early summer the following year. Once established, the plant self-sows. When dividing, plant the root crown at soil level (as for strawberry plants) to discourage root rot. It is best grown on a dry sunny bank, in a rockery, or in the crevice of a dry wall.

Malva alcea 'Fastigiata', hollyhock mallow, is very similar to musk mallow but more robust, growing to 3 ft. (0.9 m) and spreading as wide, like a bush. It is best used as a background or corner planting in a border, or a shrubby accent outside the garden. Covered all summer with medium pink, glistening bells from head to toe, it will call attention to itself wherever it is grown. It, too, can be raised from seeds sown outdoors in the fall, blooming the following summer.

Malva moschata (Plate 54), musk mallow, to 24 in. (61.0 cm), is a hardy perennial native to Europe and naturalized in neglected fields throughout North America. Its intricately cut, green leaves are soft and velvety, exud-

Plate 55. *Malva moschata* 'Alba', musk mallow. Midsummer, Gardner farm. White variant was grown from a pasture weed. Photo, Alan Dorey.

193

ing a musky fragrance—*moschata* means musk-scented. Its loose, bell flowers, clustered mainly at the top of the plant, may be pure white ('Alba', Plate 55), light pink, or soft rose-mauve ('Rosea'), with wavy-edged, delicately-veined, shimmering petals. It has properties similar to the common mallow and was used as a substitute for the same medicinal applications; a tincture from the leaves is used for bee stings. Musk mallow is a grand plant for beds or borders. Its bushy form complements vertical spikes, its soft colors blend with bright reds and strong purples or harmonize with pastels and gray-leaved artemisias. New flower buds form at the base of the plant even before the old flowers are spent, so plants are in perpetual bloom all summer. It can be raised from seeds sown outdoors in the fall; plants bloom the following summer.

Matricaria recutita

> One tablespoonful to be taken at bed time.
>
> Beatrix Potter
> *The Tale of Peter Rabbit*

Asteraceae, Aster Family
German chamomile

Annual
Site and soil: sun; well-drained
Landscape use: bed and border, edge and hedge, ground
    cover, naturalized herb, rock work
Height: 24–30 in. (61.0–76.2 cm)
Flower: white and yellow, small, daisy-like in cluster
Bloom season: early summer to midsummer

German chamomile, originating in Europe and western Asia, is a branching plant with feathery, rather shiny leaves on erect stems which sprawl over time. The small, daisy-like flowers, $1/2$–1 in. (1.3–2.5 cm) across, consist of a hollow, yellow center, becoming conical as it matures, ringed by numerous white petals. From early summer to frost the flowers are produced in profusion. The common name is derived from the Greek *chamos* for ground, and *melos*, for apple, which accurately describes the plant's low-growing habit and the flowers' apple scent, which grows stronger when they are dried. Because of its widespread herbal use in Germany, chamomile came to be associated with that country.

Plate 56. *Matricaria recutita,* German chamomile. Early summer, Gardner farm. It blooms all summer, when some flowers are harvested for tea. Photo, Alan Dorey.

German chamomile should not be confused with the very similar Roman chamomile, *Chamaemelum nobile*, a perennial of milder-climate distribution. When the double-flowered form of Roman chamomile, *C. nobile* 'Flore Pleno', was introduced to western Europe from Spain, it temporarily supplanted German chamomile as the healing herb of choice. Having similar properties, both herbs were used to treat the same ailments: fevers, digestive problems, headaches, skin inflammations, and insomnia. The most famous herbal application concerns the case of Peter Rabbit, whose mother gave him a stiff dose of German chamomile tea. Its use as a general sedative, especially for colicky children, is preserved in the 1954 edition of *The New Settlement Cookbook*. Today, German chamomile is raised as a field crop in Europe, harvested two or three times a season to meet the demand for its medicinal use. An improved strain from Germany, *Matricaria recutita* 'Bodegold', developed for commercial production, is sturdier and more erect, with larger flowers and greater medicinal properties.

In the landscape, German chamomile excels at the corners or near the edges of raised beds, where its bloom-laden, lax stems spill over and soften sharp edges. Because of its drought resistance, it grows well on exposed sunny banks or among rocks, where it revels in the sun and thin soil. It is a graceful edge along driveways or cement walks where the soil is usually very dry.

The dust-like seeds can be sown directly on the soil surface in the fall or early spring, or they can be raised indoors 6–8 weeks before the last frost, to germinate in 5 to 21 days at 55°F (13°C) when exposed to light. Plant out seedlings by clumps in early spring, spaced 6 in. (15.2 cm) apart in full sun and well-drained soil. Plants may become worn out by mid- to late summer, so it is a good idea to make two sowings. Plants produce more flowers if the soil is not overly rich. Snapping off flower heads encourages flower production, so one might as well dry them for tea.

Dried chamomile, especially the double-flowered Roman chamomile, enriches citrus-scented potpourri. To dry German or Roman chamomile, gently pull or snap off flowers from their stems when the petals just begin to turn back and the centers are raised or conical. Lay them to dry on a cookie sheet in a just-warm oven (I use the pilot light warmth in a gas oven). To make tea, steep 1–2 teaspoons dried herb in 1 cup boiling water for a few minutes using a tea egg. Add sugar or honey to taste, but no milk. German chamomile makes a sweeter tea, but both chamomiles are bitter if steeped too long. Try steeping 1 teaspoon dried chamomile with 1 teaspoon dried lemon balm. Both teas aid digestion and are relaxing except for anyone allergic to ragweed or any member of the aster family.

Related plants of interest. Seeds and plants of German chamomile are widely available from general seed and herb sources. Richters Herbs has introduced the *Matricaria recutita* 'Bodegold' strain. Roman chamomile seeds and plants are available from herb sources, and double-flowered *Chamaemelum nobile* 'Flore Pleno' plants will be at herb sources. Seeds of

Plate 57. *Anthemis tinctoria*, dyer's chamomile. Midsummer, dye bed, Country Lane Herbs and Dried Flowers. Photo, Brian Oke and Gisèle Quesnel.

197

dyer's chamomile are available from general seed sources, and the cultivars from perennial plant nurseries.

Anthemis tinctoria (Plate 57), dyer's chamomile or golden margeurite, is
a short-lived perennial whose golden flowers have been used since the
Middle Ages to produce a yellow dye. With dense, finely cut foliage, pungent when crushed, and masses of golden daisies 2 in. (5.1 cm) wide and
produced all summer, it is invaluable for beds, borders, and rock gardens.
It also is an excellent cut flower. Indoors, start seeds as for German chamomile, but speedy germination requires 70°F (21°C) and takes 8–14 days.
Space seedlings 12 in. (30.5 cm) apart in well-drained soil, not overly rich,
in full sun. Like German chamomile it is drought resistant, but in warmer
regions give it some shade and more moisture. 'Kelwayi' has brighter yellow, larger flowers; 'Moonlight' has pale, lemon yellow flowers; and the
very similar *A. sancti-johannis* has more finely cut foliage and orange flowers. Since seed grown plants are variable, deadheading is required to keep
the cultivars pure. After a few seasons, plants die out in the middle; propagate new ones by division from plantlets that form at the base of the
mother plant or by stem cuttings in the spring, which will flower the same
season. Try dyer's chamomile with purple-spiked salvias, especially *Salvia
officinalis*, and hyssop (*Hyssopus officinalis*) in mixed plantings.

Chamaemelum nobile, Roman chamomile, native to Western Europe, is
a perennial that grows by creeping rhizomes that create thick mats of ap-
ple-scented, ferny foliage. In early summer or a little later, each 9–14 in.
(22.9–35.6 cm) stem bears one, sometimes two daisy-like flowers $^{3}/_{4}$–1 in.
(1.9–2.5 cm) wide, quite similar in appearance to those of German chamomile, although the ray petals are less numerous and the central cone is
solid. It can be an attractive flowering ground cover around shrubs. Grow
it in rock gardens, along paths and entrances, or anywhere it is liable to be
stepped on to release its fragrance. The more heavily scented, double-flowered 'Flore Pleno' can be grown in a container for patio, deck, or entryways.
Roman chamomile grows best with even moisture and cool conditions; it
will not survive winters where moisture gathers around its roots. Propagate
by root division in the fall or early summer. In severe cold winter climates,
cover the planting with mulch. 'Flore Pleno' should always be grown and
propagated from roots, since seeds produce a large number of single flowers. It prefers a richer, moist soil. Both kinds are hardy in Zone 4.

Monarda

Lamiaceae, Mint Family
Bergamot, horsemint

Perennial
Site and soil: sun, partial shade; evenly moist,
  dry
Hardiness: Zones 4–10
Landscape use: accent, bed and border,
  container, naturalized herb
Height: 2–5 ft. (0.6–1.5 m)
Flower: scarlet, lilac, tubular in whorl
Bloom season: midsummer to late summer

> Wild bergamot . . . riots in pale and bloomy profusion along our country roadsides, and the grander kind . . . in its newest raiment of Cambridge Scarlet, is a prideful ornament of select gardens.
>
> Louise Beebe Wilder
> *The Fragrant Garden*

Bee balm and wild bergamot belong to a group known collectively as bergamots because their scent is similar to the bergamot oil extracted from
the tropical tree *Citrus aurantium*; they are also known as horsemints because of their coarseness. The genus is named for Nicholas Monardes, a
Spanish physician of the sixteenth century and the author of a book about
New World plants and their uses.

While they are very similar in their structure and properties, bee balm
and wild bergamot grow in opposite habitats. Bee balm, *Monarda didyma*
(Plate 58), prefers the moist and shaded woodlands and bottom lands
from New England to Georgia and Tennessee. Its spreading underground
runners create mats of aromatic, tapering, toothed leaves that send up
many square-sided stems. These are topped by striking, bright, round
flower heads held by red-tinged bracts. Each head, about 2 in. (5.1 cm)
across and often stacked in tiers, is surrounded by narrow, tubular florets
that give the whole flower a shaggy appearance. Bee balm's scent, sweet
and citrus with a hint of spice, is easily released by brushing the plant. Despite its common name, bees seldom visit the plant since the flowers' nectar is hard for them to reach. It is very attractive, however, to hummingbirds.

In contrast, wild bergamot, *Monarda fistulosa* (Plate 59), grows in the
dry, open ground of abandoned fields and mountainous areas from New

England south. A shorter, more slender plant, its two-lipped, lilac-pink flowers are arranged the same way as those on bee balm, but these are smaller, with shorter tubes, enabling bees to easily reach the nectar. Wild bergamot has a sharper, mintier aroma than its showier cousin.

Bee balm and wild bergamot were used for food, flavoring, and medicine to alleviate stomach and bronchial ailments by North American Indians and, later, the settlers. Bee balm, also known as Oswego tea, after the

Plate 58. *Monarda didyma*, bee balm. Midsummer, Gardner farm. Hummingbirds find it very attractive. Photo, Alan Dorey.

Oswego Indians who introduced it to European colonists, was once brewed in place of the common black tea in protest against British import duties prior to the American Revolution.

For many years *Monarda* 'Cambridge Scarlet' was the only cultivar available to the home gardener. Brighter than bee balm and more adaptable to cultivation than wild bergamot, it is still one of the best reds. But now, there are many choice cultivars resulting from the cross between red bee

Plate 59. *Monarda fistulosa*, wild bergamot. Midsummer, Gardner farm. Bees and butterflies find it very attractive. Photo, Alan Dorey.

201

Plate 60. *Monarda* 'Croftway Pink'. Midsummer, Gardner Farm. Bees find it very attractive. Photo, Alan Dorey.

balm and lilac wild bergamot. The available color range includes the deep, dark red of 'Mahogany', the deep, bluish lilac of 'Blue Stocking', the very popular, dusty pink 'Croftway Pink' (Plate 60), the brighter pink 'Marshall's Delight' (Plate 61)—bred for mildew resistance at Agriculture Canada's Morden, Manitoba, research station and named to honor the late H. H. Marshall, who initiated the breeding program—the spectacular, large-flowered 'Violet Queen', and the 'Snow Queen'. 'Petite Delight' (Plate 62) with many whorls of lavender-pink flowers is the first really short type, growing only 10–12 in. (25.4–30.5 cm) tall, introduced from Agriculture Canada in time to celebrate bergamot as the International Herb Association's Official Herb of the Year for 1996. The seed strain Panorama Mix offers the whole range of colors except white. The bright pink rose-geranium-scented bee balm (tetraploid *M. fistulosa*), discovered by H. H. Marshall, is tall and vigorous with an open, airy habit; it grows best in partial shade where summers are very hot.

Anything but coarse, these adaptable horsemints are becoming very popular with herb enthusiasts and the general gardener for their beautiful, long-lasting flowers, enticing aromas, and moderate, upright habit.

Plate 61. *Monarda* 'Marshall's Delight'. Late summer, Morden, Manitoba, Canada. It is resistant to powdery mildew. Photo courtesy of Agriculture Canada, Morden Research Station.

Feature one of them in an island bed with *Achillea ptarmica* 'The Pearl' and yellow sundrops (*Oenothera fruticosa*), and later with white phlox. I let it colonize near the kitchen window where its flowers appear even more vivid against the white clapboards. *Monarda* 'Croftway Pink' and purple and dark pink selections from Panorama Mix bring new, welcome colors during the heat of the season when other plants flag. They bloom well into late summer, first with early, azure monkshood (*Aconitum*), then with rudbeckia. Make a sunny accent by pairing wild bergamot and wild marjoram (*Origanum vulgare* subsp. *vulgare*), which can be left on their own except for a rough perimeter mowing.

Bergamot seeds germinate in 14 days or less from seeds sown at 70°F (21°C) just covered with the sowing medium. If seeds are started indoors in January, plants might blossom the first season, otherwise expect flowers the following season. It is advisable to grow the cultivars from plants or roots to ensure there is no color variation. Divide plants every 3 years or when the central mat becomes hard and unproductive; dispose of the old roots and replant the vigorous side growth in the spring, spacing plants 12 in. (30.5 cm) apart. Flowering can be extended by cutting off spent blooms along with their stems to encourage new buds to form in the axils of the lower stems. Powdery mildew, a common affliction of bergamots, is triggered by roots left dry for an extended period and by a lack of air circulation, especially in late summer. These plants, except for wild bergamot, prefer moisture in the soil and will grow in sun or partial shade. Partial shade, though, promotes longer lasting flowers with more intense color.

Plate 62. *Monarda* 'Petite Delight', the first dwarf type. Late summer, Morden, Manitoba. Photo courtesy of Agriculture Canada, Morden Research Station.

All types of bergamots can be used in tea, either added to black tea or brewed alone, but use only a few leaves. Add the petals to salad or to fruit cups. Use the fresh or dried leaves of bee balm, lemon bergamot, and Mexican bergamot as you would bay leaf to flavor meat dishes. All types are long-lasting cut flowers. The flower and seed heads can be dried for bouquets and wreaths—the red types keep their bright color. Add dried leaves and flowers to potpourri.

Plate 63. *Monarda austromontana*, Mexican bergamot. Midsummer. Photo courtesy of Thompson and Morgan.

Related plants of interest. Several native bergamots deserve more attention for their long flowering season and beautiful flowers. Plants and seeds of the bergamots are available from general, specialty, and herb sources. Look for seeds or plants of mountain mint from specialty seed or plant sources.

Monarda austromontana (Plate 63), Mexican bergamot, growing to 24 in. (61.0 cm), bears tiered, mauve flowers in masses that are very attractive to bees. The tapered, oregano-scented leaves are used in Mexico to season meat dishes. Native to Mexico, it is best grown like lemon bergamot.

Monarda citriodora, lemon bergamot, sometimes referred to as lemon mint, grows to 24 in. (61.0 cm) in the Appalachian Mountains and bears the characteristic whorled blooms in rosy lilac and occasionally white. These are especially showy because of their size—3 in. (7.6 cm) across—stacked position, and loosely open florets. The whole plant has a strong lemon-mint aroma when lightly brushed. In warm regions lemon bergamot may grow as a biennial, but in areas colder than Zone 7, it is best to treat it as an annual which may self-sow. Plants are easily raised from seed sown indoors in late winter. Or, try growing lemon bergamot in a container, which can be moved indoors for the winter. A heavy flowering type, 'Lambada', is a more vigorous plant to 3 1/2 ft. (1.1 m), suitable for a perennial border.

Monarda punctata, dotted monarda or dotted horsemint, bears dense, tiered whorls of yellow flowers spotted with purple and held by showy white or lilac bracts on stems 18–24 in. (45.7–61.0 cm) tall. It is found growing wild in sandy soils from New York to Florida to Texas. The plant has a strong thyme scent and was grown in the United States as a thyme substitute during World War I when the European cultivation of thyme was disrupted. Dotted monarda, suitable for naturalizing in dry conditions, grows as an annual, biennial, or short-lived perennial hardy in Zone 5. It can be raised like lemon bergamot and will self-sow once established.

Monardella odoritissima, mountain monarda, is a diminutive plant by bergamot standards, its creeping stems reach 15 in. (38.1 cm), bearing upright, 2 in. (5.1 cm), lilac-rose flowers. The very fragrant mountain monarda has a minty aroma, a combination of peppermint and pennyroyal. It grows best in dry soil and is a good candidate for a rock garden or rockery, where it enjoys conditions similar to its wild habitat, from Washington State to New Mexico. Give this plant winter protection or grow it as an annual like lemon bergamot.

Myrrhis odorata

Apiaceae, Celery Family
Sweet cicely, anise fern, giant chervil, sweet bracken

Perennial
Site and soil: partial shade, shade; evenly moist
Hardiness: Zones 3–10
Landscape use: accent, bed and border, edge and hedge,
    ground cover, naturalized herb
Height: 2–4 ft. (0.6–1.2 m)
Flower: white, wide umbel in cluster
Bloom season: spring to early summer

> **For its beauty it deserves to be in every garden.**
> Gertrude Jekyll
> *Wood and Garden*

Native to Europe and naturalized in the English countryside, *Myrrhis odorata* is the only species in the genus. Do not confuse it with species of *Osmorhiza*, North American native woodland plants with similar physical characteristics and properties, also known as sweet cicely.

Sweet cicely is an underused garden plant of great elegance and beautiful design, with its mounds of leaves and tall, dramatic flowering stalks, each in perfect proportion to the other. Every part of this admirable plant is sweetly aromatic and infused with an anise-like flavor. Ferny mounds of apple green, downy leaves, spotted white on their undersides, grow from deep, thick taproots. In late spring, their branching stalks bear wide, almost flat, white, compound umbels like a giant Queen Anne's lace. After about 2 weeks the frothy blooms are quickly followed by a multitude of 1 in. (2.5 cm) long, sharply ridged and pointed, green seeds that turn black in maturity. The handsome foliage carries on all season, well into the fall.

The names associated with *Myrrhis odorata* draw attention to its sweetness—it contains 40 percent sugar—and its anise or licorice flavor, as well as to its fernlike appearance. It has been cultivated at least since the sixth century, mostly for the food offered in all its parts, but also for medicine to treat cough, consumption, and other ailments. The oily seeds, once described by John Parkinson as "sweet, pleasant, and spicie hot," (1629) were also pressed into service to make an aromatic furniture polish.

Plant sweet cicely in a woodland garden as background for yellow cowslips (*Primula veris*) and wild bleeding heart (*Dicentra eximia*), all mulched in a sea of pink-flowered herb robert (*Geranium robertianum*). Or establish it in a generous border paired with the blue-flowered comfrey (*Symphytum caucasicum*), both displaying full bloom at the same time and enjoying the same habitat. Use it as an all-season accent in a shady spot, underplanted with spring bulbs. An all-white planting of sweet cicely, Solomon's seal (*Polygonatum multiflorum*), and dead nettle (*Lamium maculatum* 'White Nancy') would brighten up the dullest, shadiest spot. It can also be used as a leafy ground cover or a soft, low hedge.

Sweet cicely is most at home in moist, humusy soil in shaded conditions, although it will grow in partial shade or even sun if the soil is cool and damp. Dry soil and the onset of hot weather yellows the leaves and shortens an already brief bloom. To grow sweet cicely from seed, freeze it

Plate 64. *Myrrhis odorata*, sweet cicely. Early summer, Country Lane Herbs and Dried Flowers. Photo, Brian Oke and Gisèle Quesnel.

for 1 to 3 months before sowing outside in early spring. Space plants 24 in. (61.0 cm) apart in early spring. Once established, sweet cicely's long taproot makes it inadvisable to try to transplant mature plants, but it will self-sow, producing seedlings that can be transplanted if desired. However, unless you intend to use the seeds or seedlings, it is best to promptly cut the spent bloom stalks—they are undeniably attractive—or they will drop their seeds to the ground and produce an army of seedlings. Seeds and plants of sweet cicely are widely available from general seed and herb sources.

The delicately patterned leaves of sweet cicely can be pressed and used in floral designs. The plant's anise flavor combines well with most fruits, even reducing the amount of sugar necessary to sweeten stewed fruit, especially rhubarb and gooseberries. Simply add a handful of finely cut leaves to the fruit before cooking, then add sugar to taste. The green seeds can be eaten like candy. Louise Hyde of Well-Sweep Herb Farm in New Jersey developed the following recipe for sweet cicely coffee cake:

Sweet Cicely Coffee Cake
4 large sweet cicely leaves chopped fine
$3/4$ cup sugar
3 tablespoons flour
1 large can crushed pineapple, unsweetened
1 12-ounce can almond paste
2 cups Bisquick mix
2 tablespoons margarine
3 tablespoons sugar
$1/2$ cup milk

Make a dough using the last four ingredients. Spread it out flat on a greased jelly roll pan 11 in. × 17 in. (27.9 cm × 43.2 cm). Spread almond paste over the dough, then sprinkle it with the chopped sweet cicely leaves. Mix the drained pineapple with the flour and sugar, and spoon this mix over the leaves. Sprinkle extra sugar on top if desired. Bake at 400°F (205°C) for 30 to 40 minutes. Cut into squares.

Nepeta ×faassenii

Lamiaceae, Mint Family
Catmint

Perennial
Site and soil: sun, partial shade; evenly moist and well-drained
Hardiness: Zones 3–10
Landscape use: bed and border, container, edge and hedge, ground cover, rock work
Height: 12–36 in. (30.5–91.4 cm)
Flower: lavender-mauve, blue-violet, tubular in spike
Bloom season: early summer to midsummer

This catmint, sometimes referred to as mauve catmint, is a hybrid resulting from the cross between the Caucasian *Nepeta racemosa* and the southern European *N. nepetella*. It is an upright billowy plant with gray-green leaves, noticeably serrated at their edges. The small, nectar-rich flowers are tubular in form and lavender-mauve in color, on loosely packed spikes. The plant has similar properties to catnip, *N. cataria*, though to a lesser degree. While the plant oils are said to repel insects, especially ants, the blooms attract bees and butterflies as well as cats who may roll on the plants and even nibble the leaves but do not seem compelled to destroy them. Catmint leaves and flowering tops are used, like catnip, to make teas that soothe headaches and have a calming effect. Most catmints are excellent, long-lasting cut flowers, and dried catmint flowers are often added to potpourri for scent and color.

Dwarf catmint, or Persian ground ivy, a form of *Nepeta ×faassenii* often offered as *N. mussinii*, is a useful form growing to 12 in. (30.5 cm) tall and wide. Its lavender-blue flower spikes have a cinnamon fragrance and its soft, gray-green foliage a clove-like aroma. Cultivars worth growing include *N. ×faassenii* 'Blue Wonder', a compact, upright type, 18–24 in. (45.7–61.0 cm) tall with early blooming, rich blue flower spikes; 'White Wonder' is its mirror image in white. 'Six Hills Giant' is a vigorous plant to 3 ft. (0.9 m) tall that develops a 4 ft. (1.2 m) sprawl if not checked. It is larger in every way than the other catmints and produces many flowers in a pretty violet-blue. The much smaller 'Dropmore' grows 8–10 in. (20.3–25.4 cm) tall and wide, with spikes of purple-blue flowers; 'Dropmore' is usually described as a taller plant reaching 18–24 in. (45.7–61.0 cm). Since variation is a characteristic of the catmints, gardeners often complain that the plant they grow bears little resemblance to the one they expected. But all the catmints are desirable for their abundance of flowers—offered in a second round if the plant is cut back—drought resistance, and reliability in both cold and warm climates.

Catmints are marvelous for softening harsh edges in the landscape. For this purpose plant them to spill over paths, around rocks, and against or over stone walls. Dwarf catmint is a good choice for rock crevices. To substitute for lavender (*Lavandula angustifolia*), plant a thick hedge of catmint to line a stairway or the entrance to a building. In the border catmints are incomparable edging material, making bands of soft color that complement virtually all shades of flowers and foliage. Upright forms are striking among mounds of feverfew (*Tanacetum parthenium*) or mats of silver-leaved lamb's ears (*Stachys byzantina*). They also combine well with achilleas, especially the pale yellow *Achillea* 'Moonshine'. Dwarf catmint is a weed-smothering ground cover often used to underplant pink roses. All catmints combine well with pink flowers, such as peonies, pinks (*Dianthus*), and the bright trailing soapwort (*Saponaria ocymoides*). Place potted specimens in a sunny spot near entryways or on patios.

Sow seeds of catmint 6–8 weeks before the last frost at 60°F (21°C) to germinate in 7 to 10 days, or sow seeds in the fall in a cold frame where they will germinate in the spring. Set plants of all types in the ground in the spring 12–15 in. (30.5–38.1 cm) apart, wider for 'Six Hills Giant'. Catmints will grow and produce the most flowers in moist soil as long as they are well-drained and the plants have full sun, though partial shade is appreciated in warmer areas. Cut flowering stalks back to the mound of foliage after the first bloom to stimulate a second flowering in late summer or early fall, for some types; doing so will also prevent straggly growth. Trim plants again in early spring before flower buds have formed near the basal leaves. Plants are propagated by division in the spring or stem cuttings in the spring or midsummer, after the first flowering. Dwarf catmint will self-sow.

Related plants of interest. Seeds or plants of dwarf catmint are available from some general and specialty seed and herb sources. Seeds of *Nepeta nervosa* and *N. sibirica* are occasionally offered by specialty seed sources. The other catmints can be obtained from perennial plant and herb sources.

Nepeta camphorata (Plate 65), 24–30 in. (61.0–7.6 cm) tall, from Greece, is richly aromatic. Its small white flowers marked with pinkish purple spots grow in long spikes; the foliage is silvery gray. This is a frost-tender plant in Zone 7.

Nepeta ×*faassenii* 'Souvenir d'Andre Chaudron' is a stocky upright plant 24–30 in. (61.0–76.2 cm) tall, with pointed, dark green leaves and large, loose, deep violet-blue flowers 1 $^1/_2$ in. (3.8 cm) long.

Plate 65. *Nepeta camphorata*. Midsummer. Photo courtesy of Thompson and Morgan.

Nepeta grandiflora is the tallest and perhaps the showiest of catmints, on 3 ft. (0.9 m) reddish stems, sprawling to 4 ft. (1.2 m) wide with a profusion of rosy-purple spikes above narrow, gray-green leaves that have a sweet, minty aroma. This catmint dries well with its aromatic, reddish stems and flower bracts.

Nepeta nervosa, Himalayan catmint, is very compact, to 24 in. (61.0 cm) with 6 to 8 in. (15.2–20.3 cm) flower spikes of a soft, light blue and prominently veined, pointed, glossy leaves.

Nepeta sibirica is a robust plant, 18–36 in. (45.7–91.4 cm) tall with lavender flowers in whorls that first appear in midsummer and last until the fall.

Nigella damascena

Ranunculaceae, Buttercup Family
Love-in-a-mist, devil-in-a-bush, wild fennel

Annual
Site and soil: sun; well-drained
Landscape use: bed and border, edge and hedge
Height: 18 in. (45.7 cm)
Flower: five sky-blue, white petals encircled by
   threadlike bracts
Bloom season: midsummer to late summer

> The colour is a pure, soft blue of a quality distinctively its own.
> Gertrude Jekyll
> *Annuals and Biennials*

The intriguing name love-in-a-mist aptly describes the flower's unusual structure. Its sky-blue, lightly veined petals, actually sepals, and projecting stamens are surrounded by finely divided, leaf-like bracts; further down the wiry stem, fennel-type leaves swirl to give the whole plant an airy grace. Love-in-a-mist is attractive in every stage, from round, puffed bud to opened flower—1$\frac{1}{2}$ in. (3.8 cm) across—to pod, when, as its petals drop, the fruit becomes an inflated, reddish, striped balloon. As the pod matures and slits open at its top, a multitude of small, black seeds fall to the ground, assuring the flower's renewal. It is these black seeds, important in many cultures for their uses, that suggested the genus name *Nigella*, diminutive for black from the Latin *niger*; the name *damascena* indicates this species' Mediterranean origin.

The spicy seeds of all nigellas are important ingredients in curries and spice blends, and are sprinkled on breads and rolls like poppy seeds. The seeds are also used to treat digestive problems and to repel moths. In North America, the dried pods are important in the dried flower and craft trade.

Love-in-a-mist was one of Gertrude Jekyll's favorite flowers. The enduring strain of Miss Jekyll Hybrids attests to her devotion. She wrote in *Annuals and Biennials*, "The variety Miss Jekyll is the result of many years' careful selection, and may be said to be the best garden Nigella" (1916). She may be right, for although other cultivars have been introduced, none is so evocative of the delicate beauty of the flower as the semidouble, soft blue of *Nigella damascena* 'Miss Jekyll'. Selections from this cultivar include an all white and a rose version; flowers of all these are larger than the species, opening to 2 in. (5.1 cm). The reliable, double-flowered 'Persian Jew-

Plate 66. *Nigella damascena*, love-in-a-mist. Midsummer, Country Lane Herbs and Dried Flowers. Pods will be harvested for dried bouquets and wreaths. Photo, Brian Oke and Gisèle Quesnel.

els' extends the color range to include not only light blue, white, and rose, but also pink, mauve, and purple; its flowers are large, 2$^1/_2$ in. (6.4 cm), as are the pods, but plants are somewhat shorter, reaching 15 in. (38.1 cm). Dwarf cultivars such as 'Dwarf Moody' and 'Shorty Blue' are semidouble, violet-blue, and no taller than 6–8 in. (15.2–20.3 cm).

Love-in-a-mist's delicate and spreading form is best seen to advantage among annuals or lower-growing perennials near the front of the bed or border. If successive sowings are made, it will continue to provide a touch of blue all season, one that is particularly effective behind silvery or gray-leaved plants such as the low-growing dusty millers (*Pyrethrum ptarmiciflorum, Centaurea cineraria*, and others). The dwarf types with their more compact habit suggest a role for love-in-a-mist as a miniature hedge or edge. I grow *Nigella damascena* 'Miss Jekyll' in a cutting bed, where it is massed in front of bright orange and yellow calendulas.

In cool climates, sow seeds outdoors in the spring after the soil warms; seeds germinate in 8 to 16 days at 60°F (16°C). In warm climates, sow seeds in the fall for spring bloom. Space plants 12 in. (30.5 cm) apart and do not attempt to transplant extras—it is possible but the mortality rate is high. Spacing is especially important if you want to raise plants with large pods. If harvesting, be sure to leave some plants to self-sow. Where the season is long enough, sow seeds two or three times a month for successive bloom. Plants thrive in sunny but not hot conditions in ordinary garden soil.

All the nigellas are good cut and dried flowers at any stage. For fresh flowers, cut stems before the flowers are fully open, and as the petals fall observe the forming pod. For dried flowers, cut when the flowers are just open. The bracts will remain a green ruff around the flower, and even though the petals shrivel, their color, especially blue, is attractive in pastel-dominated posies and arrangements. For dried pods, cut stems when the pods are green with burgundy stripes, well before they turn brown and split open. Trim off the branching stems to avoid entanglement, bunch the stems together with an elastic, and hang them to dry away from light.

Related plants of interest. Seeds of love-in-a-mist and its cultivars are readily available from general, specialty, and some herb sources; look for other types from specialty and herb seed sources.

Nigella hispanica (Plate 67), Spanish fennelflower, is an arresting, showy type on 15 to 18 in. (38.1–45.7 cm) stems with large flowers 2½ in. (6.4 cm) across. The petals are a distinctive purple-blue with prominent, maroon stamens. The pods are inflated and horned. Plants need more heat to mature than love-in-a-mist and should be started indoors in plant cells or peat pots so that their roots will not be disturbed by transplanting; plant them outdoors after danger of frost has passed.

Nigella orientalis 'Transformer', yellow nigella, is unusual for its small, yellow-green, ½ in. (1.3 cm) flowers on 12 to 20 in. (30.5–50.8 cm) stems. Before drying, the pods can be turned inside-out to make them look like flowers.

Nigella sativa, black cumin, nutmeg flower, or Roman coriander, is the bitter fitch, the Hebrew *ketzah*, mentioned in the Bible (Isa 28:27). This plant, while the most herbally useful, is the least decorative of the nigellas. The flowers, over 1 in. (2.5 cm) across, are whitish green with the usual busy interior of colored stamens and pistils. The seed pod is large and bulging, with anthers or horns at its tip. The seeds are spicier, more aro-

Plate 67. *Nigella hispanica*, Spanish fennelflower. Late summer, Gardner farm. Photo, Alan Dorey.

matic than other species, and need rich soil and a long growing season to develop. This would be a good type to plant in a garden of cooking herbs and spices, where its dainty form would show off at the front of the planting of darker forms. Black cumin is the best for culinary uses, such as sprinkling the seeds on breads and cakes.

Ocimum basilicum var. *purpurascens*

Lamiaceae, Mint Family
Purple basil

Annual
Site and soil: sun; well-drained
Landscape use: bed and border, container, edge and
   hedge
Height: 8–24 in. (20.3–61.0 cm)
Flower: pinkish lilac, two-lipped in whorl on
   terminal spike
Bloom season: midsummer to late summer

> **Even the flowers of the purple basils are worthwhile, lavender-pink in pleasing contrast to the dark leaves.**
> Helen Van Pelt Wilson and Léonie Bell
> *The Fragrant Year*

Basil, originally from tropical Asia and Africa, is widely cultivated for its clove-scented leaves. In different cultures, some types are used medicinally to treat stomach complaints and in the household to repel insects. The essential oil is used in the perfume industry. Purple basil, a natural variant of the common or sweet green basil, *Ocimum basilicum*, has been selected and cultivated for its appearance and flavor. Its glossy leaves are a rich purple on 18 to 24 in. (45.7–61.0 cm) branching stems of a dull purple, almost black. The flowers, too, are different from the white petals of common green basil. Each bloom is exquisite with its broad, light purple upper lip and narrow, cupped, light pinkish lilac lower lip that fans out like a shelf on which the white-tipped stamens gracefully sweep out of the flower. These blooms, tucked into the axils of the leaves, appear on terminal spikes 12 in. (30.5 cm) or longer. Although the flowers are small, the plant gains effect with its whole ensemble, the contrast between purple buds, stems, and bracts against small, delicate, two-toned blooms. When lightly brushed, the plant exudes a sharper, spicier aroma than common green basil.

The basils have been addressed by herb writers from the days of Dioscorides to the present. Common sweet basil was being grown in North America by 1775, when it was advertised for sale in the *Virginia Gazette*. Purple basil and a dwarf bush form, *Ocimum basilicum* 'Minimum Purpurascens', have been grown by herb enthusiasts on this side of the Atlantic since at least the 1930s.

Ocimum basilicum 'Dark Opal' (Plate 68), developed at the University of Connecticut in mid-century, was an All-America Selection in 1962, hailed as something very new. It was more compact than the older type, growing 12–15 in. (30.5–38.1 cm) tall to 12 in. (30.5 cm) wide. Since then, plants offered under this name usually grow as tall as 24 in. (61.0 cm) and tend to have some green streaking in their leaves. Reversion is often a problem with seed strains unless they are periodically reselected. 'Red Rubin', reselected in Europe from 'Dark Opal', is more uniform in its dark color and very much like what 'Dark Opal' must have been at first. 'Purple Ruffles', a 1986 All-America Selection, also selected from 'Dark Opal', is a distinct variation on the purple theme, with heavily ruffled, almost fringed, dark purple leaves and showy whorls of pink to rose-lavender flowers.

The dwarf bush purple basil *Ocimum basilicum* 'Minimum Purpurascens' travels under a variety of names, among them 'Purpurascens Nana', 'Miniature Purple', and 'Purple Bush'. For years this strain was lost to the trade, but it was restored by Cyrus Hyde of Well-Sweep Herb Farm in New Jersey after crossing large-leaved purple basil with a tiny, green-leaved, miniature basil and carefully selecting their offspring. This process resulted in *O. basilicum* 'Well-Sweep Miniature Purple Basil'. It is a delightful and dainty plant, like a miniature bush, with small, oval, dark-purple-mahogany leaves and whorls of tiny pink flowers in large spikes at the top of the plant. All are variable when grown from seed.

The most unusual purple basil is *Ocimum* 'African Blue' (Plate 69), discovered by chance at Companion Plants herb nursery in Ohio in 1982. It is a hybrid of *O. kilmanscharium* × *O. basilicum*. A stunning plant almost as wide as it is tall, 3 ft. (0.9 m), it is the largest of the purple basils. Leaves are dark green with purple veining, giving them a bluish cast, and the long, showy flower spikes are purple. The plant has a sweet camphor scent passed on from *O. kilmanscharium*, camphor basil, a medicinal herb in Kenya, and can be used as a culinary herb. As Companion Plants coproprietor Peter Bouchard points out, unlike other basils that die after they go to seed,

Plate 68. *Ocimum basilicum* 'Dark Opal', purple basil. Late summer, Country Lane Herbs and Dried Flowers. Photo, Brian Oke and Gisèle Quesnel.

Plate 69. *Ocimum* 'African Blue', purple basil. Midsummer, Country Lane Herbs and Dried Flowers. Some of the prolific flower spikes will be dried for wreaths. Photo, Brian Oke and Gisèle Quesnel.

'African Blue' behaves more like a tender perennial, putting out new leaf growth throughout the season. This basil is mostly sterile and is only sold as plants.

Other basils have aromas and flavors that break away from the ordinary basil. *Ocimum basilicum* 'Cinnamon Basil', growing 18–30 in. (45.7–76.2 cm), is a stocky plant with bright green leaves on cinnamon-colored stems. It has dark purple flower spikes. 'Licorice Basil', 24–36 in. (61.0–91.4 cm), has long, narrow, green leaves outlined in purple and flower spikes of an attractive light purple. 'Siam Queen', an All-America Selection for 1997, is an improved form of Thai basil, a variant of *O. basilicum* that is used to flavor Thai and Vietnamese dishes. A vigorous plant reaching 3 ft. (0.9 m), its bright green, anise- or licorice-scented leaves grow on red stems. By midsummer these are embellished with densely packed, pink-violet flower spikes. These cultivars are increasingly available from general seed and herb sources; watch for improved, reselected seed.

Basil has been called the queen of the herb garden. The purple basils are particularly beautiful, possessing striking foliage color, lovely flower spikes, and varied landscaping possibilities. *Ocimum basilicum* 'Dark Opal' and 'Purple Ruffles' are very attractive in containers. Where early summer is cool (Zone 4), keep these indoors or in a greenhouse until temperatures warm, then set them out in a sheltered spot, perhaps a dooryard space in a mixed herb and flower planting among shades of pink—yarrows (*Achillea millefolium*), poppies—and white—sweet alyssum (*Lobularia maritima*), white mugwort (*Artemisia lactiflora*), nicotiana—with black and dark-eyed pink hollyhocks (*Alcea rosea*) in the background. Elsewhere, tubs of green sweet basil and bright orange and yellow nasturtium (*Tropaeolum*) are wonderful complements to the dark purples. Purple bush basil creates an incomparable edging or frame for a culinary planting—one could devote it entirely to basils—or for a bed of sun-loving annuals. *Ocimum* 'African Blue' gets center stage among lower-growing thymes, origanums, and the silver accents of lamb's ears (*Stachys byzantina*) in a sunny perennial garden.

The purple basils, even more than the green, require even heat and careful handling—the less the better—in their early growth. They also need a longer growing season, so start plants from seed indoors 6–8 weeks before the last expected frost. To avoid having to transplant seedlings after they have germinated, sow seeds directly into plastic cells, where seedlings will develop a block of roots that will not be disturbed by later transplanting. Cover seeds just twice their diameter with the sowing medium. Germination, speeded by bottom heat, starts in 4 days at 70°F (21°C) or slightly warmer. Thin out extra seedlings by cutting them off at their base with a sharp scissors, because pulling them up will disturb the others. While thinning, remove seedlings with green or streaked leaves, though sometimes streaking only develops later. Plant outdoors when warm temperatures prevail and when seedlings are 3 in. (7.6 cm) tall, spacing plants 8–12 in. (20.3–30.5) apart or more, depending on type. Pinch off tops to encourage bushiness when plants are 5–6 in. (12.7–15.2) tall. During the season, cut flower spikes for bouquets—the stems will root in water—to effectively prune plants and encourage more flower production. *Ocimum* 'African Blue' can be propagated in 5 to 10 days by stem cuttings in the usual rooting medium or simply in water. In cool climates, where basils do not usually set seed, plants can be wintered indoors, for which the bush type is especially suited.

The flower spikes can be cut for fresh and dried bouquets, and the dried flower heads add color and scent to potpourri. Leaves of all types can be used interchangeably with green basils in most dishes. The leaves of *Ocimum basilicum* 'Cinnamon Basil' and 'Licorice Basil' are especially good in fruit desserts. Use the leaves of all types for vinegars to use in salads, stir fries, and fruit desserts. To make purple basil vinegar place as many leaves as desired in a wide-mouth, glass jar with a non-metallic lid; pour white vinegar over the leaves and let them steep on a sunny windowsill. Almost at once the purple color will infuse the vinegar. After 2 to 3 weeks, strain and rebottle.

Origanum vulgare subsp. *vulgare*

Lamiaceae, Mint Family
Wild marjoram

Perennial
Site and soil: sun, partial shade; well-drained
Hardiness: Zones 4–9
Landscape use: accent, bed and border, ground cover,
   naturalized herb
Height: 30–36 in. (76.2–91.4 cm)
Flower: pink, white, tight cluster in small spike
Bloom season: midsummer to fall

> The air around was filled with the fragrance of its purple flowers and the humming ecstasy of honey bees hovering over their rich nectar.
>
> Helen Noyes Webster
> *The Herbarist*

The hardiest and tallest of the origanums, wild marjoram grows as a garden escape in the American Northeast, where it was introduced from Europe for its medicinal uses. A shallow-rooted plant, it grows a tight, spreading mat of downy, oval, 1 in. (2.5 cm) leaves. Erect square-sided stems, typical of the mint family, rise up from the mat, bearing at the top of the plant tight clusters of two-lipped, pink flowers with prominent stamens. Although the individual flowers are small they are held by rosy, purple-tipped bracts that magnify their effect. The contrast of dark buds with light colored flowers and colorful bracts gives wild marjoram its ornamental appeal over a long season. The pungently scented flowers are very attractive to bees.

Wild marjoram is mainly a medicinal plant, but where conditions are favorably dry and sunny its leaves develop enough flavor for culinary uses. Teas have been used to treat indigestion and nervousness—teas of all members of the mint family have a calming effect. The caustic extracted oil was used to soothe toothaches and to treat horses. The medicinal uses of wild marjoram are being studied in Europe, where hundreds of possibly useful chemicals have been identified.

It is a valid injunction to grow desired origanums from plants rather than from seeds in order to be sure of the plants' characteristics. But variants can be very desirable. In this way, I was inadvertently introduced to a type of wild marjoram often described as showy oregano (not to be confused with the true showy oregano, *Origanum libanoticum*). Bushy in form,

18 in. x 18 in. (45.7 cm x 45.7 cm), it bears masses of the familiar, dark-bracketed, pink flowers, more vibrantly colored than wild marjoram, with moderately scented foliage that turns purple by fall. *Origanum vulgare* subsp. *vulgare* 'Humile' is a dark-green-leaved ground cover to 8 in. (20.3 cm) tall with lilac-pink flowers. It needs a very sunny exposure to flower well.

Plate 70. *Origanum vulgare* subsp. *vulgare*, a showy oregano seed-grown variant. Midsummer, Gardner farm. Photo, Alan Dorey.

In rich soil, wild marjoram will quickly learn to disregard the confines of a flower border or bed. I have had a love-hate relationship with it for years—removing it, then inviting it back again—until I let it naturalize with bee balm (*Monarda didyma*) close to the planned landscape. There, it is near enough to be admired, yet not so close as to overrun less vigorous types. I have also naturalized it in poor ground near one of our bee hives at the woodland's edge. Here it grows with no attention whatsoever where few other plants could establish themselves. Its ability to colonize in such conditions recommends its use for erosion control on steep banks or slopes, where the "ramifying" roots, as Helen Webster described them, hold the soil. It can also be grown as a ground cover, although the flowers would be sacrificed. The dwarf form is a choice treasure for a sunny border or bed or a sun-exposed rock garden or rockery. Try showy oregano in a hanging basket.

Sow seeds of wild marjoram indoors in late winter or early spring, where seeds will germinate in 10 days or less if sown on the surface of the medium and exposed to light. Plant seedlings outside after danger of frost has passed, spacing plants 12–18 in. (30.5–45.7 cm) apart. Wild marjoram grows best in full sun, in dry, somewhat alkaline soil, but it will grow under almost any conditions. Plants are easily propagated by dividing the mat in early spring. If plants are cut back after blooming the mat will regain its leafy vigor and remain attractive well into late fall.

The long-stemmed origanums make good cut flowers and dried flowers for winter bouquets. All types dry well for crafts and are useful for texture in potpourri. The leaves of wild marjoram can be used for tea. The leaves of showy oregano or the stronger dittany of Crete, *Origanum dictamnus*, can be used for flavoring in tomato sauces and all pasta dishes. Make an herb butter by simmering, for 5 minutes on low heat, 4 ounces butter with 2 teaspoons dried herb leaves—use about twice the amount of fresh leaves. Strain, and refrigerate the butter in a container until it is needed. Use this on hot pasta or on thick slices of toasted Italian bread. Try adding a little fresh, pressed garlic to the butter before brushing it on the bread.

Related plants of interest. Seeds of wild marjoram are widely available, and plants are available from herb sources. Hybrids and cultivars are available from herb and perennial plant sources specializing in uncommon types.

All the following origanums should be grown from roots or purchased plants. Propagate by making 3–4 in. (7.6–10.2 cm) stem cuttings from soft basal growth in the spring or early summer before plants are in their vigorous growth period. Hardiness is determined more by humidity than by temperature. Origanums can survive colder temperatures in the arid con-

Plate 71. *Origanum dictamnus*, dittany of Crete. Midsummer, Country Lane Herbs and Dried Flowers. It was wintered in a greenhouse then planted in bed of flowers for drying. Photo, Brian Oke and Gisèle Quesnel.

ditions of the West, for instance, than in the same temperatures of the more humid East. Quick drainage and an open, sunny site are required for all.

Origanum dictamnus (Plate 71), dittany of Crete or hop marjoram, from the mountains of Crete, is grown as an annual in areas colder than Zone 7 or 8. One of the few showy types with culinary use (its thick, woolly leaves have a sweet pennyroyal-thyme flavor), it sends out trailing stems to 12 in. (30.5 cm) from established plants. Bright pink flowers with projecting stamens appear in pairs, held at the tip of layered, light green, cone-shaped bracts (similar to flowers of the hop vine, *Humulus lupulus*).

Dittany of Crete was one of the favorite herbs of the late Madeleine Siegler of Maine, a professional herb grower, who grew it very successfully for many years in a hanging basket outdoors in the summer—it flowered by August—and on a sunny window in winter. Once a year she replanted it in a professional growing medium, Pro-Mix, fertilized it every other month with a liquid plant food, and made 5 in. (12.7 cm) cuttings in the late winter, rooting them in water, then planting them in small pots filled with Pro-Mix.

Origanum 'Kent Beauty', is a trailing herb whose stems bear round, silver-veined leaves and pink to purple, coned flower bracts, like hops. It should be treated like a tender perennial in climates colder than Zone 8.

Origanum laevigatum 'Herrenhausen' has become one of the most popular introductions for its masses of showy, purplish pink flowers in 4 in. (10.2 cm) clusters on reddish stems 24 in. (61.0 cm) tall. Its maroon bracts seem designed to match the mats of maroon-toned foliage, whose color deepens in the fall. 'Herrenhausen' is hardy in Zone 5 and is choice for any bed or border, where it will attract flocks of butterflies, with late-blooming salvias from midsummer to frost.

Origanum leavigatum 'Hopleys' grows to 24 in. (61.0 cm) or taller with red-violet, clustered flowers and is suitable for midborder along with pastel hues. The flowers are suitable for drying. A vigorous type, it grows well in heat; it is hardy at least in Zone 7.

Origanum libanoticum, true showy oregano, grows in a wide mound with tiny, pink flowers in long spikes on creamy bracts. In climates harsher than Zone 7 it is suitable for a basket hanging outdoors in the summer and indoors in the winter. In warmer regions, its trailing stems will drape gracefully over a stone wall.

Paeonia officinalis

Paeoniaceae, Peony Family
Common peony, crimson peony, grandma's peony

Perennial
Site and soil: sun, partial shade; well-drained
Hardiness: Zones 2–8
Landscape use: accent, bed and border, edge and hedge
Height: 24 in. (61.0 cm)
Flower: purplish red, white bowl in terminal head
Bloom season: spring to early summer

The common peony, native to southern and central Europe, bears tightly wrapped, round buds that open to globe- or bowl-shaped flowers 5 in. (12.7 cm) wide. Single-petaled and dark crimson, they show numerous golden stamens within. Its sturdy stems arise from deeply cut, dark green, glossy foliage. The type that has been cultivated in British gardens since the sixteenth century is fully double and usually crimson, but double whites and pinks are also of antique vintage. Their flowers—masses of petals—are similar in shape to a giant rose, some as wide as 10 in. (25.4 cm). In Ireland the double sorts were called peony-roses.

Several species of peony have a reputation for healing, a characteristic preserved in the genus name which is associated with a healing god of Greek mythology. The name *officinalis*, meaning "from the apothecary," points to the common peony's ancient use as a medicinal herb for treating jaundice, kidney and bladder problems, and nervous afflictions such as epilepsy. *Paeonia officinalis* was known as the female peony, as distinct from *P. mascula*, or male peony. According to some authorities these were so named either because of their use in treating female or male afflictions, or because of the differences in their leaf and root size. Today, with its powerful and dangerous alkaloids, the common peony is regarded as poisonous for internal consumption. Extracts from the plant are still occasionally used in the manufacture of dyes and plastics.

Despite the introduction in the nineteenth century of many peony hybrids that arose from crossing the common peony with the scented, white Chinese peony, *Paeonia lactiflora*, the old-fashioned common peony in its double-flowered form is still grown, valued for its ease of culture, depend-ability, and large, round blooms. Some worthy cultivars include *P. officina-lis* 'Alba Plena', double white and early, 'Rosea Superba', double pink, and the ultimate cottage garden peony, 'Rubra Plena', a rich double crimson. As the flowers of each of these mature, the petals open to reveal the golden stamens within.

Combine the common peony with iris in the middle of the border of a generous cottage garden—only one plant is needed. Or grow it as a dra-matic accent in the corner of a formal raised bed, where the foliage and round blooms will soften the bed's angular lines. In the foreground of a shrubbery—but not too near, since the shrubs will rob the peonies of much-needed nutrients and moisture—its flowers will show to advantage against the dark background, and its bronzing foliage will be attractive into the fall. Old-fashioned plantings often included daffodils and pe-onies together; planting peonies is a good method for hiding the ripening daffodil leaves. The common peony also makes a fine all season hedge to line a driveway or walkway or to divide a garden into rooms. In some tra-ditions, the peony is a bride's plant—slips are taken by the young bride from her mother's plant and replanted in the brides' new home. Many old specimens still thrive on front lawns or near entrances.

The common peony will bear prolific blooms for many decades with a minimum of attention, but care should be given to the planting site and the soil. Choose full sun, except in warmer climates where some shade is appreciated, and enriched and well-drained soil. Dig a hole twice as wide as necessary to accommodate the roots and refill it, adding and mixing in 1 bushel (352 liters) of well-rotted compost and 1 pound (0.5 kg) of bone meal. Add $^1/_2$ cup (125 ml) of horticultural lime if the soil is very acid. Let the soil settle. In the fall plant the roots, each with three to five buds, $1^1/_2$ in. (3.8 cm) deep, but only 1 in. (2.5 cm) deep where the soil is heavy. Space the holes 3 ft. (0.9 m) apart and lightly mulch plants the first year, keeping them well-watered. After blooming, cut down the flowering stalks so seed heads do not form and lightly fertilize the plants with high phos-phate fertilizer (5-10-5) or 1 cup (250 ml) bone meal mixed with wood ashes. Do not use fresh manure and do not allow any of the fertilizers to come in contact with the stems of the plants.

To avoid diseases, cut all foliage to the ground in the fall. Plants need no dividing but if you want to propagate them, lift plants in the fall and wash the roots so the eyes are visible. Separate roots with a sharp knife and replant pieces with three to five eyes, the eyes facing upward. Do not despair if your peonies do not flower right away. Give them 3–5 years to attain the mature growth necessary for full-flowering. If they fail to flower at all, however, the cause is probably too deep planting or too dry soil.

Peonies require staking because of the heavy flower heads. Install hoops or linking stakes before or when the buds develop. Or place chicken wire on the ground, covering an area as wide or a little wider than the expected width of the plant, through which the fresh shoots will grow. Pull the wire upwards to support the plant in bloom. However, experienced peony growers admit that nothing will support double-flowered peonies after a rain.

For cut flowers, cut peony stalks when the buds are nearly open. The flowers will last at least a week indoors. Only cut stems on mature plants and be sure to leave three complete sets of leaves on each stem, for these are vital for the plant's future growth.

Related plants of interest. Peonies are available from perennial plant and specialty nurseries. The common peony and the tree peony are not as widely available as the hybrids.

Paeonia lactiflora, Chinese peony, was introduced to the West in the late eighteenth century in cultivated form—it had been the subject of improvement in China since 1086. In its wild form, the flowers are large, single petaled, white, and fragrant. In Chinese medicine preparations of the roots are used, among other things, to lower fevers and blood pressure. Hybrids between it and the common peony appeared by the mid-nineteenth century, laying the foundation for many modern cultivars that are valued for their double and fragrant flowers. Some of the older ones are still considered the best: 'Festiva Maxima' (1851) is early blooming, its white petals flecked with crimson; 'Duchesse de Nemours' (1856) blooms in mid-season, with white flowers and a faint yellow center; 'Felix Crouse' (1881), late-blooming, is deep rosy red.

Paeonia mascula (Plate 72) is the ancient medicinal known as the male peony or coral peony, introduced to Britain perhaps from the Mediterranean area, used exclusively until the introduction of the common peony. It is still found growing around monasteries, where it was valued for its culinary as well as medicinal properties; its coral-colored seeds were used to flavor meats. In 1991, working as a volunteer in the Jerusalem Botanical Garden, I saw for the first time this beautiful plant with large, crimson, single-petaled flower heads and brilliant yellow stamens on 24 in. (61.0 cm) stems with deeply cut, glossy foliage. It is a rare, protected wildflower in Israel. The coral peony is available from perennial plant nurseries, and *P. mascula* subsp. *arientina* may be available from specialty growers.

Paeonia suffruticosa, tree or mountain peony, is a shrub from Asia. Growing to 4 ft. (1.2 m), its green, closely branching stems bear semidouble flowers in a range of colors, including pink, red, white, purple, and yellow. The petals are noticeably cupped and fluted, and the leaves are light green and finely divided. Its bark is used in Chinese medicine to treat fevers and ulcers, among other disorders. Cultivation is similar to other peonies; windy sites should be avoided. Cut off dead blooms but do not cut back woody branches. It expands to 3 ft. (0.9 m) across as it matures, but may take 4–5 years to attain full size. It is hardy in Zone 3.

Plate 72. *Paeonia mascula*, coral peony, a rare protected flower. Spring, Mt. Meron, Israel. Photo courtesy of the Society for the Protection of Nature in Israel.

Papaver

Papaveraceae, Poppy Family
Poppy

Annual
Site and soil: sun; well-drained
Landscape use: bed and border, container, naturalized
   herb
Height: 24–36 in. (61.0–91.4 cm)
Flower: white, lilac, mauve, pink, red, solitary cup
Bloom season: midsummer to late summer

Most poppies have medicinal and culinary uses. Those with the greatest history of use are the Mediterranean opium poppy, *Papaver somniferum* (Plates 54 and 73), and the European corn poppy, *P. rhoeas* (Plate 74). The opium poppy, most famous for its narcotic properties, has also provided oil, seeds, flour, straw, even baby rattles, as well as cures for diarrhea. Corn poppy petals, once gathered by the millions to use in cough syrups, were an important food dye. This is the familiar Flanders Field poppy, whose brilliant, blood-red color reminds us of fallen soldiers on Veteran's Day.

The opium poppy is the taller plant on strong, dull green stems with jagged-edged, clasping, dull green leaves, for which it is also called lettuce poppy. Flowers, sometimes 4–6 in. (10.2–15.2 cm) across in double types, form at the top of the stem, with smaller ones tucked in side branches. The heavy, dull green buds droop then become erect, revealing just a colorful tip of the flower to come. Shortly after the sepals part, they are thrust off by the emerging bloom. Freed from their confinement, the tightly packed, silky petals unfurl, at first forming a large cup, blotched with dark purple or white at its base, then loosening and falling apart. The oval, green seed head that remains swells to great size as it matures—as large as a golf ball—eventually turning grayish brown in maturity. Finally, thousands of small, round seeds fall to the ground from openings at the top of the capsule under its hat-like top, thus assuring the plant's longevity. The whole process, from a colorful hint of the flower in its emerging tip to the revelation of the seed head, can be observed in a single day.

The corn poppy is a shorter plant, bristly in all its parts. Wiry, hairy stems grow up gracefully from hairy, light green, divided leaves; even the sepals, enclosing the flower, are covered with fine hairs. The drooping buds point upward as they get ready to release their burden of brilliant, crinkly-leaved petals, each with a black blotch at its base. Its seed pods are considerably smaller than those of the opium poppy.

Both these poppies and their variants have been cultivated as ornamentals for hundreds, even thousands, of years. The sixteenth-century John Gerard described double-flowered and feathered forms of the opium poppy in a mixture of colors from white and red to dark purple. In feathered types, the petals are long and narrow, forming shaggy heads. Eighteenth-century literature describes a double black, actually dark purple, poppy that two centuries later has been introduced as "new." Most of these old variants are available today, sometimes offered as *Papaver laciniatum*, double feathered types, or *P. paeoniflorum*, peony or carnation forms such as the Paeonia-flowered Hybrids.

Variants of the corn poppy have been grown at least since the seventeenth century. By the eighteenth century there were double reds edged with white, and by 1880, Rev. Henry Wilkes had developed the type which is named for the English village where he lived, the Shirley Poppies. Both

Plate 73. *Papaver somniferum*, opium poppy, self-sown variant. Midsummer, Gardner farm. Photo, Alan Dorey.

Plate 74. *Papaver rhoeas*, corn poppy. Midsummer, Cricket Hill Herb Farm. Photo, Judy Kehs.

single and double plants in the strain are more compact, 16–18 in. (40.6–45.7 cm) tall, with larger flowers, 2–3 in. (5.1–7.6 cm) across, than the wild type. More than anything, Shirleys are synonymous with dainty, fairy-like, fluted cups in tissue-paper pastels—white, rose, salmon—as well as red, with picotee or banded edges and white at their base. This strain was the result of many years of considerable patience in breeding. More recently, variations on the Shirley theme, *Papaver rhoeas* 'Mother of Pearl' and 'Angels Choir', extend the color range to include lilac and frosted colors with frills and banding and semidouble and fully double flowers on stems 10–30 in. (25.4–76.2 cm) tall.

The opium poppies can be grown in a variety of situations, massed in a generous perennial planting or combined in a more confined space with musk mallow (*Malva moschata*), which will cover the opium poppy leaves as they wither. Opium poppies grow in difficult situations—poor, dry soil—and can be naturalized among other carefree annuals like the deep blue bachelor's button (*Centaurea cyanus*) and bright yellow coreopsis. Coming up here and there from self-sown plants, their silky blooms, first the singles, then the doubles, enliven an herb or vegetable garden with candy-store colors—raspberry, watermelon, deep red, lilac, mauve, dark pink. These old-fashioned flowers from "grandmother's garden" are at home among old-fashioned roses, being slender enough to grow up between the roses, and then be pulled up after they have bloomed. As the fascination with "black" flowers grows, the black double poppy *Papaver somniferum* 'Black Peony' could be established in the theme garden with black tulips, hollyhocks, basils, and diminutive violas, with complementary pinks or contrasting oranges and yellows. Black plantings, far from depressing, are arresting and dramatic.

The graceful corn poppies and Shirley types are enjoying a revival of interest, too, for their old-fashioned, antique look, popular in cottage garden plantings with larkspur (*Consolida, Delphinium*), annual lobelias, and sweet alyssum (*Lobularia maritima*). The shortest forms are nice in containers where they draw attention to their airy grace. I grow them in a fluted, iron, truck tire rim sunk in a bed of annuals that include garden opium poppy variants in the background.

Sow seeds outside in full sun (opium poppies can take some shade) before the last frost in the spring; these poppies grow best in cool temperatures. Just press the seeds into the moistened soil. In Zone 8, where summers are very hot, sow seeds in the late fall for late winter or early spring bloom. In climates with harsh winters, poppy seeds can also be sown in the fall for early summer bloom. If seeds of the opium poppy are sown both in the fall and in early spring, there will be flowering plants for a good part of the summer. It is important to thin plants 9–12 in. (22.9–30.5 cm) apart, because crowding produces spindly plants with smaller flowers and pods. To prevent too much self-sowing, cut back or pull up plants after they have bloomed, unless you want to save the seed heads. Tag stems of favorite colors if you want to save their seeds, otherwise, self-sown poppies are variable. Shirley types are not as vigorous as opium poppies and will need to be renewed from fresh seed more frequently. To ensure a full range of colors, buy reselected seeds.

Poppy seeds can be used in baking without incurring their narcotic properties. All the flowers are lovely in fresh bouquets if picked with their tips just showing. Add dried petals to potpourri; use dried seed pods of the opium poppy in dried bouquets and wreaths. To harvest the seed pods, cut stalks while the stems are still green and the pod is green but enlarged; cut off branching stems and brush off leaves; and lay the stems on newspaper out of direct light until they are dry.

Related plants of interest. Seeds of the Shirley Poppies are available from general seed sources; seeds of opium poppies are available from specialty and some general seed sources. Seeds of the unimproved corn poppy and *Papaver commutatum* 'Lady Bird' are harder to find; look for them in specialty, herb, and wildflower sources.

Papaver commutatum 'Lady Bird' is a showier version of the corn poppy with large, crimson, black-blotched flowers on 18 in. (45.7) stems. It is dazzling when massed with an edging of white petunias. Introduced by Thompson and Morgan in 1876, it deserves more attention.

Perovskia

Lamiaceae, Mint Family
Russian sage

Perennial
Site and soil: sun; sharply drained, well-drained
Hardiness: Zones 3–8
Landscape use: accent, bed and border, edge and hedge,
 naturalized herb, rock work
Height: 3–4 ft. (0.9–1.2 m)
Flower: blue, lavender-blue, tubular in whorl
Bloom season: late summer to fall

From small beginnings, the merest hint of silver sprouting from bare stems by early May, Russian sage grows as wide as it is tall by late summer, when the entire plant is covered with small, gray, serrated leaves along its silvery stalks and a multitude of tiny blue or lavender-blue flowers on slender spikes. The form of the plant is billowing and airy, its scent is camphorous with a spicy note. *Perovskia atriplicifolia* has soft blue to lavender-blue flowers; *P. abrotanoides* has more violet flowers and noticeably fringed leaves; *Perovskia* 'Hybrida', a cross between the above two species, has longer flower spikes of lavender-blue and more fringed leaves than *P. atriplicifolia*. The cultivars *P. atriplicifolia* 'Blue Spire' and 'Longin' (named after Longin Zeigler, proprietor of a Swiss nursery) also have deeply cut foliage, lavender-blue flowers, and a more upright habit. 'Filigran', from Germany, has feathery foliage, an erect habit, and long, blue flower spikes.

Russian sage is neither Russian nor a sage, but it is named for a Russian general. It is native from Afghanistan to Tibet where it grows in rocky open places, and it is called sage because of its sage-like aroma. Russian sage has had a curious history in the West since its introduction in 1904. Over the decades, such gardening authorities as Gertrude Jekyll, Russell Page, and Helen Fox have commented on it, yet it remained obscure even as late as 1990, when it was still referred to as relatively unknown. Finally, in 1995, it was named Plant of the Year by the Perennial Plant Association, leading gardeners unanimously to regard it as an outstanding plant.

But is it an herb? Herb growers are torn between wanting to grow this desirable, aromatic plant, and hesitating to admit it to true herb status. At most, it is relegated to the category of ornamental, where various salvias and alliums also reside, too beautiful to ignore, yet lacking the credentials of a truly useful plant. In common with many of the so-called ornamental herbs, Russian sage has a history of use where it is indigenous: its flowers are eaten fresh, and the aromatic leaves are used like tobacco as a euphoriant. Gardeners, in any case, are wild about Russian sage for its appearance and its uses in the landscape. It is the incarnation of an easy-to-grow, low-maintenance, oversized, rosemary-scented lavender that looks good at all seasons, even in the winter when its silvery white branches are bare.

Russian sage dominates the scene wherever it grows; it only asks for room—the more upright forms need less. It can be grown as a billowy hedge, a single accent outside the garden, or a focal point within. It goes with rocks, a rock wall, or a rock outcropping, as in its native habitat. Its silvery gray foliage and lavender-blue flowers complement and improve every conceivable color, from the brightest to the lightest pastels, as well as white. Russell Page first saw Russian sage used to soften bright orange and crimson; Helen Fox thought the violet-blue flowers and silvery foliage effective when mingling among rue's (*Ruta graveolens*) bluish foliage and bright yellow flowers; I grow it near pink mallows (*Malva*). One of the most effective accent plantings is the wide bush growing on a rise between house and driveway, where it can be seen from afar in full bloom. Planting white and lilac-blue alyssum at its feet gives Russian sage a complementary framework for its hemispheric flower spikes, the tiny lilac-blue below echoing the color above. Like other silvery or woolly plants it is wonderfully drought-resistant.

Space plants 24 in. (61.0 cm) apart in sharply drained, ordinary garden soil—not overly rich—in full sun. In the spring cut back old stalks on established plants to 8 in. (20.3 cm) to promote new growth. In rich soil, Russian sage may need propping with linking stakes. To propagate, make stem cuttings during the summer. Where winters are harsh, it is most important to grow plants in well-drained conditions or they may not survive.

All the sage impostors, above and below, are good cut and dried flowers; the seed heads of the Jerusalem sages can be dried too. The dried leaves and flowers of all types can be added to potpourri.

Related plants of interest. Russian sage is mainly available from perennial plant nurseries and some herb sources; note that what is offered as *Perovskia atriplicifolia* may be the hybrid form. The following *Phlomis* species appear from time to time as plants or seeds from specialty seed sources, perennial plant nurseries, and a few herb sources.

Phlomis fruticosa, Jerusalem sage, like *Perovskia*, is not really a sage, nor does it grow in Jerusalem, although it is native to the Mediterranean region. It has been known in the West as Jerusalem sage since the sixteenth century, and it and other species have been used to adulterate true sage. When crushed, the large, pebbly leaves look the same as true sage, but the flavor is missing. "Jerusalem" seems to be a generic term for several species; of the nine *Phlomis* species native to Israel, three are called some sort of Jerusalem sage. The one species I saw in Jerusalem, golden phlomis, *P. aurea*, is very similar in appearance to *P. fruticosa* (and to real sage): the woolly bush spreads to 3 ft. (0.9 m) with gray-green, pebbly leaves and straight stems with large, top whorls of bright yellow flowers. It and the hardier *P. russelliana* look the same and prefer the same conditions—light, well-drained soil and sun, with partial shade in warmer regions. *Phlomis russelliana* is hardy in Zone 4 or 5. A very attractive, pink-flowered, Eurasian species used for food, *P. tuberosa*, tuberous Jerusalem sage, grows to 6 ft. (1.8 m) tall. Both the Jerusalem sages, *P. fruticosa* and *P. tuberosa* bloom later and are hardy in Zone 6. All types are drought-resistant, providing interest in the landscape all season with their evergreen leaves and showy spikes; even the seed heads are attractive. Plant them in sheltered spots near doorways.

Polemonium

Polemoniaceae, Phlox Family
Jacob's ladder

Perennial
Site and soil: sun, partial shade, shade; evenly moist
  and well-drained
Hardiness: Zones 3–9
Landscape use: bed and border, naturalized herb, rock work
Height: 24–30 in. (61.0–76.2 cm)
Flower: blue, violet, white bell or cup in cluster
Bloom season: spring to early summer

Polemoniums, distributed in Europe, Asia, and North and South America, are known by the name Jacob's ladder because of the way their leaves are arranged on either side of arching stems, like rungs on a ladder. The old cottage garden favorite Jacob's ladder, *Polemonium caeruleum* (Plates 75 and 76), is a mounded, upright plant with abundant clusters of 1 in. (2.5 cm), delicate, blue flowers in late spring. These are bell or cup-shaped, their golden stamens reaching out beyond the flower petals; the flowers are set off nicely by the feathery foliage typical of the genus. This plant was considered old-fashioned by the turn of the century. *Polemonium caeruleum* 'Blue Pearl', 18 in. (45.7 cm) tall with light blue flowers, is considered an improvement over the older type. 'Album' is pure white, rather rare, and choice.

Polemonium reptans, also known as spring polemonium, spring valerian, or Greek valerian, is one of several native polemoniums. It grows in moist woodlands and the margins of damp meadows from New York to Georgia. It is called Greek, some say, because the flower is blue and white like the Greek flag, and valerian because of the similarity of its leaves to those of true valerian, *Valeriana officinalis*. It is considered creeping because of its rhizomatous growth. It is a slowly spreading, sprawling plant on weak stems 8 in. (20.3 cm) tall with showy clusters of violet flowers, their white stamens not showing beyond the petals. Also, it blooms 2 weeks earlier than the upright species, in midspring.

239

Both species are greatly valued for their beautiful, early, and long-lasting bloom, as well as ease of cultivation. As herbs, both have medicinal histories based on their astringent properties. In Europe, polemoniums were used to treat fevers, nervous complaints, and epilepsy. The native polemoniums were Indian medicinals of long standing used for similar

Plates 75 and 76. *Polemonium caeruleum*, Jacob's ladder. Early summer, Gardner farm. Photo, Alan Dorey.

purposes, as well as to treat bronchitis and related conditions. The Indian name translates as "smells like pine," a reference to the root's fragrance.

Rock garden expert H. Lincoln Foster loved all polemoniums and suggested planting a variety of them in a shaded rock garden or rockery. Try planting the taller, upright form in dappled shade among chartreuse lady's mantle (*Alchemilla mollis*) and bright yellow cowslips (*Primula veris*). Either type could be naturalized in a woodland or semiwoodland setting, interplanted with tulips and daffodils (*Narcissus*) for a spectacular season of spring bloom. My husband first saw spring polemonium many years ago in Wisconsin, growing wild on a woodland slope. The delicate beauty of its flowers in this setting suggests other landscaping possibilities. As spring cut flowers polemoniums are highly valued, especially as colorful filler for small posies of pansies (*Viola* ×*wittrockiana*), forget-me-nots (*Myosotis*), and sweet woodruff (*Galium odoratum*).

Sow seeds outdoors in the spring or fall, or set plants in the ground 12–18 in. (30.5–45.7 cm) apart in early spring, in well-drained, moist, humusy soil in partial shade. Polemoniums will grow well in full sun, too, but only if the soil is moist. In full sun, however, their bloom period will be shortened. They favor cool growing conditions. Divide clumps every 3 years, just after they have flowered, to maintain their vigor. If left alone, the low, sprawling spring polemonium will readily self-sow. Jacob's ladder is most widely available, as seed or plants, from seed, perennial plant, and herb sources. Look for spring polemonium from perennial plant and wildflower sources.

Polygonatum multiflorum

Liliaceae, Lily Family

Solomon's seal, David's harp, European Solomon's seal

Perennial

Site and soil: partial shade, shade; evenly moist

Hardiness: Zones 3–8

Landscape use: accent, bed and border, ground cover,
naturalized herb, rock work

Height: 3 ft. (0.9 m)

Flower: white-tinged light green, elongated bell in cluster

Bloom season: spring to early summer

The common name Solomon's seal describes an interesting group of plants native to Europe, Asia, and North America. Their thick and knobby, rhizomatous roots are scarred from each season's growth with circular rings that look like seals, hence the origin of their name. The European Solomon's seal, an especially heavily flowering type, bears clusters of two to five small, slightly fluted and bell-shaped flowers in late spring, delicately rimmed with mint green and lightly scented. On gracefully arched and flexible stems, the flowers droop in a long descending line from the axils of glossy, pointed leaves that are so angled as to provide a frame and a contrast for the little bells. The flowers are followed in the summer by blue-black berries that are quickly harvested by birds. The foliage remains green all summer, gradually turning to golden buff by late fall, staying into the winter.

John Gerard ascribed the origin of the plant's common name to Solomon who was wise enough to appreciate the healing virtue of its roots and so set his seal of approval on them. The roots were used in preparations to treat wounds, and various parts of the plant were used in cosmetics and to treat skin irritations. These uses may be traced to the soothing substance allantoin, derived today from other plants and used in the treatment of external wounds. In the East, Solomon's seal is used to lower blood sugar in the treatment of diabetes and to treat heart disease. The spear-like young shoots have been cooked like asparagus as a potherb, and the starchy roots have been eaten as a vegetable and ground into flour. Species native to

North America were used extensively by the Indians as well as by early settlers. Try using the young growing tips in salad and cooking the shoots. Also, the flowering stems are handsome cut flowers and the foliage is prized in bouquets all season.

This elegant plant brings architectural grace to any semiwild, naturalized planting or to a formal shaded border. It consorts well with low-growing pansies (*Viola ×wittrockiana*), violets, and cowslips (*Primula veris*), as well as middle-height plants such as lady's mantle (*Alchemilla mollis*), sweet cicely (*Myrrhis odorata*), and hostas of all types. It is well paired with shrubs such as azaleas and rhododendrons that prefer the same soil and site, and it is effective in a foundation planting of shrubs. I grow Solomon's seal under the spreading limbs of an old tree-like lilac bush behind columbine (*Aquilegia*), bistort (*Polygonum bistorta*), and hostas.

Plant roots of Solomon's seal in the spring or fall in deep, moist, rich soil in partial shade. Space them 12–18 in. (30.5–45.7 cm) apart and 1 in. (2.5 cm) deep, with the growing shoots just below the surface of the soil. Propagate by division in the early spring by cutting a piece of root with at least one bud. The shoots increase slowly but steadily in a growing circle.

Related plants of interest. The various Solomon's seals are available from perennial plant and wildflower nurseries and some herb sources.

Polygonatum biflorum, small Solomon's seal, is a slender native species that grows from Connecticut to Florida and Texas and is adaptable to sunnier and drier growing conditions. It grows 12–36 in. (30.5–91.4 cm) bearing creamy white flowers in pairs in late spring. It is well suited to container culture or to edging a woodland path, where its more delicate beauty would not be overlooked. It was a widely used North American Indian medicinal, the root tea to aid digestion and other preparations to treat coughs, arthritis, and to alleviate pains and bruises.

Polygonatum commutatum, giant Solomon's seal, grows from New Hampshire to Georgia in moist woodland, and is well named for its 6 ft. (1.8 m) height. The scented flowers bloom in late spring in clusters of two to ten, a pale yellow tinged with green. It grows best in light to deep shade and with sustained moisture. It is a striking background or accent plant for a formal or naturalized setting. It is hardy in Zone 4.

Polygonatum humile, Japanese Solomon's seal, from Asia, grows 6–10 in. (15.2–25.4 cm) tall with heart-shaped, vertically grooved leaves and greenish white bell flowers in midspring. It is beautiful in a shaded rock garden or as a ground cover, and it is hardy in Zone 4.

Polygonatum odoratum 'Variegatum' is a very desirable type from Japan, 18–24 in. (45.7–61.0 cm) tall with soft green leaves trimmed with white and pairs of greenish white flowers. The sweet scent is very pronounced in the evening, making it a candidate for the evening or moonlight garden. It blooms early and is especially recommended for warm climates, Zones 9 and 10.

Polygonum bistorta

> The poly-gonum has fine deep pink bottle brush flowers which last a long time.
>
> Margery Fish
> *Gardening in the Shade*

Polygonaceae, Buckwheat Family
Bistort, adderwort, patience dock, snakeweed

Perennial
Site and soil: sun, partial shade, shade; evenly moist, boggy
Hardiness: Zones 3–8
Landscape use: accent, bed and border, naturalized herb
Height: 24–36 in. (61.0–91.4 cm)
Flower: clear pink, slender, terminal spike
Bloom season: spring to early summer

Bistort, an Old World herb, is one of the showiest members of the genus, naturalized in wet meadows of Nova Scotia and eastern Massachusetts. Its peculiar s-shaped or twisted rhizomatous roots—the species name is Latin for twice twisted—give rise to a mound of distinctive, slightly wrinkled, tapering leaves that diminish in size as they grow up slender, 16 in. (40.6 cm) stems. The stems are topped in late spring by dense, 3 in. (7.6 cm) spikes of cylindrical heads, tightly packed with many tiny flowers, whose protruding stamens give them the appearance of fluffy pokers. They are sweetly scented like hawthorn (*Crataegus*) and very attractive to butterflies.

As an herb, bistort has a long history of curative powers derived, for the most part, from its extraordinarily astringent, tannin-packed roots. Once used to tan leather, many root preparations dry up mouth and gum sores and cure diarrhea. The young shoots were eaten as a vegetable, especially in bistort pudding, a traditional dish served as a spring restorative at Easter.

As a garden subject, bistort has been unjustly neglected, even by herb fanciers, despite its ease of culture and long-lasting flower display. In Britain, where it is a common wildflower, it is a highly desirable perennial in the improved form *Polygonum bistorta* 'Superbum' (Plate 77). Bistort is the ultimate accent plant, a strong grower that can be counted on to elicit favorable comment when its pink, bottle-brush flowers, held well above an impressive mound of tongue-shaped, blue-green leaves, make their appearance in late spring. It is bold enough to be grown as a single specimen in any damp ground, or pair it with sweet cicely (*Myrrhis odorata*) or—as it is grown at Sissinghurst Castle—with the bushy Russian comfrey (*Symphytum ×uplandicum*), a background plant smothered in dangling, pinkish blue trumpets. Try bistort in a sunny island bed with *Geranium* 'Johnson's Blue', mountain bluet (*Centaurea montana*), and sweet rocket (*Hesperis matronalis*). All draw bees and butterflies. I grow bistort elsewhere, too, natu-

Plate 77. *Polygonum bistorta* 'Superbum', bistort. Early summer, Graymalkin Farm. Butterflies find it very attractive. Photo, Brian Oke and Gisèle Quesnel.

ralized in light woodland with cowslips (*Primula veris*), in boggy ground with chives (*Allium schoenoprasum*), and in shade with hostas. It thrives anywhere except in dry conditions, adding its beauty of flower and form to any planting.

Plants of bistort are easily established from rhizomes in early spring or early fall in moisture-retentive soil in sun, light shade, or shade. Where summers are very hot, partial shade will prolong bloom, which should last a month or more. Space plants 24–36 in. (61.0–91.4 cm) apart. Although bistort increases easily by its creeping roots, it seldom becomes invasive; extra or unwanted growth can be chopped off at any time and established elsewhere. One of bistort's most endearing characteristics is its ability to survive transplanting at any stage of its growth. If flowering stalks are cut back after blooming, it will flower again in the fall.

Related plants of interest. The cultivar *Polygonum bistorta* 'Superbum' is becoming more widely available from perennial plant sources. The following dwarf ground cover and its cultivars are available from the same sources.

Polygonum affine, dwarf lace plant, with similar astringent properties, is an effective spring-blooming ground cover, growing to 10 in. (25.4 cm) with 3 in. (7.6 cm), rosy spikes and light green, glossy foliage. To establish it as a ground cover, space plants 12 in. (30.5 cm) apart. 'Dimity' is a choice cultivar with light pink and crimson flowers; 'Darjeeling Red', a favorite of Margery Fish, bears deep pink spikes of bloom that gradually change to crimson over a long blooming period.

Primula veris

Primulaceae, Primrose Family
Cowslip, fairy cups, herb Peter, key flower, paigle

Perennial
Site and soil: sun, partial shade; evenly moist
Hardiness: Zones 4–8
Landscape use: bed and border, naturalized herb, rock
  work
Height: 8 in. (20.3 cm)
Flower: bright yellow funnel in umbel
Bloom season: spring to early summer

> I love cowslips not only for their scent but also for the admiration they always arouse.
>
> Rosemary Verey
> *The Scented Garden*

Of the 400 species of *Primula* distributed throughout the Northern Hemisphere, none has been more celebrated for its simple beauty and usefulness than the cowslip, a common wildflower of moist English meadows and woodlands. The clusters of 5 to 12 bright yellow flowers appear in midspring, nodding on stems that grow up from a basal rosette of 8 in. (20.3 cm) long, crinkled and tapering leaves. Each ½ in. (1.3 cm), fluted flower, held by a pale green, inflated calyx, is scented with a warm sweetness similar to the season itself, emanating from an orange dot that appears at the base of each of its petals. The buds are erect, but the flowers in bloom hang down like a bunch of keys on a ring—the origin of some of its common names—then become upright after fertilization so their seeds are not lost before they mature.

Formerly known as *Primula officinalis*, the apothecary herb, this species has had an extraordinary number of medicinal and culinary uses. Its leaves and flowers and roots were used for salad, conserves, pickles, teas, cough medicines, ointments, and the legendary cowslip wine, for which bushels of flowers were picked annually. The cowslip's ability to appease so many afflictions stems from its mildly narcotic properties. Well into the nineteenth century, great quantities of flowers were picked to make a fluffy cowslip ball used at May Day and other spring festivals. It is a wonder any cowslips were left in the wild. Their populations were certainly reduced. As with all plants of the primrose family, the young leaves and flowers of cowslip can be added to salad, and the flowers can be candied in the same way as those of *Borago officinalis*.

The great value of the cowslip as a garden plant, besides its natural beauty and pleasant scent, is that it is very hardy and undemanding and will persist even in unfavorable growing conditions. Variations in color

Plate 78. *Primula veris*, cowslip. Spring, Gardner farm. Photo, Alan Dorey.

are confined to the orange and red range. Double flowers of a form called hose-in-hose are sometimes seen in older gardens and are very choice.

Cowslips draw attention to themselves in any setting because of their upright form and bright flowers. They combine well with ferns in a naturalized situation or a shaded border. In my own garden they bloom into early summer in filtered shade among English daisies (*Bellis*), forget-me-nots (*Myosotis*), Jacob's ladder (*Polemonium*), and pansies (*Viola* ×*wittrockiana*). Established in light woodland, they seem most happy among lungwort (*Pulmonaria officinalis*), bistort (*Polygonum bistorta*), and herb robert (*Geranium robertianum*).

The easiest way to raise cowslips is to sow the seeds, uncovered, in a cold frame in the fall. Plant the seedlings the following spring, spaced 6–12 in. (15.2–30.5 cm) apart in well-prepared, humusy, moist soil in partial shade or sun. For the maximum number of flowers per cluster, divide the plants every 3 years just after blooming, being sure to water and mulch them during drought periods or until they are well established.

Related plants of interest. The wild species are available as seeds or plants from specialty seed sources, perennial plant nurseries, and herb sources. The polyantha primroses are widely available as seeds or plants.

Primula elatior, oxslip, is a natural hybrid between *P. veris* and *P. vulgaris*. It is appreciated for its small, graceful, sulfur yellow flower clusters blooming in midspring on 8 to 12 in. (20.3–30.5 cm) stems. In each cluster, the outside flowers face down and the center flowers up—all are unscented. It tolerates drier growing conditions than other primroses and creates an effective sheet of bloom when massed.

Primula ×*polyantha*, the polyantha primrose, carries both *P. veris* and *P. vulgaris* in its bloodline. It is usually scented and has herbal applications similar to its illustrious parents. It is, however, short-lived and not as easy to maintain, because it demands perfect drainage. On the plus side, the polyantha primroses are earlier blooming and come in a range of brilliant and lovely colors including lilac, purple, crimson, blue, pink, red, and cream, some laced with gold and silver, some with bright golden eyes. The hardiest strain, 'Pacific Giant', is well named with large, free-blooming clusters of upward-facing flowers almost 3 in. (7.6 cm) across on 8 to 10 in. (20.3–25.4 cm) stems. To grow from seeds, prechill them in the refrigerator for 48 hours, then sow them indoors, uncovered, to germinate at

70°F (21°C) in 10 to 40 days. Gardeners may consider it easier to grow these as annuals in areas where they do not long survive.

Primula vulgaris (Plate 79), English primrose, a hardy wildflower of English pastures and woodlands, was originally cultivated as a salad herb and vegetable and has many medicinal applications similar to those of the cowslip. It is an earlier-blooming plant on shorter, 3 to 6 in. (7.6–15.2 cm), stems with oblong leaves and wide open, upward-facing, lightly fragrant flowers about 1½ in. (3.8 cm) across. These are a soft yellow with deeper yellow centers, one flower per stem. The English primrose needs moist but very well-drained soil and will die if this condition is not met. Beautiful variants, dark rose with yellow centers, can be found in older gardens; 'Old Rose' is double-flowered with deep rose, carnation-like flowers in abundance, each delicately edged with white. Double Primrose Hybrids, an F_1 hybrid seed strain, produces variable, semidouble, yellow flowers over a long period. Tuck any of these in front of the border or in a rock garden.

Plate 79. *Primula vulgaris*, English primrose, seed-grown variant. Spring, Gardner farm. Photo, Alan Dorey.

Prunella vulgaris

Lamiaceae, Mint Family
Self-heal, all-heal, blue curls, herb carpenter, hook-heal

Perennial
Site and soil: sun, partial shade; well-drained, evenly moist
Hardiness: Zones 4–9
Landscape use: ground cover, naturalized herb, rock work
Height: 3–20 in. (7.6–50.8 cm)
Flower: purple-blue, small, open-mouthed, in whorls on
　spike
Bloom season: early summer to late summer

The Eurasian self-heal is a humble weed, widely naturalized in North America, often found growing in damp fields, pastures, and lawns. In such conditions it reaches only 3 in. (7.6 cm) in height, but in fertile soil it may grow much taller. In all circumstances, its blocky, stout flower heads are its most interesting feature. Nicholas Culpeper rightly compared the head or spike of small, open-mouthed flowers in whorls to an ear of corn. At first, the comparison seems stretched, but in the head's maturity it is most descriptive. The flower's broad upper lip, hooded in shape and deep velvety purple in color, overhangs a three-lobed lower lip that is so hairy on the middle lobe that it appears fringed. Bees come to harvest the nectar buried deep within the flower's throat, also effecting fertilization, after which the flower drops off the head but leaves its dark bracts behind so that by fall, when all the flowers have finally opened and fallen, the head resembles a diminutive, well-picked ear of corn. Since the flowers do not all open at once, the plant's blooming period extends over the whole summer. Plants increase rapidly by runners, the oblong, 1 in. (2.3 cm) leaves forming dense mats of growth that are especially encouraged when mowed, much to the exasperation of those who try by this means to banish it from their lawns.

Self-heal's history is preserved in its names. According to the *Doctrine of Signatures*, it advertised its ability to treat throat ailments by the design of its flowers—an open mouth. During the sixteenth century it gained prominence when it was used extensively to treat an outbreak of quinsy, an acute inflammation of the tissues surrounding the tonsils, in the German Imperial Army, by which it became known as brunella—Latinized to prunella—from the German for "the browns," which described a patient's brown-coated tongue at the height of infection. Like bugle (*Ajuga*), which it resembles in its herbal properties, self-heal is an astringent, traditionally used as a soothing gargle and to heal external wounds. Because of its country use as a convenient styptic it was known as hook-heal or herb carpenter. From its diversity of uses it gained the reputation as all-heal. Research suggests it also has antibiotic properties.

Through countless summers I tramped over the little self-heal until finally I discovered that this pasture weed, if grown in garden soil and used with discretion, gains great appeal with its massed flower spikes, whose ef-

Plate 80. *Prunella vulgaris*, self-heal, wild. Midsummer, Gardner farm. Photo, Alan Dorey.

fectiveness is lost in the wild. It is a good choice for naturalizing anywhere in the sun, especially in a natural rocky outcropping. Grown as a ground-hugging, weed-smothering cover, it blooms over a long period, taking up the slack of spent, spring-flowering ground covers. The fancier sorts extend its landscaping uses. Also, the cultivars are good cut flowers for small bouquets, and the dried heads with their stalks are nice in small dried posies or tussie-mussies.

Sow seeds of self-heal in the spring in ordinary garden soil in the sun, setting plants 16 in. (40.6 cm) apart. In warmer areas, self-heal appreciates a moist, richer soil and some shade. Plants self-sow and can also be propagated by division in the spring or fall. Control its spread by mowing around the planting during the season.

Related plants of interest. Seeds or plants of the wild self-heal are available from herb sources. The *Prunella grandiflora* subsp. *pyrenaica* cultivars can be found in perennial plant sources; the *P. grandiflora* Pagoda Series is offered as seed from general seed and herb sources.

Prunella grandiflora, large self-heal, is the type grown for its larger, 1 in. (2.5 cm) flowers, deep violet with a whitish tube, especially choice in the cultivars *P. grandiflora* subsp. *pyrenaica* 'Loveliness' (pale violet-blue), 'Pink Loveliness', and 'White Loveliness', which grow 8–12 in. (20.3–30.5 cm) tall and are sometimes listed under *P. webbiana*. The *P. grandiflora* Pagoda Series expands the self-heal repertoire to include, besides pink, dark blue, white, cream, and rose-red. Any of these are stunning when combined with bugles (*Ajuga*) to create a rich carpet of colors and textures all season. Do not hesitate to plant the cultivars in beds or borders, since their growth is not difficult to control, in a rock garden, or in containers in sunny or semishaded areas. Grow from plants or start seeds indoors 8–10 weeks before the last frost; just cover seeds, which should germinate in 30 to 60 days at 55–65°F (13–18°C). The 'Loveliness' cultivars are hardy in Zone 4; the Pagoda Series is hardy in Zone 6.

Pulmonaria officinalis

Boraginaceae, Borage Family

Lungwort, common lungwort, hundreds-and-thousands, Jacob and Rachel, soldiers and sailors, spotted cowslip

Perennial

Site and soil: partial shade, shade; evenly moist

Hardiness: Zones 3–9

Landscape use: bed and border, edge and hedge, naturalized herb, rock work

Height: 12 in. (30.5 cm)

Flower: pink, blue, violet, white, small trumpet in cluster

Bloom season: spring to early summer

The European lungworts are a fascinating group of plants for their herbal history, pretty and changing flowers, and handsome foliage. *Pulmonaria officinalis*, once a healing herb of wide repute, carries out the basic lungwort design. In early spring, even through drifts of snow, its dark pink bud-tips begin to show, highlighted against the earthy mass of last year's growth. The stems, arising to 12 in. (30.5 cm) or less, bear clusters of small, trumpet-shaped flowers that open pink and quickly change to purple, then blue, and finally, having spent their generous store of shades, fade to white and close. There are always several different-colored flowers on each stem, giving rise to many common names—those above are just a sampling—which play on this theme. Unlike other species, the leaves of the common lungwort appear at the same time as the flowers, though they are small and inconspicuous. As the plant matures, however, the basal leaves grow in importance. Somewhat heart-shaped and tapering, covered with down, and spotted or splotched with gray to their tips, they remain in evidence all season and survive hard frosts before finally expiring.

The common lungwort is an exemplar of the herbs listed in the ancient *Doctrine of Signatures,* which purported that a plant advertised its curative powers by its physical characteristics. Since lungwort has spotted, lung-shaped leaves it was so named and was used to treat all sorts of bronchial and lung problems. The plant does have soothing properties, so it may have relieved the discomfort of sore throats and similar minor complaints. Water distilled from the plant is considered effective balm for sore or tired eyes. An extract from lungwort is an ingredient in vermouth.

Lungwort is the first flowering plant to make its appearance in our Nova Scotia gardens, so we watch for signs of life at the most unpromising time, early April, when the ground is still frozen, snow lingers in drifts, and bitterly cold winds scour the Island. Anxiously watching for any sign of spring, it is a never-failing joy to spy the very first pink bud. In a day or two the little trumpets are blowing in the cruel wind, just as Margery Fish saw them in her English garden in March. As the spring sun warms the earth, the long-lasting trumpets become a mass of blooms, a shimmering haze of violet, inviting our honeybees to enjoy an early and plentiful source of nectar. Flowering lasts a full month.

I first discovered lungwort as a ground cover, its traditional use, and there is no denying that it speedily and effectively carpets the ground by means of its rhizomes, for which it is rightly named hundreds-and-thousands. It is useful around shrubbery and trees, particularly if it is underplanted with spring bulbs—plenty of daffodils golden and glorious. It also excels as an edge, instead of stones or bricks, for any type of planting; it both frames the plants within and provides a barrier against grass and weeds.

Plant roots of lungwort in partial shade or even full sun if the soil is moist. Water them well and mulch them if conditions are dry. Only one thing will kill lungwort: dry winds in drought conditions. Propagate plants by division in early fall, watering them well. In a sunny situation, especially one that is exposed, the foliage will benefit from mowing after the blooms are spent. Fresh leaves grow in about a week. Foliage and flowers retain best color and appearance in shaded situations.

Related plants of interest. Since lungworts readily hybridize, their offspring cannot always be accurately determined. The cultivars below are listed as they usually appear in catalogs. The lungworts are available from perennial plant and herb sources, but *Pulmonaria* 'Salmon Glow' is rare.

Pulmonaria angustifolia, blue lungwort, is characterized by narrow, solid green leaves and brilliant blue flowers, rich pink in bud. Pair this lungwort with spring yellows: forsythia, daffodils (*Narcissus*), and leopardsbane (*Doronicum*). It is recommended for rock gardens, where it makes a dramatic splash of color. The best cultivar is 'Azurea', 8–12 in. (20.3–30.5 cm) tall.

Pulmonaria montana, Christmas cowslip, is the earliest to bloom, not by Christmas, but by the end of February in Zone 6. The flowers, on 12 in. (30.5 cm) stems, are salmon-red in tight clusters, tucked into soft green foliage, usually unspotted. 'Redstart' is brick red with unspotted foliage.

Pulmonaria saccharata, Bethlehem sage—a reference calling on the "wise" meaning of the word—closely resembles the common lungwort but its leaves are more heavily spotted, especially in the well-known 'Mrs Moon' (Plate 81), named not for its moon-splashed leaves but for the wife of illustrator H. G. Moon, a friend of William Robinson. 'Sissinghurst White', sometimes listed under *P. officinalis*, has pure white flowers, turning pink, and heavily spotted leaves. 'Janet Fisk' is similar to 'Mrs Moon' but the

Plate 81. *Pulmonaria saccharata* 'Mrs Moon', Bethlehem sage. Spring, Robison York State Herb Garden, Cornell Plantations. Photo, Diane Miske, Cornell Plantations.

leaves appear to be painted silver. 'Roy Davidson' has sky-blue flowers and beautifully mottled, rather narrow leaves that never look weary. 'Pink Dawn' (Plate 82) has white-spotted leaves and pink flowers. All are hardy in Zone 3.

Pulmonaria 'Salmon Glow', of uncertain origin, has large, scarlet-red flower heads and is hardy in Zone 4 or 5.

Plate 82. *Pulmonaria saccharata* 'Pink Dawn', Bethlehem sage. Spring, Joseph Hudak garden. Photo, Joseph Hudak.

Rosa gallica 'Officinalis'

Rosaceae, Rose Family
Apothecary's rose, red rose of Lancaster

Shrub
Site and soil: sun; evenly moist and well-drained
Hardiness: Zones 4–10
Landscape use: accent, bed and border, edge and
  hedge
Height: 3 ft. (0.9 m)
Flower: crimson, semidouble in cluster
Bloom season: early summer to midsummer

Throughout history, roses have been singled out and elevated above all flowering plants as a gift from the angels, adored and admired for their beauty and fragrance, valued, too, as food and medicine. The red rose of antiquity, later known as the apothecary's rose, exemplifies those types that were selected from the wild so long ago that their original forms are unknown; others of these are the Alba or white rose and the Damask rose.

A rose of singular beauty, the apothecary's rose is a low, spreading bush 3 ft. (0.9 m) tall and as wide, with nearly thornless stems and handsomely veined, dull green, toothed leaves. Loosely doubled, but crisply petaled, the flowers are almost contemporary in appearance. Deep crimson and 3–4 in. (7.6–10. 2 cm) wide when fully opened, they reveal a mass of bright golden stamens in their centers. Spent blooms are followed by small, teardrop-shaped, brick red fruits that remain on the bushes all winter.

The apothecary's rose, the oldest form of *Rosa gallica* in cultivation, may have been introduced to the West from Damascus before the thirteenth century. It was especially valued for its perfume and medicinal applications—the red petals, high in tannin, have soothing properties. The fresh flowers carry a pure rose fragrance that is intensified when the petals are dried, the scent lasting a long time even when the dried petals are powdered. There was a great demand for red rose petals from Greek and Roman times into the nineteenth century. Provence, the center of red rose petal production, exported 10 tons (9072 kg) of dried petals to the United States alone in the mid-nineteenth century. In the North American home

Plate 83. *Rosa gallica* 'Officinalis', apothecary's rose, forming a hedge. Midsummer, Gardner farm. Photo, Alan Dorey.

of that period, petals from home-grown plants provided a pharmacopeia themselves, supplying roses for syrups and infusions to soothe sore throats, heal mouth sores, and, when infused in vinegar, to lessen the pain of headaches. All sorts of wines, teas, waters, lotions, jellies, jams, conserves, and potpourris were created from its petals and fruits to nourish the body and cheer the soul.

Although once-blooming, the apothecary's rose and its desirable cultivars offer abundant and scented flowers for 3 weeks to a month, and, just as important, they are reliably hardy. The sport *Rosa gallica* 'Rosa Mundi' (introduced before 1581) has more tightly doubled flowers, its petals splashed with several shades of dark and light pink. *Rosa* 'Charles de Mills' (date of introduction unknown) has rich reddish purple blooms so doubled that they appear quartered, a term used to describe types whose mass of petals seem to be packed into four separate sections. *Rosa* 'Tuscany' or 'Old Velvet' (introduced before 1820) has double, very dark crimson, almost black blooms, a striking contrast to the golden stamens within.

If kept trimmed and free of suckers, the low form of the apothecary's rose makes it suitable for a mixed planting. I once visited an appealing garden where a fine collection of old roses, including the apothecary's, were featured in a series of small beds, each one liberally planted with old-fashioned perennials such as foxglove (*Digitalis*), Canterbury bells (*Campanula medium*), lupines (*Lupinus*), sweet William (*Dianthus barbatus*), pinks (*Dianthus*), and pansies (*Viola* ×*wittrockiana*), all of which bloom at the same time. All forms of the apothecary's rose are beautiful in rose beds, in mixed plantings, and in hedges. Try it as a wide, informal hedge that will be glorious in bloom and always the subject of admiration. A single specimen, contained by mowing around it, makes a handsome accent in the landscape, in a sunny, open site.

Roses in general thrive in an open, sunny site with good air circulation that discourages fungus disease. The old roses grow well in heavy, moist, though well-drained, soil. Before planting, soak the roots in water for at least 2 hours. The planting holes should be 15–18 in. (38.1–45.7 cm) wide, 12–18 in. (30.5–45.7 cm) deep, and 30 in. (76.2 cm) apart. Mix 1 bushel (352 liters) of rotted compost or manure with the soil and add 1 cup (250 ml) of bone meal. Make a cone of the soil, over which the roots should be placed pointing downward. Trim away weak or crossed roots, then fill in the hole, tamping down the soil to eliminate air pockets; leave a depression around the plant for watering. Where winters are severe, grafted roses must be well covered with 1 to 2 in. (2.5–5.1 cm) of soil over the graft—the swelling on the lower stem—otherwise the graft could be damaged, leaving the undesirable rootstock to take over.

It is important in the rose's early life to provide it with plenty of water; a seasonal mulch will help to conserve moisture. Every spring after the plant is established scratch into the surrounding soil a handful of bone meal and ½–1 cup (125–250 ml) general garden fertilizer; also spread 2 or 3 shovelsful of compost around the base, not close to the stem. Spring pruning is minimal; just trim away crossed, dead, or unwanted stems and suckers. To propagate, take stem cuttings just after flowering and plant them in a prepared bed of sandy soil outside; mulch and water them over the summer, and they should be ready to replant by the following spring. An easier way to propagate this and other old roses is to pull suckers straight up out of the ground, cut them back by at least half, and replant them at once.

An easy and enjoyable way to "use" roses is to cut them for indoor bouquets, simultaneously performing a service by keeping bushes trimmed. Use clippers and cut the stems at a slant just above a set of leaves. Choose roses in every stage, from the just opening bud to fully opened flowers— a mix lends interest. They combine well with tansy (*Tanacetum vulgare*) foliage, especially curly tansy (*T. vulgare* var. *crispum*), sprigs of chartreuse lady's mantle (*Alchemilla mollis*), sprays of blue *Anchusa* or *Cynoglossum*, and double white feverfew (*Tanacetum parthenium* cultivars). Save the petals from the spent bouquet for making potpourri, or pick fresh ones and spread them out on cookie sheets near a gentle source of heat, turning them occasionally. When they are crispy dry, follow the directions below (which can be applied to making any potpourri).

Potpourri

Mix 1 teaspoon essential oil with 3 tablespoons orrisroot (granular or pinhead) and allow to blend in a covered jar for 3 days, shaking occasionally. Add mixture to 1 quart of dried petals. Place the petals and scented orrisroot in a tightly closed container away from light and shake it every other day for 6 weeks before opening. To vary, add pieces of dried orange peel and mixed spices such as crushed cloves and cinnamon, and supplement the rose petals with other dried flowers for color, texture, and scent. The potpourri can be placed in open bowls or specially lidded jars and stirred or shaken occasionally to release the scent.

The dark red rose petals release their color in jellies and vinegar. All scented petals are delicious—they taste as roses smell. They can be candied as the flowers of *Borago officinalis,* and enjoyed as garnishes on salads or desserts or in open-faced sandwiches. For example, spread thinly sliced, whole wheat bread with sweet butter and cover with clean petals—cut out the white base for it is somewhat bitter—then lightly sprinkle with a cinnamon-sugar mix.

Related plants of interest. All the roses are available from specialty rose nurseries and some herb sources.

Rosa rugosa, rugosa or Japanese rose, was introduced to the United States in the late 1800s for its resistance to salt spray; it is now naturalized along the coastline from the Canadian Maritimes to Cape Cod. It is a vigorous,

Plate 84. *Rosa rugosa* 'Rubra Plena', rugosa rose. Early summer, Gardner farm. Photo, Alan Dorey.

rugged, upright rose 8 ft. (2.4 m) tall with bristly, thorny stems and attractive dark green, ribbed and wrinkled foliage—*rugosa* means wrinkled. The crinkly petaled flowers, from rose to white, are 2–3 in. (5.1–7.6 cm) across, and moderately fragrant. They bloom profusely in early summer and less generously again in the fall. Rugosas bear outstandingly beautiful hips, orange or rosy red, 1 in. (2.5 cm) wide and crowned with erect sepals. The late fall foliage, a coppery bronze, is an added bonus. Growth requirements are similar to the apothecary's rose, but plants are tolerant of dry, sandy soil and wind. They make wonderful tall, informal hedges or specimen plants. 'Alba' is pure white, 'Rubra' is violet-red, and the semi-double, strongly clove-scented 'Rubra Plena' (Plate 84) is dark pink.

In traditional Chinese medicine preparations from the flowers and fruits are used to promote blood circulation, ease the pains of rheumatism, and provide a tonic to regulate the vital energies. The hips, besides their ornamental value in the late fall and winter, are a source of vitamin C and pectin and are used to make jellies and teas. They are a mild laxative and diuretic.

Some of the most desirable rugosa cultivars are the older ones. *Rosa* 'Blanc Double de Coubert' (introduced 1892), of tree-like proportions at 7 ft. (2.1 m), is one of the most outstanding white roses of all time, its flowers strongly fragrant and double, with their golden centers still apparent. It blooms later than *R. rugosa*, continuing into the fall with the late flowers appearing among the fruits formed from the first blush of bloom. It is grown as a hedge or specimen. *Rosa* 'Frau Dagmar Hartopp' (introduced 1914) is quite compact, a low, wide bush suitable for the garden, 2–5 ft. (0.6–1.5 m) tall, with continuous bloom throughout the summer. Its flowers are striking silvery-pink, golden-centered, single, 3 in. (7.6 cm) wide, and very fragrant, followed by large hips. *Rosa* 'Hansa' (introduced 1905) is a refined version of 'Rubra Plena', 6 ft. (1.8 m) tall with very double, dark reddish purple flowers, 3–4 in. (7.6–10.2 cm) across, intensely clove-scented, followed by large hips. It blooms early and late with a few flowers in between and is suitable for hedge or specimen planting.

Rosmarinus officinalis

Lamiaceae, Mint Family
Rosemary

Shrub
Site and soil: sun; sharply drained, well-drained
Hardiness: Zones 7 or 8–10
Landscape use: accent, bed and border, container, edge and
    hedge, ground cover, rock work
Height: 2–8 ft. (0.6–2.4 m)
Flower: light blue, dark blue, violet-blue, pink, white, small, two-lipped
    in cluster
Bloom season: spring to early summer

Rosemary's natural home is by the Mediterranean Sea—its Latin name means, literally, dew of the sea—in areas known as *maquis* that support shrubby growth and low trees. Under warm, sunny conditions, with sufficient moisture, bushes may reach considerable height and girth, but in a pot it usually grows 2–4 ft. (0.6–1.2 m). A handsome plant, hardy between 15 and 20°F (−9 and −7°C), with a thick woody trunk in older specimens, its leaves are needle-like to 1¹/₂ in. (2.5–3.8 cm) and strongly veined with a single line that divides one narrow half from the other. Slightly rolled under at their margins and crowded along stems in pairs, the undersides of the leaves are white and hairy, almost silvery, and the top of the leaves green, leathery, and somewhat pebbly in texture. Flowers, borne in clusters on the previous year's growth, in leaf axils near the tops of the stems, are two-lipped like other members of the mint family. But these are rather unusual in that the middle lobe of the lower lip is noticeably enlarged and bowl-like and spotted within. Stamens protrude from each flower, gracefully reaching out to form an arc, like a tiny orchid. Bloom color varies from blue in the species form, to a brighter blue in the creeping kind, *Rosmarinus officinalis* 'Prostratus', and to dark blue, pink, or white in other cultivars. The plant in flower has a spicy, piny, sharp, and warm aroma that draws a multitude of bees, who produce from its nectar the choicest of honey.

Rosemary has been a popular herb since ancient times. It has been strewn and burned in incense like lavender, brewed in teas to soothe nerves, headaches, stomach disorders, and colds, distilled for perfumes, cosmetics, and medicines, and infused in alcohol for a treatment for rheumatism known as Hungary water. Its culinary uses, too, have ancient origins, most often associated with the cooking or grilling of rich meats such as lamb, beef, and pork. Contemporary research credits rosemary as an effective carminative, to dispel intestinal gas, and antispasmodic, to calm nervous and muscular spasms. Rosemary oil is used as a food preservative.

Rosemary is also for remembrance. The details of herbal lore are often regarded solely as fancies of the past, by which we, in our superior wisdom, are bemused and charmed. Yet that lore preserves the mundane but interesting conditions of historic daily life, the knowledge of which may lead us to better understand the customs and traditions maintained in our

Plate 85. *Rosmarinus officinalis*, rosemary. Spring, University of Washington, Seattle, Center for Urban Horticulture. Where it can be grown in the ground all year, rosemary usually blooms in the spring; elsewhere bloom times vary. Photo courtesy of the University of Washington Center for Urban Horticulture.

present lives. Rosemary was used on ceremonial occasions, such as weddings and funerals, because its leaves were evergreen—hence always useable—and because their peculiar structure caused them to retain their fragrance and freshness after being picked, longer than any other aromatic herb. Such characteristics suggested the enduring values of fidelity and remembrance: "Be't for my bridal or my burial," wrote the poet Robert Herrick, expressing a long-established, familiar tradition.

So extraordinary is rosemary's appeal—its full, shrubby growth even in a pot, its spicily pungent leaves, its occasional bursts of magical blooms, its romance—that the great number of gardeners who live in very un-Mediterranean climates will go to almost any length to maintain plants from one season to another. The most ingenious and bizarre strategies have been advanced since colonial times for wintering rosemary, including storing pots in a dark cellar (certain to bring early death), wrapping them in burlap to store in a greenhouse, placing them in pits in the ground, covering them with baskets, building whole greenhouses around them along a south-facing wall. The method of choice for most gardeners in climates harsher than Zone 8 is to place pots on a sunny windowsill.

The relative hardiness of rosemary is a subject of great interest to aficionados. Great hopes have been raised for *Rosmarinus officinalis* 'Arp', introduced in 1973 and named after Arp, Texas where it was found by Madalene Hill. It has been hailed as the hardy rosemary, the only one that might be able to grow in the ground and survive a harsh winter. Reputed to be hardy to −10°F (−23°C), which is Zone 6, possibly Zone 5, it is a more sprawling form than the species, with gray-green leaves and light blue flowers, growing to 5 ft. (1.5 m). Its performance, however, has been inconsistent.

Finding the best flowering rosemarys among the many cultivars is difficult given the variables of climate, day length, and maturity, all factors in encouraging flower production. In my experience, rosemary blooms indoors in midwinter and may bloom again in the spring or early summer when set outdoors. Elsewhere, rosemarys may bloom in the summer and even rebloom in the fall, depending on climatic and cultural conditions.

In hot, dry, frost-free areas rosemary's drought resistance is invaluable. The upright rosemarys are distinctive shrubs or hedges, very attractive when fronting a wall, lining a broad stairway, or marking entrances, where their penetrating aroma will be noticed when brushed. The columnar, straight-growing sorts such as *Rosmarinus officinalis* 'Tuscan Blue' (Plate 86) and 'Majorca Pink' can be used for formal plantings; smaller, more compact kinds such as 'Blue Boy' can be incorporated into a border. The trailing or prostrate and semiupright forms can also be grown in the foreground of a border or among rocks, at the foot of walls, or as a ground cover. The very wide-spreading 'Lockwood de Forest' is stunning in hanging baskets. Gardeners in climates where rosemary is not hardy can sink a potted rosemary into the ground to be the centerpiece of an island herb bed in the spring. Just dig out the pot each fall to winter the plant indoors. While the flowers will not be as prolific as they would be elsewhere, they are a pretty blue and the plant's habit and form will add to the garden; it looks wonderful in a large tub on a deck, too.

Plate 86. *Rosmarinus officinalis* 'Tuscan Blue', rosemary. Late winter, greenhouse, Cricket Hill Herb Farm. Photo, Deb Kehs.

Rosemary is variable when grown from seed, but doing so is not difficult. Sow seeds indoors in late winter or early spring, uncovered, at 70°F (21°C); with bottom heat, germination should occur within a week, otherwise expect it to take 21 days. At all stages, keep soil evenly moist; the potting soil should be amended with both sharp sand and vermiculite. Outside, young plants should be spaced 12–18 in. (30.5–45.7 cm) apart, mature plants 3–4 ft. (0.9–1.2 m), depending on type, in full sun—though in a hot climate, rosemary will tolerate partial shade—and soil slightly alkaline or neutral. Most importantly, plant in very well-drained soil; water should never be allowed to collect around rosemary's roots. The site should have good air circulation but be protected from wind; after low temperatures, winter wind is a major factor in limiting rosemary's hardiness. Presoaked clay pots are recommended for container-grown rosemary. Outdoors, these should be fertilized every 2 weeks.

To protect branches from winter damage, wrap the plants as you would other shrubs, tying the material so the branches are lifted upward; be sure to leave the top of the plant uncovered. For *Rosmarinus officinalis* 'Arp', winter it indoors for a season so it attains some size and a good root system before attempting to winter it in the ground in colder areas. When plants are indoors, give them at least 4 hours of direct sun a day—or 12 hours of strong artificial light—and a cool spot at approximately 60°F (16°C). Dry heat will cause the needles to drop.

It may take 3 years for rosemary plants to bloom from seed. If plants are heavily harvested for their leaves, flower production will suffer since flowers occur on the previous season's growth. Eventually, rosemary becomes woody and both leaf and flower production is sparse, so new plants should be propagated. Take stem cuttings any time during the summer from a 4–5 in. (10.2–12.7 cm) sprig of vigorous new growth at the top of the plant. These root in moist sand in 6 weeks or less. Layering to produce more plants can be done easily in the spring—branches should be pegged down and mounded over with earth. These should form roots by fall, when they can be clipped from the mother plant and potted. When a plant outgrows its container, move it to one 3–4 in. (7.6–10.2 cm) larger and reduce the roots by a third before repotting. Repot in the spring so a good root system is developed by the time rosemary is brought indoors, otherwise, plants may be unable to absorb water properly, which is a common cause of plant failure. Water deeply with room temperature water whenever soil is dry to the touch.

Rosemary flowers and leaves add a bracing scent to potpourri. The flowers are edible and can be used to embellish desserts, but the leaves have more flavor and are used for cooking, especially with pork and lamb dishes. Rosemarys vary in flavor, making some types more suitable for cooking than others. For a change, add a small amount of chopped leaves to the dough of sugar cookies, biscuits, breads, or rolls. Add the chopped and bruised leaves to butter or use them to flavor jelly, which makes a deliciously unusual condiment with a main course or a spread on biscuits or crackers, alone or with cream cheese. The following recipe can be used to make a jelly of any herb, changing the juice to suit the desired flavor:

Herb Jelly

Place 1 cup finely cut, fresh rosemary leaves in a saucepan, bruise them with the bottom of a heavy glass, add 2 cups water, orange juice, or sherry to the herbs, and slowly bring the mixture to a boil. Turn off the heat and let the herbs steep, covered, for 15 minutes, occasionally bruising the leaves again to release more flavor, then strain out the leaves. To 1 1/2 cups of this infusion, add 2 tablespoons vinegar, 3 1/2 cups sugar, and a dash of salt. Bring this mixture to a rolling boil that cannot be stirred down. Stir in 1 pouch or 1/2 bottle of liquid pectin and reboil the mixture for 1 minute, stirring constantly. Remove from heat, let settle, skim if necessary, and pour into scalded jelly jars and seal at once. Makes about seven 1/4 pint jars.

Related plants of interest. Seeds of the species are widely available from general seed sources. The cultivars are available from herb sources.

Rosmarinus officinalis 'Alba Heavy Leaf' is vigorous to 4 ft. (1.2 m) with distinctive, true white flowers. Described as hardy to 15°F (−9°C), experience suggests it may be even hardier.

Rosmarinus officinalis 'Blue Boy', a dwarf prostrate type with small, light green leaves, has light blue flowers and a bushy habit, growing 2–4 ft. (0.6–1.2 m). It looks good in containers and is hardy to 15°F (−9°C) with protection. It is a good winter bloomer indoors.

Rosmarinus officinalis 'Collingwood Ingram' has an upright form 24–36 in. (61.0–91.4 cm) tall, spreading 4 ft. (1.2 m) wide. With brighter blue flowers than the species and a more spreading habit, it makes a tall ground cover or a handsome tub plant with gracefully curving stems. It is hardy to 20°F (−7°C) with protection.

Rosmarinus officinalis 'Gorizia', an upright type to 4 ft. (1.2 m) with unusually broad leaves and light blue flowers, is a Thomas DeBaggio introduction, named after the town in Italy where one of his customers found it. It is hardy to 15°F (−9°C).

Rosmarinus officinalis 'Lockwood de Forest', Santa Barbara rosemary, was a chance seedling in the garden of the family for whom it is named; it probably resulted from a natural cross between *R. officinalis* and *R. officinalis* 'Prostratus'. It is a vigorous plant with flowers more prolific than either parent in a lovely robin's-egg blue. Semiupright in habit and woody, it grows 12–24 in. (30.5–61.0 cm) tall and 4–8 ft. (1.2–2.4 m) wide, spreading over banks and draping itself over walls. It is hardy to 20°F (−7°C).

Rosmarinus officinalis 'Majorca Pink' is a stiff, upright type 2–4 ft. (0.6–1.2 m) tall with what DeBaggio describes as "dazzling blooms of amethyst-violet." It is hardy to about 15°F (−9°C) with protection.

Rosmarinus officinalis 'Prostratus' is the archetypal creeping rosemary from which many other cultivars have come. I saw it used extensively for landscaping in Jerusalem, edging all banks, grounds, and roadways, always in bloom. It is a darker blue than the species, about 18 in. (45.7 cm) tall and 4½ ft. (1.4 m) across, and a useful ground cover. In colder regions, it is attractive in hanging baskets or urns. It is hardy to 20°F (−7°C).

Rosmarinus officinalis 'Severn Sea' is semiupright with light blue flowers in profusion. It is hardy to 15°F (−9°C).

Rosmarinus officinalis 'Tuscan Blue' (Plate 86), tall and upright to 8 ft. (2.4 m) or more, bears clear violet-blue flowers and larger leaves than the species. It is a vigorous grower rated as the second hardiest rosemary after 'Arp', hardy to 10°F (−12°C).

Ruta graveolens

Rutaceae, Rue Family
Rue, herb-of-grace

Perennial
Site and soil: sun; well-drained
Hardiness: Zones 4–9
Landscape use: accent, bed and border, edge and
   hedge
Height: 3 ft. (0.9 m)
Flower: yellow, conical star in loose cluster
Bloom season: midsummer to late summer

> A shrub of rue is a handsome addition to any garden, because of its shining, blue-green . . . leaves and its curious yellow-green flowers, which cover the shrub in mid-summer.
>
> Helen Noyes Webster
> *Herbs*

Rue is a low, wide plant found on dry, rocky limestone slopes in Mediterranean regions. Its lacy blue-green foliage, segmented into oval lobes, grows from a woody base, giving the plant a bushy appearance. From midsummer until fall the top of the plant is covered with small, bright yellow flowers in comb-like clusters that are very attractive to butterflies. These flower heads, often gilded, are regularly dried for bouquets. Each small, incurving flower surrounds a prominent, greenish center; when the petals fall, knob-like green pods are left behind, giving the whole plant a decorative air over a long season.

From its association with church services, where it was used as a brush to sprinkle holy water, rue earned the name herb-of-grace. Its reputation throughout all the different cultures of Europe as a charm or repellent against evil spirits, has its origin in rue's strong, pungent odor that comes from the oil glands found on its leaves and flowers and from the acrid juice in its stems. The genus name, from the Greek *reuo*, meaning to set free, may refer to its mystical use or its medicinal application in treating a number of ailments from rheumatism to expelling worms. It is still regarded as a folk remedy for indigestion, but it can be poisonous and should not be ingested.

The unimproved species is still the best for flowering, since new cultivars focus exclusively on the foliage, which is admittedly very handsome. Although rue has always enjoyed prominence in the herb garden since the herb revival movement of the 1930s, it has also been popular in England, where it was once a staple of the knot garden. One seventeenth-century writer suggested a planting of rue with pennyroyal (*Mentha pulegium*), marjoram (*Origanum*), chamomile (*Chamaemelum nobile*), daisies (*Bellis*), and violets, enclosed by evergreens. Such a planting would be a bit difficult to manage, perhaps, but it suggests possibilities. Rue is a handsome perennial with varied advantages to offer a garden setting, but it has been generally underused, not only because of its confinement as an herb, but because it has been regarded primarily as a foliage plant. I grew rue for several years before coming to value its bright midsummer bloom that lasts well into the fall, even through light snow. It retains its interest even as its desiccated flowers are blown about in the wind, refusing to be displaced. Try rue at the front of an island bed where it will make a lovely mound of foliage all season, a contrast for bright yellow daisy flowers, such as calendula and golden margeurite (*Anthemis tinctoria*), and the purple spikes of hyssop (*Hyssopus officinalis*). When it flowers, rue's mound is trans-

Plate 87. *Ruta graveolens*, rue. Midsummer, Graymalkin Farm. Photo, Brian Oke and Gisèle Quesnel.

formed by its bright yellow crown of flowers, a long-lasting counterpoint to the spiked forms of purple and blue sage (*Salvia viridis* and *S. farinacea*). With its low, shrubby form it is invaluable in creating a garden's underlying structure, and for this function it can be grown as a hedge around taller plants, as a corner marker, or at the edge of a winding path in a large island bed. In northern areas rue usually grows only to 30 in. (76.2 cm).

Rue flowers best in full sun, although it will grow in partial shade, in well-drained, light soil. Moist soil is said to produce the bluest leaves, but in my experience, moist soil is also responsible for rue's early demise. Plants can be grown from seeds sown indoors in late winter at 60–70°F (16–21°C), where they should germinate in 10 to 14 days. Set out seedlings after all danger of frost has passed, spacing them 18 in. (45.7 cm) apart, farther apart in warmer regions. In the spring, only cut back hard stems when new growth appears. In colder regions, plants may die back over the winter, but they usually grow up again as temperatures warm. Propagate by carefully dividing roots of established, but not overly woody, plants early in the season after they have put on new growth. Self-sown seedlings should be nursed along—kept well weeded—until they are robust enough to take care of themselves, otherwise, the fragile little plants could be overwhelmed by nearby vegetation.

Under certain conditions, the action of sunlight on the oils in the plant's leaves can cause skin irritation to anyone handling them. The intensity of the oil increases in older plants, so wear gloves if you have sensitive skin or notice any rash. In over 20 years of handling rue, I have not been bothered, but the warning should not go unheeded.

Related plants of interest. Seeds or plants of rue are widely available, but fringed rue is very hard to find.

Ruta chalapensis, fringed rue, is taller than *R. graveolens* with larger flowers and teardrop-shaped foliage. I was bowled over to discover its dramatic and exuberant bloom while on a trip to Israel, where it grows on the hillsides with very tall wild fennel. In early spring, approximately late March, plants are crowned with flocks of swallowtail butterflies, a decorative touch to the golden flowers beneath. Interestingly, rue's reputation as a charm knows no geographical boundaries, for in the Galilee it is grown in folk gardens to bring good luck. Also, rue leaves are used in curing olives. Upon returning home, I learned that fringed rue can be grown even in the

Northeast, where flowering had been reported from late June through late July and sporadically all summer in a Zone 5 garden. Fringed rue is a tender perennial hardy to Zone 8, so plants must be wintered indoors or cuttings made during the summer to bring indoors. I have grown this rue successfully from seed gathered in Israel. 'Dimension Two' is a very desirable prostrate form with blue, fringed foliage and frilly, yellow flowers.

Salvia

> **The salvias are an interesting group—all pretty attractive, in my estimation.**
>
> Judy Kehs
> Cricket Hill Herb Farm
> Rowley, Massachusetts

Lamiaceae, Mint Family
Salvia, sage

Perennial
Site and soil: sun; well-drained
Hardiness: Zones 7–10
Landscape use: accent, bed and border, container, naturalized herb, rock work
Height: 2–5 ft. (0.6–1.5 m)
Flower: red, blue, purple, tubular, in spike
Bloom season: late summer to fall

Of the 900 species of *Salvia* distributed throughout the world, very few are cultivated in our gardens, not because they are not beautiful, but because the group has been dominated by only a few kinds, especially *S. splendens*, the ubiquitous bedding plant. Herb fanciers, individuals like Richard Dufresne, a specialist and collector of rare and unusual salvias, herb nurseries, and display gardens, however, have been quietly expanding the repertoire. Some, like pineapple sage, *S. elegans* and bog sage, *S. uliginosa*, were popular at the turn of the century; others are entirely new with relatively unknown hardiness. The late-blooming ones fall into two groups, the frost-tender fruit salvias and the hardier fall salvias. All are drought resistant and offer exquisite spikes of tubular flowers, some with colorful, long-lasting calyxes, as well as handsome foliage from smooth and bright green to textured and aromatic. All will attract hummingbirds, butterflies, and bees in search of late nectar.

The fruit salvias, native to Mexico, are pineapple sage and *Salvia dorisiana* (Plate 88), fruit-scented sage, both named for their fruit-scented leaves. Pineapple sage grows to 4 ft. (1.2 m) or taller—in the ground, half that in a tub—on fuzzy stems covered with medium green, pointed leaves,

Plate 88. *Salvia dorisiana*, fruit-scented sage. Late winter, greenhouse, Cricket Hill Herb Farm. Where it can be grown outdoors all year, it blooms in late summer or fall. Photo, Deb Kehs.

topped by loose, 8 in. (20.3 cm) spikes of brilliant, though unscented, long, narrow, red flowers that have been compared to firecrackers. These are especially attractive to hummingbirds. *Salvia elegans* 'Honey Melon' is a smaller plant to 2 ft. (0.6 m) with a more lax habit, shorter, broader, melon-scented leaves, and the same brilliant flowers; 'Frieda Dixon' is a compact form to 3 ft. (0.9 m) with coral-red flowers. All are hardy in Zone 8, where they begin to bloom by midsummer; in Zone 7 they enjoy a short bloom period outdoors before frost; and elsewhere they begin blooming as soon as they are brought inside before the first frost. *Salvia dorisiana* grows to 4 ft. (1.2 m) or more in the ground and bears large, velvety, olive-green leaves and large, 2 in. (5.1 cm), bright pink, loosely tubular flowers in spikes. Both the leaves and flowers have a fruity scent, like grapefruit and pineapple combined. It blooms outdoors in late fall in Zone 10; elsewhere, it blooms indoors in midwinter.

The fall salvias, mostly hardy in Zone 8, or Zone 7 with protection, have flowers that concentrate in the blue tones, their colors especially vivid in the autumn light. *Salvia clevelandii*, cleveland or blue sage, 3 ft. (0.9 m) tall, is native to the hills of San Diego and is distinguished by its large, bergamot-like (*Monarda*) whorls of royal blue flowers widely spaced along the stem and its gray-green leaves that have a penetrating, camphorous or balsamic aroma. It has a history of use among native North American Indians for flavoring and medicinal purposes, similar to cooking sage, *S. officinalis*. *Salvia uliginosa*, bog sage, from Brazil, is a vigorous plant that spreads by runners. It has spikes of sky-blue flowers frosted with white, borne on willowy stems 4 ft. (1.2 m) tall. *Salvia leucantha*, Mexican bush or hummingbird sage, is extraordinary for its rapid growth—in a single season it reaches 3–5 ft. (0.9–1.5 m) tall and just as wide. Olive-green leaves grow on the arching, down-covered stems. Terminal spikes carry small white or purple-lipped flowers, held by soft, fuzzy, violet-lavender calyxes. Listed as hardy in Zone 9 or 10, it has been known to survive winter in colder zones. *Salvia azurea* (Plate 89), blue sage, the hardiest of the fall salvias surviving in Zone 5, is a wildflower from the Southwest and Plains states. A wide, bushy plant to 4 ft. (1.2 m) with gray-green leaves, its stems often bend from the weight of the long spikes of clear blue flowers. *Salvia azurea* 'Grandiflora', pitchers sage, has larger, deeper blue flowers.

The fruit sages grow wide and splashy in beds and borders in warmer regions. *Salvia elegans* 'Honey Melon' can be grown as a ground cover. Elsewhere grow them in containers placed along paths, near entrances, on patios or decks—wherever their leaves will be brushed to release their fruity aromas. The hardier sages are the glory of the fall border, when combined in background plantings with creamy-plumed grasses (*Miscanthus* and *Pennisetum*) or the arching sprays of creamy white mugwort (*Artemisia lactiflora*). Their blue or purple flower spikes combine well with virtually all late-blooming flowers, especially pink mallows (*Malva*) and yellow achilleas. Where they are reliably winter hardy, they, especially cleveland and pitcher's sage, can be naturalized in dry areas. All the sages benefit from being grown near rock walls or in natural rock outcroppings.

The fruit and fall salvias can be grown from seed the same way as common sage, but in cooler regions it is wiser to buy plants. All do best in full sun and well-drained soil; the fruit sages prosper in rich loam. Perfect

Plate 89. *Salvia azurea*, blue sage. Late summer, Joseph Hudak garden. Photo, Joseph Hudak.

drainage is crucial for wintering salvias, particularly where they are marginally hardy; where sharp drainage is assured they sometimes survive beyond their usual hardiness limit. Cut back woody plants in the spring to encourage fresh growth; clip plants during the season to maintain compact growth. In rich soil, some salvias may need staking, especially pitcher's sage which has fairly weak stems; otherwise, plants can be dwarfed by cutting them back to about half their size in late July. A heavy mulch is advisable where plants are marginally hardy. Where plants are not hardy, make stem cuttings in the summer and winter these indoors; pineapple sage roots in water. To winter whole plants indoors—smaller ones are more successful—cut them back to about 8 in. (20.3 cm), then dig up the plants and move them inside by stages. Move potted salvias indoors without cutting them back and they will bloom. Consider growing the frost-tender salvias as annuals since most are fast growing.

The leaves and flowers of the fruit sages flavor and decorate salads, fruit cups, and beverages. The flowers of *Salvia dorisiana* are especially delicious; they can be snipped into cream cheese spreads and even added to bread dough. The leaves and flowers can be steeped in vinegar. The leaves of cleveland sage, black sage, and other aromatic sorts can be used for seasoning or teas. The dried leaves and flowers of all kinds can be added to potpourri. The salvias are also fine cut flowers.

Related plants of interest. Many different salvias are offered in nurseries and catalogs, a few more of which are listed below. Visit herb nurseries and display gardens to become acquainted with their diversity. The hardier sorts are available from perennial plant nurseries. Seeds of native salvias are available from specialty and wildflower seed sources.

Salvia greggii, rocky mountain or autumn sage, is a dainty shrub to 18 in. (45.7 cm) or taller with peppery scented leaves. It grows wild in Mexico as well as the American Southwest and is valued for its small stature and large flowers in choice colors, including peach and deep pink, as well as shades of red and yellow. It is hardy in Zone 9, but some of the hybrids developed from it, such as *Salvia* 'Plum Wine' (*S. greggii* var. *rosea* × *S. lemmonii*) and *Salvia* 'Raspberry Royal' (*S. greggii* × *S. lemmonii*) are hardy in Zone 8.

Salvia guaranitica, from South America, grows to 3 ft. (0.9 m) and has lightly anise-scented leaves with brilliant blue flowers that are very attractive to hummingbirds. Listed as hardy in Zone 8, it can winter in Zone 7 if protected. The hybrid *Salvia* 'Purple Majesty' (*S. guaranitica* × *S. gesneraeflora*) is hardier and quite spectacular, with bright green leaves and large, 3 in. (7.6 cm), purple flowers on long spikes.

Salvia mellifera, black sage, is not black at all. It is a tall shrub to 7 ft. (2.1 m) in its native southern California habitat, but in a pot it grows to a manageable 3 ft. (0.9 m). It bears nectar-rich, light lavender-blue flowers and aromatic, glossy green leaves that can be used for teas or seasoning.

Salvia pomifera, Greek apple sage, is named for the cherry-sized, round "fruits" that grow on its stems; they are actually scars from insect stings. It is a shrubby plant 3 ft. (0.9 m) tall with textured, aromatic, scalloped leaves and terminal spikes of two-lipped flowers—the upper lip violet-blue, the lower one mid-blue, the calyx often reddish purple. In ancient times, the apples, preserved like a candy, were exported from Crete to Israel; the dried galls are sold as a medicinal in Crete.

Salvia fruticosa, triloba or Greek sage, forms the same kind of fruits as Greek apple sage. When in Israel, I tasted the fresh, juicy apples of the native plant. This sage is also 3 ft. (0.9 m) tall and branching, with terminal spikes of pink or mauve, two-lipped flowers. Its rough, gray-green leaves are often used as a substitute or adulterant for cooking sage, and like many salvias, it has a history of use in folk medicine. Both Greek and Greek apple sage are hardy in Zone 9 or 10, where they bloom in early spring.

Salvia dominica, dominica sage, is my favorite sage of the eastern Mediterranean. The plant glows from the many silvery leaves and the calyxes around the two-lipped, white and light yellow flowers. Its gray-green leaves are also hairy and aromatic. Greek apple, Greek, and dominica sage are all regarded as possible models for the first menorah (see Ex 25:31–38 for a botanical description). In their native habitat the candelabras of bloom are outlined against rocky cliffs and large rocks, an effective way to grow or naturalize them where conditions allow. Dominica sage is grown in Britain, but I am eagerly awaiting its introduction to North America.

Salvia verticillata, whorled clary sage, is one of the hardier showy sages. The cultivar 'Purple Rain' is mounding and compact to 24 in. (61.0 cm) with velvety, oval leaves. It shows its profusion of purple, tightly whorled flowers all summer. It is hardy in Zone 4.

Salvia officinalis

Lamiaceae, Mint Family
Sage, garden sage, common sage, cooking sage

Perennial
Site and soil: sun; well-drained
Hardiness: Zones 4–9
Landscape use: bed and border, container, edge and
    hedge, rock work
Height: 30 in. (76.2 cm)
Flower: violet-blue, deeply tubular in whorl
Bloom season: early summer to midsummer

Of all the *Salvia* species distributed throughout the world, only *S. officinalis* is known simply as sage, with no qualifying description. A shrubby Mediterranean plant, its white-woolly stems are covered with 2 in. (5.1 cm), gently tapered, pebbly textured leaves, apple-green at first and grayish green in maturity. In its second year of growth it bears a terminal spike, half as tall as the plant itself, that carries many small, loosely arranged, two-lipped flowers that bloom in early June for at least a month, attracting bees and hummingbirds to its nectar-rich blooms. The plant's scent is strong, not unpleasantly, with camphorous overtones.

Sage's fame as a medicinal is preserved in its common and Latin names, derived from *salveo,* meaning "I save." From ancient times, sage was employed to treat everything from snake bites and warts to infertility and amnesia. John Gerard considered it to be a "brain herb," associated with fortifying and strengthening mental powers. Like all strongly scented herbs, it is rich in essential oils, suggesting a range of uses. As an effective astringent, sage is still listed in the U.S. Pharmacopeia for treating bleeding gums and sore throats. Possibly anti-bacterial in action, sage may have other, yet undiscovered, applications.

Sage is a proven carminative, to dispel intestinal gas, and for this reason is often paired in cooking with fatty meats or beans, to which dishes it imparts a peppery and pungent taste. It is also used to flavor cheese. Sage honey is highly regarded; the potential yield from a single plant is rated by honey producers in the 4–6 range on a scale of 1–10.

Sage's well-deserved reputation as a useful plant has, unfortunately, obscured its ornamental qualities as a low-maintenance, drought-resistant, hardy perennial of easy culture, with evergreen, attractive foliage and early summer flowering wands. It is a plant similar in design and color to those approved ornamentals in the same genus. Sage is usually relegated to the vegetable patch, grown there in rows as an annual, its tender, first-season leaves harvested for cooking. Then the plant is discarded because the

Plate 90. *Salvia officinalis*, common sage. Midsummer, Gardner farm. Photo, Alan Dorey.

leaves of second-year plants are not as abundant. Most gardeners, including herb enthusiasts, never get to see sage's second year offering of vertical bloom, an asset in any planting.

Sage associates well with the yellows, blues, and pinks of early summer, with golden daylilies (*Hemerocallis*), soft yellow *Achillea* 'Moonshine', rainbow-tinted iris, low mounds of rosy-flowered pinks (*Dianthus*), and soft blue hardy geraniums, as well as the gray-green-leaved nepetas and lavenders (*Lavandula angustifolia*). The elegant *Salvia officinalis* 'Albiflora' and 'Rubriflora' belong here as well, with their white-flowered spikes and reddish purple flowers, respectively. The compact 'Nana', to 12 in. (30.5 cm) with smaller leaves, is happy among rocks, in a container, or at the front of any planting. Try garden sage's blue wands among dyer's chamomile (*Anthemis tinctoria*), whose prolific, yellow, daisy-like flowers sprawl around and between the upright sage stalks, complementing the latter's foliage all season.

Indoors, sow seed 6–8 weeks before the last frost at a depth of ¼ in. (0.6 cm), where they should germinate in 4 to 12 days at 70°F (21°C). Or sow seed directly outside 2 weeks before the last frost, in full sun and well-drained, not overly rich, garden soil, spacing plants 18–24 in. (45.7–61.0 cm) apart. Plants should be well-watered in their early growth, but mature plants will withstand drought conditions. The following spring, clip back to signs of life to stimulate fresh growth; also clip back after flowering to maintain a compact habit and to encourage a strong main stem for wintering. For the plant's survival where winters are harsh, do not harvest leaves in late summer or fall. After two or three seasons, plants become woody and twisted, sparse in their production of leaves and flowers. Propagate by seeds, cuttings, or division in early summer, or by layering leafy stems whenever there is sufficient growth. Cultivars should be propagated vegetatively. Seeds or plants of sage are widely available from general seed and herb sources, and the cultivars are available mainly from herb sources.

To use sage in the kitchen, add fresh chopped or pulverized dry leaves to cottage cheese, or to any game, pork, poultry, or cheese dishes. For tea, steep ½ teaspoon dried leaves with ½ teaspoon dried chamomile in 1 cup boiling water; add honey to taste. The flowering stems are excellent cut flowers and dry well.

Salvia sclarea

Lamiaceae, Mint Family
Clary sage, clear eye

Biennial
Site and soil: sun; well-drained
Hardiness: Zones 4–9
Landscape use: accent, bed and border
Height: 3–4 ft. (0.9–1.2 m)
Flower: white, lilac, pale blue, two-lipped in whorl
Bloom season: early summer to midsummer

> **When it is in bloom it is one of the handsomest plants in the border.**
> Helen Fox
> *The Years in My Herb Garden*

Clary sage is an Old World medicinal native to southern Europe. Its first season produces a mound of velvety, nearly heart-shaped, puckered leaves at least 12 in. (30.5 cm) in length and 3–4 in. (7.6–10.2 cm) wide. As if this were not enough, the following season it sends up a candelabra of long flowering stalks, each small flower made significant by its glistening, rosy-pink or mauve bract. These are decorative even after the flowers have faded, giving the plant a long season of interest. Clary sage exudes a strong, musky aroma when lightly touched. Surprisingly, its extracted oil, used in perfumery and cosmetics, is pleasantly grape-scented. Clary sage's use as an eyewash is preserved in its species and common name from the Latin *clarus,* to clear. During its bloom period—more than a month, beginning around late June—it is often visited by hummingbirds.

This sage is one of those plants that is grown in its original form, to which additions or subtractions would seem to be superfluous, except for the cultivar *Salvia sclarea* 'Turkestanica', Turkish sage, that has larger bluish or pinkish white flowers, violet bracts tinged with green, and slightly larger leaves.

Clary sage's long history of use as a medicinal and culinary herb—John Parkinson describes how to make clary fritters with its substantial leaves—has relegated it to the herb garden or the reconstructed colonial garden. Its beauty of foliage and flower in perfect balance highly recommends this sage for general landscaping. As a gardener with a discerning eye for color and form, Gertrude Jekyll recognized its value, as she did of all plants whether or not they were regarded by others as ornamentals. Clary sage, she observed, is "a medicinal herb of the old gardens, but is valuable in flower borders where good colour arrangements are desired" (1916).

Plate 91. *Salvia sclarea*, clary sage. Early summer, Graymalkin Farm. Photo, Brian Oke and Gisèle Quesnel.

I have grown clary sage for many years—searching the ground for seedlings has become a spring ritual—in a mixed, informal planting of flowers and herbs, where its pastel spikes enjoy association with foxglove (*Digitalis*), veronica, and hyssop (*Hyssopus officinalis*), as well as with the bushy, pink musk mallow (*Malva moschata*). It creates a bold, upright accent by a stone wall, where it also enjoys the heat, with curly tansy (*Tanacetum vulgare* var. *crispum*), an unblooming, lacy foliage herb of arching form. In common with other downy-leaved plants, clary sage withstands the drought-like conditions of a dry, sunny, exposed site, reminiscent of its native habitat. Here, where other plants would suffer, it thrives, showing off its foliage and flowers to advantage. Where space permits, massed plants are effective; in a generous border, three plants would create a wide swathe. In a more confined space, one plant is sufficient.

Sow seeds indoors 8–10 weeks before the last frost, just lightly pressing them into the soil since light speeds germination. At 70°F (21°C), germination, which can be irregular, should occur in 4 to 21 days. Avoid overwatering at all stages, both in its early growth and in the garden. Choose a well-drained, sunny spot and plant out seedlings, spaced 2 ft. (0.6 m) apart, after all danger of frost has passed. To help the plants survive the winter, avoid overrich, moist soil. Cut back stalks after blooming, but leave some for self-sowing. Where winters are severe, give first-year plants some protection. To ensure clary sage's seasonal appearance, raise new seedlings every year.

All the salvias are exceptional cut flowers. For dried flowers, the blue salvias keep their color better than lavender (*Lavandula angustifolia*). Use the scented flowers for potpourri and the furry leaves in fresh nosegays.

Related plants of interest. Clary sage is widely available from herb sources. The following are hardy types (Zone 4 or 5) that can be grown from seed, except where noted. They are available from specialty seed sources and the best perennial and herb nurseries.

Salvia argentea, silver sage, native to southern Europe and Bulgaria, is similar in its appeal and growth habit to clary sage and like it, is usually grown as a biennial. The first year, silver sage produces rosettes of wrinkled, larger-than-life leaves in a mound, each enormous leaf heavily covered with silvery-white, silky down. The next year, a multitude of thin stalks bear clouds of near-white, wispy flowers, each one supported by a pinkish white bract, growing in whorls. The flower stalks should be cut back right after the blooms are spent in order to encourage the vigor of the show-stopping foliage, a long-season asset. Silver sage is a striking accent among the blues and purples of early summer. Like clary sage, it is drought resistant.

Salvia glutinosa, Jupiter's distaff, is a minty-scented perennial from Europe, 24 in. (61.0 cm) tall and just as wide, which flowers in late June and persists all summer, bearing a mass of small, pale, citron-yellow flowers — an unusual color among sages — with light brown markings. The fuzzy green leaves are so rich in essential oils that they are sticky to the touch. The common name comes from the stems' use in spinning. A rather sprawling plant that self-sows, it is best used in informal plantings.

Salvia pratensis, meadow sage or meadow clary, is a variable, musk-scented perennial of European origin that grows to 3 ft. (0.9 m) and begins blooming by late May with long sprays of packed, lavender-pink flowers from a neat rosette of gray-green foliage. The flowers are light blue-lilac in the cultivar 'Haematodes'. Bloom continues into the fall if the spent stalks are cut back. It is invaluable in the perennial border for its free-flowering habit and long season. Its dark seeds, mucilaginous when soaked in water, were once used like clary sage as an eye wash. Its honey yield is rated as high as the flowers of common cooking sage. Still, "It looks more like a flower than an herb," observed one herb authority, perhaps in embarrassment.

Salvia ×*superba* includes a group of hybrids, some of which may also be listed under *S. nemerosa,* all of which are grown from plants. They are compact types 18–24 in. (45.7–61.0 cm). The musk-scented 'East Friesland', the most popular, bears heavily packed, deep violet flower spikes enhanced by maroon bracts. At Well-Sweep Herb Farm in New Jersey, Zone 6, it flowers two or three times a season when cut back. 'May Night', with dark violet-blue spikes, blooms earlier, as its name suggests. 'Rose Queen' with red-violet to rose-pink flowers grows on rose-tinted stems. Try all these with yellow yarrow (*Achillea* 'Moonshine'); I grow 'East Friesland' to great effect with the gray, needle-leaved Roman wormwood (*Artemisia pontica*). Propagate by division or stem cuttings.

Salvia viridis

Lamiaceae, Mint Family
Painted sage, annual clary, purple-top

Annual
Site and soil: sun; well-drained
Landscape use: bed and border, edge and hedge
Height: 18–24 in. (45.7–61.0 cm)
Flower: purple, pink, white, petal-like, terminal
    bract
Bloom season: midsummer to late summer

> *Salvia horminum*
> **is often called Blue-
> beard, from the
> purple-blue bracts,
> the flowers being
> less conspicuous.**
> Margaret Brownlow
> *Herbs and the Fragrant
> Garden*

A native of Mediterranean regions, painted sage or annual clary is quite unlike its larger cousin, clary sage. It is a slender plant, whose interest resides solely in the top portion of the stem, in its vividly-colored, petal-like bracts. These, flushed green at their base and darkly veined, entirely obscure the tiny, two-lipped flowers—in the same shade as the bracts—hidden in leaf axils along the stem (bees, however, find them of great interest). The top bracts are smaller, upright tufts, flushed with white. The seeds, which have the same mucilaginous properties as clary sage, were used in the same way, especially as an eyewash.

Painted sage is a descriptive name for a plant whose many stems look as if they had been dipped in a bucket of bright paint, but it has traveled under several different names during its long history of cultivation in the West. Thomas Jefferson called it horminum sage after its Latin name, now obsolete, *Salvia horminum* (Betts and Perkins 1986); *horminum* means sage in Greek. By 1835 the London seed house of Flanagan and Nuttings was advertising it as "Red Top" or "Purple Top" (Newcomb 1985). In 1916, in *Annuals and Biennials*, Gertrude Jekyll referred to it by its old Latin name, *S. viridis*, praising the cultivar 'Bluebeard'. By the 1950s, in Margaret Brownlow's *Herbs and the Fragrant Garden*, "Bluebeard" was synonymous with the plant itself. In herb circles, however, it was, and is, most often known as annual clary.

Despite this history which would seem to indicate familiarity, painted sage is not well known, neither as a colorful annual nor as an herb. In the annual salvia class, it has been overrun by the ubiquitous scarlet sage, *Salvia splendens*; among herb growers it has been overshadowed by its big cousin. I had to travel halfway around the world, to Israel, to become familiar with it and to appreciate its beauty. There it is part of the annual carpet, a vivid patch of purple among the brilliant yellows, blues, pinks, and reds of the exuberant Middle Eastern spring of February through April.

After returning home I began to grow whatever seeds were available, first *Salvia viridis* 'Tricolor Mix' in blue, pink, and cream, then 'White Swan'; 'Claryssa', in the usual range of purple, pink, and white, is different only in its somewhat larger showy bracts. I saved seeds of the pink from these

Plate 92. *Salvia viridis*, painted sage. Midsummer, Country Lane Herbs and Dried Flowers. Photo, Brian Oke and Gisele Quèsnel.

mixtures myself, and then noticed 'Pink Sundae', which Margaret Brown-low knew. Since then, I have also noticed 'Blue Bird', possibly the reappearance of 'Bluebeard' in a more compact form.

The virtues of painted sage are beginning to be appreciated by the general gardener looking for easy to grow, colorful, and adaptable plants that are at home with other annuals or that fill in a perennial bed. Thomas Jefferson featured the purple in a mixed border with white snapdragons and red corn poppies, a planting worth repeating (Betts and Perkins 1986). I grow the purple type in a cutting bed for drying—it dries navy blue and is highly prized—and all three colors in a perennial garden, where they are separately massed at the front with calendulas. For drying, pick painted sage when it is brightest, before seeds form. Painted sage prefers to grow in cool, moist conditions, which, in cooler climates, means a long growing season. Well into late fall the colorful bracts are still quite vivid, especially in the lighter shades, where the dark veining is most apparent.

Sow seeds indoors 6–8 weeks before the last frost, sowing seed on the surface of the growing medium; they will germinate at 70°F (21°C) in 3 to 12 days. Plant seedlings outside after the last frost, spacing plants 6–8 in. (15.2–20.3 cm) apart. Once planted, painted sage will self-sow for years; the purple will dominate unless controlled.

Related plants of interest. The following two salvias, both native to North America, are also significant for discerning herb and general gardeners for their long season of bloom and ease of culture. Unlike other showy types that cannot be relied upon to bloom from seed during the growing season, both Texas sage and mealycup sage can be grown as annuals; they can be perennials in warmer regions as indicated. They are grown like painted sage, but should be started 10–12 weeks before the last frost date, since they need a longer growing season. They and painted sage are available from general seed sources, but *Salvia* 'Indigo Spires' is available only from the best perennial and herb plant nurseries.

Salvia coccinea 'Lady in Red' (Plate 1), Texas sage, sometimes called scarlet sage, is a shorter, compact, and earlier blooming plant than the species, and was an All-America Selection for 1992. Although dwarf, growing only 12–15 in. (30.5–38.1 cm), it is not a stiff plant, unlike true scarlet sage, and its intense red flowers, white in bud, are borne in loose spikes that grow up from attractive, musk-scented leaves. Try 'Lady in Red' in a large tub paired with a bright, yellow mound of signet marigold (*Tagetes tenuifolia*) for bloom that lasts until frost. The transformation of Texas sage continues with elegant variations, the best of which are 'Coral Nymph' and 'Snow Nymph', 24–36 in. (61.0–91.4 cm), with airy habit and stature that are beautiful in a perennial border or among herb greenery in the late summer. Texas sage, hardy in Zone 8, is very attractive to hummingbirds, and can be grown in sun or light shade.

Salvia farinacea, mealycup sage or blue salvia, is a lovely wildflower from New Mexico and Texas. The small, velvety blue flowers are packed in long spikes along slender blue stems, each little flower held in a calyx that looks as if it had been dusted with flour, which gave rise to the common name, mealycup. Silvery gray foliage at its base perfectly complements the plant in bloom. 'Victoria', the hardiest type—I have tested it to 28°F (−2°C)—is a compact plant to 18 in. (45.7 cm), still unsurpassed for its densely packed, violet-blue flower spikes and early bloom. 'Mini Victoria' to 12 in. (30.5 cm) is a boon to gardeners in colder climates for its earlier bloom in midsummer. *Salvia* 'Indigo Spires' (*S. farinacea* × *S. longispicata*) is outstanding in the perennial border, with long blue flower spikes on stems to 4 ft. (1.2 m). Grow this cultivar from plants, not seeds. Mealycup sage, hardy in Zone 6 or 7, is very popular with bees and butterflies. It also makes exceptional fresh and dried cut flowers; for drying, pick when all but the top of the spike is just open.

Sanguinaria canadensis

Papaveraceae, Poppy Family
Bloodroot, redroot, snakebite, sweet slumber

Perennial
Site and soil: partial shade, shade; evenly moist and
  well-drained
Hardiness: Zones 3–8
Landscape use: bed and border, naturalized herb, rock work
Height: 4–12 in. (10.2–30.5 cm)
Flower: white, solitary goblet
Bloom season: spring to early summer

> **One of the earliest and most beautiful spring flowers.**
> Maude Grieve
> *A Modern Herbal*

Bloodroot is one of a group of exquisite flowers known as spring ephemerals, whose short-lived blooms are here today and gone tomorrow (Plate 6. See p. 49). The only species in the genus, it grows in rich, open woods and slopes across Canada and from New England to Florida and Nebraska. In early spring, the rhizomes send up a single stem or scape with the flower bud enfolded by a solitary leaf. As the leaf unfurls, the flower stem grows to 12 in. (30.5 cm), bearing a single, goblet-shaped bloom of eight to twelve narrow, waxy, white petals, sometimes tinged with pink at their base, with many tassel-like golden stamens within. As the petals fall, the 3 in. (7.6 cm) seed pods quickly form, concealed by an umbrella of pale green foliage, grayish on the underside, lobed, and as broad as 10 in. (25.4 cm) across. By midsummer the foliage dies back and there is little sign that bloodroot ever marked the spot.

Both the Latin and common names preserve bloodroot's most famous characteristic, the rhizome's thick crimson sap, used by North American Indians as a skin dye—the root is still used to dye material red. Preparations of the roots were used to treat warts, tumors, and ringworm. The caustic nature of the plant extract suggests its use in treating dental plaque, but since bloodroot contains powerful alkaloids and is potentially poisonous, it should never be used for self-medication.

Watching for the first signs of bloodroot to poke through cold ground is as great a sport as lungwort-watching, though it requires greater diligence, for once the scape with the enfolded bud has appeared it is not long before the flower opens and disappears. A season's close observation reveals that only a few clumps can give almost 3 weeks of bloom, as new flowers open and old ones pass by; in rainy and cloudy weather the goblets close, giving the appearance of candle flames. The double-flowered *Sanguinaria canadensis* 'Multiplex' (Plate 93) is a great boon to the gardener for its longer lasting solid white blooms, in which all the stamens have been transformed into petals.

The best way to grow bloodroot is to find a habitat its likes—filtered shade is best—and leave it alone to prosper. Try it under a tree with wild bleeding heart (*Dicentra eximia*), lungwort (*Pulmonaria officinalis*), and Jacob's ladder (*Polemonium*). Their foliage will cover the bare ground left by bloodroot. It is also beautiful when massed on a slope with wild bleeding heart or planted against stones to show off first its flowers, then its spreading foliage.

Bloodroot is tricky to grow because of its placement needs. On the one hand, it needs sun for maximum bloom, but on the other hand, shade for its roots. It likes moisture, but not too much since the rhizomes may rot. The best strategy is to plant it near a tree, shrub, or rockery, or in any setting where other plants will offer some shade later in the season, but where the sun can easily reach the young plant. A deciduous tree offers an encouraging habitat since it will only be partially in leaf when bloodroot blooms. Plant roots spaced 6 in. (15.2 cm) apart, buried 1 in. (2.5 cm) deep with the bud end pointing upward, in moderately moist and well-drained soil that is enriched annually with leaf mold or rotted compost. Once planted, bloodroot should be left alone because it increases slowly. It spreads by self-sowing—seedlings may appear some distance from the original planting—and by creeping rhizomes, which can be divided in the fall. It is as tricky to collect seeds at the proper stage of maturity—when they are brownish—as it

Plate 93. *Sanguinaria canadensis* 'Multiplex', double-flowered bloodroot. Spring, Robison York State Herb Garden, Cornell Plantations. Photo, Diane Miske, Cornell Plantations.

is to keep an eye on the emerging flower. Seed pods are sometimes concealed by the large leaves and should be harvested before they split open. Plant seeds in a cold frame, then plant out the seedlings the following spring.

Seeds of bloodroot are available from herb and wildflower sources, and plants are available from perennial plant and herb sources. *Sanguinaria canadensis* 'Multiplex' is offered by the best perennial plant nurseries, sometimes as 'Flore Pleno'.

Sanguisorba canadensis

Rosaceae, Rose Family
Canadian burnet

Perennial
Site and soil: sun, partial shade; evenly moist, boggy
Hardiness: Zones 3–9
Landscape use: accent, bed and border, naturalized
  herb
Height: 4–5 ft. (1.2–1.5 m)
Flower: creamy white, shaggy in cylindrical spike
Bloom season: late summer to fall

> There is a handsome species . . . with tall spikes of white blossoms . . . attractive enough for perennial flower gardens.
> Gertrude Foster
> *Herbs for Every Garden*

Canadian burnet, the only North American native species in the genus, grows in swamps and bogs and along roadsides from Labrador to Indiana to the mountains of Georgia. By late summer it appears as a mass of 8 in. (20.3 cm), bottle-brush spikes atop tall, slender, upright stems. The dense clusters of small, white flowers—actually petal-like sepals, each with a pale green, central stripe—are decorated with prominent stamens which give the whole spike a shaggy appearance. Since the lower flowers open first, the top of the spike may be bare. Rounded and velvety bright green, the spike complements the toothed and divided long, arching leaves of the same color that grow up from a basal rosette.

Its genus named is derived from the Latin *sanguis*, blood, and *sorbeo*, to absorb, and refers to the plant's use for healing wounds, both internal and external, with its tannin-rich roots and leaves. It shares this characteristic with the other plants in the genus, most notably the Old World herb, *Sanguisorba officinalis*, great burnet, and *S. minor*, salad burnet. Since the leaves must be cooked first to remove their bitterness, Canadian burnet has not been used for food to the extent of its better known relatives (Facciola 1990). The young leaves of great burnet, for example, can be used to flavor salads and cream cheese spreads. Also, all the burnets are good filler in fall bouquets.

The garden virtues of this native plant include late and long bloom through light frosts and the ability to grow in wet or ordinary garden soil, in sun or partial shade—in other words, Canadian burnet is an adaptable plant. Yet it has been largely ignored, both as a perennial flower and an interesting herb. I first became aware of Canadian burnet when I saw the ver-

Plate 94. *Sanguisorba canadensis*, Canadian burnet. Early fall, Cabot Trail, Cape Breton Island, Nova Scotia, Canada. Photo, Patricia Dix.

tical white spires growing among late asters and goldenrod on a bank near the shoulder of the road far from human habitation. I returned in the spring and dug a small root which grew well and expanded to form a naturalized planting in my own landscape with New England asters (*Aster novae-angliae*). In the garden proper it grows with bright yellow and bronze rudbeckias, a pleasing combination of colors and forms. Canadian burnet in full fall bloom makes an elegant accent under the high, spreading limbs of a large tree. Combine it with blue autumn monkshood (*Aconitum henryi*) or plant it as a background for another undervalued relative, *Sanguisorba obtusa*, Japanese burnet, a lower-growing species.

Plant roots of Canadian burnet in the early spring or fall, spaced 24 in. (61.0 cm) apart, in sun or partial shade. It is described as a plant for wet, even boggy soil, but it can also grow in drier soil, as it sometimes does in the wild. Cut back stalks at the end of the season; propagate by division every 3 years or as necessary. It can be grown from seed but I have never seen them available.

Related plants of interest. Burnet plants are available from perennial plant nurseries and wildflower and herb sources.

Sanguisorba dodecandra, mountain burnet, is native to the subalpine meadows of northern Italy. It is similar to Canadian burnet in form but is shorter at 3 ft. (0.9 m), with 3 in. (7.6 cm), greenish yellow spikes above a rosette of serrated leaves. It grows in moist soil and is hardy in Zone 6. This is a good choice for warmer areas.

Sanguisorba obtusa, Japanese burnet, is an alpine meadow flower that begins to bloom a little earlier than Canadian burnet, in late summer rather than fall. It grows to 4 ft. (1.2 m) with a bushier, less vertical form. Its fuzzy, rose-colored plumes, 4 in. (10.2 cm) long, arch gracefully over rosettes of grayish green, toothed foliage. It grows best in moist soil in sun or partial shade, which will help it to hold its color longer, and it is hardy in Zone 4.

Sanguisorba officinalis, great burnet, of Eurasian origin, is a wildflower of damp meadows. It grows to 3 ft. (0.9 m) on narrow, leafless stems, from a wide basal rosette of paired leaflets that look as if they had been trimmed with pinking shears. The summer-blooming flowers, borne mainly at the top of the stem, are dark red to purplish and club-shaped. An herb "from the apothecary" it was once esteemed for healing wounds. Its leaves, like those of salad burnet, have a cucumber-like flavor and a long history as a salad seasoning. Sow seeds outdoors in early spring or late fall on the soil surface; they need light and low temperatures, under 60°F (16°C), to germinate. It is a background plant in the border or one to establish in a wet meadow with Canadian burnet.

Santolina

One of the most ornamental of all herbs.

Adelma Simmons
Herb Gardening in Five Seasons

Asteraceae, Aster Family
Santolina

Shrub
Site and soil: sun; sharply drained
Hardiness: Zones 6–8
Landscape use: accent, bed and border, edge and hedge, ground cover, rock work
Height: 18–24 in. (45.7–61.0 cm)
Flower: golden yellow, lemon-yellow button in terminal head
Bloom season: early summer to midsummer

Santolinas are small evergreen shrubs from the Mediterranean area. The old favorite, beloved of Tudor-style knot gardens, is *Santolina chamaecyparissus*, lavender cotton or gray santolina, whose species name means dwarf cypress. Its older name, *incana*, means white or woolly. Both these names call attention to the plant's well-known characteristics: a mounded form with silvery white leaves. The name "lavender cotton" combines the plant's sharp, camphorous aroma with its cotton-soft foliage.

Gray santolina may spread 3–4 ft. (0.9–1.2 m) wide over time, with round, whitish, branching stems growing to 24 in. (61.0 cm) or more from a thick woody base, forming a dense bush. Leaves are beautifully silvered, so downy, intricate, and serrated like a comb that they look like white coral. From late June through midsummer the mound of foliage is crowned by golden buttons, rayless disk flowers globular in shape, 3/4 in. (1.9 cm) wide. These rise about 6 in. (15.2 cm) above the plant in such abundance that they seem to be borne in clusters, yet there is only one golden button to each long, leafless stem. Two forms are especially free flowering: the dwarf, compact *S. chamaecyparissus* 'Nana', 6–8 in. (15.2–20.3 cm) tall, and 'Pretty Carrol', a compact hybrid between 'Nana' and the species, 10–20 in. (25.4–50.8 cm) tall with pale yellow flowers.

Another useful herb in this genus is *Santolina rosmarinifolia*, green santolina (Plate 95). It is a counterpoint to gray santolina in foliage color, with brilliant green leaves. It has the same button flowers, only pale or lemon yellow, from late June to late July. It grows 18–24 in. (45.7–61.0 cm) tall and, like gray santolina, is wide, spreading to 3 ft. (0.9 m) in maturity. Its scent is pungent with resinous overtones. There is much confu-

Plate 95. *Santolina rosmarinifolia*, green santolina. Midsummer, Country Lane Herbs and Dried Flowers. Photo, Brian Oke and Gisèle Quesnel.

sion surrounding the nomenclature of green santolina, which is often listed as *S. virens* or *S. viridis*. The cultivar *S. rosmarinifolia* 'Primrose Gem' is also commonly sold as green santolina, but it has flowers of a more subdued yellow. Green santolinas are hardier than the gray-leaved kinds.

Santolinas have been used traditionally as insect repellents among stored woolens, with lavender (*Lavandula angustifolia*) and southernwood (*Artemisia abrotanum*) in the mixture known as Guarde Robe, once popular in France. In common with wormwood (*Artemisia absinthium*) and other bitter-tasting herbs, gray santolina was used as a vermifuge to expel worms, especially from children. Modern research suggests their antiseptic and antibiotic properties. The santolinas' extracted oils are used in perfumes.

Unlike herbs that were introduced to Western Europe because of their medicinal or culinary qualities, the santolinas were valued solely for their hedge-making abilities. Their willingness to be trimmed and maintained as stiff upright shrubs kept many gardeners unaware of their varied uses in the landscape. Santolinas are impressive at the front of a border, island bed, or rock garden, where they create low mounds of beautiful foliage all summer and clouds of assorted and plentiful yellow blooms for at least a month. Plants complement the colors, forms, and fragrance of salvias, nepetas, and lavenders (*Lavandula angustifolia*). The gray and green can be interplanted for great effect anywhere in the landscape, as long as the site is sunny, open, and dry. Naturalize them on a sunny bank or rockery, where they attain their greatest height and width; use them to outline a broad stairway or path; or group them together near entrances to create a low wall around a sunny patio or deck.

Santolinas are slow to mature so they are usually purchased as plants. They are offered by perennial plant nurseries, but the greatest selection is from herb sources. Set them out in late spring 18–24 in. (45.7–61.0 cm) apart, or 12–15 in. (30.5–38.1 cm) for a hedge. The site should be sunny, the soil light, sandy, and well-drained. Santolinas do not tolerate moist conditions in the least; they also suffer in hot, humid climates where they are best grown at higher altitudes. In those hot and humid climates mature plants should be cut back by half in the spring; in colder climates prune lightly. Cut back flowering stalks after they are spent, but do not trim or prune plants heavily in the fall, since fresh foliage appears on old wood the following season.

Where winters are harsh, heavy snow may break stems and bitter cold may cause the outer stem tips to die back—sometimes severely—but plants usually rejuvenate. Hardiness is variable, largely depending on a favorable, sheltered, growing site. Some gardeners in regions as harsh as Zones 4 and 5 report that they keep santolinas for years by heaping them with sand before the ground freezes in the fall. Plants can also be protected with evergreen boughs; snow is the best cover. Propagate plants by division in the spring, by layering stems with sand in the fall, or by taking stem cuttings during the summer and wintering them indoors in small pots, where they will develop a good root ball that transplants well.

Trim the leafy stems of santolina throughout the season to dry for potpourri or sachets. Mix dried leaves in equal quantities with lavender and southernwood to use as an all-purpose moth repellent. Fresh leaves create pretty, outer ruffles in fresh or dried posies or tussie-mussies. The long-stemmed flowers dry well and are prized for dried arrangements. Both leaves and flowers are used in wreaths and other floral arrangements, where their aroma is also an asset.

Saponaria officinalis

Caryophyllaceae, Pink Family
Soapwort, bouncing bet, fuller's herb

Perennial
Site and soil: sun, partial shade; evenly moist
Hardiness: Zones 3–9
Landscape use: accent, bed and border, naturalized
   herb
Height: 24–36 in. (61.0–91.4 cm)
Flower: light pink, rose-pink, loose in terminal cluster
Bloom season: midsummer to late summer

> On summer evenings the fragrance of the flowers is so intense that they were described by one old writer as "fulsomely sweet."
>
> Elizabeth Lawrence
> *Gardening for Love*

Although native to Europe and Asia, soapwort is naturalized in great patches along roadsides and railroad tracks and in damp meadows and waste places, especially in the mid-Atlantic states and throughout the Midwest. Growing by means of its creeping, underground roots, it creates wide mats of shiny-leaved, pointed green foliage, which is a source of lather-producing saponin. By midsummer or earlier, clusters of ragged-petaled flowers, each one held by a puffed calyx, appear atop thick-jointed stems. In the evening their clove-like scent attracts their pollinator, the hawkmoth.

Soapwort, used since ancient times in the fulling of wool cloth, was introduced to the New World in the early eighteenth century, probably because of its well-known cleansing properties—it is still used to clean old, delicate fabrics—as well as its ability to soothe skin irritations. By the nineteenth century, no longer needed, it became a wildflower. The double-flowered types, long cottage garden favorites in England, were soon introduced into American gardens as ornamentals. Their popularity is preserved in the innumerable folk names they gathered—bride's bouquet, goodbye summer, lady-at-the-gate. Highly adaptable to a variety of conditions, soapwort was grown from north to south, from east to west. But by the 1930s it was disappearing from gardens once more, literally tumbling over banks to grow in roadside ditches as a garden escape. Today, double soapwort is being sought once more for its relaxed beauty and scent, very much a contemporary plant. Two popular double forms are *Saponaria officinalis* 'Rosea Plena' (Plate 96) in light pink and 'Rubra Plena' in a deeper rose-pink.

One of the best ways to take advantage of this vigorous herb is to establish it as an accent planting outside the garden proper; one still sees it grown this way in older gardens, often by a doorway or gate, where its strong evening scent will be appreciated. In these locations it is contained by mowing, which should be done every time the grass is cut during the summer. I allow it to grow among perennials in a cottage garden planting with summer phlox, bergamots (*Monarda*), rue (*Ruta graveolens*), and hyssop (*Hyssopus officinalis*), but I do need to watch that it does not overspread its welcome. The single soapwort is easier to naturalize than the double-flowered type. If you have a damp spot where little else will grow, let it spread as wide as you want and control by roughly mowing around the colony.

It is true that soapwort is adaptable, but it grows best in evenly moist conditions in full sun, where its pink flowers have the best color. Plants grown in partial shade are usually near white. The single type can be grown from seed sown outside in a covered cold frame to germinate over the winter; or sow seeds in the spring, when germination should take about 10 days. Double-flowered soapwort is usually sterile and grown from roots.

Space plants 12 in. (30.5 cm) apart in early spring or fall. In a garden setting, soapwort may need to be divided every year.

As a cut flower, several sprigs of soapwort, especially the double form, will fill a room with fragrance. To produce a lather for hand or face wash-

Plate 96. *Saponaria officinalis* 'Rosea Plena', double-flowered soapwort. Late summer, Gardner farm. Photo, Alan Dorey.

ing, especially convenient when working outdoors, rub a minimum of ten leaves together; dwarf soapwort will also produce lather. To make 4 gallons (15.2 liters) of sudsy wash water to clean fine or old fabrics like lace, grow a patch of *Saponaria officinalis* 2 × 4 ft. (0.6 × 1.2 m). To prepare the soap, chop roots, stems, and leaves of the plant into small pieces; soak them briefly in warm water and stir until suds form (Buchanan 1987). To use this soap, soak fabric in cold water, then lay it on a flat surface. Using a circular motion, gently rub the fabric surface with a sponge dipped in the frothy soapwort solution.

Related plants of interest. All the soapworts are available from perennial plant and herb sources.

Saponaria ×*lempergii* 'Max Frei' (*S. cypria* × *S. haussknechtii*) is a more refined and compact perennial soapwort to 6 in. (15.2 cm) tall, with very showy, bright pink flowers that bloom longer than any other of the soapworts. It is most suitable for the front of a perennial border backed by blue

Plate 97. *Saponaria ocymoides*, dwarf soapwort. Early summer, Graymalkin Farm. Photo, Brian Oke and Gisèle Quesnel.

salvias for a stunning, long-lasting effect. Grow it the same as dwarf soapwort; it is hardy in Zone 5 or 6.

Saponaria ocymoides (Plate 97), dwarf soapwort, creeping soapwort, or rock soapwort, is a trailing perennial plant 8–10 in. (20.3–25.4 cm) tall with similar lather-producing properties. In early summer it produces a brilliant mound of small, bright pink flowers in loose sprays, especially beautiful spilling over rocks or when used as a ground cover. Unlike its taller cousin, it must have dry conditions—light, quickly draining soil—to survive a harsh winter. To grow from seed: prechill seeds for 3 weeks, then sow them on the medium surface about 12 weeks before the last frost. Germination takes 7–21 days at 70°F (21°C). Plant seedlings outside in the spring in full sun, spacing them 4–8 in. (10.2–20.3 cm) apart. Propagate by division. Dwarf soapwort is hardy in Zone 3.

Satureja montana

Lamiaceae, Mint Family
Winter savory

Perennial
Site and soil: sun; sharply drained
Hardiness: Zones 5–9
Landscape use: edge and hedge, ground cover, rock work
Height: 12–24 in. (30.5–61.0 cm)
Flower: pinkish white, tubular in terminal spike
Bloom season: midsummer to late summer

> Flowers . . . are tiny and give the appearance of a plant covered with a light fall of snow.
>
> Rosetta Clarkson
> *Herbs: Their Culture and Uses*

Winter savory, so called because of its perennial nature, as distinct from the annual summer savory, *Satureja hortensis,* is native to the Mediterranean region. An upright miniature bush, woody at its base, its many stems are covered with glossy, dark green, pointed leaves. From midsummer to fall the plant is topped off with tiny, whitish or pale pink, two-lipped flowers that are each spotted purple on the lower lip—bees find them very attractive. The sprinkling of its pale flowers in short, upright spikes has given rise to the many comments that compare winter savory's bloom to a light snow fall.

Both savorys were among those used by the seventeenth-century settlers of New England. Credited with stimulating appetite and aiding digestion, they were traditionally added to vegetables, especially beans, and rich meats. The leaves of winter savory are sharper in flavor than those of summer savory, with a spicy, thyme-like overtone. In northeastern Canada, winter savory is the one preferred by local Acadians.

With its evergreen leaves, upright habit, and low stature, winter savory was a favorite hedge plant in Tudor knot gardens, which suggests its use to outline a formal herb planting. It can also be used to edge an informal garden of flowers, where its own snowy bloom is a definite advantage. Used to growing on dry, rocky hillsides in its native habitat, winter savory is well suited to a rockery, a natural outcropping, or a rock garden.

Two other forms of winter savory are well worth growing, not only for their profuse bloom, but also for their uses in the landscape: *Satureja montana* 'Nana', dwarf winter savory, 8 in. (20.3 cm) tall, and *S. montana* subsp. *illyrica*, creeping savory, 2–4 in. (5.1–10.2 cm) tall, a fully prostrate mound of curving branches and relatively large, cascading, white flowers. Both of

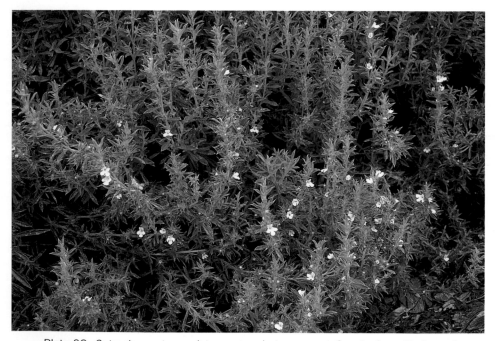

Plate 98. *Satureja montana*, winter savory. Late summer, Country Lane Herbs and Dried Flowers. Photo, Brian Oke and Gisèle Quesnel.

these savorys are at home among rocks or in containers; creeping savory shows off in a hanging basket.

Sow seeds indoors 6–8 weeks before the last frost, just pressing them into the surface of the medium; germination should occur in 20 days, probably less, at 70°F (21°C). Outside, after the last frost, space plants 10–12 in. (25.4–30.5 cm) apart, closer for the shorter types. None of the winter savorys will winter over in moist, poorly drained soil; sharp drainage and full sun are required for success with these plants, similar in their cultural needs to thyme. Clip them back to new growth in the spring; do not clip in the fall, especially in harsh climates, as added winter protection.

The savorys are delicious in herb butter used to flavor fish dishes; simply brush the herb-infused butter over the broiled fish as it comes out of the oven. Add fresh or dried savory leaves to poultry, beef, vegetable, and cheese dishes, and to bread dough.

Related plants of interest. Seeds and plants of winter savory and plants of dwarf and creeping savory are available from herb sources. Seeds of summer savory are widely available from general seed and herb sources.

Satureja hortensis, summer savory, should not be overlooked for its ornamental qualities. Since its leaves are harvested before the plant comes into bloom, when they have the most flavor, the dark purple flowering tops are missed with their 18 in. (45.7 cm) stems packed with tiny, pink flowers. The wide-spreading, mature plant, when massed, looks like lavender (*Lavandula angustifolia*) and can be grown attractively around rocks, at the base of stairs, by a stone wall, or in a perennial, annual, or mixed border. Summer savory often self-sows from season to season. Sow seeds outside in the spring, or start plants indoors 4 weeks before the last frost, growing them the same as winter savory, but spacing plants 6–8 in. (15.2–20.3 cm) apart.

Solidago

Asteraceae, Aster Family
Goldenrod

Perennial
Site and soil: sun; well-drained
Hardiness: Zones 3–10
Landscape use: accent, bed and border, ground
  cover, naturalized herb, rock work
Height: 1–6 ft. (0.3–1.8 m)
Flower: gold, white, small, daisy-like in cluster
Bloom season: late summer to late fall

"Everyone knows the goldenrods—but very few know them," observes the wildflower authority Harold Rickett (1963). They are difficult to sort out, one from the other, particularly since they readily hybridize. Of the more than 100 species of *Solidago*, most are native to North America. They are a familiar sight in late summer in overgrown, once-cultivated fields and along roadsides, but they also grow at the wood's edge, in woodland thickets, and even by the seashore. Tiny, golden, thinly rayed, daisy-like flowers—white in silver-rod, *S. bicolor*—are tightly packed into straight spikes, one-sided and wavy plumes, slender and club-shaped wands, or flat-topped heads on unbranching, rather woody stems. Leaves vary from narrow and toothed to oblong and smooth-edged, and in *S. odora*, sweet goldenrod, they are anise-scented. Height varies, too, from the very tall, rough-leaved *S. rugosa* to the diminutive, alpine *S. cutleri*, less than 12 in. (30.5 cm) tall. None of these are responsible for the allergic reaction, hay fever, that is often attributed to them, since its pollen is sticky and can only be transferred by insects; the true culprit is ragweed, *Ambrosia artemisii*.

The genus name, from *solidare*, meaning "one that makes whole," attests to its healing virtues. Preparations from the native North American goldenrods and European goldenrod, *Solidago virgaurea*, have been used to heal wounds and alleviate coughs and fevers. The flowers have laxative properties, but the seeds were used to treat diarrhea. The golden flowers were used to dye homespun wool.

Although they are not very well known as garden plants, Europeans consider the bright yellow goldenrods very desirable in the flower border, and they have produced many cultivars. The most successful, in my opinion, are those that retain the airy grace of the wild forms; the least successful are those that have large, overbright, oversize flowering heads on short, dumpy plants. The goldenrods are gaining in interest in North America for their late, bright bloom, attractiveness to butterflies, and graceful, natural forms.

I first became aware of goldenrod's landscaping possibilities when I saw it grown in a great drift by the administration building of the Newfoundland Botanical Garden. Under the brilliant direction of Bernard S. Jackson, butterfly habitats had been created all over the Garden, in open woods as well as in high traffic areas. I was struck by the planting of wild *Solidago graminifolia*, lance-leaved goldenrod, a lovely golden accent against the weathered boards of the building. No longer was goldenrod an unwanted field weed, but a desirable ornamental. Less vigorous wild species such as *S. rigida*, stiff goldenrod, to 5 ft. (1.5 m), grow by clumps rather than running roots and create handsome splashes of gold at the back of the border or island bed. The anise-scented sweet goldenrod, to 24 in. (61.0 cm), throws long sprays of golden bloom and is suitable for a bed, border, or accent by itself. Another garden sort is the magnificent *S. rugosa*, wrinkled goldenrod, with a multitude of pendulous, one-sided, golden sprays. In the garden, goldenrods combine with rudbeckias, echinaceas, or in a generous setting, with fountains of *Miscanthus*. In a naturalized setting, goldenrods show off to advantage among New England asters (*Aster novae-angliae*) and Joe Pye-weed (*Eupatorium maculatum*). Blooming may begin in late July and last until November.

Wild species can be grown from seed sown indoors 6–8 weeks before planting outdoors or sown outdoors in the early spring or late autumn; germination takes 14–42 days at 50°F (10°C). Seedlings or purchased roots should be planted outside early—a light frost will not hurt them—in well-drained soil, not overly rich. As one observes in nature, the most lovely plumes arise in dry, unfertilized fields. Cut back plants after flowering to prevent, or at least discourage, self-sowing. Divide plants every 3–4 years or as necessary. Some goldenrods may need staking in windy sites or where soil is rich.

Goldenrods are good cut and dried flowers; cut the stems when the flowers are freshly opened. All types have a sweet aroma when dried and can be added, sparingly, to potpourri. I first saw the process of dying yarn with goldenrod demonstrated outdoors, where nearby plants were plucked and immersed in a cauldron, heated by a wood fire. The procedure is not difficult. Prepare the wool for dyeing by tying it in loose skeins. Wash it in lukewarm water, then place the wet wool in 3 gallons (11.4 liters) water with a mordant of 4 ounces (113 g) alum and 1 ounce (28.3 g) cream of tartar. Extract the dye from the plants by covering flower tops with water and simmering them until the color has been extracted; you will need at least 1¼ gallons (4.8 liters) of water per 3½ ounces (99.2 grams) of wool. Strain and cool the liquid to lukewarm, then add the mordanted wool and simmer until the dye has penetrated the fiber, for 20 to 40 minutes. Rinse the wool in very warm water, adding salt or vinegar to the last rinse water.

Plate 99. *Solidago* ×*hybrida*, goldenrod, a self-sown variant of low forms originally grown from seed. Midsummer, Joseph Hudak garden. Photo, Joseph Hudak.

Hang the skeins to dry. The color will vary from bright shades of yellow to tan, according to the maturity of the flowers and the strength of the dyeing solution.

Related plants of interest. Seeds of goldenrods are available from specialty seed sources. Plants of sweet goldenrod are available from herb sources; others are available from perennial plant nurseries.

Solidago canadensis 'Golden Baby', Canada goldenrod, is clump forming with golden plumes. It grows to 24 in. (61.0 cm) and is early blooming, probably of hybrid origin (*S. canadensis* × *S. virgaurea*). If allowed to seed itself, the offspring, often referred to as *Solidago* ×*hybrida* (Plate 99), may be taller but are still desirable.

Solidago sempervirens, seaside goldenrod, is a spectacular, vigorous, late-blooming type to 6 ft. (1.8 m). It bears arching, one-sided golden plumes and is suitable for naturalizing, especially in coastal locations since it is tolerant of salt spray. Growing it in dry soil will produce a more compact form.

Solidago sphacelatus 'Golden Fleece', 18 in. (45.7 cm) tall, can be grown in a border, rock garden, or as an all-season ground cover. Its leaves are glossy and heart-shaped, its golden flowers borne in delicate sprays. It is late-blooming, though, and probably not worth growing for bloom in climates more harsh than Zone 5 or 6.

Solidago virgaurea 'Cloth of Gold' is primrose yellow, 18–24 in. (45.7–61.0 cm) tall, and early. It is quite suitable for a garden situation.

Stachys officinalis

> It is a pretty woodland plant.
>
> Maude Grieve
> *A Modern Herbal*

Lamiaceae, Mint Family
Betony, bishopswort, wood betony, woundwort

Perennial
Site and soil: sun, partial shade; evenly moist and well-drained
Hardiness: Zones 4–9
Landscape use: bed and border, naturalized herb
Height: 24–36 in. (61.0–91.4 cm)
Flower: reddish purple, tubular in whorl
Bloom season: midsummer to late summer

A native of open woodland and moist fields from Scotland to the Mediterranean and from Spain to the Caucasus, betony is an herb of antiquity. Distinctive rosettes of coarse, dark green, and heavily veined leaves — nearly heart-shaped and strongly aromatic—grow up from woody rhizomes. The erect stems bear short, densely filled spikes of small flowers in clustered whorls, twenty to thirty flowers in a cluster. The spikes are interrupted, appearing mostly at the top of the plant, but also further down the stem in smaller whorls, each one growing out of a pair of short, scallop-edged leaves that are miniature versions of the basal foliage. The merest brush releases the plant's strong musk-mint scent. Bees are drawn to betony when it is in full bloom.

As an official herb "of the apothecary" betony was once considered a cure-all used internally in teas to cure headaches and externally in poultices to heal wounds, among many other ailments. In its day, it was always at hand as a staple of the monastery garden—hence its name bishopswort. Like other herbs that were widely used to alleviate many afflictions, it was endowed with magical powers to ward off evil. Betony was "good for the man's soul or for his body," according to an early medieval herbal by Apelius (Grieve 1931).

As an ornamental, betony has been overlooked, perhaps overshadowed, by its silver-leaved relative, lamb's ears, *Stachys byzantina*, which is a shame because betony has a lot to offer. It is an easygoing plant with a long and significant flowering period. And its basal foliage is handsome at all seasons. Betony is perfect for an informal cottage garden planting, attractive near the middle of the border with clary sage (*Salvia sclarea*). Or it can be naturalized in a moist but well-drained spot with elecampane (*Inula helenium*). These two, planted together, are handsome accents anywhere in the landscape, especially at the edge of light woodland. With its upright spikes and bright color betony is also suitable for an herb or medicinal garden of more subtle foliage plants.

Sow seeds indoors 8–10 weeks before the last frost at 70°F (21°C); they should germinate in 15 to 30 days. Or buy plants and space them 12–18 in. (30.5–45.7 cm) apart in humusy soil, in full sun or light shade; where winters are severe, moist soil conditions should be avoided. Cut the spent flowering stalks to encourage more blossoming, which may continue to the fall. Take advantage of cutting the flower stalks before they are spent, since all betonys are long-lasting cut flowers.

Related plants of interest. Betony is available from herb and specialty seed sources. Great-flowered betony is available from the best perennial plant nurseries.

Stachys macrantha, great-flowered betony, blooms in early summer. It was a favorite of Marjory Fish who considered it a familiar, but always wel-

Plate 100. *Stachys officinalis*, wood betony, in sun (See also Plate 4, p. 30–31). Midsummer, Cricket Hill Herb Farm. Photo, Judy Kehs.

come, cottage garden plant. An old country name, the king-in-splendour, is wonderfully descriptive of this compact betony with stiff stems to 24 in. (61.0 cm) and showy, rosy purple flower spikes that grow up from crinkled leaves. Despite its obvious merits it is seldom grown in the herb or flower garden. Try it at the front of a mixed border among a spreading cloud of white, double-flowered feverfew. 'Superba', the type grown by Fish, has large flower spikes; 'Alba' has lovely, pure white flower spikes, a nice contrast to the dark green foliage; and 'Rosea' has clear pink flowers. Great-flowered betony needs well-drained soil and full sun, except where summers are very hot.

Symphytum

> **Over many weeks . . . it unfurls coiled spirals of buds and hangs out a succession of small . . . bright blue bells.**
>
> Patrick Lima
> *The Harrowsmith Illustrated Book of Herbs*

Boraginaceae, Borage Family
Comfrey, bruisewort, knitback, knitbone

Perennial
Site and soil: sun, partial shade; evenly moist
Hardiness: Zones 3–9
Landscape use: accent, bed and border, naturalized herb
Height: 2–4 ft. (0.6–1.2 m)
Flower: mauve, crimson, white, blue bell in drooping cluster
Bloom season: spring to early summer

Two species exemplify comfrey, both as a healing herb and an ornamental. The better known medicinal is *Symphytum officinale*, English comfrey, of Eurasian origin. Rangy in its growth, to 3 ft. (0.9 m) or more, it grows from a deep, fleshy taproot. The basal leaves are large, coarse, but not unattractive, and prominently veined, reduced in size further up the stem. The rose-tipped buds are arranged gracefully in arched coils at the tips of branching stems. Gradually, by late spring and early summer, the coils are gently released and the $1/2$ in. (1.3 cm) bells bloom in a mass, changing from rose to purple-crimson as they mature. Red comfrey, a more compact form, 18–24 in. (45.7–61.0 cm) tall with crimson flowers, is usually of-

312

fered as a separate species, *S. rubrum*. Of the two exemplifying species, the best known ornamental is *Symphytum caucasicum* (Plate 101), small blue comfrey, from the Caucasus. It is a robust plant, too, despite its common name, although not as rangy and with more generous, slightly larger flowers of a beautiful, horizon blue. Both comfreys draw hummingbirds.

Since ancient times, comfrey has been used to heal bruises and broken bones. This singular ability is preserved in its many folk names, as well as its Latin name, which is derived from a Greek word meaning to unite.

Plate 101. *Symphytum caucasicum*, small blue comfrey. Early summer, Gardner farm. Photo by Alan Dorey.

Comfrey leaves and roots contain allantoin and choline, two substances which promote healthy growth of red blood corpuscles. At one time, preparations from the plant were taken internally for various complaints, but this use is now discouraged because if taken in quantity, comfrey could be carcinogenic. Some kinds, however, are highly regarded cattle fodder. Comfrey is still considered beneficial for the external treatment of bruises. Also, its roots yield a yellow-brown dye.

As a garden plant, comfrey is valued for its commanding presence whether in leaf, bud, or flower, for its month-long-lasting blooms, and for its virtual indestructibility. Over 20 years ago, the herb writer Adele Dawson gave me a few roots of blue comfrey, and it and its many descendants have survived untold hazards. Once, our resident bull took a midnight stroll through the herb garden, trampling everything in his wake. He took special interest in the comfrey, which was just about to bloom, and ground it to a pulpy mass with his massive head. Although it did not bloom that spring, it soon regrew a thick clump of long, handsome leaves and put forth a few blossoms in late summer.

Small blue comfrey grows advantageously in a variety of situations. In an island garden it is the centerpiece for late spring and early summer, rising above and complementing the vertical, pink spikes of bistort (*Polygonum bistorta*) and the frilly, white saucers of sweet cicely (*Myrrhis odorata*); I have naturalized it along our lane in full sun, on a shaded woodland slope with sweet violets (*Viola odorata*), and in a wet ditch near a bee hive —it is an excellent source of nectar. Wherever it is grown, it calls attention to itself; our visitors invariably ask its name and are surprised to learn it is the humble healing herb, comfrey, so beautiful when smothered in blue bells.

Think carefully before planting comfrey because, with its long taproot, it means to stay. Sow seeds in early spring, or in spring or fall set plants 24 in. (61.0 cm) apart in moist soil and partial shade. If the soil is rich, comfrey will need staking. To dwarf growth, plant comfrey in drier soil and a sunny situation. Cut back the plants after bloom for a fresh mound of leaves and late summer repeat bloom. In a garden, comfrey should be divided at least every 2 years.

Since the plants decompose quickly and are nutrient-rich, comfrey makes great compost or even mulch. If used for the latter purpose, be sure seed heads are not included. To ease muscular tension, add an infusion of comfrey to bath water: steep ¼ cup dried leaves in 1 quart boiling water for 30 minutes, then strain. For a simple poultice to soothe bruises, apply fresh leaves to the sore spot, then cover them with a warm, moist towel.

Related plants of interest. The comfreys are available from perennial plant and herb nurseries.

Symphytum grandiflorum, dwarf comfrey, once known as *Pulmonaria lutea,* is an elegant, low-growing plant 6–16 in. (15.2–40.6 cm) high with fuzzy, rich green leaves that form a thick carpet, even in dry, shady conditions, making it useful for colonizing around shrubs. The drooping, elongated, tubular flowers are creamy yellow and very showy. The buds of 'Hidcote Blue' are tipped with blue, then open creamy white.

Symphytum ×uplandicum, Russian comfrey, is a natural hybrid between *S. officinale* and *S. asperum* and is the type used for cattle fodder. It is also a grand plant, growing as tall as 6 ft. (1.8 m) in the optimum conditions of moist soil and partial shade, bearing rose-purple blooms in heavy clusters. It provides a wonderful background for lower growers but needs plenty of room. At Sissinghurst Castle it is paired with bistort (*Polygonum bistorta*).

Tagetes tenuifolia

Asteraceae, Aster Family
Signet marigold

> **A most beautiful plant . . . as round as a ball.**
> *Vick's Catalogue and Floral Guide*
> Spring 1865

Annual
Site and soil: sun; well-drained
Landscape use: bed and border, container, edge and hedge, rock work
Height: 6–12 in. (15.2–30.5 cm)
Flower: lemon yellow, tangerine, daisy-like in mound
Bloom season: midsummer to late summer

The signet marigold, descended from a Mexican wildflower, was transformed into the ultimate bedding plant of the Victorian era. The small, five-petaled yellow daisies, no more than 1 in. (2.5 cm) wide on 24 in. (61.0 m), branching stems, were considerably dwarfed. The brilliant, domelike mounds that resulted are quite suitable for mass plantings, but even a single plant gains its effect from the seemingly endless numbers of flowers that are produced from midsummer through several light frosts — these marigolds are slightly hardier than other types of marigolds. The signet marigold's ferny foliage is aromatic with a distinctive, unforgettable, citrus aroma, easily released by lightly brushing the plant.

With the decline in formal mass bedding schemes, the signet declined in popularity until being almost entirely obscured in the modern era by the many larger-flowered African and French marigolds. But signets are being rediscovered as flavoring herbs as well as appealing plants with a variety of landscaping uses. The most enduring cultivars are *Tagetes tenuifolia* 'Lemon Gem' (Plate 1), 'Tangerine Gem' (Plate 102), and 'Little Giant', the last with dark purple splotches at the base of its golden petals. My favorite is the hard-to-find 'Lulu' (Plate 103), truly dwarf at 8 in. (20.3 cm), with a mass of lemon-yellow daisies. Other types are variable, in my experience, growing 6–12 in. (15.2–30.5 cm). Interest in signets is reflected

Plate 102. *Tagetes tenuifolia* 'Tangerine Gem', signet marigold. Midsummer, Country Lane Herbs and Dried Flowers. Photo, Brian Oke and Gisèle Quesnel.

Plate 103. *Tagetes tenuifolia* 'Lulu', signet marigold, and *Tropaeolum majus* Double Gleam Hybrids, semitrailing nasturtium. Late summer, Gardner farm. Photo, Avinoam Danin.

in the development of new, more compact cultivars with a greater color range, as in 'Paprika' with pimento-red petals edged with gold.

It has been a delight to grow signets for many years. I plant them to edge a culinary garden where their bright color contrasts well with herb greenery—parsley, marjoram, basil. I grow them in tubs, either alone for a bright accent, paired with dwarf crimson nicotiana, or with the dwarf *Salvia coccinea* 'Lady in Red' (Plate 1). The tubs are placed in high traffic areas, along paths and near doorways, where the signets will be noticed. Those who pass invariably brush the plants, releasing their uncommon perfume that never fails to stop visitors in their tracks. "What is that plant?" they always ask, looking back with astonishment and oohing and aahing at the brilliant mound of bloom. Signets are wonderful rock garden plants, always attractive in foliage, always bright in bloom.

Signets require a longer growing season than other marigolds. Where summers are hot and long, seeds can be sown in the ground when temperatures warm, otherwise it is best to start plants indoors 8–10 weeks before the last frost. Barely cover the seed and germination will occur at 70°F (21°C) in 5 to 14 days, sometimes less. Space seedlings 6–8 in. (15.2–20.3 cm) apart after the last frost. The plants benefit from deadheading, which is easily accomplished by lightly drawing a cupped hand along the top of the plant; care should be taken, however, since the stems are brittle. Saved seed may not produce the same characteristics as the original, especially in dwarf plants.

Flowers and leaves of signet marigold release their citrus flavor in floral vinegars, which are easy to make by first steeping the flowers and leaves in white vinegar until the desired flavor is achieved, then straining the liquid through two layers of cheesecloth. Floral vinegars can be added to salads of all types and to fruit desserts, especially fresh fruit cups. They can also be used as skin freshener, for which purpose steep with the marigolds any type of mint leaves and sprigs of southernwood (*Artemisia abrotanum*). Then dilute the vinegar with an equal amount of water before adding it to wash or bath water.

Related plants of interest. Seeds of signet marigolds are available from general seed sources. Seeds or plants of Mexican mint marigold are available from specialty seed and herb sources.

Tagetes lucida, Mexican mint marigold, is a tender perennial in climates more harsh than Zone 7 or 8. Similar to the wild signet marigold except for its narrow, anise-scented leaves, it is often grown as a tarragon substitute in warm climates where that plant is difficult to grow. In cold climates, Mexican mint marigold almost never blooms, either outdoors or indoors, so its ornamental value is considerably reduced. There is little cause to hope for an earlier-blooming type due to problems of light and temperature sensitivity. The flavorful leaves, though, may still be enjoyed. Use them wherever an anise scent is desired, in sauces and herb butters and in chicken and fish dishes. In warm regions, sow seeds indoors 6 weeks before the usual outdoor spring planting time, and in late spring plant seedlings spaced 12 in. (30.5 cm) or more apart to account for their sprawl. Once established, Mexican mint marigold reseeds itself by late fall after flowering; also, stems will root in water.

Tanacetum parthenium

Asteraceae, Aster Family
Feverfew

> Its reputation as a garden flower is secure.
> Jim Wilson
> *Landscaping with Herbs*

Perennial
Site and soil: sun, partial shade; well-drained
Hardiness: Zones 4–9
Landscape use: bed and border, container, ground cover, rock work
Height: 24 in. (61.0 cm)
Flower: white and yellow, white, daisy-like flower or pompon in cluster
Bloom season: early summer to midsummer

At first glance, the Eurasian feverfew seems almost identical to chamomile (*Matricaria recutita*) because of the similarity of their daisy-like flowers and general form. But on closer inspection, these plants are noticeably different. Feverfew is more erect with smoother, less ferny, lighter green foliage that carries a pungent, medicinal scent that is evident throughout the plant, even in its seeds. The 1 in. (2.5 cm) flowers with flat, rather than cone-shaped, yellow centers surrounded by short, stubby, white petals are borne in profusion almost all summer on branched sprays.

The double, white *Tanacetum parthenium* 'Flore Pleno' (Plate 105) or 'Plenum', has been known since the sixteenth century. It is a pompon flower, wholly white, very similar in appearance to *Achillea ptarmica* 'The Pearl'. Its flowering sprays, once popular in bridal bouquets, earned it the name bridal rose.

The name feverfew is a corruption of the Latin *febrifuge*, meaning fever, and draws attention to the herb's primary past use as a fever-reducer, as recorded by Charlemagne in 812 (Webster 1942). It has other applications, among them the treatment of rheumatism and of headaches, for which it has generated contemporary interest as an effective treatment for migraines. It should not, however, be used for self-treatment.

Feverfew has an odd place in our gardening tradition. Herb gardeners tend to grow the single species type; the double white can often be found in older gardens, loved for its profusion of pure white flower sprays; but gardeners, in general, are more familiar with the bedding versions, which are described as annuals and sometimes listed under *Matricaria*. These

Plate 104. *Tanacetum parthenium*, feverfew. Midsummer, Country Lane Herbs and Dried Flowers. Photo, Brian Oke and Gisèle Quesnel.

bedding plants are valued for their low, mounded forms smothered in flowers all summer: *Tanacetum parthenium* 'Santana Lemon' to 7 in. (17.8 cm) has yellow button flowers, thinly rayed; 'Snowball' to 12 in. (30.5 cm) carries a multitude of tight, ivory buttons; and 'White Stars' grows 6–9 in. (15.2–22.9 cm) tall, its white, star-shaped flowers similar in shape to those of cushion mums.

The taller feverfews are grand filler plants in the perennial bed or border, useful to tone down bright reds and purples. Their bushy forms complement more vertical perennials such as salvias, foxgloves (*Digitalis*), and veronicas. The double white grows nicely in several different plantings, in full sun and partial shade, with deep orange calendulas and purple-topped painted sage (*Salvia viridis*). The unimproved, single, daisy-like form can be a ground cover under a bank of roses where it will carry on all summer, forming buds at its base while still blooming at its top. The low, neater, mounded sorts can be grown as low edging for annuals or perennials, or use them to line driveways or enhance foundation plantings.

Plate 105. *Tanacetum parthenium* 'Flore Pleno', double-flowered feverfew. Midsummer, Gardner farm. Photo, Alan Dorey.

They also look great around steps, at the base of rocks, in rock gardens, or in tubs with bright yellow or orange signet marigolds (*Tagetes tenuifolia*) for landscape accents.

Feverfew is a short-lived perennial that is often grown from seeds that produce flowering plants the first season; the double-flowered forms usually come true. Sow the fine seeds indoors 6–8 weeks before the last frost at 70° F (21° C) on the surface of the soil; germination takes 10–15 days or less, even with old seed. Or sow the seeds outdoors when the soil has warmed. Space plants 18–24 in. (45.7–61.0 cm) apart for tall types and 12–15 in. (30.5–38.1 cm) for the shorter kinds. The soil must have excellent drainage; if moisture gathers around their roots in the winter, plants do not survive, although seedlings may be found in their vicinity. Feverfew becomes woody after a few seasons and should be propagated from the young shoots that grow near the bottom of the mother plant in early spring. Shear plants back in midseason to prevent legginess in the taller kinds and to stimulate more blooms. The fast-growing, bedding sorts are usually grown as annuals.

The old, double, white feverfew is an especially fine cut and dried flower. The young leaves and stems of crown daisy, *Chrysanthemum coronarium*, can be eaten raw in salads, stir fried or parboiled, or used to season soups. The dried, ground flowers of dalmatian pyrethrum, *Tanacetum cinerariae-folium*, can be made into an insecticide by mixing 1 tablespoon (15 ml) into 2 quarts (2 liters) hot water that has been infused with a little soft soap.

Related plants of interest. Seeds and plants of the species and double white feverfew are available from herb sources. Seeds of the annual bedding versions are offered by general seed sources. Seeds and plants of dalmatian pyrethrum and crown daisy are available from specialty seed and herb sources.

Chrysanthemum coronarium, crown daisy, is an easily grown annual, 18–36 in. (45.7–91.4 cm) tall. It is a bushy, vigorous plant with abundant, yellow daisies 2 in. (5.1 cm) across, and deeply cut, toothed, green foliage. A friend gave me seeds, calling the plant by its oriental name, *shunginku*, advising me to eat the young, spicy-flavored leaves. I was delighted by the flowers and recognized the plant as one of the "flowers of the field," plants described in the Bible as a metaphor for mortality. In the Middle East it blooms profusely, covering fields and roadsides with a yellow carpet in midwinter, but disappears with the onset of spring and hot temperatures. In my northern garden, it persists all summer. Sow seeds, covered ¹/₄ in. (0.6 cm) deep, outdoors when the soil has warmed or indoors 6–8 weeks before the last frost. Grow this in a mixed border, or among the edible herbs or vegetables. There are many cultivars, bred for their edible leaves.

Tanacetum cinerariaefolium, dalmatian pyrethrum, is a hardy perennial, 12–24 in. (30.5–61.0 cm) tall, with shining, 1 in. (2.5 cm) daisy-like flowers of white rays with yellow centers and handsome silvery gray, finely cut foliage. The flowers are the main commercial source for insecticidal pyrethrum. It is a sun-loving plant that should be mulched over the winter to ensure its return where winters are harsh.

Tanacetum coccineum, painted daisy, was once widely gathered for its use in the insecticide pyrethrum, but it is now grown for its pretty flowers, their petals painted in different colors—pink and shades of red. It grows to 30 in. (76.2 cm) with attractive ferny foliage. Painted daisy is perennial, bearing prolific flowers if given full sun, well-drained soil, and heat. Cut plants back for later bloom.

Tanacetum vulgare

Asteraceae, Aster Family
Tansy, bitter buttons, golden buttons

Perennial
Site and soil: sun, partial shade; evenly moist, well-drained
Hardiness: Zones 4–9
Landscape use: accent, edge and hedge, naturalized herb
Height: 3 ft. (0.9 m)
Flower: yellow button in cluster
Bloom season: late summer to fall

> Long ago this was one of the most important herbs and a highly decorative plant in every garden.
> Audrey Wynne Hatfield
> *The Weed Herbal*

Tansy is an Old World herb naturalized throughout North America along roadsides, in fields, and at old homesteads. It is a vigorous plant that grows by creeping rhizomes. At first just a ferny, green mound, its straight stems bear long, arching, finely divided leaves all the way to the top of the plant by late summer. The flower clusters or corymbs, about 4 in. (10.2 cm) wide, are dense with many small buttons, each ½ in. (1.3 cm) across, of tightly compressed disk florets. At first the buttons are light in color and waxy in appearance, but as the florets open, the buttons become bright yellow and concave in shape. As their season progresses, the buttons become convex, then flat, and finally turn brown as the seeds mature and disperse. The whole plant is strongly aromatic, with a fresh, penetrating, peppery-camphorous aroma.

Its species name, *vulgare*, meaning common, tells the story of tansy, a folk herb par excellence. It has been used since ancient times to strew, to repel bugs, to stimulate appetite, to dye material a clear yellow-green, to flavor foods in place of expensive spices, and even to preserve corpses. It was this latter use from which its genus name is believed to be derived, from the Greek *athanatoia*, meaning immortality; shortened to *thansa*, it then suggests the common name.

On Cape Breton Island off the northeastern tip of Nova Scotia, tansy still grows at Highland Scottish settlement sites dating from the late eighteenth century, sometimes lingering in the shade of a spruce forest, more often thriving in the rich soil of an abandoned farm site. Here one sees handsome stands, a mass of bright yellow buttons above the bright green, plume-like foliage. Though it is highly invasive, there is no denying tansy's appeal. The cultivar *Tanacetum vulgare* 'Goldsticks', with larger flower heads on long stems for cutting, is longer flowering than the species. Curly tansy, *T. vulgare* var. *crispum*, herbally the same as common tansy, is grown mainly for its lovely foliage, since it rarely blooms.

Do not be beguiled by the attractive, ferny seedlings. Tansy should never be planted in the garden proper. If grown in the right place, however, a place where it can be controlled, it can give much pleasure and even solve landscaping problems. A tansy hedge is beautiful, in or out of bloom, and is easily controlled by mowing, as long as there is grass growing on either side; or it very effectively will line a driveway. It can also be used as a single accent by a wall, fence, shed, or any structure, as long as it can be controlled by mowing. The problem arises when the hedge or accent is no longer needed or wanted. Tansy, in this sense, is truly immortal. Bear this quality in mind when establishing tansy in the first place. Another strategy is to let tansy go, to naturalize it in an open, sunny spot where its bright buttons and plumes can be admired, but where it cannot interfere with other plantings. Remember that naturalized plantings are not wholly maintenance-free. They need to be roughly mown, as with a scythe or brush hook, and, in the case of tansy, the ground should be loamy and moist for best flower production.

Sow seeds outdoors in late fall to germinate the following spring. Space seedlings 12–24 in. (30.5–61.0 cm) apart in loamy soil in sun or partial shade, though sun is better for sturdy plants and bright flowers. Once established, you should have a lifetime supply of plants; make root divisions in the spring. I have never found it necessary to stake plants, but be forewarned about the possibility, especially in a windy, exposed site where the soil is rich.

The medicinal uses of tansy are discouraged for it could be toxic, but a small amount of chopped leaves can safely be used to add peppery flavor to food; try adding a small amount to scrambled eggs. Common tansy is a superb cut flower; and for dried flowers, cut the stems when the buttons are just becoming convex. The dried leaves of all types can be added to potpourri or used for room freshener: add a small handful to a saucepan of boiling water and let it simmer, uncovered. The leaves and flowers of all types can be used for moth repellent when mixed with equal parts wormwood (*Artemisia absinthium*) and southernwood (*Artemisia abrotanum*).

Related plants of interest. Seeds and plants of common tansy are widely available from herb sources. Seeds of *Tanacetum vulgare* 'Goldsticks' are available at select sources. Silver tansy is available from perennial plant and herb sources, but *T. ptarmicifolium* 'Silver Feather' is rare.

Tanacetum niveum, silver tansy, is a terrific landscaping plant that is very underused. It has silvery, finely cut foliage and, by midsummer, masses of small, daisy-like flowers with white rays and yellow centers. Growing to 3 ft. (0.9 m) tall and just as wide, silver tansy is hardy in Zone 5.

Tanacetum ptarmicifolium 'Silver Feather', silver-lace tansy, is native to the Canary Islands and is grown as an annual in areas colder than Zone 8 or 9. It reaches 18 in. (45.4 cm) with silvery, feathery leaves, as its name indicates, and a crown of button flowers in late summer. It can be grown from seeds or cuttings. It has been reclassified at least three times, most recently from the genus *Chrysanthemum*.

Thymbra spicata

Lamiaceae, Mint Family
Spiked thymbra, za'atar

Shrub
Site and soil: sun; sharply drained
Hardiness: Zones 8–10
Landscape use: accent, bed and border, container, naturalized herb, rock work
Height: 12–22 in. (30.5–55.9 cm)
Flower: rose-pink, tubular on spike
Bloom season: late summer to fall

Spiked thymbra is an erect, low-growing shrub to 24 in. (61.0 cm) native from Greece to Israel. It is called spiked thymbra for the plant's small, showy, tubular flowers that grow in 1 to 4 in. (2.5–10.2 cm) spikes at the tips of its square-stemmed branches. These are densely covered with dark green, narrow foliage that is strongly camphor scented, a combination of oregano and thyme.

Although still rare in the nursery trade, it is commonly grown by North American immigrants, mostly from Syria and Lebanon, who use it as a flavoring herb and call it za'atar. To confuse matters, za'atar is also the name of a spice blend in which spiked thymbra may be the main flavoring ingredient, depending on the blend's country of origin, with roasted sesame seeds, ground sumac fruits, and salt. This mixture is traditionally baked into pita bread after first being thinned with olive oil (see recipe below). Spiked thymbra may also be a common constituent of grocery store oregano because of its excellent flavor and long shelf life. It has many uses in the folk medicine of the Mediterranean region. An old custom, still practiced, is to eat a small amount of the leaves every day for 40 days to build up an immunity to snake bites.

Although a newcomer to cultivation in North America, spiked thymbra was grown in the late 1940s by Helen Fox, an early champion of the ornamental value of many herbs. She grew it from seed as an annual in her Westchester County garden in New York, and although not as robust nor as aromatic as it would have been if grown in California, she was pleased by its neat appearance and lovely whorls of stalkless flowers tinged with rose.

Unless it is grown as an annual, in hard winter climates spiked thymbra should be grown in containers that can be taken indoors in the fall before heavy frost. Outdoors, pot-grown plants can be grouped with others, such as Spanish lavender (*Lavandula stoechas*), blue sage (*Salvia clevelandii*), and dittany of Crete (*Origanum dictamnus*). These should be placed near entrances or on patios and decks where their mingled scents and contrasting flowers will be most appreciated. Where spiked thymbra can be grown in the ground over the winter, it is most striking in a natural outcropping of rocks, naturalized among bright mats of creeping red thyme (*Thymus pulegoides* 'Kermesinus'). Under these conditions, similar to those in its native habitat, it will thrive. In a perennial herb and flower border, or in a formal, raised-bed herb planting, spiked thymbra's neat growth is an asset.

Spiked thymbra can be grown from seeds, but they are hard to find. Sow them in potting soil fortified with vermiculite or sharp sand for quick drainage; mist, rather than water, the soil, and mist emerging seedlings. Seeds take up to 21 days to germinate at 70°F (21°C). Outside, space young plants 8 in. (20.3 cm) apart or mature plants 12–18 in. (30.5–45.7 cm) apart. It is better to keep plants indoors or in a greenhouse until temperatures warm. Spiked thymbra needs full sun and an alkaline to neutral soil, sharply drained and dry. It will survive light frosts, but should be protected from heavy freezing. Winter container-grown plants indoors near a cool, sunny window or in a greenhouse. Clip back branches in the spring to encourage fresh growth near the base of the plant. Propagation is difficult, but can be achieved by stem cuttings or layering.

All za'atar herbs can be used like oregano—to flavor butter or meat, vegetable, egg, cheese, and pasta dishes. For the ultimate pleasure, bake them into the crust of homemade pita bread. The best pita I have ever had was in the Bedouin village of Shibli at the foot of Mount Tabor in Israel, where it is baked in an outdoor oven called a *taboun,* a rectangular tin box open at the front with a narrow firebox at one side. Inside the taboun is a manually operated revolving wheel on which the pita is baked. Each one passes through the flames in turn until it is lightly browned and the za'-atar-and-olive-oil coating is sizzling. A very hot oven and the following directions will produce the nearest thing.

Herbed Pita Bread

1 tablespoon traditional baking yeast
1 scant tablespoon salt
2 tablespoons sugar
3 cups water
6–7 cups unbleached white flour
2 heaping tablespoons za'atar spice blend (spiked thymbra, roasted
    sesame seeds, ground sumac fruits, and salt)
olive oil

Mix the za'atar spice blend with olive oil for spreading consistency. Mix the yeast, salt, and sugar with ½ cup warm water, cover, and let stand for 10 minutes; stir the mixture to make sure the yeast is dissolved—it should be foaming. Add the rest of the water and 4 cups of flour, then mix the dough vigorously, adding flour as needed to make it stiff. Knead 5 minutes, then cover the bowl and let the dough rise in a warm place until doubled. Preheat oven to 450°F (230°C). Pinch the dough, cut it into twelve pieces (or six if you want larger rounds) and roll out each piece to ¼ in. (0.6 cm) thick. Place as many as will conveniently fit on a lightly greased cookie sheet, patting each one into a roughly round shape, then gently press little indentations into the top of the dough to hold the za'atar and olive oil mixture. Brush the dough with the mixture, then bake immediately for about 8 minutes. The pita crust should be golden brown and the oil sizzling (Gardner 1992).

Related plants of interest. All the za'atar plants are available from the best herb nurseries; Bible hyssop, *Origanum syriacum,* is the most widely available.

Thymus capitatus, conehead thyme, is another za'atar herb from the Mediterranean region with similar growth habits and cultural requirements. The lavender-mauve flowers are very showy, growing at the tips of 8 to 10 in. (20.3–25.5 cm), stiff, upright branches. It is a compact little bush with a dense mass of tiny blooms, each with prominent stamens. Bees are very attracted to the flowers. Conehead thyme is well suited to formal plantings such as knot gardens. The abundant, small-leaved foliage is spicily thyme-scented with savory overtones and is used for flavoring the same way as spiked thymbra.

Origanum syriacum (Plate 106), also known as *O. maru* or *Majorana syriaca*, is the one and only true za'atar. Known as Bible hyssop for the several references to it throughout the Hebrew Bible, it is an ancient Jewish symbol of modesty and an important medicinal and flavoring herb. Literally growing between the rocks in its native habitat, it thrives where most plants would fail, thus its association with modesty and humility. In its early growth, it looks very much like sweet marjoram (*Origanum marjorana*) or oregano (*Origanum vulgare*), with small, downy, heart-shaped leaves. But as it matures, it becomes a hairy gray shrub with woody stems, each topped by small, white flowers in dense spikes. Called in Arabic *za'-atar*, and in Hebrew *ezov*, this is the herb of choice to flavor the spice blend za'atar. Its flavor is sweeter, less peppery or thyme-flavored, than the various substitutes.

In colder regions Bible hyssop is decorative, but much subdued, in a hanging basket or in tubs placed near the bright yellow or orange signet

Plate 106. *Origanum syriacum*, Bible hyssop, wild. Spring to early summer, Neot Kedumim, Biblical Land Reserve, Israel. Elsewhere it blooms from early summer to late summer in the ground or in containers. Photo courtesy of Neot Kedumim.

marigolds (*Tagetes tenuifolia*) for a contrast of foliage, flowers, and scent. Hardy in Zone 8 or 9, Bible hyssop can be naturalized in a rockery with Roman hyssop (*Satureja thymbra*) and Spanish lavender (*Lavandula stoechas*), both false hyssops, as they grow in their native habitat. As long as a dry, rocky terrain is provided, these herbs will flourish.

Satureja thymbra (Plates 107 and 108), whorled savory or Roman hyssop, another za'atar herb, has entered the nursery trade probably from Greece. I first saw it growing on the slopes of Mount Carmel in Israel. It is very aromatic, like oregano but spicier, growing 12–18 in. (30.5–45.7 cm) tall with many upright stems that bear small-petaled, pink flowers in whorls from the middle to the top of the stem. The flowers are encircled with upturned, pointed leaves, giving the top of the plant the appearance of a decorative urn. Called *za'atar parsi*, Persian za'atar, or *za'atar romi*, Roman za'atar, in Arabic, the plant is also known as Roman hyssop, another of the false hyssops mentioned in the Talmud. Roman hyssop is false in the sense that it is not the hyssop, *Origanum syriacum*, mentioned with no qualifying name throughout the Bible.

Plates 107 and 108. *Satureja thymbra*, whorled savory, wild. Spring, Mt. Carmel, Israel. Elsewhere it blooms in late summer. Photo, Avinoam Danin.

Whorled savory or Roman hyssop has a rich history of use in Middle Eastern folk medicine as a cure-all for various internal and external complaints. In common with the other za'atar herbs, it can be used as a substitute in the spice blend if Bible hyssop is not available. Grown like spiked thymbra, its landscaping uses are similar—it is perfect among rocks. At Neot Kedumim in Israel, where Biblical habitats are recreated,

the false hyssops and the true hyssop are naturalized together in a memorable planting. They are also used for general landscaping at the base of a broad stairway.

Thymus

The flowers look like amethysts and rubies.

Helen Fox
The Years in My Herb Garden

Lamiaceae, Mint Family

Thyme

Perennial, shrub
Site and soil: sun; sharply drained, well-drained
Hardiness: Zones 4–10
Landscape use: bed and border, container, edge and
        hedge, ground cover, naturalized herb, rock work
Height: 1–12 in. (2.5–30.5 cm)
Flower: pink, rose, lavender, crimson, white, small, tubular in leaf axil
Bloom season: early summer to midsummer

There are two basic forms of thyme: the small, upright shrub and the low, creeping sort. The types that fall between these two forms are hard to categorize—they are semiupright, spreading, and mounding at the same time. Their nomenclature is very confusing for the ordinary gardener and the specialist alike.

The bush thyme with which most gardeners are familiar is *Thymus vulgaris*, cooking thyme, descended from a wild Mediterranean species, improved over centuries of cultivation. It grows no more than 12 in. (30.5 cm) tall, spreading as wide with age, forming a woody base from which grow many erect, twiggy branches covered with needle-like, shiny, dark green leaves. From early summer to midsummer the diminutive shrub is covered with light pink or white, two-lipped flowers tucked into leaf axils at the top of the plant and borne in profusion. At flowering time, also the time of the greatest concentration of thymol, the essential oil that gives cooking thyme its familiar, peppery mint flavor and scent, bees come in great numbers to harvest nectar.

The creeping thymes, often confused with one another, are hardy and vigorous. *Thymus praecox* subsp. *arcticus* (Plates 5, p. 43, and 50, p. 176–177) is native in Greenland and from Scandinavia to northwestern Spain. It grows flat to the ground from a woody base, forming tight mats of tiny leaves with hairs at their margins and stems no taller than 3 in. (7.6 cm). It produces a multitude of tiny, lavender-purple flowers that bloom in sheets early in the summer. The name *praecox*, meaning early, describes its bloom season. The other thyme usually considered creeping exhibits mixed characteristics of habit. *Thymus pulegoides*, most often known as mother-of-thyme, is distributed throughout Europe. It is variable, mounding or spreading out in wide sheets, growing 4–10 in. (10.2–20.3 cm) tall, with glossy, rather rounded leaves that are larger than most thymes, and abundant, long-lasting clusters of lavender-pink flowers. The whole plant is very aromatic. Both *T. pulegoides* and *T. praecox* subsp. *arcticus* are called creeping thyme, mother-of-thyme, or wild thyme; they even may be undifferentiated and listed under *T. serpyllum*, a name that means creeping. Where they are naturalized on hillsides, they appear from a distance like a field of heather. And they are both very attractive to bees.

The genus name is derived either from the Greek *thumos*, which means courage, or *thymon*, to fumigate. Both explanations are probable enough given thyme's many traditional uses as a fortifying and bracing herb to treat coughs and respiratory illnesses, earaches, migraines, and digestive problems, and as a fumigator, as in the burning of incense or the strewing of herbs. Thymol is a proven disinfectant against bacteria and fungi, credited with being able to kill bacilli in 40 seconds. Today it is used to flavor mouthwashes, dentifrices, and medicines. Several thyme species, primarily *Thymus vulgaris*, have well-deserved reputations as culinary herbs. Their pungent, peppery, mint flavor is outstanding in meat dishes, stews, and sauces. Thyme honey, golden amber in color and slow to crystallize, has a long-lasting, minty flavor.

Depending on climate and growing conditions, virtually all thymes bloom prolifically. They are effective in a variety of landscaping situations. Formerly considered strictly for the herb garden, thymes, in their infinite variety, are beginning to be appreciated as versatile and beautiful plants that offer attractive foliage and massed bloom from early summer through fall, depending on type.

Even the traditional culinary thyme varies in habit, flower, leaf color and general hardiness. *Thymus vulgaris* 'Narrow Leaf French', also offered as 'German Winter', 'French Summer', or 'Greek Gray', to 12 in. (30.5 cm) tall, has pink flowers, grayer leaves than the species, and a sweeter scent and flavor. 'Broad Leaf', English thyme, has pale pink flowers, grows to 8 in. (20.3 cm) tall with a semicreeping habit, and is hardier than the species; it has larger, more rounded bright green leaves that are not as strongly scented as the species. The earlier-blooming 'Orange Balsam' with white or pale pink flowers is more citrus in aroma, due to the presence of different essential oils. Those citrus-scented essential oils are carried through the hybrid cross between *T. vulgaris* and *T. pulegoides* to lemon thyme, *T.* ×*citriodora*. It grows to 12 in. (30.5 cm) tall with leaves a bright green that hints of gold and with flowers pale lilac; the whole plant is intensely lemon scented. *Thymus* ×*citriodora* 'Aureus', or golden lemon thyme, a mutation of lemon thyme, has variegated, bright yellow-green leaves, a semi-upright habit, 8–12 in. (20.3–30.5 cm) in height, and pale purple flowers crowded in its axils. The leaves gradually turn green by the time the plant flowers, then revert to green and gold by fall. All forms of *T. vulgaris* and the lemon thymes are marginally hardy in Zone 4.

Some of the showiest variants are offspring of *Thymus praecox* subsp. *arcticus*. The lightly scented 'Alba', often sold as 'White Moss', has diminutive, white flowers that create a sheet of bloom over a mat of bright green leaves from early to late June. 'Annie Hall', one of the earliest to bloom, has fragrant, pink flowers; the pink-flowered 'Britannicus' (Plate 109), Britannia thyme, forms a fuzzy mat of silvery leaves and smells like lemon and thyme combined; 'Coccineus', or 'Creeping Red Thyme', one of the flashiest of all thymes with profuse red or magenta flowers over a dark green mat of leaves, is well scented and blooms from late June to the fall; and 'Pink Chintz', lightly scented with a buttery flavor, is valued not only for its long-lasting mantle of lavender-pink flowers set off by silvery leaves, but also for its later summer to fall bloom. *Thymus praecox* subsp. *arcticus* and its cultivars are the hardiest of thymes, surviving in Zone 4.

The best forms for flowering among *Thymus pulegoides* include: 'Fosterflower', named for Gertrude Foster, or 'White Creeping Thyme', 4–6 in. (10.2–15.2 cm) tall, which blooms in late summer; 'Kermesinus', or 'Creeping Red Thyme' (though it is not the same plant as *T. praecox* subsp. *arcticus* 'Coccineus', above), bears brilliant magenta or rose-purple flower spikes and blooms just after 'Fosterflower'; 'Oregano Thyme', 6–10 in. (15.2–25.4 cm) tall, is semiupright and late blooming, from mid- to late summer, with lavender-pink flowers over large, rounded leaves that have a thyme-oregano scent. *Thymus pulegoides* and its cultivars are hardy in Zone 4 or 5.

By choosing different kinds, gardeners can enjoy flowering thymes from early summer well into the fall. Shrub types, which spread as wide as their height if untrimmed, thrive in open, sunny, raised beds. They combine well with bright signet marigolds (*Tagetes tenuifolia*), dwarf nepetas, taller salvias, and mounds of rue (*Rue graveolens*) and santolinas for a variety of forms and colors. Thymes also show off when grouped along stone walls or pathways as a low, informal hedge. They can be grown among rocks or in tubs on a sunny patio. The creeping thymes are choice ground covers; underplanted with spring and fall bulbs they carpet the ground around shrubs and roses or between steps and pavings. The low-

Plate 109. *Thymus praecox* subsp. *arcticus* 'Britannicus', Britannia thyme. Midsummer, Country Lane Herbs and Dried Flowers. Photo, Brian Oke and Gisèle Quesnel.

growing *Thymus praecox* subsp. *arcticus* is best for foot traffic. The most vigorous thymes, *T. praecox* subsp. *arcticus* or *T. pulegoides*, but not their cultivars, are best for naturalizing on a dry, sunny bank where they hold soil to prevent erosion.

Indoors 8–10 weeks before the last frost, sow seeds of species on the surface of the soil, where they should germinate at 70°F in 15 to 30 days, or sooner with bottom heat. One week before the last frost, plant seedlings outdoors, spacing them 8–12 in. (20.3–30.5 cm) apart, but no more than 10 in. (25.4 cm) for a ground cover. Establish the cultivars from plants. The best site for all thymes is light, quickly draining, and early-warming soil in full sun in colder climates and partial shade in warmer climates. Shrub types are susceptible to fungus disease when exposed to excessive moisture, so give them good air circulation. Cut back plants after flowering to maintain tidy growth and encourage fresh leaf production; severely trim shrub thymes in the spring to stimulate fresh growth.

Shrub types become woody in 3–4 years or less, after which they will need to be divided in the spring or replaced by stem cuttings from non-flowering shoots in early summer. When propagating variegated thymes, be sure to carefully select the most variegated shoots. Creeping thymes are easily layered since the stems are already lying on the soil, but be careful when heaping dirt over them to leave the tips of the branches exposed to air. Mulch thymes lightly where severe winter weather or exposure to wind may cause the tops of plants to die back. If plants do suffer winter damage, they may recover after a spring clipping.

Harvest the flavoring thymes when the plants are just in bloom. The strongly scented leaves are used in the all-purpose blend of fresh herbs called *fines herbes* with chives, tarragon, parsley, and chervil, and fresh or dry in *bouquet garni* with celery, parsley, and bay leaf for flavoring soups and sauces. Thyme flavor goes well with all meat dishes; lemon-scented thymes are used for fish. Thyme jelly, made with grape juice, is delicious. Thyme is best dried by placing leafy stems on a cookie sheet in a just warm oven or near a gentle source of heat until the leaves can be stripped. Although a good sized thyme bush yields a small amount of dried leaves, these are so intensely flavored, only a little bit is needed in any dish. All scented thymes can be added to potpourri.

Related plants of interest. Seeds of common cooking thyme, *Thymus vulgaris*, are widely available from general seed sources; the greatest variety of thymes are offered by herb sources.

Thymus brousonetti, Moroccan thyme, is semiupright, spreading, and mounding to 12 in. (30.5 cm) high with flower spikes 2 in. (5.1 cm) in length, very large for thyme. These are densely packed with light pink flowers like little trumpets, blooming in spring and early summer. A pine-scented thyme, it is hardy in Zone 8 with protection. Grow it in containers outdoors and winter it inside where it makes a fine houseplant.

Thymus herba-barona, caraway thyme, 1–4 in. (2.5–10.2 cm) tall, is a creeper with a profusion of deep rose flowers over a mat of shiny, dark green leaves. It flowers early in the summer and sporadically later. It is traditionally used to flavor a baron of beef (double loin), as its Latin name suggests. It is very hardy in Zone 4.

Thymus leucotrichus 'Peter Davis Thyme', 3–4 in. (7.6–10.2 cm) tall, is a spicily scented, spreading mat with pink flowers that bloom from late spring to mid-June. It is hardy in Zone 6.

Thymus 'Linear Leaf Lilac', Marshall thyme, is a 3–8 in. (7.6–20.3 cm) tall, lightly scented creeper with narrow, gray-green foliage, smothered in lavender flowers in early summer. It is hardy in Zone 4.

Thymus pseudolanuginosus or *T. praecox* 'Languinosus', woolly thyme, is drought resistant because of its small, down-covered gray leaves that form woolly mats about 1 in. (2.5 cm) high. But it is also more susceptible to fungus because of the moisture the mats retain. The faster growing *T. pseudolanuginosus* 'Hall's Woolly Thyme' is more generous with its pale pink to white flowers in early summer. Plant this thyme in rock crevices, between pavings, or draping over stone walls. It is hardy in Zone 4.

Tropaeolum

The flours are dispersed throughout the whole plant, of colour yellow . . . unto the backe-part of the same doth hang a taile or spurre.

John Gerard
The Herball

Tropaeolaceae, Nasturtium Family
Nasturtium, Indian cress

Annual
Site and soil: sun; well-drained
Landscape use: accent, bed and border, container, edge and hedge, ground cover
Height: 8 in. to 6 ft. (20.3 cm to 1.8 m)
Flower: red, orange, yellow, single, spurred funnel
Bloom season: midsummer to late summer

Garden nasturtiums are descended from two wild species from South America, the low, scrambling *Tropaeolum minus* and the tall, twisting *T. majus* (Plate 110). Both share succulent, light green stems with round, shield-shaped leaves, from which comes the genus name based on the Greek for *trophy*. The crinkled, five-petaled flowers are outfacing and held by five sepals; the upper sepal forms an elongated, nectar-laden spur. All parts of the plant have a peppery taste quite similar to watercress.

The various forms created by crossing these two species has resulted in low, semitrailing, and tall climbers in a brilliant assortment of colors—cream, gold, salmon, rose, peach, scarlet—some flowers darkly spotted at their bases, some ruffled, doubled, and spurless, 2–3 in. (5.1–7.6 cm) across. Some have marbled leaves. The double-flowered types are especially fragrant, like spiced perfume; their scent is freely carried on the warm, summer air.

Originally grown for food as a substitute for watercress and as a condiment for meat from its pickled buds, nasturtiums were mainly ornamentals by the 1860s. By the early 1900s, after being eclipsed for several decades, the climbing type became popular for growing over trellises and arbors—the old-fashioned look was then in fashion. Now nasturtiums of all types are popular as both ornamentals and herbs, welcomed back to the fold in the wake of growing interest in edible flowers. In addition to their beauty and delicious flavor, nasturtiums are reputed to have antiseptic properties useful in treating infections; they are also high in vitamin C.

I have grown many nasturtiums over the years, and I find virtue in each of them. *Tropaeolum majus* 'Double Dwarf Jewel' makes a fine edge for an exposed, sunny planting of annuals. By midsummer they have spread out to form a wide, weed-smothering mat of circular foliage embellished by dazzling flowers. The large-flowered 'Empress of India'—a late nineteenth-century cultivar with blue-gray foliage and deep orange-scarlet flowers—and the marbled-leaved Alaska Hybrids grow well in tubs. Set the tubs on top of variegated goutweed (*Aegopodium podagraria*), an irrepressible ground cover that is improved by overplanting with bright, potted annuals. The Double Gleam Hybrids (Plate 103), discovered in California in the 1920s, are must-haves. These are very double- and large-flowered in soft colors, semitrailing, very fragrant, and good in containers set by entrances and near paths. I have the tall climbing nasturtium planted in a large barrel by an old shed where it scrambles up to and over the roof in true cottage garden style, with white sweet alyssum (*Lobularia maritima*) foaming at its base (Plate 111). And, without support, I let the climber 'Jewel of Africa'—a cultivar with all the nasturtium flower colors over speckled and striped leaves—trail over the ground. The spurless Whirly-

Plate 110. *Tropaeolum majus*, nasturtium. Midsummer, edible flower bed, Country Lane Herbs and Dried Flowers. Photo, Brian Oke and Gisèle Quesnel.

bird Hybrids are easier than the others to integrate into a mixed border because of their upward-facing, round flowers in soft colors. One of the most
effective ways to use nasturtiums is as a long border on either side of a
steep stairway; the foliage forms a thick hedge, allowing a rippling wave of
bright flowers to descend, uninterrupted, from the top to the bottom of
the stairs.

Nasturtium seeds are large and round, easy to handle, and perfect for
the beginner. But care is needed in planting them. To succeed, nasturtiums
need warm, well-drained soil, not overly rich. (Too rich soil produces a
fine crop of leaves at the expense of flower production.) On the other
hand, nasturtiums grow best in cool weather. There is a fine line between
planting the seed early enough to catch the cool weather, yet waiting until the soil is warm enough. If seeds are planted too early, they may rot. A
minimum of 65°F (18°C) is needed for germination, which should occur
in 7 to 12 days or less. Where summers are very hot and winters are frost-
free, plant seeds in early fall for winter bloom. Drop several seeds every
6–8 in. (15.2–20.3 cm) for short types and 12 in. (30.5 cm) for climbing
types, pressing them firmly into the soil so seeds are covered to twice their
depth. They need darkness to germinate. Since the climbers need a longer
season, these may be started indoors in plant cells or any container where
their roots will not be disturbed by transplanting. Use a strong spray of
cold water to dislodge aphids; cut back attacked plants if they are badly in-
fested.

Pick tender leaves and fresh flowers of nasturtiums all season for salads
and sandwiches; be sure to inspect flowers for insects. Stuff the larger types
with a dab of egg, chicken, or tuna salad and serve them as appetizers.
Cottage cheese thinned with yogurt makes a good spread on thinly sliced,
whole wheat or rye bread; gently press an opened flower onto the spread.
Steep flowers in white vinegar to release their warm, red color and peppery
flavor. After straining, use nasturtium vinegar in salads, pickled eggs, or
wherever a light peppery flavor is wanted. An older custom is to decorate
a table centerpiece with a garland of flowers.

Related plants of interest. Nasturtium seed is widely available from general seed sources; the old-fashioned climber and some of the older cultivars can also be found in specialty seed sources. Select sources offer the

Plate 111. *Tropaeolum majus*, climbing nasturtium, and Lobularia maritima, sweet alyssum, growing together in a half barrel. Late summer, Gardner farm. Photo, Avinoam Danin.

marbled-leaved climber, *Tropaeolum majus* 'Jewel of Africa', and tuberous nasturtium.

Tropaeolum tuberosum, a vine type from Peru, bears orange, red, and yellow flowers and has edible, tuberous roots with a peppery flavor and vanilla-like aroma. The tubers, about the size of a small carrot, should be dug before frost. They can be boiled, sautéed, added to stews, pickled, or sliced thin and eaten raw.

Valeriana officinalis

> Towering above the usual herbage . . . the crowning masses of light-coloured flowers, make the plant conspicuous.
>
> Maude Grieve
> *A Modern Herbal*

Valerianaceae, Valerian Family
Valerian, garden heliotrope, true valerian

Perennial
Site and soil: sun, partial shade; evenly moist, well-drained
Hardiness: Zones 3–10
Landscape use: accent, bed and border, naturalized herb
Height: 3–5 ft. (0.9–1.5 m)
Flower: pale pink, flat, terminal umbel
Bloom season: early summer to midsummer

The widely distributed valerian forms a mound of handsome, dark green leaves its first year. These are deeply cut, each set precisely opposite one another in seven to ten pairs, like the rungs of a ladder. The second year and thereafter, hollow, ribbed stems are produced, carrying leaves that almost disappear at the top of the plant, where the flowers are borne in early summer. The pinkish white heads, flattish, 2–4 in. (5.1–10.2 cm) wide when fully opened, are composed of tightly compressed tubes or funnels. In full bloom, valerian exudes a heavy, sweet, musky fragrance similar to that of heliotrope, *Heliotropium arborescens*, a tender, purple-flowered bedding plant with which it is sometimes confused. True valerian may also be confused with red valerian, *Centranthus ruber*, a member of the same family.

For at least 2000 years, preparations from valerian's roots have been used to treat hysteria, epilepsy, depression, and insomnia, ailments for which its effectiveness has been proven by modern research. In Europe, valerian, as the medicine from the plant is known, is a popular over-the-counter drug more effective than Valium, its proponents claim. Cats are attracted to the disturbed roots, which are stronger in aroma than the flowers, which attract flocks of butterflies.

Valerian's value for the gardener lies in its tall, massed flowers on self-supporting stems, its hardiness, its ability to grow in almost any soil, and its heady perfume, which is associated with the sweet, warm breath of early summer, of fields of red clover, and of banks of elder blow. The planting of valerian most memorable for me was at the back of a small grouping of white-flowered plants on a slight rise. There its tall wands swayed above Siberian iris (*Iris sibirica*), foxglove (Digitalis), and peach-leaved

Plate 112. *Valeriana officinalis*, valerian, close-up. Midsummer, Gardner farm. Photo, Alan Dorey.

Plate 113. *Valeriana officinalis*, valerian. Early summer, Graymalkin Farm. Photo, Brian

Oke and Gisèle Quesnel.

bellflower (*Campanula persicifolia*), wafting a sweet aroma over the whole area. I grow it near the back of an informal cottage garden, where its bloom season coincides with lower growing blue borage (*Borago officinalis*), pink mallows (*Malva*), and purple veronicas. Valerian's pale pink flowers are foils for flaming red oriental poppies (*Papaver orientale*), for bright blue anchusas, and for all the bellflowers, especially the bright purple clustered bellflower (*Campanula glomerata*). It is a good choice for a meadow planting in the sun or along a semishaded area at the edge of woodland. If you like its strong fragrance, which is particularly noticeable in the evening, plant it close to traffic areas along paths and near entrances. It makes a good cut flower, too.

Indoors, sow seeds 10–12 weeks before the last frost, just covering them. Germination at 70°F (21°C) takes 21–25 days; or sow seeds outdoors in early spring. Space plants 15–24 in. (38.1–61.0 cm) apart, depending on their size, in almost any garden soil, on the moist side if possible. Valerian grows well where summers are cool. Once established, it self-sows with abandon, turning up for many years in cement cracks, gravel driveways, and similar habitats, even when discouraged; cut back plants after blooms are spent and before seeds have formed. The easiest way to propagate valerian is by taking basal cuttings from the side shoots in the spring or fall. To reduce its spread in confined circumstances, chop out excess growth or replace with young plants.

Related plants of interest. Plants and seeds of valerian can be obtained from herb sources; seeds of red valerian are offered by specialty seed and herb sources. Plants are available from perennial plant nurseries.

Centranthus ruber, red valerian or Jupiter's beard, is a short-lived perennial native to southern Europe, belonging to the valerian family. Some authorities claim its flowers yield a diuretic tonic and its roots have sedative properties similar to valerian's. In Europe, the leaves and roots are eaten as vegetables. Chaucer called it setwall because of its preference for the chalky limestone rubble of old buildings. Red valerian is outstanding in a garden and spectacular hanging from a dry wall, because of its long-lasting flowers that are fluffy, rose-pink in terminal clusters on 24 to 36 in. (61.0–91.4 cm) stems from early to late summer if plants are kept trimmed of spent flowers. The honey-scented blooms attract butterflies and are good cut flowers. Cultivars include 'Roseus' with salmon to red flowers and the white 'Albus'. Like valerian, red valerian grows best where summers are cool, preferring a light, well-drained soil and full sun; rich soil produces large plants at the expense of flower production. Sow seeds indoors the same way as valerian, 8 weeks before the last frost, and propagate as for valerian. Red valerian is hardy in Zone 4.

Veronica

Scrophulariaceae, Figwort Family
Speedwell

Perennial
Site and soil: sun; well-drained
Hardiness: Zones 4–10
Landscape use: bed and border, ground cover,
    naturalized herb, rock work
Height: 2–30 in. (5.1–76.2 cm)
Flower: blue, purple-blue, lavender, wheel-like in spike
Bloom season: early summer to midsummer

> **Venus governs this plant and it is . . . used both outwardly and inwardly.**
> Nicholas Culpeper
> *Culpeper's Complete Herbal*

The speedwells, growing wild in the Northern Hemisphere, are roughly categorized as low, fast-growing creepers with mat-forming leaves and taller, more slowly spreading mat- or clump-forming kinds. These share a similarity of design in their small, roundish, four-petaled flowers—the lower petal smaller and narrower than the others and more pointed at its tip—usually purplish or blue, often veined. The flowers grow on spikes of various lengths that are either tucked into leaf axils or borne atop each stem like a graceful vase that swells out at its base and gently tapers to a point, its tip often curved to one side. Each spike, no matter how small and slender, whether densely or loosely packed, looks full, almost fluffy, due to the long stamens that protrude from the center of each tiny bloom. The creepers generally bloom earlier, beginning in late spring; the medium to tall types begin to flower in early or midsummer and may continue well into fall.

The speedwells in general have astringent properties. At least twenty species have been used as drugs, foremost among them common speedwell, the herb of the apothecary, *Veronica officinalis*. A wildflower naturalized in dry fields, open woods, and on dry banks in North America, it sends out prostrate, hairy stems to 18 in. (45.7 cm) with toothed-edged, mat-forming leaves. The delicate, pale blue flower spikes, 1–2½ in. (2.5–6.4 cm) in length, grow straight up from the leaf axils. The medicine prepared from its flowers was called veronica and was regarded in Europe as a cure-all, although its main use was in a tea to treat coughs and respiratory ailments; its medicinal use has since become obsolete. Young leaves of some species were eaten in the spring as an antiscorbutic, like watercress. The common name, based on the Anglo-Saxon word "speed," as it was said upon leave-taking as a wish for good health and happiness, may refer to the plant's highly regarded healing properties or it may describe the way the tiny flowers readily fall from the spike in farewell. The genus is named for St. Veronica.

Plate 114. *Veronica prostrata*, harebell speedwell. Early summer, Graymalkin Farm. Photo, Brian Oke and Gisèle Quesnel.

More domesticated creepers include *Veronica prostrata* (Plate 114), harebell speedwell, 3–8 in. (7.6–20.3 cm) tall; its cultivar 'Heavenly Blue' has sapphire-blue flower spikes. And *V. repens,* creeping speedwell, forms a low, emerald-green mat of foliage with early blooming, light blue flowers. Some of the most elegant speedwells, the result of careful selection and breeding, are the former medicinal *V. incana,* silver speedwell, and the clump-forming, old-fashioned, purplish veronica *V. longifolia.* Silver speedwell creates slow-spreading mats of downy, gray leaves and flower spikes to 24 in. (61.0 cm), but it is usually grown more for its silvery foliage carpet than for its flowers. The hybrid *V. incana* 'Sarabande', to 12 in. (30.5 cm), however, offers less silvery foliage with more profuse, violet-blue spikes; 'Minuet', to 15 in. (38.1 cm) bears clear pink flower spikes above silvery foliage mats and blooms all summer. *Veronica longifolia* 'Sunny Border Blue' is one of the most satisfying of the clump-forming speedwells. A plant with lush, roundish foliage and a compact habit to 30 in. (76.2 cm) high, it produces many dark blue spikes that bloom from June until frost if the spent stalks are cut back; 'White Icicle', an inverted icicle in shape, is densely packed with pure white flowers on compact plants to 18 in. (45.7 cm) that bloom from midsummer to fall.

Despite their marginal medicinal uses, veronicas of all types are usually well represented in herb gardens and are well known to the general gardener for their versatility and long-lasting flower spikes. The taller speedwells make fine cut and dried flowers. The blue flowers are prized for potpourri and dried flower crafts.

The creepers are splendid, low-maintenance ground covers, great for covering otherwise weedy spots that are difficult to mow, such as odd corners or the bases of containers or tubs. Common speedwell is the choice for naturalizing on a dry bank, as it grows in the wild. The mat-forming speedwells can be underplanted with spring and fall bulbs, or grown at the edge of pavings and at the base of walls. The more domesticated creepers grow down over rocks creating carpets of blue in late spring. The compact, mat-forming *Veronica incana* 'Sarabande' and 'Minuet' are fine edges at the front of the border. The blue and white flower spikes of *V. longifolia* are stunning when paired with the dainty lemon daylily (*Hemerocallis lilioasphodelus*) or combined with blue and purple nepetas and salvias, pink musk mallows (*Malva moschata*), yellow coreopsis, all yarrows (*Achillea*), and finally, the rudbeckias.

Sow seeds of common or creeping speedwell, available from herb or specialty seed sources, outside in the spring, then thin seedlings to 12 in. (30.5 cm) apart. Pinch off faded flowers to encourage new growth. Start cultivars from plants, which can be found in perennial plant and herb sources, and space them 12–15 in. (30.5–38.1 cm) apart, depending on type. Cut back spent stalks to encourage flower production and maintain compact growth. Divide plants in the spring or fall every 3 years or as needed as they become overcrowded, or take stem cuttings in the spring or summer. Common speedwell grows well in dry, well-drained soil and full sun; the other speedwells grow best in well-drained but moisture retentive soil, also in sun although they will tolerate partial shade.

Veronicastrum virginicum

> If you would enjoy a new showy perennial in your herb garden, this . . . plant may be the answer.
>
> Madeleine Siegler
> *Herbal Treasures*

Scrophulariaceae, Figwort Family
Culver's root, bowman's root, tall speedwell

Perennial
Site and soil: sun, partial shade; well-drained
Hardiness: Zones 3–8
Landscape use: accent, bed and border, naturalized herb
Height: 5 ft. (1.5 m)
Flower: white, pale pink, tubular in spike
Bloom season: late summer to fall

The only species in the genus, Culver's root is a North American native that grows in rich woods, thickets, and meadows from Vermont to Manitoba and south to Florida and Texas. At first glance it appears to be an oversize veronica, as it was once classified, with which it does share a family resemblance. Its name, with the suffix *astrum*, meaning false, suggests the association. Culver's root also looks something like bugbane (*Cimicifuga racemosa*), but in the end, it is in a class by itself. Its slender spikes, less rounded than bugbane's and more plentiful, are tightly packed with small, snapdragon-like, tubular flowers, each four-lobed with two protruding stamens. The spikes are tapered and gently curved, appearing at the top of the plant, creating a candelabra effect with one spike above surrounded by multiple spikes below. The opened flowers at the bottom are fuzzy in appearance, the packed buds at the top are smooth and tight. Its green, toothed leaves, an attractive foil for the flowering wands above, grow in whorls around the unbranched stem, rather than in opposite pairs as on veronicas.

Culver's root is named for the doctor who learned of its uses from the North American Indians and introduced the plant to the settlers. The dried root was used primarily to treat intestinal and liver disorders: "In this you have a herbal medicine superior to most of the popular preparations and one that has been used for generations" (Hutchens 1991). The roots, however, contain leptandrin, a very powerful cathartic and emetic; they should never be self-administered in any form.

Plate 115. *Veronicastrum virginicum*, Culver's root. Late summer, Massachusetts. Photo, Joseph Hudak.

Despite its history of use in North America, adaptability to cultivation, late bloom, and stately appearance, Culver's root has been ignored as an herb and underused as a garden plant. Culver's root's flowering candelabras are elegant at the back of a border behind blue great lobelia (*Lobelia siphilitica*) and late salvias. Feature it in an island bed among lower-growing rudbeckias, establish it as an accent in front of a shrubbery, or naturalize it at the woodland's edge with other late-blooming, native plants such as goldenrods (*Solidago*) and asters. Two worthy cultivars are *Veronicastrum virginicum* 'Album', which has pure white spikes and foliage that appears deeper green, and 'Albo-rosea', brushed with pink. Also, the spikes are long-lasting cut flowers and can be dried for winter arrangements.

Culver's root is available as seed or plants from specialty seed sources and perennial and wildflower plant nurseries. Sow seeds outdoors in early spring or autumn, just pressing them into the soil since they need light to germinate. When the weather is still cool, transplant seedlings, spacing them 18 in. (45.7 cm) apart in any well-drained, humusy soil in sun or partial shade. Culver's root spreads by forming clumps, which can be divided in late fall or early spring. Each piece of root should have at least one eye; set it at the soil surface and mulch over the winter. Although Culver's root can also be increased by stem cuttings taken in the summer, root division is the fastest and easiest way to establish flowering plants. Grow the cultivars from roots, which are hard to find, but are available from perennial plant nurseries.

Vinca minor

Apocynaceae, Dogbane Family
Periwinkle, joy-of-the-ground, lesser periwinkle, running myrtle, sorcerer's violet

Perennial
Site and soil: sun, partial shade, shade; well-
   drained
Hardiness: Zones 4–9
Landscape use: ground cover
Height: 6 in. (15.2 cm)
Flower: violet-blue, white wheel in leaf axil
Bloom season: spring to early summer

> However ubiquitous it is as a ground cover, it can never be said to be "common," for it carries at all seasons a quality of refinement and poise.
>
> Wayne Winterrowd
> "North Hill: A Garden in the Making"
> *Horticulture*

Periwinkle, native to central Europe and western Asia, is an evergreen plant with trailing shoots 12–24 in. (30.5–61.0 cm) long. These shoots easily root along the surface of the soil, sending out new trailing stems in various directions, all covered with glossy, dark green, oval leaves. Erect stems carry the flat, five-petaled, wheel-shaped, usually violet-blue, 3/4 in. (1.9 cm) flowers in early spring. Both the Latin and common names come from the Greek word meaning to bind, for which there are two standard interpretations. One is that binding refers to the plant's healing properties; the other refers to the way its stems bind down other plants growing in their vicinity. Both explanations are apt, for periwinkle has an ancient reputation for staunching blood—a country name is cut-finger—and it is the ultimate weed-smothering ground cover.

The hardy periwinkle has been grown in North America since colonial times, perhaps brought over for its medicinal properties. Modern research has confirmed its ability to stop bleeding, to lower blood pressure, and to improve memory disorders, but it should never be used in any form for self-medication. Its frost-tender cousin, *Vinca major*, greater periwinkle, trailing and evergreen, is similar in habit and herbal properties. The most familiar and popular form of periwinkle is the unimproved old blue, *V. minor* 'Bowles's Variety'. It is a very hardy and vigorous sort, with broader foliage and a profusion of larger and bluer flowers. The white 'Alba' is also large-flowered, but not as vigorous; the more compact 'Atropurpurea' has beautiful, dusty rose flowers; and 'Gertrude Jekyll', a choice cultivar, is very dwarf and dainty with white flowers that bloom well even in dry, sunny conditions.

Periwinkle has no rival for quickly creating a rich, lustrous carpet that, once established, needs little attention. But keep track of it, for both *Vinca minor* and *V. major* can choke out native vegetation if not controlled. A clichéd but always pleasing theme is to let it spread into a large circle underplanted with yellow and purple crocuses and plenty of bright yellow daffodils beneath a tall tree. Periwinkle can also be established on steep slopes, as a woodland path, to carpet a tight corner—the best for this purpose is *V. minor* 'Gertrude Jekyll'—or anywhere that is difficult to mow. The seventeenth-century John Parkinson recommended it as a ground cover for a clematis-covered bower, an idea worth pursuing.

Periwinkle is adaptable to different soils and sites but prefers loose, humusy, well-drained soil high in potash. In colder climates, it takes more sun but grows well in shade, too. For a quick cover, space plants 6–8 in.

Plate 116. *Vinca minor*, periwinkle. Spring, Joseph Hudak garden. Photo, Joseph Hudak.

(15.2–20.3 cm) apart. To propagate, dig up the matted clumps, cut them apart, and plant the divisions, watering them well. Divide at any time, provided new plants are watered well. Control the planting by mowing around the planting or digging up unwanted new growth.

Related plants of interest. Plants of periwinkle are available from many perennial plant nurseries. Seeds of Madagascar periwinkle, which may be listed under *Vinca rosea,* are available from general seed and herb sources.

Catharanthus roseus,* Madagascar periwinkle, is a tender perennial usually grown as an annual. It has the same wheel-shaped flowers, increased by breeding to 2 in. (5.1 cm) across, in white and shades of red, often with a darker eye. Plant extracts are used as an insulin substitute and for treating cancer, especially Hodgkin's disease. Tests indicate its use to kill nematodes in the soil in the same way as French marigolds (*Tagetes patula*). Improved cultivars have reduced the 24–36 in. (61.0–91.4 cm) plant to 6 to 18 in. (15.2–45.7 cm). Plants bloom in masses all summer, and are drought, pollution, and heavy rain resistant. They are used for bedding in the same way as impatiens, for sun or partial shade, for growing under shrubs, and for planting in containers and hanging baskets. Sow seeds 10–12 weeks before the last frost and provide bottom heat to 80°F (27°C) for best germination in 6–23 days. Plant seedlings 9 in. (22.9 cm) apart outdoors after the last frost.

Viola odorata

Violaceae, Violet Family
Sweet violet, garden violet

Perennial
Site and soil: partial shade, shade; evenly moist
Hardiness: Zones 4–8
Landscape use: bed and border, container, ground
  cover, naturalized herb, rock work
Height: 6–8 in. (15.2–20.3 cm)
Flower: deep blue, white, solitary butterfly shape
Bloom season: spring to early summer

The sweet violet, of Eurasian and North African origin, has been cultivated in many countries for centuries, its basic form unchanged. Short, thick rhizomes growing from deep roots send out above-ground runners that root every 3–5 in. (7.6–12.7. cm), creating new plants wherever they go. In early spring, a multitude of narrow stems arise from thick basal clumps of glossy, veined, nearly heart-shaped leaves, 2½ in. (6.4 cm) wide. Each stem holds a delicate, five-petaled flower, ¾ in. (1.9 cm) across, with two upright petals like wings, and two lower petals on either side of a broader petal that extends backward to form a spur. The broad petal acts as a landing pad for insects who are guided to the nectar within. Despite each flower's relative insignificance, a single plant gains great appeal by its habit of blooming in showy bouquet-like bunches.

According to the many legends that surround the sweet violet, it sprouted from the blood of the boaster Ajax, or it sprang up around the Goddess Io to provide her with food when she was turned into a heifer by Jupiter. Homer, Virgil, even Napoleon with his famous promise, "I will return in the spring with the violets," were fulsome in their praise of this floral symbol of modesty.

As a plant of use and delight, the sweet violet is unrivaled. John Gerard, John Parkinson, and Nicholas Culpeper, writing in the sixteenth and seventeenth centuries, all extolled the virtues of sweet violets for their uses in food and medicines as well as for their beauty (Leighton 1986). Since ancient times their perfume has been distilled to scent or flavor cosmetics, wines, sweet liqueurs, and sweet waters, uses that have been largely replaced by synthetic chemicals since it takes 220 pounds (99.8 kg) of flowers to produce 2 ounces (56.7 grams) of essential oil. A syrup of violets is still recommended as a mild laxative or cough syrup. The plant also contains salicylic acid, the active ingredient in aspirin, which gives credence to its ancient use to soothe headaches.

The most perfumed types are the original purple and the white variant *Viola odorata* 'Alba', but some hybrids are also scented and offer large, prolific, longer lasting blooms. 'Royal Robe', one of the best, has rich purple flowers 2½ in. (6.4 cm) wide, pansy-like in form when fully opened; 'Rosina' is smaller-flowered but is a beautiful deep pink; 'White Czar' is pure white with prominent, purple throat veining; and the very hardy 'Queen Charlotte' has large, blue flowers 1½ in. (3.8 cm) across.

For many years I pulled up the thick, leafy clusters of white sweet violets that grew uninvited in my garden, shading out other plants and moving into empty spaces. Then one spring lovely drifts of delicate blooms and glossy foliage appeared from a multitude of plants that had settled in the receptive soil around a nearby tree trunk where I had once tossed the unwanted plants. I had never given the old whites a chance to show off their beauty, but in the right place they became a point of interest in the spring landscape. Try naturalizing sweet violets on a lightly wooded slope where their leaves will be the glossiest and the flowers more long lasting. Choice cultivars should be shown off at the front of a bed or border, in a shaded rockery, or in containers. Sweet violets are prime candidates for a scented garden, but their fabled aroma is delicate and fleeting. To get the maximum benefit, plant a large patch about 100 sq. ft. (9.3 sq. m), but if space does not allow, establish sweet violets close to living areas by entrances, along paths, and near patios and decks.

The easiest way to start seeds is to sow them in a cold frame and let them germinate over the winter—they need exposure to freezing. Set out plants in early spring 12 in. (30.5 cm) apart in moist, humusy soil in partial shade or shade. Sweet violets will grow in sun if the soil is evenly moist; overrich soil will produce leaves at the expense of flowers. Propagate by division after the plants have bloomed or in the fall.

Both sweet violets, a symbol for modesty, and *Viola tricolor*, Johnny-

Plate 117. *Viola tricolor,* Johnny-jump-up. Early summer, Toronto. Photo, Brian Oke and Gisèle Quesnel.

jump-up, for happy or sad thoughts, are prized for fresh nosegays or tussie-mussies. The flowers of both are edible and can be candied as described for *Borago officinalis*. Fresh violets are sweet and crisp and are a nice embellishment when lightly pressed into chocolate frosting or inserted with a bit of stem into fresh fruit cups.

Related plants of interest. Seeds of sweet violets are available from specialty seed sources; plants are available from perennial plant and herb sources. Seeds of Johnny-jump-up are available from general seed and herb sources. Look for the choice cultivars from specialty seed sources.

    Viola tricolor (Plate 117), Johnny-jump-up or wild pansy, a short-lived perennial or biennial, is the most carefree of all violas and an old cottage garden favorite. It bears flowers that resemble miniature hearts or faces whose colors are always changing since the plants readily hybridize. The archetypal, five-petaled flower is purple, yellow, and creamy white with pencil-thin whiskers or veins radiating from a golden center. My favorite is a dark velvety purple with a golden eye, grown from seed many years ago but now hard to find; 'King Henry' has large flowers, violet, sky-blue, and gold; 'Helen Mount', also large-flowered, is purple, lavender, and yellow; 'Prince John' is pure yellow. The whole plant has properties that stimulate metabolism, originating the country name heartsease, and ameliorate chronic skin problems such as eczema. Plant seedlings 6 in. (15.2 cm) apart in moist soil and partial shade in beds or borders, along pathways, in rock gardens, or in containers where they make good filler around other plants. They will grow where they like, however, since the ripe seed capsules burst open, shooting forth their many seeds to germinate in unlikely spots, literally jumping up between pavings, under stairways, in the lawn, always appreciated for their unfailing cheerfulness. Shear back plants in early summer for repeat bloom from late summer or fall into late fall. They languish in the heat of high summer unless given some shade.

Common Name Cross-reference

aconite, *Aconitum napellus*
adderwort, *Polygonum bistorta*
alkanet, *Anchusa*
all-heal, *Prunella vulgaris*
alumroot, *Geranium maculatum*
angelica, *Angelica archangelica*
    Korean, *Angelica gigas*
anise fern, *Myrrhis odorata*
annual clary, *Salvia viridis*
archangel, *Angelica archangelica*
    yellow, *Lamium galeobdolon*
    silver, *Lamium galeobdolon* 'Her-
      mann's Pride'
autumn lilac, *Aconitum carmichaelii*

basil, *Ocimum*
    dwarf bush, *Ocimum basilicum*
    'Minimum Pupurascens'
    purple, *Ocimum basilicum* var. *pur-
      purascens*
    Thai, *Ocimim basilicum*
bee balm, *Monarda didyma*
bee bread, *Borago officinalis*
bergamot, *Monarda*
    lemon, *Monarda citriodora*
    Mexican, *Monarda austromontana*
    wild, *Monarda fistulosa*
betony, *Stachys officinalis*
    great-flowered, *Stachys macrantha*
    wood, *Stachys officinalis*
bishopswort, *Stachys officinalis*

bistort, *Polygonum bistorta*
bitter buttons, *Tanacetum vulgare*
bitter fitch, *Nigella sativa*
black cumin, *Nigella sativa*
blood flower, *Asclepias curassavica*
bloodroot, *Sanguinaria canadensis*
bloodwort, *Geranium robertianum*
blue curls, *Prunella vulgaris*
blue sailors, *Cichorium intybus*
borage, *Borago officinalis*
bouncing bet, *Saponaria officinalis*
bowman's root, *Veronicastrum virginicum*
bridal rose, *Tanacetum parthenium*
bride's bouquet, *Saponaria officinalis*
bridewort, *Filipendula ulmaria*
broom
    dyer's, *Genista tinctoria*
    Scotch, *Cytisus scoparius*
    warminster, *Cytisus* ×*praecox*
bruisewort, *Symphytum*
bugbane, *Cimicifuga racemosa*
    kamchatka, *Cimicifuga simplex*
bugle, *Ajuga*
    carpet, *Ajuga reptans*
    pyramid, *Ajuga pyramidalis*
bugleweed, *Ajuga reptans*
    tufted, *Ajuga genevensis*
bugloss, *Anchusa*
    common, *Anchusa officinalis*
    Italian, *Anchusa azurea*
    viper's, *Echium vulgare*

burnet
Canadian, *Sanguisorba canadensis*
great, *Sanguisorba officinalis*
Japanese, *Sanguisorba obtusa*
mountain, *Sanguisorba dodecandra*
salad, *Sanguisorba minor*
butterfly weed, *Asclepias tuberosa*

calamint, *Calamintha grandiflora*
alpine, *Acinos alpinus*
lesser, *Calamintha nepeta*
showy, *Calamintha grandiflora*
calendula, *Calendula officinalis*
caper bush, *Capparis spinosa*
cardinal flower, *Lobelia cardinalis*
blue, *Lobelia siphilitica*
carnation, *Dianthus*
carpenter's weed, *Ajuga reptans*
catmint, *Nepeta ×faassenii*
dwarf, *Nepeta ×faassenii*
Himalayan, *Nepeta nervosa*
mauve, *Nepeta ×faassenii*
catnip, large, *Calamintha grandiflora*
celery, wild, *Angelica archangelica*
chamomile, *Matricaria recutita*
dyer's, *Anthemis tinctoria*
German, *Matricaria recutita*
Roman, *Chamaemelum nobile*
cheeses, *Malva sylvestris*
chicory, *Cichorium intybus*
chives, *Allium schoenoprasum*
Chinese, *Allium tuberosum*
corkscrew, *Allium senescens* var. *glaucum*
garlic, *Allium tuberosum*
silver curly, *Allium senescens* var. *glaucum*
clear eye, *Salvia sclarea*
cobbler's bench, *Lamium maculatum*
cohosh, black, *Cimicifuga racemosa*
comfrey, *Symphytum*
dwarf, *Symphytum grandiflorum*
English, *Symphytum officinale*
middle, *Ajuga reptans*

red, *Symphytum rubrum*
Russian, *Symphytum ×uplandicum*
small blue, *Symphytum caucasicum*
coneflower
black sampson, *Echinacea angustifolia*
purple, *Echinacea purpurea*
convall-lillie, *Convallaria majalis*
cool tankard, *Borago officinalis*
cowslip, *Primula veris*
American, *Caltha palustris*
Christmas, *Pulmonaria montana*
spotted, *Pulmonaria officinalis*
creeping Jenny, *Lysimachia nummularia*
crocus
autumn, *Colchicum autumnale*
saffron, *Crocus sativus*
showy autumn, *Colchicum speciosum*
Culver's root, *Veronicastrum virginicum*
cut-finger, *Vinca minor*

daisy
crown, *Chrysanthemum coronarium*
painted, *Tanacetum coccineum*
dalmatian pyrethrum, *Tanacetum cinerariaefolium*
dame's rocket, *Hesperis matronalis*
David's harp, *Polygonatum multiflorum*
deadmen's bells, *Digitalis purpurea*
devil-in-a-bush, *Nigella damascena*
dewcup, *Alchemilla mollis*
dittany of Crete, *Origanum dictamnus*
dropwort, *Filipendula vulgaris*
dwarf lace plant, *Polygonum affine*

echinacea
narrowleaf, *Echinacea angustifolia*
pale purple, *Echinacea pallida*
elecampane, *Inula helenium*
fringed, *Inula magnifica*
Himalayan, *Inula royleana*
evening rocket, *Hesperis matronalis*

fairy candles, *Cimicifuga racemosa*
fairy cups, *Primula veris*

fairy's glove, *Digitalis purpurea*
fairy's thimble, *Digitalis purpurea*
false salvia, *Lamium maculatum*
fennel, wild, *Nigella damascena*
feverfew, *Tanacetum parthenium*
foxglove, *Digitalis*
   Grecian, *Digitalis lanata*
   merton, *Digitalis* ×*mertonensis*
   purple, *Digitalis purpurea*
   rusty, *Digitalis feruginea*
   straw, *Digitalis lutea*
   yellow, *Digitalis grandiflora*
fuller's herb, *Saponaria officinalis*

garden heliotrope, *Valeriana officinalis*
garlic
   golden, *Allium moly*
   oriental, *Allium tuberosum*
geranium
   big root, *Geranium macrorrhizum*
   fox, *Geranium robertianum*
   spotted, *Geranium maculatum*
   wild, *Geranium maculatum*
ghost plant, *Artemisia lactiflora*
giant chervil, *Myrrhis odorata*
gillyflower, *Dianthus*
golden buttons, *Tanacetum vulgare*
golden marguerite, *Anthemis tinctoria*
goldenrod, *Solidago*
   alpine, *Solidago cutleri*
   Canada, *Solidago canadensis* 'Golden
     Baby'
   European, *Solidago virgaurea*
   lance-leaved, *Solidago graminifolia*
   seaside, *Solidago sempervirens*
   stiff, *Solidago rigida*
   sweet, *Solidago odora*
   wrinkled, *Solidago rugosa*
goodbye summer, *Saponaria officinalis*
gow choy, *Allium tuberosum*

heartsease, *Viola tricolor*
herb carpenter, *Prunella vulgaris*
herb-of-grace, *Ruta graveolens*

herb Peter, *Primula veris*
herb robert, *Geranium robertianum*
holigold, *Calendula officinalis*
hollyhock, *Alcea rosea*
   black, *Alcea rosea* 'Nigra'
   rugosa, *Alcea rugosa*
holyoke, *Alcea rosea*
honeywort, *Cerinthe*
hook-heal, *Prunella vulgaris*
hop vine, *Humulus lupulus*
   Japanese, *Humulus japonicus*
horse-heal, *Inula helenium*
horsemint, *Monarda*
   dotted, *Monarda punctata*
hundreds-and-thousands, *Pulmonaria
   officinalis*
hyssop, *Hyssopus officinalis*
   anise, *Agastache foeniculum*
   Bible, *Origanum syriacum*
   blue giant, *Agastache foeniculum*
   giant, *Agastache*
   Mexican giant, *Agastache mexicana*
   Mexican lemon, *Agastache mexicana*
   rock, *Hyssopus officinalis* subsp. *aris-
    tatus*
   Roman, *Satureja thymbra*
   yellow giant, *Agastache nepetoides*

Indian cress, *Tropaeolum*
inula
   Caucasian, *Inula orientalis*
   swordleaf, *Inula ensifolia* 'Compacta'
iris
   blue flag, *Iris versicolor*
   crested, *Iris cristata*
   Florentine, *Iris germanica* var. *floren-
    tina*
   white flag, *Iris germanica* var. *floren-
    tina*
   yellow flag, *Iris pseudacorus*

Jacob and Rachel, *Pulmonaria officinalis*
Jacob's ladder, *Polemonium, P. caeruleum*
Johnny-jump-up, *Viola tricolor*

joy-of-the-ground, *Vinca minor*
junn jui choi, *Artemisia lactiflora*
Jupiter's beard, *Centranthus ruber*
Jupiter's distaff, *Salvia glutinosa*

key flower, *Primula veris*
kingcup, *Caltha palustris*
king-in-splendour, *Stachys macrantha*
knitback, *Symphytum*
knitbone, *Symphytum*

lady-at-the-gate, *Saponaria officinalis*
lady's bedstraw, *Galium verum*
lady's mantle, *Alchemilla mollis*
  dwarf, *Alchemilla erythropoda*
  alpine, *Alchemilla alpina*
lamb's ears, *Stachys byzantina*
large-rooted cranesbill, *Geranium mac-*
  rorrhizum
lavandin, *Lavandula ×intermedia*
lavender, *Lavandula angustifolia*
  English, *Lavandula angustifolia*
  French, *Lavandula stoechas*
  hardy, *Lavandula angustifolia*
  Spanish, *Lavandula stoechas*
  true, *Lavandula angustifolia*
lavender cotton, *Santolina chamaecy-*
  parissus
leek
  Chinese, *Allium tuberosum*
  lady's, *Allium cernuum*
  lily, *Allium moly*
lily-of-the-valley, *Convallaria majalis*
lion's foot, *Alchemilla mollis*
lobelia, great, *Lobelia siphilitica*
love-in-a-mist, *Nigella damascena*
lungwort, *Pulmonaria officinalis*
  blue, *Pulmonaria angustifolia*
  common, *Pulmonaria officinalis*

mallow
  blue, *Malva sylvestris*
  common, *Malva sylvestris*
  high, *Malva sylvestris*

hollyhock, *Malva alcea* 'Fastigiata'
  jagged, *Alcea rosea*
  marsh, *Althea officinalis*
  musk, *Malva moschata*
  poppy, *Callirhoe involucrata*
  tree, *Malva sylvestris* subsp. *mauritiana*
  zebrina, *Malva sylvestris* 'Zebrina'
marjoram, *Origanum*
  hop, *Origanum dictamnus*
  wild, *Origanum vulgare* subsp. *vulgare*
marsh marigold, *Caltha palustris*
Martha Washington's plume,
  Filipendula rubra 'Venusta'
marybud, *Calendula officinalis*
May lily, *Convallaria majalis*
meadowbright, *Caltha palustris*
meadow clary, *Salvia pratensis*
meadow runnagates, *Lysimachia num-*
  mularia
meadow saffron, *Colchicum autumnale*
meadowsweet, *Filipendula*
Mexican mint marigold, *Tagetes lucida*
milfoil, *Achillea millefolium*
mint
  Korean, *Agastache rugosa*
  lemon, *Monarda citriodora*
monarda
  dotted, *Monarda punctata*
  mountain, *Monardella odoritissima*
  rose-scented, *Monarda fistulosa*
moneywort, *Lysimachia nummularia*
monkshood, *Aconitum napellus*
  autumn, *Aconitum henryi*
  azure, *Aconitum carmichaelii*
  English, *Aconitum napellus*
mosquito plant, *Agastache cana*
mother-of-the-evening, *Hesperis matro-*
  nalis
mountain balm, *Calamintha grandiflora*
mugwort
  common, *Artemisia vulgaris*
  sweet, *Artemisia lactiflora*
  white, *Artemisia lactiflora*

nasturtium, *Tropaeolum*
nigella, yellow, *Nigella orientalis* 'Transformer'
nosebleed plant, *Achillea millefolium*
nutmeg flower, *Nigella sativa*

onion
  autumn wild, *Allium stellatum*
  nodding, *Allium cernuum*
  prairie, *Allium stellatum*
  Siberian, *Allium ramosum*
oregano, *Origanum vulgare*
  showy, *Origanum vulgare* subsp. *vulgare*
  true showy, *Origanum libanoticum*
orris, *Iris germanica* var. *florentina*
Oswego tea, *Monarda didyma*
our lady's tears, *Convallaria majalis*
oxslip, *Primula elatior*

paigle, *Primula veris*
pansy, *Viola ×wittrockiana*
parsnip, wild, *Angelica archangelica*
patience dock, *Polygonum bistorta*
peony
  Chinese, *Paeonia lactiflora*
  common, *Paeonia officinalis*
  coral, *Paeonia mascula*
  crimson, *Paeonia officinalis*
  female, *Paeonia officinalis*
  grandma's, *Paeonia officinalis*
  male, *Paeonia mascula*
  mountain, *Paeonia suffruticosa*
  tree, *Paeonia suffruticosa*
periwinkle, *Vinca minor*
  greater, *Vinca major*
  lesser, *Vinca minor*
  Madagascar, *Catharanthus roseus*
Persian ground ivy, *Nepeta ×faassenii* 'Dwarf Catmint'
phlomis, golden, *Phlomis aurea*
pink, *Dianthus*
  border, *Dianthus caryophyllus* × *D. plumarius*

  Cheddar, *Dianthus gratianopolitanus*
  China, *Dianthus chinensis*
  clove, *Dianthus caryophyllus*
  cottage, *Dianthus plumarius*
  fringed, *Dianthus superbus*
  Indian, *Lobelia cardinalis*
  sand, *Dianthus arenarius*
pleurisy root, *Asclepias tuberosa*
polemonium, spring, *Polemonium reptans*
poppy, *Papaver*
  corn, *Papaver rhoeas*
  Flanders Field, *Papaver rhoeas*
  lettuce, *Papaver somniferum*
  opium, *Papaver somniferum*
  Shirley, *Papaver rhoeas* Shirley Poppies
pot marigold, *Calendula officinalis*
primrose
  English, *Primula vulgaris*
  polyantha, *Primula ×polyantha*
purple-top, *Salvia viridis*

queen-of-the-meadow, *Filipendula ulmaria*
queen-of-the-prairie, *Filipendula rubra*

radicchio, *Cichorium intybus*
rattletop, *Cimicifuga racemosa*
red robin, *Geranium robertianum*
redroot, *Sanguinaria canadensis*
Roman coriander, *Nigella sativa*
rose
  apothecary's, *Rosa gallica* 'Officinalis'
  Japanese, *Rosa rugosa*
  red, of Lancaster, *Rosa gallica* 'Officinalis'
  rugosa, *Rosa rugosa*
rosemary, *Rosmarinus officinalis*
  Santa Barbara, *Rosmarinus officinalis* 'Lockwood de Forest'
rue, *Ruta graveolens*
  fringed, *Ruta chalapensis*
running myrtle, *Vinca minor*

sage, *Salvia*, *S. officinalis*
autumn, *Salvia greggii*
Bethlehem, *Pulmonaria saccharata*
black, *Salvia mellifera*
blue, *Salvia clevelandii*, *S. azurea*
bog, *Salvia uliginosa*
clary, *Salvia sclarea*
cleveland, *Salvia clevelandii*
common, *Salvia officinalis*
cooking, *Salvia officinalis*
dominica, *Salvia dominica*
fruit-scented, *Salvia dorisiana*
garden, *Salvia officinalis*
Greek, *Salvia fruticosa*
Greek apple, *Salvia pomifera*
horminum, *Salvia viridis*
hummingbird, *Salvia leucantha*
Jerusalem, *Phlomis fruticosa*
meadow, *Salvia pratensis*
meadow clary, *Salvia pratensis*
mealycup, *Salvia farinacea*
Mexican bush, *Salvia leucantha*
painted, *Salvia viridis*
pineapple, *Salvia elegans*
pitcher's, *Salvia azurea* 'Grandiflora'
rocky mountain, *Salvia greggii*
Russian, *Perovskia*
scarlet, *Salvia coccinea* 'Lady in Red',
    S. splendens
silver, *Salvia argentea*
Texas, *Salvia coccinea* 'Lady in Red'
triloba, *Salvia fruticosa*
tuberous Jerusalem, *Phlomis tuberosa*
Turkish, *Salvia sclarea* 'Turkestaniana'
whorled clary, *Salvia verticillata*
salvia, blue, *Salvia farinacea*
sampson root, *Echinacea purpurea*
santolina
    gray, *Santolina chamaecyparissus*
    green, *Santolina rosmarinifolia*
savory
    creeping, *Satureja montana* subsp.
        illyrica
    dwarf winter, *Satureja montana* 'Nana'

ornamental, *Calamintha grandiflora*
showy, *Calamintha grandiflora*
summer, *Satureja hortensis*
whorled, *Satureja thymbra*
winter, *Satureja montana*
sekka-yama-negi, *Allium senescens* var.
    glaucum
self-heal, *Prunella vulgaris*
    large, *Prunella grandiflora*
setwall, *Centranthus ruber*
shunginku, *Chrysanthemum coronarium*
sicklewort, *Ajuga*
signet marigold, *Tagetes tenuifolia*
silver-rod, *Solidago bicolor*
snakebite, *Sanguinaria canadensis*
snakeroot, *Cimicifuga racemosa*
snakeweed, *Polygonum bistorta*
sneezewort, *Achillea ptarmica*
soapwort, *Saponaria officinalis*
    creeping, *Saponaria ocymoides*
    dwarf, *Saponaria ocymoides*
    rock, *Saponaria ocymoides*
soldiers and sailors, *Pulmonaria offici-
    nalis*
soldier's woundwort, *Achillea millefolium*
Solomon's seal, *Polygonatum multiflorum*
    European, *Polygonatum multiflorum*
    giant, *Polygonatum commutatum*
    Japanese, *Polygonatum humile*
    small, *Polygonatum biflorum*
sops-in-wine, *Dianthus caryophyllus*,
    D. plumarius
Spanish fennelflower, *Nigella hispanica*
speedwell, *Veronica*
    common, *Veronica officinalis*
    creeping, *Veronica repens*
    harebell, *Veronica prostrata*
    silver, *Veronica incana*
    tall, *Veronicastrum virginicum*
spiked thymbra, *Thymbra spicata*
spotted dead nettle, *Lamium maculatum*
squawroot, *Cimicifuga racemosa*
star flower, *Borago officinalis*
star-of-Persia, *Allium christophii*

string-of-sovereigns, *Lysimachia num-mularia*
succory, *Cichorium intybus*
sunflower, *Helianthus annuus*
  common, *Helianthus annuus*
  Maximilian's, *Helianthus maximilianii*
  showy, *Helianthus* ×*laetiflorus*
  wild, *Inula helenium*
swallowort, *Asclepias tuberosa*
swamp milkweed, *Asclepias incarnata*
sweet alyssum, *Lobularia maritima*
sweet Annie, *Artemisia annua*
sweet bracken, *Myrrhis odorata*
sweet cicely, *Myrrhis odorata*
sweet John, *Dianthus superbus*
sweet rocket, *Hesperis matronalis*
sweet slumber, *Sanguinaria canadensis*
sweet wormwood, *Artemisia annua*

tansy, *Tanacetum vulgare*
  curly, *Tanacetum vulgare* var. *crispum*
  silver, *Tanacetum niveum*
  silver-lace, *Tanacetum ptarmicifolium* 'Silver Feather'
tceqa, *Helianthus annuus* 'Hopi Black Dye'
thousand-leaf, *Achillea millefolium*
thyme, *Thymus*
  basil, *Acinos arvensis*
  Britannia, *Thymus praecox* subsp. *arcticus* 'Britannicus'
  bush, *Thymus vulgaris*
  caraway, *Thymus herba-barona*
  conehead, *Thymus capitatus*
  cooking, *Thymus vulgaris*
  creeping, *Thymus praecox* subsp. *arcticus*, *T. pulegoides*
  English, *Thymus vulgaris* 'Broad Leaf'
  golden lemon, *Thymus* ×*citriodora* 'Aureus'

lemon, *Thymus* ×*citriodora*
Marshall, *Thymus* 'Linear Leaf Lilac'
Moroccan, *Thymus brousonetti*
mother-of-, *Thymus praecox* subsp. *arcticus*, *T. pulegoides*
wild, *Thymus praecox* subsp. *arcticus*, *T. pulegoides*
woolly, *Thymus pseudolanuginosus*

valerian, *Valeriana officinalis*
  Greek, *Polemonium reptans*
  red, *Centranthus ruber*
  spring, *Polemonium reptans*
  true, *Valeriana officinalis*
violet
  garden, *Viola odorata*
  sorcerer's, *Vinca minor*
  sweet, *Viola odorata*

witloof, *Cichorium intybus*
wolfsbane, *Aconitum lycoctonum, A. napellus*
wonder honey plant, *Agastache foeniculum*
woodruff
  oriental, *Asperula orientalis*
  sweet, *Galium odoratum*
woundwort, *Stachys officinalis*

yama-rakkyo, *Allium thunbergii*
yarrow, *Achillea millefolium*
  fern-leaved, *Achillea filipendulina*
  woolly, *Achillea tomentosa*
yomogi-na, *Artemisia lactiflora*

za'atar, *Origanum syriacum, Thymbra spicata*
  Persian, *Satureja thymbra*
  Roman, *Satureja thymbra*

Herbs in Bloom from Spring to Fall

The following four seasons from spring to fall are based on approximate bloom times in Zones 5 and 6; gardeners in warmer or colder growing regions should adjust accordingly.

Spring (mid-March through May)

Ajuga
Alchemilla mollis
Allium schoenoprasum
Caltha palustris
Convallaria majalis
Cytisus scoparius
Dianthus
Galium odoratum
Geranium robertianum
Iris germanica var. *florentina*
Lamium maculatum
Myrrhis odorata
Paeonia officinalis
Polemonium
Polygonatum multiflorum
Polygonum bistorta
Primula veris
Pulmonaria officinalis
Rosmarinus officinalis
Sanguinaria canadensis
Symphytum
Vinca minor
Viola odorata

Early summer (June)

Allium schoenoprasum
Anchusa
Angelica archangelica
Borago officinalis
Calendula officinalis
Digitalis purpurea
Filipendula
Hesperis matronalis
Hyssopus officinalis
Lavandula angustifolia
Lysimachia nummularia
Malva sylvestris
Matricaria recutita
Nepeta ×*faassenii*
Prunella vulgaris
Rosa gallica 'Officinalis'
Salvia officinalis
Salvia sclarea

Santolina
Tanacetum parthenium
Thymus
Valeriana officinalis
Veronica

Midsummer (July)

Achillea millefolium
Aconitum napellus
Alcea rosea
Asclepias tuberosa
Calamintha grandiflora
Cichorium intybus
Cimicifuga racemosa
Echinacea purpurea
Humulus lupulus
Inula helenium
Lobelia cardinalis
Monarda
Nigella damascena
Ocimum basilicum var. *purpurascens*
Origanum vulgare subsp. *vulgare*
Papaver
Ruta graveolens

Salvia viridis
Saponaria officinalis
Satureja montana
Stachys officinalis
Tagetes tenuifolia
Tropaeolum

Late summer to fall (August to the first frost, September or October)

Agastache foeniculum
Allium tuberosum
Artemisia lactiflora
Capparis spinosa
Colchicum autumnale
Helianthus annuus
Lobelia siphilitica
Perovskia
Salvia
Sanguisorba canadensis
Solidago
Tanacetum vulgare
Thymbra spicata
Veronicastrum virginicum

Herb Sources

The following is a list of retail plant and seed sources that offer significant selections of herbs. Most of them have catalogs and mail-order services. Some of the sources have display gardens, which are good places to see many herbs in bloom; contact them to find the best time or season to visit.

General seed sources

Chiltern Seeds
Bortree Stile
Ulverton, Cumbria LA12 7PB
U.K.

Geo. W. Park Seed Co.
Cokesbury Road
Greenwood, South Carolina 29647-
0001
U.S.A.

Johnny's Selected Seeds
Foss Hill Road
Albion, Maine 04910-9731
U.S.A.

Pinetree Garden Seeds
Box 300
New Gloucester, Maine 04260
U.S.A.

Stokes Seeds
P.O. Box 548
Buffalo, New York 14240-0548
U.S.A.
Public garden.

Stokes Seeds Ltd.
39 James Street, Box 10
St. Catharines, Ontario L2R 6R6
Canada

Sutton Seeds
Hele Road
Torquay, Devon TQ2 7QJ
U.K.

Territorial Seed Co.
P.O. Box 157
Cottage Grove, Oregon 97424
U.S.A.

Thompson and Morgan
P.O. Box 1308
Jackson, New Jersey 08527-0308
U.S.A.

Thompson and Morgan Ltd.
Poplar Lane
Ipswich, Suffolk 1P8 3BU
U.K.

W. Atlee Burpee and Co.
300 Park Avenue
Warminster, Pennsylvania 18974
U.S.A.

Watkins Seeds Ltd.
P.O. Box 468
New Plymouth 067 86-800
New Zealand

Specialty seed sources
These sources are most likely to carry seeds for open-pollinated types, hard-to-find seed strains, native plants, wildflowers, and exotics.

Abundant Life Seed Foundation
P.O. Box 772
Port Townsend, Washington 98368
U.S.A.
Specializes in preserving rarely offered wild and old-fashioned flowers and herbs. Public garden.

Diggers Mail Order
105 Latrobe Parade
Dromana, Victoria 3936
Australia
Specializes in herbs, bulbs, and old-fashioned plants.

Flowery Branch
P.O. Box 1330
Flowery Branch, Georgia 30542-1330
U.S.A.
Specializes in old and new seed strains.

The Fragrant Path
P.O. Box 328
Ft. Calhoun, Nebraska 68023
U.S.A.
Specializes in fragrant, old-fashioned flowers and wildflowers.

J. L. Hudson
Star Route 2, Box 337
La Honda, California 94020
U.S.A.
Specializes in rare seeds, including native and Old World herbs.

Le Jardin du Gourmet
P.O. Box 75
St. Johnsbury, Vermont 05863
U.S.A.

King's Herbs
P.O. Box 19-084
Avondale, Aukland
New Zealand
Specializes in standard and unusual herbs, cottage garden plants, and gourmet and oriental vegetables.

Kings Herb Seeds
P.O. Box 14
Glenbrook, New South Wales 2773
Australia

Ornamental Edibles
3622 Weedlin Court
San Jose, California 95132
U.S.A.
Specializes in vegetables and edible flowers.

Phoenix Seeds
P.O. Box 9
Stanley, Tasmania 7331
Australia
Specializes in nonhybrid seeds.

Plants of the Southwest
Route 6, Box 11A
Santa Fe, New Mexico 87501
U.S.A.
Offers landscaping information. Demonstration gardens in Albuquerque.

Seedhunt
P.O. Box 96
Freedom, California 95019-0096
U.S.A.
Specializes in seeds of drought-tolerant herbs and perennials, including many salvias.

Seeds of Change
Box 15700
Santa Fe, New Mexico 87506-5700
U.S.A.

Select Seeds
81 Stickney Hill Road
Union, Connecticut 06076
U.S.A.
Specializes in old-fashioned flowers.

Shepherd's Garden Seeds
30 Irene Street
Torrington, Connecticut 06790
U.S.A.
Specializes in flowers and herbs among the European vegetable strains.

Specialty Seeds
24 Jolimont Terrace
Jolimont, Victoria 3002
Australia

William Dam Seeds
Box 8400
Dundas, Ontario L9H 6M1
Canada
Specializes in European herbs.

Perennial plant sources
These sources offer fine cultivars of plants whose herbal nature often is overlooked; they may have separate listings of culinary herbs. Also look for herbs at nurseries specializing in native plants, wildflowers, plants for specific habitats, or exotics, although herbs may not be designated as such.

Canyon Creek Nursery
3527 Dry Creek Road
Oroville, California 95965
U.S.A.

Carroll Gardens
P.O. Box 310
444 East Main Street
Westminster, Maryland 21157
U.S.A.

Corn Hill Nursery
R.R. 5
Petticodiac, New Brunswick E0A 2H0
Canada
Display gardens. A good source for roses.

Logee's Greenhouses
1421 North Street
Danielson, Connecticut 06239
U.S.A.
Specializes in indoor plants.

Prairie Moon Nursery
Route 3, Box 163
Winona, Minnesota 55987
U.S.A.
Specializes in plants and seeds of native species.

Shady Oaks Nursery
112 Tenth Avenue Southeast
Waseca, Minnesota 56093
U.S.A.
Offers information about growing in shade.

White Flower Farm
Route 63
Litchfield, Connecticut 06750-0050
U.S.A.
Public garden.

Specialty herb sources
These sources often sell both plants and seeds and carry the greatest assortment of lavenders, rosemarys, salvias, and thymes.

Cheshire Herbs
Fourfields
Forest Road
Nr. Tarporley, Cheshire CW6 9ES
U.K.

Companion Plants
7247 North Coolville Ridge Road
Athens, Ohio 45701
U.S.A.
Display beds.

Country Lane Herbs and Dried Flowers
R.R. 3
Puslich, Ontario N0B 2J0
Canada
Display gardens.

Cricket Hill Herb Farm Ltd.
74 Glen Street
Rowley, Massachusetts 01969
U.S.A.
Display gardens.

Dabney Herbs
Box 22061
Louisville, Kentucky 40222
U.S.A.

Fox Hollow Herbs and Heirlooms
P.O. Box 148
McGrann, Pennsylvania 16226
U.S.A.
Specializes in cottage garden flowers and herbs.

Goodwin Creek Gardens
P.O. Box 83
Williams, Oregon 97544
U.S.A.
Specializes in flowers for drying, fragrant plants, and herbs.

Graymalkin Farm
16839 The Gore Road
R.R. 3
Caledon East, Ontario L0N 1E0
Canada
Specializes in herbs and flowers for drying.

Hartman's Herb Farm
Old Dana Road
Barre, Massachusetts 01005
U.S.A.
Public garden.

Hedgerow Herbs
8 Pannau Street
Rhandirmwyn Nr. Llandovery, Dyfed
SA2 0NP
U.K.

The Herbary and Scented Garden
  Nursery
89 Station Road
Herne Bay, Kent CT6 5QQ
U.K.
Specializes in plants to attract butterflies and bees.

The Herbfarm
32804 Issaquah–Fall City Road
Fall City, Washington 98024
U.S.A.

Hollington Nurseries
Woolton Hill
Newbury, Berkshire RG15 9XT
U.K.
Display gardens.

Iden Croft Herbs
Frittenden Road
Staplehurst, Kent TN12 0DH
U.K.
Display gardens.

Margery Fish Plant Nursery
East Lambrook Manor
South Penharton, Somerset TA13 5HL
U.K.
Specializes in unusual cottage garden plants and herbs.

Nichols Garden Nursery
1190 North Pacific Highway
Albany, Oregon 97321-4598
U.S.A.
Public garden.

Richters Herbs
P.O. Box 26, Highway 47
Goodwood, Ontario L0C 1A0
Canada
Specializes in plants and seeds of unimproved species and new cultivars.

The Rosemary House
120 South Market Street
Mechanicsburg, Pennsylvania 17055
U.S.A.
Public garden.

Sandy Mush Herb Nursery
Route 2 Surret Cove Road
Leicester, North Carolina 28748
U.S.A.

Suffolk Herbs
Sawyers Farm
Little Cornard
Sudbury, Suffolk CO10 0NY
U.K.
Specializes in oriental vegetables and herbs from around the world.

Sunnybrook Farms
P.O. Box 6
9448 Mayfield Road
Chesterland, Ohio 44026
U.S.A.

T. DeBaggio Herbs
923 North Ivy Street
Arlington, Virginia 22201
U.S.A.

VanHevelingen Herb Nursery
2324 Jodi Court
Newberg, Oregon 97132-1378
U.S.A.

Well-Sweep Herb Farm
317 Mt. Bethel Road
Port Murray, New Jersey 07865
U.S.A.
Public garden.

Wrenwood of Berkeley Springs
Route 4, Box 361
Berkeley Springs, West Virginia 25411
U.S.A.
Public garden.

Bulb sources

Cruickshank's Inc.
1015 Mount Pleasant Road
Toronto, Ontario M4P 2MI
Canada

MClure and Zimmerman
108 West Winnebago
Box 368
Friesland, Wisconsin 53935
U.S.A.

Rose sources

Antique Rose Emporium
Route 5, Box 143
Brenham, Texas 77833
U.S.A.

Heritage Rose Gardens
16831 Mitchell Creek Drive
Fort Bragg, California 95437
U.S.A.

The Roseraie at Bayfields
P.O. Box R
Waldboro, Maine 04572
U.S.A.

Pickering Nurseries, Inc.
670 Kingston Road
Pickering, Ontario L1V 1A6
Canada

Vintage Gardens
2833 Old Gravenstein Highway South
Sebastopol, California 95472
U.S.A.

Further sources may be found in the current edition of the following books:

The Andersen Horticultural Library's Source List of Plants and Seeds. Chanhassen: Minnesota Landscape Arboretum.

Gardening by Mail and *Taylor's Guide to Specialty Nurseries,* by Barbara J. Barton. Boston: Houghton Mifflin.

The Herb Companion Wishbook and Resource Guide, by Bobbi A. McRae. Loveland, Colorado: Interweave Press.

Northwind Farm's Herb Resource Directory, by Paula Oliver. Shevlin, Minnesota: Northwind Farm Publications.

The Plant Finder. London: Royal Horticultural Society.

The Seed Search, by Karen Platt. Sheffield, England.

Bibliography

Adams, James. 1987. *Landscaping with Herbs*. Portland, Oregon: Timber Press.

Armitage, Allan. 1993. *Burpee Expert Gardener Series: Allan Armitage on Perennials*. New York: Prentice Hall.

Art, Henry W. 1986. *A Garden of Wildflowers*. Pownal, Vermont: Storey Communications.

Bauersfeld, Marjorie. 1959. *The Herbarist*, no. 25.

Bennett, Jennifer, Pat J. Tucker, and Marnie Flook. 1988. Rock gardens. *Harrowsmith* (July/Aug.): 71–77.

Betts, Edwin M. and Hazelhurst Bolton Perkins. 1986. *Thomas Jefferson's Flower Garden at Monticello*, rev. ed. Charlottesville: University Press of Virginia.

Bloom, Alan. 1986. Transatlantic advice. *Horticulture* (Apr.): 30–35.

Bonar, Ann. 1985. *The Macmillan Treasury of Herbs*. New York: Macmillan.

Bown, Deni. 1988. *Fine Herbs for a Beautiful Garden*. London: Unwin Hyman Ltd.

Bown, Deni. 1995. *The Herb Society of America Encyclopedia of Herbs*. New York: Dorling Kindersley.

Bremess, Lesley. 1989. *The Complete Book of Herbs*. Montreal: Reader's Digest Association.

Brickell, Christopher and Fay Sharman. 1986. *The Vanishing Garden*. London: John Murray and the Royal Horticultural Society.

Brown, Jane. 1982. *Gardens of a Golden Afternoon*. New York: VanNostrand Reinhold.

Brownlow, Margaret E. 1957. *Herbs and the Fragrant Garden*. Kent, U.K.: The Herb Farm.

Buchanan, Rita. 1987. *The Weaver's Garden*. Loveland, Colorado: Interweave Press.

Buchanan, Rita, ed. 1995. *Taylor's Guide to Herbs*. New York: Houghton Mifflin.

Cannon, John and Margaret Cannon. 1994. *Dye Plants and Dyeing*. Portland, Oregon: Timber Press.

Clarkson, Rosetta. 1942. *Herbs: Their Culture and Uses*. New York: Macmillan.

Clebsch, Betsy. 1997. *A Book of Salvias: Sages for Every Garden*. Portland, Oregon: Timber Press.

Crockett, James Underwood. 1971. *The Time-Life Encyclopedia of Gardening: Annuals*. Alexandria, Virginia: Time-Life Books.

Crockett, James Underwood. 1971. *The Time-Life Encyclopedia of Gardening: Bulbs.* Alexandria, Virginia: Time-Life Books.

Crockett, James Underwood. 1972. *The Time-Life Encyclopedia of Gardening: Perennials.* Alexandria, Virginia: Time-Life Books.

Crockett, James Underwood and Ogden Tanner. 1977. *The Time-Life Encyclopedia of Gardening: Herbs.* Alexandria, Virginia: Time-Life Books.

Culpeper, Nicholas. [1652] n.d. *Culpeper's Complete Herbal.* Reprint. London: W. Foulsham and Co.

Dana, Mrs. William Starr. [1893] 1963. *How to Know the Wild Flowers.* Reprint. New York: Dover.

Danin, Avinoam. 1980. The resourceful caper. *Israel-Land and Nature,* vol. 5, no. 4 (Summer): 138–141.

Danin, Avinoam. 1984. The seven-branched "menorah," apples of the Cretans and the Isle of Caphtor. *Israel-Land and Nature,* vol. 10, no. 1 (Fall): 27–29.

DeBaggio, Thomas. 1989. Hardy lavenders. *The Herb Companion* (Apr./May): 10–14.

DeBaggio, Thomas. 1990. Rosemary and its culture. *Herb Companion* (Dec./Jan): 34–37.

DeBaggio, Thomas. 1994. *Growing Herbs.* Loveland, Colorado: Interweave Press.

DeBaggio, Thomas. 1996. New for '96. *The Herb Companion* (Feb./Mar.): 44–50.

Deno, Norman C. 1993. *Seed Germination: Theory and Practice.* State College, Pennsylvania: Norman C. Deno.

Dobelis, Inge N., ed. 1986. *Magic and Medicine of Plants.* Pleasantville, New York: Reader's Digest.

Dominick, Anne Westbrook. 1992. Herbal aspirin. *The Herb Companion* (Aug./ Sept): 36–39.

Dowden, Anne Ophelia. 1979. *This Noble Harvest: A Chronicle of Herbs.* Cleveland and New York: William Collins Publishers.

Earle, Alice Morse. 1901. *Old Time Gardens.* New York: Macmillan.

Emerson, Ralph Waldo. Hamatreya. Cited in *The Gardener's Quotation Book,* edited by Jennifer Taylor. 1992. New York: Barnes and Noble Books.

Facciola, Stephen. 1990. *Cornucopia: A Source Book of Edible Plants.* Vista, California: Kampong Publications.

Fish, Margery. [1961] 1983. *Cottage Garden Flowers.* Reprint. London: Faber and Faber.

Fish, Margery. [1964] 1980. *Ground Cover.* Reprint. London: Faber and Faber.

Fish, Margery. [1964] 1983. *Gardening in the Shade.* Reprint. London: Faber and Faber.

Flannery, Harriet B. 1976. Ornamental characteristics of selected herbs and a key to their identification. Master's thesis, Cornell University.

Foster, Gertrude B. 1976. *Herbs for Every Garden.* London: The Garden Book Club.

Foster, Gertrude B. 1981. Know the chamomiles. *The Herb Grower,* vol. 34, no. 1:8–9.

Foster, Gertrude B. and Rosemary Louden. 1980. *Park's Success with Herbs.* Greenwood, South Carolina: George W. Park Seed Co.

Foster, H. Lincoln. [1968] 1982. *Rock Gardening.* Reprint. Portland, Oregon: Timber Press.

Foster, Steven. 1984. *Herbal Bounty! The Gentle Art of Herb Culture.* Salt Lake City: Peregrine Smith Books.

Foster, Steven. 1992–1993. Chamomile. *The Herb Companion* (Dec./Jan.): 64–68.

Foster, Steven and James A. Duke. 1990. *A Field Guide to Medicinal Plants.* Boston: Houghton Mifflin.

Fox, Helen M. 1933. *Gardening with Herbs for Flavor and Fragrance.* New York: Macmillan.

Fox, Helen M. 1953. *The Years in My Herb Garden.* New York: Macmillan.

Fox, Helen M. 1958. Some uncommon herbs of ornamental value. In *Handbook on Herbs,* edited by Frederick McGourty. 1972. Plants and Gardens Series, vol. 14, no. 2. Brooklyn: Brooklyn Botanic Garden.

Fox, Helen M. 1959. Color in the herb garden. *The Herbarist,* no. 25: 34–48.

Freeman, Margaret B. 1943. *Herbs for the Medieval Household.* New York: Metropolitan Museum of Art.

Friend, Rev. Hilderic. 1883. *Flowers and Flower Lore.* London: George Allen and Co. Ltd.

Gardner, Jo Ann. 1992. *The Heirloom Garden.* Pownal, Vermont: Storey Communications.

Gardner, Jo Ann. 1992. Za'atar. *The Herb Companion* (Oct./Nov.): 47.

Gardner, Jo Ann. 1993. Flowering herbs. *Horticulture* (Feb.): 44–49.

Gardner, Jo Ann. 1994. One grower's experience: 'Lady' lavender. *The Herb Companion.* (Feb./Mar): 32–33.

Gardner, Jo Ann. 1994. Covering new ground: Old World herb ground covers. *Harrowsmith* (June): 50–55.

Gardner, Jo Ann. 1997. *Living with Herbs.* Woodstock, Vermont: The Countryman Press.

Genders, Roy. 1984. *The Cottage Garden and the Old-fashioned Flowers.* London: Pelham Books.

Gerard, John. [1633] 1975. *The Herball or Generall Histoire of Plantes . . . very Much Enlarged and Amended by Thomas Johnson Citizen and Apothecarye of London.* Reprint. New York: Dover.

Gray, Asa. 1887. *Gray's School and Field Book of Botany.* New York: Ivison, Blakeman and Co.

Grieve, Mrs. M. [1931] 1971. *A Modern Herbal, Vols. 1 and 2.* Reprint. New York: Dover.

Griffiths, Mark, ed. 1994. *Index of Garden Plants: The New Royal Horticultural Society Dictionary.* Portland, Oregon: Timber Press.

Hareuveni, Nogah. 1980. *Nature in Our Biblical Heritage.* Israel: Neot Kedumim.

Hareuveni, Nogah. 1984. *Tree and Shrub in Our Biblical Heritage.* Israel: Neot Kedumim.

Harper, Pamela and Frederick McGourty. 1985. *Perennials: How to Select, Grow and Enjoy.* Los Angeles: HP Books.

Hatfield, Audrey Wynne. 1983. *The Weed Herbal.* New York: Sterling Publishing Co.

Hedrick, U. P. [1919] 1972. *Sturtevant's Edible Plants of the World.* Reprint. New York: Dover.

Hibberd, Shirley. [1871] 1986. *The Amateur's Flower Garden.* Reprint. London: Croom Helm.

Hill, Lewis and Nancy Hill. 1994. *Bulbs: Four Seasons of Beautiful Blooms.* Pownal, Vermont: Storey Communications.

Hill, Madalene and Gwen Barclay. 1987. *Southern Herb Growing.* Fredricksburg, Texas: Shearer Publishing.

Hopkinson, Patricia, Diane Miske, Jerry Parsons, and Holly H. Shimizu. 1994. *Herb Gardening.* New York: Pantheon Books.

Hudak, Joseph. 1993. *Gardening with Perennials Month by Month.* Portland, Oregon: Timber Press.

Hutchens, Alma R. 1991. *Indian Herbology of North America.* Boston: Shambala Publications.

Huxley, Anthony. 1982. *Huxley's Encyclopedia of Gardening.* New York: Universe Books.

Ingram, Timothy. 1995. Sowing fresh seed. *The Hardy Plant.* (Autumn): 40–44.

Jekyll, Gertrude. 1911. *Colour Schemes in the Flower Garden.* London: Country Life.

Jekyll, Gertrude. 1916. *Annuals and Biennials.* London: Country Life.

Jekyll, Gertrude. 1926. *Wood and Garden.* London: Country Life.

Kamm, Minnie Watson. [1938] 1971. *Old-time Herbs for Northern Gardens.* Reprint. New York: Dover.

King, Mrs. Francis. 1928. *From a New Garden.* New York: Alfred A. Knopf.

Kirkpatrick, Debra. 1992. *Using Herbs in the Landscape.* Harrisburg, Pennsylvania: Stackpole Books.

Klimas, John E. 1974. *Wildflowers of Eastern America.* New York: Alfred A. Knopf.

Kowalchick, Claire and William H. Hyton, eds. 1987. *Rodale's Illustrated Encyclopedia of Herbs.* Emmaus, Pennsylvania: Rodale Press.

Lacy, Allen. 1990. Fall salvias. *Horticulture* (Oct.): 36–39.

Lathrop, Norma Jean. 1981. *Herbs: How to Select, Grow and Enjoy.* Los Angeles: HP Books.

Lawrence, Elizabeth. 1957. *The Little Bulbs.* New York: Criterion Books.

Lawrence, Elizabeth. 1987. *Gardening for Love: The Market Bulletins.* Durham, North Carolina: Duke University Press.

Leighton, Ann. 1986. *Early American Gardens: For Meate or Medicine.* Amherst: University of Massachusetts Press.

Leighton, Ann. 1987. *American Gardens in the Eighteenth Century: For Use or For Delight.* Amherst: University of Massachusetts Press.

Leighton, Ann. 1987. *American Gardens of the Nineteenth Century: For Comfort and Affluence.* Amherst: University of Massachusetts Press.

Liberty Hyde Bailey Hortorium. 1976. *Hortus Third: A Concise Dictionary of Plants Cultivated in the United States and Canada.* New York: Macmillan.

Lima, Patrick. 1986. *The Harrowsmith Illustrated Book of Herbs*. Camden East, Ontario: Camden House.

Lord, Priscilla Sawyer. 1972. The beauty of herbs. In *Handbook on Herbs and Their Ornamental Uses*, edited by Frederick McGourty and Hester Mettler Crawford. 1972. Plants and Gardens Series, vol. 28, no. 1. Brooklyn: Brooklyn Botanic Garden.

Lust, John. 1974. *The Herb Book*. New York: Bantam Books.

McCormick, M. J. 1989. Never enough thyme. *The Herb Companion* (Apr./May): 20–23.

McGourty, Frederick, ed. 1972. *Handbook on Herbs*. Plants and Gardens Series, vol. 14, no. 2. Brooklyn: Brooklyn Botanic Garden.

McGourty, Frederick. 1989. *The Perennial Gardener*. Boston: Houghton Mifflin.

McGourty, Frederick and Hester Mettler Crawford, eds. 1972. *Handbook on Herbs and Their Ornamental Uses*. Plants and Gardens Series, vol. 28, no. 1. Brooklyn: Brooklyn Botanic Garden.

Markham, Gervase. 1613. *The English Husbandman*. Cited in *The Cottage Garden*, by Roy Genders. 1984. London: Pelham Books.

Martin, Tovah. 1989–1990. A sampler of unusual herbs. *The Herb Companion* (Dec./Jan): 30–33.

Muir, John. 1938. *The Unpublished Journals of John Muir*, edited by Linnie Marsh Wolfe. Boston: Houghton Mifflin.

Newcomb, Peggy C. 1985. *Popular Annuals of Eastern North America 1865–1914*. Washington: Dunbarton Oaks.

The New Settlement Cookbook. 1954. New York: Simon and Schuster.

Niering, William A. and Nancy C. Olmstead, eds. *Audubon Society Field Guide to North American Wildflowers*. 1979. New York: Alfred A. Knopf.

Oster, Maggie. 1991. *Flowering Herbs*. New York: Running Heads.

Painter, Gillian. 1983. Herbal irises. *The Herb Grower*, vol. 35, no. 3: 59–61.

Parkinson, John. [1629] 1975. *Paradisi in Sole Paradisus Terrestris*. Reprint. New York: Dover.

Patterson, Allen. 1972. Herbs in the ornamental garden. In *Handbook on Herbs and Their Ornamental Uses*, edited by Frederick McGourty and Hester Mettler Crawford. 1972. Plants and Gardens Series, vol. 28, no. 1. Brooklyn: Brooklyn Botanic Garden.

Pesch, Barbara B. and Ann Lovejoy, eds. 1990. *Herbs and Cooking*. Plants and Gardens Series, vol. 45, no. 4. Brooklyn: Brooklyn Botanic Garden.

Peterson, Roger Torey and Margaret McKenny. 1968. *A Field Guide to Wildflowers*. Boston: Houghton Mifflin.

Philip, Chris. 1996. *The RHS Plant Finder*, 10th ed. Derbyshire, U.K.: Moorland Publishing Co. Ltd.

Phillips, Harriet. 1984. Rosemary hardiness. *The Herb Grower*, vol. 36, no. 3: 46–48.

Phillips, Harriet. 1991. The best of thymes. *The Herb Companion*. (Apr./May): 21–29.

Phillips, Harry R. 1985. *Growing and Propagating Wild Flowers*. Chapel Hill: University of North Carolina Press.

Phillips, Rodger and Nicki Foy. 1990. *The Random House Book of Herbs.* New York: Random House.

Phillips, Rodger and Martyn Rix. 1991. *The Random House Book of Perennials, Vols. 1 and 2.* New York: Random House.

Plowden, C. Chicheley. 1968. *A Manual of Plant Names.* New York: Philosophical Library.

Potter, Beatrix. n.d. *The Tale of Peter Rabbit.* London: Frederick Warne.

Powell, Eileen. 1995. *From Seed to Bloom.* Pownal, Vermont: Storey Communications.

Ramsay, Jane. 1987. *Plants for Beekeeping in Canada and the Northern USA* London: International Bee Research Association.

Randall, John M. and Janet Marinelli, eds. 1996. *Invasive Plants: Weeds of the Global Garden.* Twenty-first Century Gardening Series, no. 149. Brooklyn: Brooklyn Botanic Garden.

Rickett, Harold William. 1963. *The New Field Book of American Wild Flowers.* New York: G. P. Putnam's Sons.

Rohde, Eleanour Sinclair. [1936] 1969. *A Garden of Herbs.* Reprint. New York: Dover.

Rollins, Elizabeth. 1989. Origanums today. *The Herbarist,* no. 55: 1–5.

Rollins, Elizabeth and Arthur O. Tucker. 1992. The other origanums. *The Herb Companion* (Feb./Mar): 23–27.

Sanecki, Kay N. 1974. *The Complete Book of Herbs.* New York: Macmillan.

Shakespeare, William. *A Winter's Tale.* In *The Pelican Shakespeare,* edited by Baldwin Marshall. Baltimore: Penguin Books.

Shaudys, Phyllis. 1986. *The Pleasure of Herbs.* Pownal, Vermont: Storey Communications.

Shaudys, Phyllis. 1990. *Herbal Treasures.* Pownal, Vermont: Storey Communications.

Shepherd, Roy E. 1978. *History of the Rose.* Reprint. New York: Earl M. Coleman.

Shimizu, Holly H. 1986. Rediscovering native American herbs. *The Herbarist,* no. 52: 49–53.

Silber, Mark and Terry Silber. 1988. *The Complete Book of Everlastings.* New York: Alfred A. Knopf.

Simmons, Adelma. [1964] 1990. *Herb Gardening in Five Seasons.* Reprint. New York: Plume.

Talmud (Babylonian). Cited in *Tree and Shrub in Our Biblical Heritage,* by Nogah Hareuveni. 1984. Israel: Neot Kedumim

Thaxter, Celia. [1894] 1988. *An Island Garden.* Reprint. Boston: Houghton Mifflin.

Trew, Christoph Jakob. 1985. *The Herbal of the Count Palatine.* London: Harrap.

Tucker, Arthur O. and Elizabeth D. Rollins. 1989. The species, hybrids, and cultivars of *Origanum* (Lamiaceae) cultivated in the United States. *Baileya,* no. 23: 14–27.

VanHevelingen, Andy. 1992. The orris iris. *The Herb Companion* (Aug./Sept): 33–35.

Verey, Rosemary. 1991. *The Scented Garden*. New York: Random House.

Verey, Rosemary. 1995. My plant of the year: *Lobelia siphilitica*. *The Hardy Plant* (Autumn): 27–31.

Vick, James and Sons. 1865. *Vick's Catalogue and Floral Guide*. Cited in *Popular Annuals of Eastern North America 1965–1914*, by Peggy C. Newcomb. 1985. Washington: Dunbarton Oaks.

Webster, Helen. 1942. *Herbs: How to Grow Them and How to Use Them*. Boston: Ralph T. Hale.

Webster, Helen. 1947. Lavenders. *The American Herb Grower*, vol. 1, no. 3 (Aug./Sept): 4–8.

Wilder, Louise Beebe. [1932] 1974. *The Fragrant Path*. Reprinted as *The Fragrant Garden*. New York: Dover.

Williamson, John. 1988. *Perennial Gardens*. New York: Harper and Row.

Wilson, Helen Van Pelt and Léonie Bell. 1967. *The Fragrant Year*. New York: Bonanza Books.

Wilson, Jim. 1994. *Landscaping with Herbs*. New York: Houghton Mifflin.

Winterrowd, Wayne. 1990. North Hill: a garden in the making. *Horticulture* (Nov.): 43–51.

Woodward, Carol H. and Harold William Rickett, eds. 1979. *New York Botanic Garden's Field Guide: Common Wild Flowers of the Northeastern United States*. Woodbury, New York: Barron's.

Wyman, Donald. 1971. *Wyman's Gardening Encyclopedia*. New York: Macmillan.

Index of Plant Names

Italicized numbers denote pages on which photographs and illustrations appear.